To Colleagues of the
Religious Research Association

American Denominational Organization

A Sociological View

Ross P. Scherer

William Carey Library

1705 N. SIERRA BONITA AVE. • PASADENA, CALIFORNIA 91104

Published by the William Carey Library
1705 N. Sierra Bonita Avenue
Pasadena, California 91104, U.S.A.
Telephone (213) 798-0819

PRINTED IN THE UNITED STATES OF AMERICA

ISBN 0-87808-173-9
Library of Congress Number 80-13859

CONTENTS

Foreword

Martin E. Marty

The denomination is a betwixt and between institution late in the twentieth century. An invention of Anglo-American Christianity, designed to make possible free and equal church life in the era of voluntary religious association, it appears to many to be obsolete. As such, one must ask whether it merits the attention the authors of this book give it.

At first glance, the denomination seems to belong somewhere "back there" with fossils, Studebaker wagons, blacksmiths, and the Grange. Nostalgia buffs may cherish recall of the days when denominations denominated theological differences. They may gather for rites to celebrate the time when denominations served as boundaries between various creeds and confessions. Tell me that someone was a Methodist in 1780 or 1880 and you tell me much about him or her. In 1980 I must know whether the Methodist is liberal or conservative; charismatic or programmatic, liberationist or capitalist or whatever.

The denomination is in trouble not merely because it does not provide boundaries or safeguard lines of confessional division. For seventy years, at least since the International Missionary Conference at Edinburgh in 1910, it has stood as a symbol for that which retards the expression of Christian unity. For most of the intervening years ecumenists have had to deal realistically with the residual power of

I

denominations even while implicitly undercutting them. Today they are no longer the chief barriers. In recent times the question of First and Second World versus Third World, or the issue of which cause or theological tendency one supports, is a greater problem for ecumenists. But denominations remain and have to be confronted.

A third source of confusion is in the competition denominations receive from two directions. On the one hand, the "para-church" has become a rival. The trend in current Christianity is for people not to congregate but to form clienteles. They follow this or that Christian shaman, guru, or celebrity, be he or she the leader of a retreat center, a mass evangelist, or a priest of the electronic church. People put their energies not into Presbyterianism but into a lay movement in or alongside it; not into Catholicism but into a charismatic cell or house; not into Lutheranism but into a Lutheran anti-abortion front. The denomination is at best a vestige or a tag-along.

On the other hand, purely individualized or—perish the word— "privatized" Christianity has also become a rival for the form of church life called the denomination. Thomas Luckmann in *The Invisible Religion* is one of many who has shown how modernity has removed the props that associations once provided. People seem to be alienated, in pursuit of loneliness, choosing isolation—especially in religion. They put together an utterly personal package drawn from who knows what sources: from remembered Sunday School faith, from the religion of a spouse, the experience of the classroom, and the moonlighting sessions with Eastern lore. They join the denominations' alumni association and give the bad mouth to weaklings who need each other in congregations. Since denominations imply some measure of bureaucratic life, they are especially beneath contempt.

So much for the mislocation of the denomination in an age when other patterns of loyalty compete for Christian attention. One could also discern percisely the opposite kind of mislocation by observing how many people in denominations act. Just as cancer cells often outpace healthy ones in growth, so diseased denominations and denomination-alism attract notice more than healthier forms of church life.

I refer here to the idolization of the denominations by factions that fight over their power and their future. Perhaps because the spoils are now so small, the survivors want to be victors and thus winners of the spoils. Virtually every major denomination today is torn apart between such factions. The *Good* News movement is *bad* news in one group; the "Concerned" element implies everyone else is "Unconcerned" in another. In one denomination the charismatics make themselves the sign of stumbling: "If you are not a Christian by being saved our way, you are at best half safe, and perhaps not saved at all." In another denomination, the majorities try to snuff out the charismatics. Traditionalists attempt to regain power in Catholicism, and moderates hold on to some in another, as the winds of the Zeitgeist blow all parties in many directions.

In the process one gets the impression that denominations really are powerful, that they are worth fighting over. They gain an importance far beyond anything that derives from their biblical or confessional rationales—if they ever had such rationales. They are placed higher in the economy of God than such human inventions ever should be. People stay in them or leave them for reasons that artificially inflate their importance.

Somewhere between these extremes there lies the real denomination, born late in Christendom and having flourished in post-Christendom during the voluntaryistic age. Whoever wants to take seriously the organization of the church, the way its institutions relate to the community of the Holy Spirit, will have to reckon with the denomination and seek to locate it properly. To do so one could use many tools: journalistic, pastoral, lay, historical, theological, and the like.

In this book a number of sociologists use the tools of their discipline and profession in order to contribute to further understanding. They know that theirs is not the only proper angle of vision, but they would protest should anyone rule out *a priori* the insights that their approach can offer.

The organization of the book looks conventional enough, since in Part I the overviewers line up for the usual Protestant-Catholic-Jewish appraisals. Yet under such ordinary-looking shells there are tantalizing puzzles and surprising findings. The choice of denominationally related agencies or subgroups is rather rich: religious orders, mission societies, theological schools, congregational models, and the life of professionals may not make up an encompassing list, but they do touch on the most sensitive areas. And the final section deals with the tensions of which I have spoken above.

In his introduction, Ross Scherer speaks of an "open systems" theory approach. This strikes me as an important alternative to evolutionary or deterministic schemes, and allows for the surprising revitalizations denominations have seen and can see. This approach, which the authors of this book tend to favor, helps us see complex bodies in even more intricate environments. In the process they provide us with virtual "do it yourself" kits so that we can carry on the work by applying what we have learned to other denominations and agencies. And we can be poised to understand the change which this book convinces us is constant, and is full of threat—and promise.

Preface

This book has taken longer than it should have to see the light of day. This in greater part has been due to the fear of contemporary publishers that modern society is no longer interested in hearing about "religious organization." I, of course, hope they are wrong. Credit for stimulating me to pursue this "new look" in the study of religious organization goes to William V. D'Antonio, University of Connecticut, then Executive Secretary of the Society for the Scientific Study of Religion, who asked me to convene a session or two on "religion" at the SSSR sections of the meetings of the American Association for the Advancement of Science, held in Chicago, in December, 1970. In the present book, there are only two survivors of the papers presented at those sessions on "Directions in Religious Organization," those by Daniel Elazar and Douglas Johnson, and only the former's is in substantially the same form. The rest of the papers have been recruited over the decade from among colleagues and friends in the religious research "community." Not everyone speaks from exactly the same perspective, but all have written in a non-partisan and ecumenical manner. Most of them are mindful also of the historical nature of churchforms and have also tried to keep an eye on the relationship of what they write to church policy.

The one regretful omission is the lack of a chapter on "Black Denominational Organization." A qualified authority had agreed to supply this chapter but never managed to come through, and it became too late to recruit a substitute.

I would like to thank Thomas M. Gannon, S.J., Chairman of Sociology of Loyola University, and the University itself for many courtesies and logistical support; Ralph D. Winter, General Director, Center for World Mission, for help in making publication possible; Martin E. Marty for writing the Foreword; and of course all the book's contributors without whom this effort would not be possible.

I think I speak for them too in hoping that this volume may modestly assist in making the third petition of the Lord's Prayer, at least from an ecclesiastical point of view, become a greater reality: "Thy will be done on earth as it is in heaven."

Ross P. Scherer

Chicago, Illinois
May 1, 1979

CONTRIBUTORS

Gary P. Burkhart is Associate Professor and Chairman of the Department of Sociology at Benedictine College (Kansas). He received the Ph.D. in sociology from the University of Kansas.

Daniel J. Elazar is Senator N.M. Peterson Professor of Political Studies, Bar Ilan University-Israel, and Professor of Political Science and Director of the Center for the Study of Federalism, Temple University. Holding a Ph.D. in political science from the University of Chicago, he is author of numerous chapters and texts in political science and of the recent *Community and Polity: The Organizational Dynamics of American Jewry* (Jewish Publication Society of America, 1976).

Thomas M. Gannon, S.J., is Professor and Chairman of the Department of Sociology at Loyola University of Chicago. He received his Ph.D. in sociology from the University of Chicago. He has served as President of the Religious Research Association and President of the Association for the Sociology of Religion and is currently a member of the Executive Committee of the International Conference of the Sociology of Religion. He is the author of many articles in professional journals and co-author of the book, *The Desert and the City* (Macmillan, 1969).

William R. Garrett is currently Professor and Chairman of the Department of Sociology at St. Michael's College, Vermont. He received the Ph.D. in the sociology of religion from Drew University. He is the Chairman of the Research and Planning Committee of the Vermont Ecumenical Council and past Chairman of the Department of Professional Ministry, Vermont Baptist State Convention. His publications include many articles in sociological journals and the chapters on "Religion" and "Family" in *Sociology: An Introduction,* edited by Reece McGee (Dryden Press, 1977). He currently is editor of *Sociological Analysis.*

Loyde H. Hartley is Professor and Dean of the Faculty of Lancaster Theological Seminary (United Church of Christ). He received his Ph.D. in the sociology of religion from Emory University and is the author of *Placement and Deployment of Professionals in the United Church of Christ.*

Garry W. Hesser is serving as Associate Professor of Sociology and Director of the Metro-Urban Studies Program at Augsburg College in Minneapolis. He received the Master of Divinity from Union Theological Seminary-NYC and the Ph.D. in sociology from the University of Notre Dame and is the author of numerous articles on urban sociology and the sociology of religion.

Douglas W. Johnson currently is Executive Vice-President of the Institute for Church Development, Inc., Ridgewood, N.J., a private consulting firm. He received the Bachelor of Sacred Theology from Boston University and the Ph.D. in the sociology of religion from Northwestern University and Garrett Seminary. He formerly served as Director of Research and Information Services, National Council of Churches, New York City. He has served as an officer of the Religious Research Association; is co-author of *Punctured Preconceptions* (Friendship Press, 1971) and *Religion in America: 1950 to the Present* (Harper and Row, 1978); and author of *The Care and Feeding of Volunteers* (Abingdon, 1978).

Gertrud Kim, O.S.B., served as Instructor in Sociology at Loyola University of Chicago, having completed her M.A. (and course work for the Ph.D.) there. She is a religious Sister of the Order of St. Benedict.

Martin E. Marty is the Fairfax M. Cone Distinguished Service Professor of the History of Modern Christianity at the University of Chicago and Associate Editor of *The Christian Century.* He received the M. Div. from Concordia Seminary (St. Louis) and the Ph.D. from the University of Chicago and is also the recipient of more than ten honorary degrees. He is past president of the American Society of Church History, formerly served as Associate Dean of the Divinity School, the University of Chicago, and currently is co-editor of *Church History.* Author of dozens of books and articles, he won the National Book Award in 1971 for *The Righteous Empire* and recently published *A Nation of Behavers* and *Religion, Awakening and Revolution.*

Everett L. Perry, "dean" of denominational researchers/planners, currently is Consultant, the Program Agency of the United Presbyterian Church in the U.S.A., New York City. He received the Ph.D. in the sociology of religion from the Divinity School, the University of Chicago. He has served as Vice President of the Religious Research Association and is the author of a host of applied studies and materials in parish sociology and planning, including *The Smaller Church Mission Study Guide* (1978).

Ross P. Scherer currently is Associate Professor of Sociology at Loyola University of Chicago, where he has also served as Chairman of the Department and currently is Director of Graduate Studies in Sociology. He received the Diploma in Theology from Concordia Seminary-St. Louis, and the Ph.D. in sociology from the University of Chicago. Previously he was Director of Research Operations and Director of Ministry Studies at the National Council of Churches, New York City. He is past President of the Religious Research Association and previously authored "The Church as a Formal Voluntary Organization," a chapter in *Voluntary Action Research 1972*, edited by David H. Smith (Lexington Books).

David S. Schuller currently is Associate Director of the Association of Theological Schools in the United States and Canada. He received his Ph.D. in sociology from St. Louis University and formerly was Professor of Practical Theology, Concordia Seminary, St. Louis. He is the author of several articles, book chapters, and is senior project director and co-author of *Readiness for Ministry* (Vol. I "Criteria" and II "Assessment," pub. by ATS in 1975 and 1976); *Ministry in America* will appear in 1980 (Harper and Row).

Kaoru Peter Takayama is Associate Professor of Sociology at Memphis State University, having received the Ph.D. in sociology from Southern Illinois University. He has authored numerous articles and co-authored *A Sociology of Mathematics and Mathematicians* (Paideia Press, 1975).

Ralph D. Winter is General Director of the Center for World Mission, Pasadena, California, and previously was Professor of World Mission, Fuller Theological Seminary. A recipient of the Ph.D. in Linguistics and Anthropology from Princeton University, he is the author of various articles in missiology.

Introduction

The Sociology of Denominational Organization

Ross P. Scherer

This is a book on the sociology of American denominational organization. Not all contributors are sociologists nor would they label themselves as such. Even among the majority who claim to be sociologists, not all work from exactly the same understanding as to just how the sociologist operates. Nevertheless, all contributors are committed to seeing denominations—or major agencies of them—as contemporary social and cultural phenomena which carry on their life within the larger environment of American society and which operate from a special sense of identity and mission. The book makes no claim to be an exhaustive treatment of all American denominations as organizational phenomena. While the writers treat major denominational "families" and important agencies, their treatments are selective. The major contribution of this book, rather, is to suggest a new viewpoint for looking at denominations, that of "open systems" theory. According to this view, denominations

are highly complex structures which, *because* they are human organizations among other organizations (though possessing a divinely given
"mission"), must continually confront competing choices which produce
conflict, strain, imbalance, or less than full satisfaction at any one point
in time. In other words, because modern society is complex and
changing, denominations too become complex and must continually face
"dilemmas" which require adjustments in goals and strategies for
mission. Like a logger riding on a turning log, they must continually act to
maintain "balance." At times, denominations can be assertive and
aggressive over against society, and at other times retreating and
withdrawing. For each choice and solution, there is a gain and there is a
price. Perhaps some sociological understanding of denominations as
open systems can aid churchmen in making better choices.

THE CURRENT SITUATION IN
CHURCH AND SOCIOLOGY

The last twenty years have been turbulent ones for the churches.
While the social setting of American religion has been "pluralistic" and
competitive almost from the beginning, the logical consequences of this
pluralism have had to await the post-World War II situation. Events
since World War II have made the "normalcy" and the internal
preoccupations of the American churches prior to that time seem tame by
comparison. With the movement of population to suburbia in the 1950s,
church membership hit an all-time peak. But the 1954 U.S. Supreme
Court decision on public school segregation along racial lines spotlighted
a national problem and symbolized a national change on which most of
the churches had been silent. The turbulence came to a head in the 1960s
with the civil rights movement, the election of the first Roman Catholic
as President of the U.S., the youth revolt against the "establishment"
and the Vietnam War, the "black manifesto," the discovery of the
phenomenon of "civil religion" (as distinguished from "denominational
religion"), the spread of pentecostal religiosity and the "Jesus" movements, the economic crunch which launched us into the 1970s, and the
phenomenon of Watergate and the resignation of an American President
in disgrace. In a more specifically ecclesiastical way, we began to see the
ecumenical impact of the "open window" unlocked after 400 years by the
Roman Catholic Church at Vatican Council II. As counterpoint, we saw
first the rise, near demise, and now altered format for merger among the
more Americanized Protestant denominations in the form of the Consultation on Church Union.

The 1970s have seemingly put American denominational organizations on the defensive. Many people, especially youth, have become
indifferent to the bodies which traditionally have nurtured their religious

faith. They however, became selectively excited over Eastern and mystical religions and pseudo-religions. Centralized denominational structures had to cut back their staffs; the movement to suburbia began to slow down; a medieval-like shift in focus to the local congregation and away from the regional and national judicatory levels set in. And yet, in the latter '70s a new calm—and possibly a renewed vigor—has begun to come over the churches. This has been accompanied by the ascendancy to power of an American President who is avowedly committed to social reconciliation and personally devoted to his own brand of denominational Christianity (Southern Baptist), and yet thus far in a non-offensive way. Whether these are signs or portents of a true religious revival is not yet clear.[1] Recently, too, we have begun to see flags of stress and caution being raised over against a number of "cults," culminating in the horror over the incredible, tragic suicide-murder of over 400 persons at the People's Temple, in Jonestown, Guiana, in November, 1978.

The last decades have also seen some twists in the fate of the behavioral sciences. If World War I was the turning point for the emergence of scientific psychology, the same can probably be said for World War II as the period of emergence of scientific sociology. The sociology of religion and the sociology of complex organizations have come of age since that time. Three professional organizations have been established in the U.S. in the 1960s for the scientific study of religion— The Society for the Scientific Study of Religion, the Religious Research Association, and the Association for the Sociology of Religion (in addition to societies for church history, missiology, etc.). Each publishes a scientific journal. The second of these has made its avowed aim to assist denominational religion in the development of organizational "policy." Meanwhile, almost the same developments have occurred with respect to the behavioral study of complex organizations. Specialized journals and textbooks on organizations regularly appear; while theoretical consensus is not yet here, some sifting and sorting of theoretical approaches to the study of organizations has begun to take place. The time, therefore, now seems ripe to attempt some rapprochement between the heretofore separate fields of the sociology of religion and the sociology of complex organizations.

The application of systematic research methods to the study of church units is not exactly new, for as far back as the 1920s and '30s H. Paul Douglass and his disciples poured forth countless studies of Protestant congregations and church agencies in various urban centers in the United States via the New York-based Institute of Social and Religious Research. These were followed by many doctoral dissertations and lesser theses both in university sociology departments and in university-related theological schools, especially at the University of Chicago. (See Everett L. Perry's comments on the early adoption of the ecological model for the study of local churches in Chapter 7.) However, while some of these studies were fairly sophisticated for the time, they often proceeded without a clear theoretical basis, or their theoretical frameworks were particularistic to church organization and probably unmindful of the fact that *all* organizations have certain common problems as they seek to cope effectively amidst changing environments. Probably the model concept most widely used in the study of religious organizaton has been the *church-sect* typology enunciated by Ernst Troeltsch, later recast as a developmental sequence by H. Richard Niebuhr, and still later detailed in numerous component dimensions by Liston Pope.[2]

Useful and informing as these concepts have been, they too are now revealed as particularistic, both in terms of the particular historical and sociopolitical situation (that of the European, "established" state-churches) and the particular institutional sector (the ecclesiastical-theological) out of which they grew. These limitations make church-sect less than universal as a vehicle for clarifying the nature of church-as-organization.

Thus, any "new look" for examining religious organizations must simultaneously be capable of seeing religious denominations *as organizations among other organizations* and thereby possessing the *same* structural attributes and processes as are *common* to all organizations; and also as *unique* and possessing distinctive attributes by virtue of their transcendent outlook and commitments. Good sociology will seek to preserve and not violate the integrity of outlook and identity possessed by any organization. Throughout church history, there have always been those who in their approach to the church-as-organization have leaned to one side or the other. Those who have followed a Doetic-like approach have denied the "natural" or human character of religious organizations in favor of viewing *only* the *divine*; others of an Arian-like bent have tended to see churches as *only natural* and human. The present volume does not deny the possibility of "the divine," but it pretends to be unable sufficiently to deal with the transcendent via sociological concepts except insofar as the "divine" is capturable in human consequences, for example, in the form of a special self-concept, special degree of commitment, special goals, or special symbolism. Thus, the sociological aim must be modest and not pretend to exhaust the total ontological reality of churchly organizations as divine-human works (see Gertrud Kim's pertinent remarks on this problem in Chapter 2).

THE "OPEN SYSTEMS" MODEL

As we said, we need an approach to the study of denominations which sees them both as organizations among other organizations and also as unique. An approach to which more and more students of organizations are currently turning is the "open systems"/contingency perspective. At this point, we prefer to refer to it only as a model, rather than as a theory, since insufficient work has yet been done to fully elaborate and test it as a tool for empirical explanation. The latter, however, is an important future objective. The open systems models is more attractive than other models because it seems usefully (1) to permit observation of both factual/objective types of data as well as more subjective "impression;" (2) to handle the interchanges between various external and internal levels of operation; (3) to admit the possibility of continuous "strain" (which under certain conditions may break out as conflict) as normal to all organizations; (4) to view seeming stability of structure as the face of "process" and all semblance of "order" as being a continually "negotiated order." Thus, proponents of the open systems view wish to include as much as possible in their perspective while simultaneously trying to minimize the amount of distortion.

While "open systems" means much more, much of its current relevance derives from its emphasis upon the relation of the organization to its *environment*. Previous models tended to see the organization as self-enclosed and having to contend with the problem of internal disorder. For being able to see the organization as a dynamic system in interchange with its environment, we probably have to thank the work of those in the field of comparative biology, for open systems originally grew out of the study of the organism and later of the individual person (psychology). Only recently, has it been applied to systems like the sociocultural, which are really "emergent" entities. As with most sociological entities, the assumption here is that emergents, such as the group, the complex organization, the community and the national society, each have a life of their own and are *not reducible* merely *to* the *sum of their parts*. This means organizations are capable of becoming ends in themselves and of being almost endowed with personality. This seems especially true of those systems termed "churches," in which members invest so much of themselves—which are viewed as transcendent in purpose and God-given. Nevertheless, while such systems as a kind of "super-being" often influence people in their actions, we must never forget that without the "parts" (the people) the system would be lifeless and inert and that the "parts" are sometimes capable of resisting and producing a different outcome. Thus, organizational outcomes are seldom automatic and should be seen as the results of negotiation (and sometimes power struggle and conflict) between leaders and leaders and between leaders and led. The popular, Islamic revolution in Iran in 1979 is a case in point.

LEVELS OF SOCIAL SCIENTIFIC ABSTRACTION

Before we further discuss how the sociologist thinks of organizations as open systems, it seems desirable to consider how the social scientist thinks as such, how he or she handles forms and appearances and through a process of abstraction broadens their meaning by generalization to a higher order of reality. In trying to classify these levels of reality, however, we run into the problem of "jargon" or terminology. Many intellectuals rebel at sociology's use of special terms and seem averse to its dealing with everyday happenings from a special viewpoint. But tool ideas are the stock in trade of any modern discipline which wishes to build a system of knowledge that is universal in acceptance and enduring in time. Proceeding from the more abstract to the less abstract, most scientific disciplines distinguish the following descending levels of concepts: paradigm, model, theory, empirical observation. Sociologists similarly make use of these.

Paradigm

A *paradigm* is one of the broadest and abstractest approaches to reality. Ritzer defines it as follows:

> A paradigm is a fundamental image of the subject matter within a science. It serves to define what should be studied, what questions should be asked, how they should be asked, and what rules should be followed in interpreting the answers obtained. The paradigm is the broadest unit of consensus within a science and serves to differentiate one scientific community (or sub-community) from another. It subsumes, defines, and interrelates the exemplars, theories, methods, and instruments that exist within it.[3]

Ritzer goes on to state that sociologists generally employ at least three different "fundamental images" of subject matter—the factist, definitionist, and behaviorist.

The *factist* ("social facts") paradigm tends to be the most dominant in sociology and tends to see society as a vast interrelation of nation-states, institutional networks, organizations, and interest groups on a large-scale basis. The sample survey or poll is the research technique most used. In this picture, the denomination would be seen as a large-scale organization connected externally to other organizations and other competing denominations and composed internally of diverse elements (diocese, districts, congregations, special agencies) connected to each other over vast expanses of territory. One of the sub-approaches (exemplars) under the factist paradigm would be that which views the denomination (and all complex organizations) as a "social system" or as a set of "role" structures. As stated, the facist paradigm is probably the one most applied in sociology, especially in analyzing large-scale forces. However, it tends to have a bias toward determinism and to view human actors as almost compelled by the environmental forces (e.g., class structure, organizational size, complexity) which surround them. If we can be aware that it is just one point of view, among others, it can serve us usefully.

The *definitionist* paradigm, according to others, more fully takes account of man's uniqueness and wholeness as a perceiving and deciding human being. It focuses less upon large-scale structures and more upon people trying to understand and make sense out of each other's meanings via intimate groups. It tends to see man less as determined and more as imposing his own world view upon outer reality. Definitional analysis would pay special attention to the beliefs and self-conceptions of religious people and their organizations on the assumption that how people *see* themselves, in relation to their fellow men and to God, affects how they will *behave*. It is obvious that this approach, valid as it may be, may ignore other, important forces influencing action. Personal observation, case study, and content analysis are the techniques of study most used.

The *behaviorist* paradigm, of the three, is probably least used in sociology and more employed in psychology. Whereas the factist approach studies the largest-scale forces, and the definitionist intermediate levels, the behaviorist focuses on the smallest kinds of exchanges between person and person and person and group, and usually by means of controlled experiments in a laboratory. Some deem it, with its emphases upon psychic costs and balances, as a kind of "sociological economics." Some behaviorists may approach man mechanistically; they seek to reduce human motivation to its basic, irreducible psychological elements. Undoubtedly, members of churches can be thought of as engaging in exchanges with others in terms of psychic costs and balances; behaviorist analysis may well shed some light, e.g., on the practices of giving and receiving within denominations. But such an approach can scarcely exhaust the total reality of religious men carrying on worship, witness, religious education, and a search for social justice within structures we call denominations.

The conclusion to this must be, then, that the various approaches/paradigms each touch a valid level of reality and that the pursuit of all three (and more) will yield the fullest degree of understanding that is possible.

Model

If a paradigm gives basic direction and provides a "fundamental image of the subject matter" we seek, a model brings us another level down to reality. A model gives a general picture, not a photograph but a general idea, of the phenomenon we want to deal with. It is a kind of "prototype," a simplified and stripped down version of something that in reality is much more detailed and unique. If you ask a small child to draw a "car," he or she will probably draw a general profile featuring a body, two wheels, windows, and a hood. We would not expect the "model" here to look like a particular "make." A descriptive model or type in social science, then, is a generalized picture of a social form with which we deal in everyday life and yet inclusive enough to cover many individual cases. Various sociologists of organizations have portrayed their preferences in their model-pictures of what successful, modern organizations are to look like. Some have likened the large-scale organizations to a machine (scientific management); others have said it is really like a big family (human relations); and others have termed it a transformation system, a complex set of processes for accomplishing certain objectives by carrying on exchanges with the "environment" outside it (open systems). As with the paradigms, the various models each also undoubtedly portray an element of the truth. Just as complex organizations vary widely (e.g., a bank vs. a YMCA), so perhaps must the "models" also vary, the more closely they try to reflect real groups.

Daniel Bell notes that in Western history the most widespread images for thinking about organizations have been those growing out of experience with the church and the army.[4] The Bible itself provides a number of metaphors for "organizing for God." In Exodus we have the image of a charismatic leader, Moses, leading a mighty column of immigrants out of captivity to the "promised land." The church as a march of immigrants has been a favorite of black preachers. Bunyan in *Pilgrim's Progress* also uses the metaphor of "Christian" on a dangerous pilgrimage. Christ in His parables frequently likened the "Kingdom of God" to a farm, a small business, a family, or some other small-scale group. St. Paul used a number of ancient world models to describe the form of religious organization, frequently comparing the struggles of believers to soldiers in an army or athletes in Olympic games. Probably most notable, however, is his identification of the early Christian movement with an organism, the human body, in which the church members comprise "the body of Christ" and who as parts are to function cooperatively with one another (1 Cor. 12: 12-31). Undoubtedly, church and military models have reciprocally influenced each other throughout history since both share the need for structure, firmness of mission and zeal, and risk.

Theory

We can now treat two other tool concepts (besides paradigm and model) briefly. Just as a model brings us another step closer to reality, *a theory* brings us even closer. "*A*" theory, (as opposed to general theoretical discussion) is a particular set of assumptions and hypotheses which are logically connected in such a way that they can explain and predict relations between two or more factors (variables). A theory, then, normally states relationships in the form of *propositions that are testable* by reference to reality (a descriptive model is not ordinarily testable).[5] Unfortunately, we have very few, if any such "theories" in the area of organizations; we may have some bits and pieces. Historically the biggest theory-type idea in the study of religious organization has been the Troeltsch-Niebuhr hypothesis that, over time and under certain conditions, a "sect" will "settle down" and become transformed into a "denomination." Considerable research has been done to test this.

Empirical Observation

At the other extreme from paradigm is the raw and unrefined *empirical observation*. Whether it is a simple observation like that attributed to Watt, that steam pressure tended to push up the lid of his mother's teakettle; or that the average rate of Sunday church attendance in the U.S. in the 1970s has been on the decline, such observations form the raw materials for any kind of testable science, including a social science of religious organization. When we begin to think systematically, therefore, about the nature of churches as organizations, we ought to be aware of the particular level of abstraction on which we are thinking; we ought to be quite explicit about the particular assumptions we are working from.

DETAILS OF THE OPEN SYSTEMS MODEL

We can now pick up where we left off earlier and examine the open systems perspective as a model for approaching the study of organizations, specifically religious organizations. What are the assumptions with which it operates? These can now be summarized in more detail as follows:[6] (1) The organization is seen as a huge transformation system, whereby its personnel procure resources (input), do something with and to them (throughput), and exchange the products (output) with other persons and organizations in the environment. (2) It is crucial for the organization and its personnel somehow to come to terms with forces in the outer "environment." For in the environment ordinarily lies its survival, as it is the main source of the organization's resources—its goals, people, finances, and security. The organization would run down (undergo "entropy") unless it were constantly reenergized from without. The environment thus also offers the constant possibility of "variety," parts of which can be incorporated into the organization. (3) The organization is capable of "mapping" and "coding" its external reality, and the mappings and codings of information are fed back and stored in the system. This means that the organization personnel's assimilations of the environment are *selective*, and only those mappings are preserved which organizational actors interpret as "successful" or "effective." (4) All this results in what some theorists term a "steady state" (even including some "slack" periods), which really is not a permanent stability but only a relative order and which exists with a latent presence of "strain." (5) The organization exists in and itself has a history. This permits experimentation with a variety of policies for pursuing mission over a period of time. When its functionaries become aware of mismatches with desired outcomes, "feedback" occurs, and this feedback serves as a stimulus for correcting actions. Thus, a certain amount of "deviance" can be expected and, in fact, actually be beneficial. (As with the body, a "mild" heart attack can serve as a salutary warning.) (6) The organization seemingly is stabilized by a "structure" of roles, rules, and understandings, but this should not cover up the fact that it really lives by a *process* of engagement—its order is a constantly *negotiated* order. (7) This means there really is no "one best way" but *many* ways to reach given objectives. This elevates the continuous importance of the human actors as decision makers and creators of policy. These then are some of the assumptions underlying the perspective of the "open systems" model.

As stated, the importance of environment is currently being underlined by contemporary theorists of organizations. Emery and Trist,[7] British industrial psychologists, have carried our understanding of environment even further by providing one of the more exciting portraits of environments in terms of differing degrees of density and complexity. They posit a fourfold classification of structural relations of organizations to each other and the vital forces around them.

Park and Burgess, University of Chicago sociologists, earlier had leaned on concepts of plant and animal ecology to understand the development of American cities; they suggested that competition was the basic process by which human population allocated land for commercial as well as residential uses. Emery and Trist go beyond this and suggest that the relations of organizations to each other, competitive or collusive, operate in time and within an environmental framework of changing density and complexity. (For example, the fast foods industry faced by an entrant into that field today is vastly different from the one faced by "McDonald's System, Inc." when it incorporated back in 1955.) One can cite many examples of the way in which "product" organizations come to dominate their situations by securing a certain percentage "share of the market." The notion of an evolution of an organizational context or "field" is thus a reasonable assumption. The field for a given set of organizations—e.g., automobile manufacturers, school systems, hospitals, purveyors of luxury goods—can develop, expand, shrink, even evaporate. We see this happen daily.

To be more specific, Emery and Trist suggest the following four, ideal type stages of development of organizational "causal textures:" (1) *Placid-randomized or -unclustered.* This is the situation in which the focal organization can hardly identify an "opposite number"—a "figure with no ground." This is the undefined situation of "pure competition" in which an organization does not even know who its competitors may be. (This stage does not last long, however, if it exists.) (2) *Placid-clustered.*

At this stage, organizations begin to define their field, to take account of rivals, to experience modifications of unrestrained competition, and to cluster but not in systematic ways. (3) *Disturbed-reactive*. At this stage, the field has grown dense with ever more entrants into the competition. Several interlinked clusters may emerge, frequently affiliated via standard-setting and regulating authorities like a "league," a "council," or a "trade association." Competition may turn into collusion, and the field may narrow down to an oligopoly of a "big three" or "four." (Compare, for example, the marked difference between the fields of metropolitan television and FM broadcasting.) (4) *Turbulent*. This involves emergence of a "true field" with a life of its own. Interactive effects of the field itself overwhelm the component parts. Multiple clusters and systems emerge, each with their own dynamics. Environmental complexity makes "step jumps" to new levels, making it nigh impossible for decision makers in individual organizations to predict outcomes. More concretely, today the near revolutionary effects of new technology and the emergence of world markets mean almost total uncontrollability and unpredictability. (For example, consider the plight of the major American auto-makers in the last few years who simultaneously have found themselves face-to-face with environmental protest movements, Federal controls upon pollution, invasion of their markets by foreign auto-makers, inflation, the rise in prices by the oil-producers, and the coming of the "energy crisis." These surely are the marks of a "turbulent field!") The reader may make his or her own application to the plight of "old-line" denominations who are faced in their ministries to youth by the invasion of Eastern religions and the rise of new cults. The diffusion and popularity of these is in part an interactive effect of U.S. military activity overseas as well as the world's becoming one market and one communications system.

The Functional Tasks of Organizations

As stated, the open systems persepective views the organization as getting something (resources), doing something with this, and then exchanging the transformed product with other agencies or persons in the environment in a continuous recycling. This implies that as they carry on their life, all organizations are faced with certain *tasks*. There is, however, no agreement on just which are the essential processes of organizations, nor which are the most important. Furthermore, some would regard the whole effort to posit such "functional tasks" or "requirements" as an exercise in tautology. Price,[8] for example, lists twenty-two processes (plus an additional eight for which he finds no existing measures); Heydebrand[9] lists twenty-four, clustering them under four categories (environment and autonomy, complexity of goal and task/program structure, internal structural differentiation, coordination and control). Champion[10] lists sixteen, clustering them under four general headings (structure, control, behavior, change). Beckford,[11] concerned specifically to adapt the open systems perspective to religious organization, has come up with four major foci—environment, resources, processes, and structures, the last one subdivided into four more (specialization, formalization, centralization, and distribution of authority).

Parsons[12] has enunciated what is undoubtedly the most renowned list of such "system requirements" in his fourfold A-G-I-L scheme: Adaptation, Goal-Attainment, Integration, and Latency ("latency" meaning the less obtrusive tasks of "pattern-maintenance" and "tension-management"). Actually, each of these is really a cluster of processes. Parsons seldom spells out details; but a liberal interpretation of the kinds of requirements involved in each might be as follows.[13] *Adaptation* means that the organization must come to terms with this environment—the warding off of external threats and the securing of "legitimacy" and the right to exist; the development and procuring of resources with which to do its work, especially funding of programs; the cooptation of a social base or constituency which can serve as the organization's source of key personnel and as audience. James Thompson has pointed to the importance of organizational gatekeepers' converting situations of "uncertainty" into "certainty." They do this either through (a) passively neutralizing environmental opposition through "buffering" and stockpiling of extra resources, "leveling" or regularizing environmentally produced fluctuations, and "forecasting" market opposition through better information, research, and polling; and/or (b) actively manipulating the environment via "vertical merger" (cooptation of rivals where possible), "horizontal merger" (cooperation in externals as necessary), and trying to influence outside "regulators" (e.g., government) to be more benign.

Goal-attainment means the political process of determining policy and program, including development of staff specialization, position/role structures, and mechanisms for allocating resources and coordinating effort. Goal-attainment also may involve minimizing uncertainty in the area of an organization's "internal technology" (e.g., in denominations, in their seminary professors' use of volatile higher critical methodology in scriptural interpretation). Administrators face the task of keeping the "leakage of uncertainty" into the inner (theological?) "technical core" to a minimum.

Thus, the imagery is of a closed system (the technical core) operating within the technical boundaries of an open system.[14]

Organizational officials thereby face the paradoxical task of trying to "have" the organizational "cake" and "eat it too"!

Integration involves attention to cohesion of the system, including providing symbolism and traditions, as well as mechanisms for handling grievance. *Latency* refers to the less obtrusive but no less important tasks of keeping the system going—recruiting new members to replace old, socializing and passing on the tradition to the new or young, handling the personal-individual problems of members so that such problems do not detract from participation in the system.

An important point which Parsons does not emphasize, however, is that organizations *seldom* have the opportunity to meet or fulfill these tasks *one at a time* but they must handle them *simultaneously*. Handling the diversity of processes required for survival or mission is not an "either or" but a "both and." Early in the life of organizations, members must devote much effort to the procurement of resources—funds, members; this makes it difficult to give equal attention to knitting the members together as a group. Nevertheless, even while giving more attention to *one* cluster of tasks, *all* must be given their due. For example, Methodism on the early American Frontier was at first primarily engaged in adapting to the peculiar nature of this environment via a new form of evangelism, a new strategy for reaching migrants scattered over a frontier—the emergence of the itinerant circuit-rider. However, it had simultaneously to be concerned about developing sufficient esprit de corps, identity, and solidarity to provide a rallying point amid the flux of the westward-moving migration. So Methodism created its "book of Discipline."

In the history of denominational development, Presbyterians are said to have worked with a more democratic government but a "monarchical Gospel;" while Methodists developed a "monarchical" government but preached a more "democratic Gospel."[15] Each group tried to balance external adaptation with each's peculiar form of identity. (See the next chapter for a more detailed view of how theology or "ideology" can be related to choice of organizational strategy and tactics.) It may be that there are varying stages in the development of an organization whereby leaders will successively have to move back and forth from one task to another, giving each need its hour and due. Organizational development and nurturing then becomes a matter of *balancing and phasing*. Some cycles may repeat themselves, some not. Sometimes, there will be major conflict with an external force—the state; sometimes, the stress will be more internal and result from discontent and dissatisfaction among the grass roots. The separate parts of requirements of an organizational thus function as part of a dynamic whole or come to be in tension with each other and with outer forces. People (and organizations?) apparently need both recognition (or security) *and* challenge; similarly, too much isolation can curb creativity—contact, while it does involve "strain," is found to be more productive.[16] Potentiality for strain is always present. With shifts in the environment, such strains can become *stresses* or out-and-out conflicts. People will not continue to tolerate such stresses indefinitely, however. They will bear them until they can adjust them and a new "steady state" is regained.

"Negotiated Order" and Structure

If it is true that all organizations today are having more and more to deal with a changing environment, if the internal order which results is more and more only a temporarily "negotiated" one, how can we characterize various kinds of organizations in terms of their internal unity, their looseness or tightness? Warren suggests that at the one extreme there are *"unit"* organizations which maintain ownership or central control over all the organization's parts (even though authority to act may be delegated downward through appropriate channels). An industrial conglomerate or a large university ("multiversity") will still be a unit organization if the central executive has veto power over any decision of subordinates. At the other extreme, Warren posits a field of organizations operating with almost total independence of each other, a situation akin to Emery and Trist's "placid-randomized" or "placid-clustered" field—he terms this a "social choice" situation.[17] In between such situations with either central control or no control, he lists two other types with partial control—the "coalition" and the "federation." The *coalition* is a cooperative arrangement between organizations whereby they share certain ad hoc program objectives, with each unit organization lending personnel to form a joint staff or "task force" but maintaining separate organizational identities. The *federation* is closer to the unit organization in that it is an "organization of organizations," with member units giving more of their autonomy to an ongoing, full time federation staff who are responsible to a federation board, and not directly to the component organization members. (See p. 42 for details of Warren's typology.) Federative organization is very common today, e.g., the AFL-CIO, the United Nations, numerous trade associations. Because of the lack of consensus and the amount of uncertainty built into such organizations of organizations, coalitions and federations can be very fragile—constituent members can withdraw at any time and pull out staff and funding overnight. This means such organizations are essentially *political* (like state or federal legislatures) and can involve constant negotiation. The staffs of federations, therefore, seem to function most effectively when given the tasks of carrying out fairly neutral, instrumental functions like research and development, providing "good offices" for facilitating the meeting together of members, or arranging for seminars on topics of common interest, etc. (See Chapter 11 for Garrison's discussion of how one such federation, the National Council of Churches, can be seen as being in a rivalry with its constituent member organizations.)

The last section of this chapter specifically treats the concept of denomination. Nevertheless, at this point a comment on the federative character of the denomination may be in order. Generally speaking, American denominations, while sometimes *appearing* to be unit organizations are really *federations* (occasionally coalitions). (Burkart clearly demonstrates this in the next chapter, as also does Winter for evangelical Protestant groups.) Most Protestant and Jewish denominational ideologies contain strong defenses of the principle of decentralization and federation. The local congregation usually owns its own property and usually makes the decisions on the hiring or termination of its professional staff. However, within Protestantdom, there are degrees of federativeness. Generally, religious organizations, because of their voluntary character, are more decentralized than business or governmental organizations. They are held together less by structure and apparatus, and more by sentiments and commitments of members and by organizational ritual and ideology ("faith"). Unquestionably, however, greater tentativeness and looseness is a growing characteristic of *all* organizations today, not just the religious ones.

THE DENOMINATION AS AN OPEN SYSTEM

With this general review of tool concepts employed in sociological thinking and the assumptions of the open systems model, the functional requirements of organizations, and structural types, we are now ready to make application of all this to denominations as open systems. To the credit of the past investigators of religious organizational phenomena, they have long worked with model concepts of religious organization. But, as noted earlier in this chapter, the major model used, the church-sect typology, is too particularistic and dated if we are truly interested in a "new look" which would help us transfer discoveries from research on *other* organizations to the field of *religious* organization. We need an approach using the *less* particular—this will actually help us to explain *more*. This new look is the open systems model. Within this model, we can make the necessary qualifications so that the integrity of any organization, even of organizations claiming a special basis of legitimacy as religious organizations do, can be preserved.

The present book conceives of the religious *denomination* as the major organizational form of religion in the modern world. The major significance of the term, "denomination" (or "denominationalism" when the environing or systemic situation is meant), relates to the *environing field* in which the denomination is found. That is, when the term denomination is used, it refers not simply to the kind of internal form but to a kind of sociopolitical environment—that of pluralism, competition, church-state detachment, and agree-to-disagree toleration.

Denominations are in part of whole the products of their environments, and this can be good or bad. They can be tamed-down sects, as in the case of Methodism; or, they can be accommodated, state-church types which have been transferred from Europe, as in the case of Catholicism, the Lutherans, and the Episcopalians.[18] Thus, the "old look" terms may still be useful in one sense—as when we refer to a particular American denomination as historically having been "church-originated" or "sect-originated." Such labels tell us something in a nutshell about the particular denomination's history, and probably also something about its contemporary ethos. Elsewhere, I have gone into more detail concerning evaluations of the denomination as a spiritual force noting that many have considered it to be activistic, pragmatic, atheological, lay-dominated, political, exclusivistic, and class-selective.[19] Much of this is probably true. However, American denominations are reflective of the sociopolitical system which has evolved in the U.S. On the other hand, positively speaking, over against the European forebears, American religiosity certainly in quantitative terms surpasses the European variety. Is it possible for quality to develop out of quantity? Are the chances for this as good if there is *less* quantity or little quantity at all?

The denomination is a new and unique ecclesiastical form which had its birth in America under the complex conditions which existed between the Revolution and the Civil War. Church historian Sidney Mead puts it well:

> The denomination, unlike the traditional forms of the Church, is not primarily confessional, and it is certainly not territorial. Rather it is purposive. And unlike any previous "church" in Christendom, it has no official connection with a civil power whatsoever. . . . Neither is the denomination a "sect" in any traditional sense, and certainly not in the most common sense of a dissenting body in relationship to an Established Church. It is, rather, a voluntary association of like-minded individuals, who are united on the basis of common beliefs for the purpose of accomplishing tangible and defined objectives. One of the primary objectives is the propagation of its point of view, which it in some sense holds to be "true."[20]

Thus, the hallmarks of the denomination are its "private," non-state character, competitive relations to those outside it, voluntaristic attachment of its members and reliance upon persuasion, being directed to specific purposes (e.g., fund-raising, evangelism), its general malleability in relation to the environing situation. As said, these characteristics may be viewed as "good" or as "bad," depending upon the criteria.

A historian like Mead sheds valuable light in distilling the denominational essence out of reading countless denominational histories. Nevertheless, if we wish to do research on religious organization using the paradigms of sociological thinking, the label "denomination" by itself does not help us very much to develop a scientific study of the internal and external operations of denominations as organizational entities.

Conventionally, denominations are classified according to the major form of church polity or internal government for which they are known— e.g., episcopal, presbyterian, congregational. Mead has commented that many operate with a mixed polity, e.g., that the Lutheran type is more properly "presbygational." However, much more objectionable than this is that such classifications are based on *formal* criteria and tend to ignore *informal*, operative patterns. As Harrison has noted for the case of the American Baptist Churches, informal, functional "bishops" lacking the formal title "bishop" may be much more powerful than those possessing such titles but lacking much real organizational power.[21] The fact of the matter is that, in an environment of denominational pluralism which has long existed in the United States (and is becoming the pattern for the rest of the free world), more denominations operate *alike* than differently. In the different traditions, they just have different labels for the same thing. Such labels are deceiving.

Let us in the final part of the Introduction to this book sketch some of the more particular implications of the open-systems model for the dynamics of the denomination as "an organization among other organizations." The open systems/contingency approach views the organization as a transformation process intimately linked with its environment. In the past, sociology textbooks written from the perspective of the "functionalist" variety of open systems typically have assigned churches in modern society the tasks of stabilizing the social order, supporting the public mores, tending to the proper socialization of the children (e.g., into the Ten Commandments), and providing "comfort" to the emotionally broken and bereaved.[22] At worst, they have tended to see organized religion as on the side of conservation, the "establishment," "privilege," or "reaction." In this view, denominations are seen as receiving toleration and resources of money and people and, in return, providing a source of stability for society.

More recently, however, sociologists and especially journalists have seen the inadequacy of this view and have been noting the "prophetic" or critical stance of at least some churchmen over against the status quo. Thus, implicitly they have begun to recognize another authentic function of religion (in addition to the "priestly" or stabilizing one)—subjecting contemporary social standards and practices to transcendent standards of "judgment." While it is probably true that American denominations probably emphasized the priestly and comfort contributions of religion during World War II and also the period of suburban settlement during the 1950s, the 1960s saw a reemphasis upon the other side in the form of church-originated protests against racial injustice and U.S. involvement in Vietnam. Thus became evident what has always been the case throughout history—the inevitability of tension between priestly and prophetic traditions of spirituality. Thus, denominational religion can be capable of providing sources for *both maintenance and* also *adaptation* of society.

Max Weber, the great German sociologist of the early twentieth century, pleaded for the autonomy of the "ideological" factor and was inclined to see religious ideas as something other than a rationalization for "material" privilege (which was the Marxian view).[23] A Protestant theologian and admirer of Weber, H. Richard Niebuhr,[24] however, emphasized the other side, the way in which American denominations in their historical developments became expressions of interests in social class, ethnicity, race, and region. Implicitly, however, both Weber and Niebuhr would agree that denominational relationship with environment is inevitably *interactive*, with *both* the denomination and the external society shaping *each other*.

Another way of putting the above (as Takayama notes in Chapter 9) is to state, in terms of Emery and Trist's "causal textures" of environment, that the denominational situation has moved from "placid-clustered" in the 1930s to "disturbed-reactive" in the 1950s and to "turbulent" in the 1960s and 1970s. As noted earlier, however, this shift in environmental textures is true also for most other organizations as well, although other organizations (e.g., business) react in different ways.

Denominations are both like other organizations and also "special." Denominations, like other organizations, have to come to terms with a number of basic "needs" or tasks. They have to adapt to environments; they have to face an open society and try to control it for their own ends, enhancing their own security and certainty. They have to attain objectives, which includes the developing of structures, strategies, and tactics for reaching them; this usually involves creation of an apparatus, staffs, leadership patterns, and communications. All also need a certain amount of internal cohesion, organizational loyalty, and resolution of internal conflicts and grievances. Finally, all organizations must solve the problems of member compliance, socialization and nurture of the young, including replacement of personnel and leadership lost through death or defection, and also the rewarding of member participation. This is a big order.

On the other hand, denominations are and operate in ways that are "special" or "different." In line with the preceding list of processes, let us note some of the differences. When it comes to the question of *adaptation* to the environment, how certain is the "legitimacy" of the churches in the public domain, where officially they are just additional, private, "voluntary associations"? While they are not primarily "market" organizations, they tend distinctly to compete in markets. Their institutional positions are not guaranteed, including their resource base; membership and commitment are at a continual ebb and flow. As Will

Rogers is said to have commented about the Supreme Court, denominational staffs have to "read the election returns" since funding is basically
a "trickle up" process going from the local congregations to middle level
judicatories, national headquarters, and finally (if any) to ecumenical
organizations. Ironically, during economic recessions, many denominations—unlike business organizations—tend to cut back on adaptive tools
like "research and development" first. Such shortsightedness would be
considered suicidal in other organizations.

Regarding the process of *goal attainment*, there may be an argument
whether denominations really have goals or are in fact "goalless."[25] If
there are goals, the extent to which these are priestly vs. prophetic is a
question. According to the open systems view, such strain from duality of
goals might actually be good. Denominations probably suffer from some
of the same, inevitable tendencies toward member apathy and toward
oligarchy of leadership experienced by other voluntary associations
(such as political parties, labor unions, and professional associations).
Denominations tend to be dispersed over wide territories; their full time
professionals sometimes experience social distance from the part time
lay "amateurs"; the grass roots can sometimes be alienated from and not
be familiar with the view as seen from central headquarters. Denominations are "people-changing" and not "product-producing" organizations. Because of political reasons—and probably for effectiveness of
essential goals—most American denominations operate with decentralized decision making. They may centralize determination of general
goals but they generally decentralize how this is worked out. As noted
before, they fit the federative or coalitional model of organization rather
than the "corporate" or "unit" type. In actual practice, they range from
the once extremely centralized Roman Catholic pattern to the decentralized, diffused operation of Judiasm. While some seem to be highly
"connectionalist" and even bureaucratized (e.g., National Council of
Churches), this may really only be a veneer in comparison with truly
bureaucratic agencies (e.g., the military, Internal Revenue Service). As
Everett Perry maintains (Chapter 7) different *structural levels* of the
denomination may have to be judged by different goal criteria. For
example, rational planning involving clearcut goals like improvement of
social and economic justice may effectively apply at the *national*
denominational level; but less rational and more expressive goals like
worship, personal fulfillment, and mutual acceptance may apply more at
the *local* congregational level. The congregation basically may be more
communal and family-like than organization-like.

When it comes to the question of *internal cohesion* or solidarity,
denominations par excellence possess unique resources. The occasional
factional fights, even schisms, only underscore the intensity and
uniqueness of denominational loyalty. The organization itself frequently

becomes "the cause"; no other organizations have such survival power. Perhaps more than other organizations, denominations are motivated by special forms of ideology or belief. Such ideological systems can act as powerful agents of socialization and control, almost creating a situation of "private government" for the members who are constrained to "be separate" and non-conformist with the external society. (This is truer of sects, of course, than of denominations.) Various contributors disagree on emphases; for example, Burkart stresses the importance of ideological purpose, while Takayama emphasizes the importance of formal constitutions and rules as critical. Nevertheless, insofar as denominational lay members carry on social roles within the society, their experiences there are fed back into the denominational system, leading to change and accommodation—this means that at the grass roots the "boundaries" are truly permeable. Thus, even here, although the watchword of denominations is "concord," "brotherhood," "harmony," and "fellowship," order also takes on the character of a "negotiated order."[26] Is concord genuine or superficial? The recent Missouri Synod brouhaha can be interpreted as a shift from an order based on informal, traditional, communal-like value consensus to a negotiated one based on explicit "politicization" of the system and employing power and coercion to achieve "unity." Takayama notes that conflicts from the environment are frequently exaggerated within after being imported into the denomination. This occurs mainly when the members are a "crosscut" or more or less representative sample of the outer society. (When a group like a sect, on the other hand, experiences "multiple status cleavage" with the society, such a group can be more internally united against an "external enemy.")

In regard to the *maintenance* tasks of the organization, perhaps no other organizations (except nationalism) have had as large a claim as the denominations have had on family, primary group, ethnic, and class in-groups as powerful agencies of socialization. As mentioned earlier, on the local level, congregations over time tend to become more communal than organizational. Thus, denominations as systems have nurtured members not simply by means of formal associations (membership in which is normally transferable), but also by building religious subcommunities of a quasi-ethnic nature (membership non-transferable). While in contemporary America, there has been much "switching" of denominational memberships (one survey showed a range of 14% to 49% for various white, Christian, American denominations),[27] today the problem for some groups may be as much "dropping out" altogether as "switching." For Catholics, the problems posed by birth into an "indelible" communal-type faith may be severe. The above observations demonstrate some of the ways in which denominations function differently from other organizations, even other voluntary organizations.

In this connection O'Dea[28] has commented on the benefits of a "healthy unadjustment" between religion and society. He notes five "dilemmas of institutionalization of religion," which are types of organizational strain with which he believes all religious organizations must inevitably live. Included are the dilemmas of "mixed motivation" (he implies that multiple motivations are unavoidable); "objectification versus alienation" (he concludes that struggle between the informal and formal are likewise unavoidable); "administrative order/elaboration" (too much elaboration gives rise to reform and protest); "concrete definition vs. substitution of letter for spirit" (the "time" problem and the need for generality vs. relevance of the particular); "conversion vs. coercion" (the problem of requirement of commitment vs. individual right to "be free"). O'Dea thinks religious organizations fluctuate between the poles of being too consoling or too conflicting; too closed or too rigid; too stabilized or too prophetic; too particularistic and divisive or too general; too infantilizing or too open to change.

Hoge has developed one of the more fruitful ways for classifying denominations according to "options" combining liberal/conservative degree of theological opinion with affirmation/transcendence of American middle-class value commitments.[29] Thus, he comes up with the following six options for denominational policy: pluralistic and culture-affirming (most of the mainline Protestant denominations); conservative and culture-affirming (Southern Baptists, conservatives in the Missouri Synod and Southern Presbyterian Church); liberal and culture-affirming (Unitarian-Universalists, YMCA, etc.); conservative and culture-transcending (some sects and "neo-evangelicals"—the Missouri "moderates" might like to see themselves classified here); liberal and culture-transcending (scattered local, communal experiments); and pluralistic transcending groups (for which he can find no empirical cases). While not specifically related to the open systems approach, his typology seems compatible with the thematic direction of the present book and needs to be studied.

CONCLUSION

If there is any one overall theme or hypothesis which should emerge from reading this book, it is the religious organization's special obsession with "unity" coupled with its attendant fragility. Unity is not a mere pragmatic goal in religious organizations but a matter of essence—they must not only pursue it—*they have to celebrate it!* This is their glory, but also their hazard and risk. Thus, the religious organization tends to be a *structurally fragile* organization. Its consensus rests directly upon a constant process of winning and keeping the "consent of the governed" and somehow hooking this to a concept of "mission." This means in turn that leadership here is more sociologically crucial than ideology. The leader as the man-in-the-middle becomes the link between the voluntary members and the mission. How can he combine consent with some sort of structure? Communication and consensus-making (politics?) thus become indispensable when the environment outside is turbulent. The leader finds informal means more effective than formal in constructing a climate of persuasion when pursuing mission. The bottom line then must be that *all denominations are coalitions* more or less. All, more or less, must face a constant state of tentativeness. To "lead" such a structure may seem impossible, but this situation does assure—as the growth of denominations in the United States shows—the greatest organizational vitality and endurance.

A Note of Caution

We close with brief attention to the problem of cautions and limitations with regard to applying the open-systems perspective to the study of religious organizations, specifically denominations.[30] The social scientist's gaze is always slanted and truncated. As he or she seeks to illuminate a particular phenomenon by seeing it in relation to more general paradigms or models (e.g., the schisms among the Southern Presbyterians or Missouri Lutherans in Chapter 9), distortion always occurs with focus. Generalized discussions like this Introduction are no substitute for comparative, empirical case comparisons. Some of the contributors to this book have made beginnings. Although reiteration may be trite, we must note again that the task before us is to see denominations both (1) as they are like other organizations and also (2) as different from them. This flows both from the scientist's own methodological integrity as well as the integrity of the data themselves.

There undoubtedly are limits to the study of the non-rational by the rational. Weber coined a phrase, the "charismatic," to handle the observation of organizational phenomena which were neither traditional nor rationally purposive. "Charismatic" or "inspired" behavior can occur in movements other than denominations (e.g., reform movements, political or nationalistic protests, etc.); however, it surely can also occur in organizations whose members attempt to relate themselves and their tasks to the transcendent. There are probably limits to the application of rationality to organizations which are basically non-economic and implicitly political, or sentiment- or value-based. Are religious organizations means or ends, or are they both? Business and government service organizations seldom voluntarily "commit suicide," but this seems possible with religious organizations (e.g., Jonestown). What happens when members of an organization—who have heretofore viewed it as *sui generis*, supernatural, non-changing, and as something awesome—suddenly discover that it is otherwise? Gary Wills says that the major revelation of Vatican II to the members of the Roman Catholic Church is that "the Church" *can change*.[31] Grappling with the juncture of religion and science-induced change is also (partly) what is troubling conservatives among the Missouri Lutherans. What all this means is that there probably must be sub-specializations within general organizational study which can faithfully take account of the peculiarities of each special institutional sector or situs, e.g., business, government, law, education, health, religion, etc. That way, knowledge can be advanced and error minimized.

Another question arises concerning how "open" religious organizations are or must be to the environment. Many religious people feel that their mandate comes from above, from "revelation," and so the religious system cannot be "open." However, they are always laboring within a context, a situation, societal "contingencies" (assuming they feel called to a "mission"). It is clear from recent events that Roman Catholicism, while seemingly "closed" for centuries, does indeed have permeable boundaries. But being or remaining "open" need not imply *capitulation* to environment. And no demeaning of mission is necessarily involved when strategies and tactics are shaped in accord with what appears to be "natural" for the times. In fact, organizations must frequently *adapt to* environment *for the sake of* mission. It is clear also that the varying levels of religious organization—local congregation, regional judicatory, national denomination, international ecumenical federation—vary in their degree of permeability. The local church, while communal and insular in some respects, is open to the impact of its lay members' experiences in the occupations and communities external to it.

The Rest of the Book

Finally, in this Introduction, there only remains the briefest task of providing a rationale for the order and contents of the rest of the book. This can be done simply, since each of the book's three major parts will be preceded by a brief interpretive introduction of that section's contents. This first introductory chapter has provided a general overview of the notion of the organization as an "open system" and its applicability to the denomination as a complex organization. Not all contributors are sociologists; neither have they all written specifically from the viewpoint of this particular model. Ideally, however, each's view is compatible with it. In Part One, Burkart, Kim, and Elazar provide a survey of the major denominational "families" in the United States, including predominantly white Protestant denominations, Roman Catholicism, and Jewish organization. In Part Two we look at a number of specific agencies and paradenominational structures, including Gannon's treatment of Catholic predominantly male religious orders; Winter's treatment of Protestant predominantly evangelical mission societies; Hartley and Schuller's analysis of the changing situation of the theological seminary; Perry's coverage of the three models successively employed in (predominantly) Protestant congregational planning—the ecological, goal, and voluntary association models; and Hesser's attempt to interpret the life and career of religious professionals in terms of organization-originated "dilemmas" or strains. Part Three specifically deals with strain and change in and among denominations. Takayama's chapter is more general and can be viewed almost as a continuation of this present Introduction, since his chapter more than the others explicitly proceeds from the open systems view and carries the application of the notion of strain further into advanced cases of conflict and splitting in denominations. His masterful analysis needs to be studied in detail for leads as to future denominational studies, a foretaste of which he gives in his case studies of the recent Southern Presbyterian and Missouri Synod schisms. The reader shouldn't overlook his summarization of what we now know in the form of propositions and hypotheses appended to the chapter. The other two chapters in the last section treat more particular aspects related to denominational change. Johnson deals with the question of disagreements between denominational leadership and the grass roots and their consequences for funding and program. Garrett in effect deals with what happens in Emery and Trist's stages III and IV, when denominations discover that others are working the same field, attempt an accommodation to each other, form a denominational "trade" association (a council of churches), and then find themselves competing with their own trade association. He makes a suggestion for resolving this strain by pointing the council in the direction of serving as an "R&D" institute for the churches, an idea with some merit. The book concludes with a brief epilogue.

Notes

1. George Gallup Jr. notes a rise in church attendance in 1976 for the first time in two decades, with 42% of Americans attending a church or synagogue in a typical week—Paul Henrickson, "A Pollster on Religion's Surge," *National Observer*, June 27, 1977. However, Gallup wonders about the depth of the revival, since "religion is *increasing* its influence on society but morality is *losing* its influence." See also the special section, "A Time of Renewal for U.S. Churches," *U.S. News and World Report*, April 11, 1977, pp. 54-72.   ·

2. Ernst Troeltsch, *The Social Teaching of the Christian Churches* (New York: Macmillan, 1931 and 1960), pp. 331-343; H. Richard Niebuhr, *The Social Sources of Denominationalism* (New York:

Meridian, 1929 and 1957); Liston Pope, *Millhands and Preachers* (New Haven: Yale University Press, 1942), pp. 117-140.

3. George Ritzer, "Sociology: A Multiple Paradigm Science," *American Sociologist* 10 (August, 1975): 156-167, quotation 157.

4. Daniel Bell, *The Coming of Post-Industrial Society* (New York: Basic/Harper Colophon, 1976), p. 276. He also notes that the modern business corporation is the one new organizational form; and that, while U.S. Steel is the prototype corporation of the first third of the twentieth century and General Motors of the middle third, IBM is the model for the *last* third.

5. Some maintain that an "explanatory model" definitely *is* testable by being operationalized in relation to empirical events.

6. This discussion is indebted to Walter Buckley, "Society As a Complex Adaptive System," pp. 490-513 in Walter Buckley (ed.), *Modern Systems Research for the Behavioral Scientist* (Chicago: Aldine, 1968); also selections in F.E. Emery, (ed.), *Systems Thinking* (Baltimore: Penguin, 1969); Daniel Katz and Robert L. Kahn, *The Social Psychology of Organizations* (New York: John Wiley, 1966). Some prefer to label this approach by the term "structural contingencies" or "contingency" theory, e.g., Curt Tausky, *Work Organizations, Major Theoretical Perspectives* (Itasca, Ill.: F.E. Peacock), pp. 61-82. See also Jeffrey Pfeffer, *Organizational Design* (Arlington Heights, Ill.: AHM, 1978). Other labels could be "situationist" or "contexualist" theory. Some even talk of a "political economy" approach which seems similar to the above.

7. F.E. Emery and E.L. Trist, "The Causal Texture of Organizational Environments," reprinted as pp. 268-281 in Merlin B. Brinkerhoff and Phillip R. Kunz (eds.), *Complex Organizations and Their Environments* (Dubuque, Iowa: William C. Brown, 1972).

8. James Price, *Organizational Effectiveness* (Homewood, Ill.: Irwin, 1968).

9. Wolf Heydebrand (ed.), *Comparative Organizations: The Results of Empirical Research* (Englewood Cliffs, N.J.: Prentice-Hall, 1973), pp. 11-29.

10. Dean J. Champion, *The Sociology of Organizations* (New York: McGraw-Hill, 1975), pp. 86-101.

11. James A. Beckford, *Religious Organization: A Trend Report and Bibliography* (The Hague: Mouton, 1975), p. 34. This is an excellent, overall assessment of the need for a "new look" in the organizational study of religion and specifically focuses on the applicability of the open systems view, including both review as well as pioneering reformulation of a direction to go. It is "must" reading and a companion piece to this book.

12. Talcott Parsons has enunciated his views on countless occasions. See, e.g., "General Theory in Sociology," pp. 3-16 in *Sociology Today,*

Problems and Prospects, Robert K. Merton et al. (eds.) (New York: Basic Books, 1959); also his "Suggestions for a Sociological Approach to a Theory of Organizations," *Administrative Science Quarterly*, 1 (June, 1956): 63-85 and 1 (Sept., 1956): 225-239.

13. For a parallel treatment with application to the problem of denominations, see the editor's "The Church As a Formal Voluntary Association," pp. 81-108 in David H. Smith et al. (eds.), *Voluntary Action Research: 1972* (Lexington, Mass.: D.C. Heath, 1972).

14. Tausky, *Work Organizations*, p. 69.

15. William Warren Sweet, *The Story of Religion in America* (New York: Harper, 1939), p. 319.

16. See writings by psychologist D.C. Pelz, "Creative Tensions in the Research and Development Climate," *Science*, 167 (July, 1967): 160-165; D.C. Pelz and F.M. Andrews, "Autonomy, Coordination, and Stimulation, in Relation to Scientific Achievement," *Behavioral Science*, 11 (March, 1966): 89-97.

17. Roland L. Warren, "The Interorganizational Field As a Focus for Investigation," pp. 313-317 in Brinkerhoff and Kunz, op. cit. (Table on p. 316 reproduced in Chapter 1 of present book).

18. See Elizabeth Nottingham, *Religion: A Sociological View* (New York: Random House, 1971), chapter 8, for expansion of this view.

19. See the Ross P. Scherer chapter in David H. Smith, et al., *Voluntary Action Research: 1972*, op. cit., p. 85.

20. Sidney E. Mead, "Denominationalism: The Shape of Protestantism in America," reprinted as pp. 70-105 in Russell E. Richey (ed.) *Denominationalism* (Nashville, Abingdon, 1977), quotation from pp. 70-71.

21. Paul M. Harrison, *Authority and Power in the Free Church Tradition* (Princeton: Princeton U. Press, 1959). However, as Takayama notes in Chapter 9, official polity may provide a certain leverage and legitimacy for church officials who wish to implement prophetic social ethical pronouncements which may be unpopular at the grass roots.

22. See, e.g., the otherwise thoughtful treatment of this problem by Kingsley Davis, *Human Society* (New York: Macmillan, 1949), pp. 521-529.

23. Max Weber, *The Protestant Ethic and the Spirit of Capitalism* (New York: Scribner's, 1930).

24. *Social Sources*, op. cit.

25. Nicholas J. Demerath III and Philip E. Hammond, *Religion in Social Context, Tradition and Transition* (New York: Random House, 1969), pp. 173-180.

26. See J. Kenneth Benson, "Editor's Introduction: Innovation and Crisis in Organizational Analysis," *Sociological Quarterly*, 18 (Winter,

1977): 3-16, especially 12, for the concept of "negotiated order" as a more realistic view of the steady state of organizations.

27. Rodney Stark and Charles Y. Glock, *American Piety: The Nature of Religious Commitment* (Berkeley: University of California Press, 1968), p. 195.

28. Thomas F. O'Dea, *The Sociology of Religion* (Englewood Cliffs, N.J.: Prentice-Hall, 1966), pp. 90-101, quotation p. 106.

29. Dean R. Hoge, *Division in the Protestant House, The Basic Reasons behind Intra-Church Conflicts* (Philadelphia: Westminster Press, 1976), pp. 123-132.

30. J. Kenneth Benson provides a trenchant review of the inadequacies of contemporary sociological research on organizations, op. cit. His article serves as overall introduction to a special issue of the *Sociological Quarterly*, "Organization Analysis: Critique and Innovation," op. cit., which needs to be studied carefully.

31. Gary Wills, *Bare Ruined Choirs: Doubt, Prophecy, and Radical Religion* (Garden City, N.Y.: Doubleday, 1972), p. 21.

Part One

Overview of Major
Denominational "Families"

Introduction to Part One

Ross P. Scherer

The chapters in Part One provide an overview of structure of the three, conventional, denominational "family" groups—Protestant, Roman Catholic, and Jewish. Structurally speaking, the Jewish groups are probably the most decentralized and least clergy-dominated; the Roman Catholic Church is the most centralized and clergy-dominated; and the Protestant groups are arrayed on a continuum between. Such comparison may be an over-simplification, however, since as Sister Kim points out, the American Catholic Church is not an autonomous denomination; furthermore, Catholic dioceses vary with the individual bishop in the autonomy allowed to their laity and constitutent clergy. The chapter authors differ somewhat in the conceptual emphases with which they approach their phenomena. Burkart employs various typologies for categorizing his Protestant cases; Kim is concerned with meaning as well as form in Catholicism, treating both in the context of change; and Elazar points to the communal as well as associational bases of Judaism.

In Chapter 1, Burkart employs a "developmental and historical" case-study approach, using the formal constitutions and organizational tables of seven Protestant denominations as his documentary data. He maintains that "ideology" is the most important causal determinant influencing "polity," although he sees ideology and practice as "in a dialectical relation." He lists eight ideological solutions to the problem of religion-world tension, each with an implication for particular organizational elaboration (see Figure 2). Theoretically, he says, a dualistic view implies organizational elaboration and hierarchic authority; a messianic outlook, either introverted withdrawal or active evangelistic attack upon the world; a secularistic view, total openness to type of form; and a predestinarian stance, irrelevance to organization. Some may criticize this as simplistic, since it tends to overlook more *informal* developments, historical accidentals, etc. whereby tactical expediencies get to be sacralized into enduring forms (viz., the names of the major Protestant denominations which are variously based on a type of polity—Episcopal, Presbyterian; a founding Reformer—Lutheran; or a spiritual approach—Baptist, Methodist, etc.). Other factors also mediate and affect the directions of structural adaptation, e.g., the social class and ethnic origins of the lay membership base and their familiarity with civil organizational models, the degree to which the denominational polity includes laymen of high social rank in its decision-making groups, geographic isolation and degree of Americanization of members, etc.

Following Warren, Burkart categorizes denominations according to the degree of their unitary vs. federative make-up and their degree of centralization of decision. He classifies his cases according to a number of types: the authoritarian coalition (the Children of God), the democratic coalition with a cooptative structure (the Churches of Christ), the moderately centralized federation (the Disciples, American Baptist Churches, and the Assemblies of God), and grossly centralized federation (Lutheran Church in America, United Methodist Church). He links all types together in a massive, developmental "organizational tree" (Figure 5), ranging from a simplified and loosely linked coalition over to complex, federative structures with increasing degrees of horizontal specialization and vertical structural control.[1] Thus, he sees Protestant groups as coalitions or federations. While not everyone in the denominations named would accept his labeling of their group, his schema nevertheless provides an exploratory grid for classifying denominations in terms of increasing centralization, complexity, and formality. Thus, he illustrates the open systems principle that there is "no (necessarily) one best way." His cases perhaps illustrate more than "test" his models of denominational development.

On the other hand, Harrison's work warns us against the illusion of formalism.[2] Organizational "myths" may blind partisans to the true state of affairs—the danger of ideological over-justification of a particular polity as the one best way. The particularism of labels for the same structural unit—e.g., "conference," "synod," "convention," "assembly," etc. for the major national, denominational decision unit—illustrates the strong power of traditions to make the same form seem unique.

Kim, in her treatment of Roman Catholic structure since Vatican II in Chapter 2, provides an in-depth analysis of a more complex but *single case*, including the problem of the integration or non-integration of *structure with meaning*. As a Sister and native Korean, she brings both familiarity (through being a participant observer) and distance (through citizenship). Her own personal ambivalence toward the contemporary directions of change in Catholicism may be evident at times in her analysis, e.g., regarding the value of conservation vs. adaptation. She asserts that rationality and charisma converged in Vatican II, demonstrating that religious organizations, while interacting with their environments, can *generate change* also *from within*.

She notes the ways in which Roman Catholicism as a denomination is different from Protestant groups—in being the eldest, largest, most international and inclusive denomination. She also points to the significance of the celibacy requirement for religious professionals, the centralization of power in a supranational authority outside the United States, and the unitary structure of Catholicism, with authority viewed not as delegated from the bottom up but from the top down. Her shrewd observation that the most significant change in connection with Vatican II came with *change in meaning*, rather than *structure*, seems crucial. Structurally, the old forms tend to persist; or if new forms have emerged, they tend to be duplicative, existing side-by-side with the old—a kind of "muddling through." Perhaps the single biggest change is the recognition of the *possibility of change* by means of "institutionalizing the change process" itself. This means that change tends to beget change. Catholicism has suddenly moved perhaps from a "placid clustered" to a "turbulent" field! She worries over the lack of recruitment to professional church occupations and the current uncertainty and lack of consensus in core beliefs.

In Burkart's spectrum of structural forms, Roman Catholicism (while unique in other ways) becomes merely "another case," at the polar maximum in authority and centralization. In practice however, it may be possible for a regional judicatory (e.g., a Catholic diocese) to operate with some autonomy when the national decision group is viewed as advisory (in this case, the U.S. Conference of Bishops). Ultimately, too, the degree of organizational voluntarization in individual Catholic parishes will be the final determining fact. Such voluntarization has always been a possibility amid the openness of American denominational pluralism; but since Vatican II, it is becoming more and more a probability. Laymen (and clergy) may still "pray," but less and less do they have to "pay and obey." Catholic churchmen would do well to carefully examine the spectrum of positions in Protestantism as a giant experimental design of possible options.

Elazar's analysis in Chapter 3 of the diffusion of decision within Jewish institutions perhaps shows the ultimacy of the decentralization process, the polar opposite of the pre-Vatican II Catholic pattern. He also raises the question of the relation of the *communal* to the *associational*, present also in Catholic and Protestant structures, but more basic to Judaism. Thus, clearly Jews are held together not only by their organizational memberships (perhaps, in fact, in spite of their loose organizational structuring), but by their loyalty to their "traditions," mostly ethnic but also specifically religious. In some ways, the Jewish situation may be viewed as a "deviant case." In almost total contradiction to the Catholic pattern, Jews lack any authoritative, worldwide organization for Jews. Par excellence, Jewish organization is based upon *persuasion*, within an informal communications network in the "Jewish community." Thus, the Jewish model is a federative one, but without visible, obvious mechanisms for cohesion.

Elazar lists four types of structural units—government-like, "roof" agencies (e.g., educational, welfare, health); localistic primary groups (synagogues and clubs—communal seemingly); general-purpose, mass-based associations (brotherhoods and sisterhoods); and special-interest organizations (synagogue federations, medical centers, cultural associations). The first two types provide resource support and maintenance; the latter two activation of program and content. In his view, synagogue membership grew after World War II but then declined, mirroring a struggle between the more "cosmopolitan" Jewish health and welfare federations and the more "localistic" synagogues. The denomination in the Jewish view, then (if it can be termed that), is extremely federative. Perhaps this antipathy to centralization is an outgrowth of the well-known Jewish view that the maximum personal freedom lies in structures that guarantee the greatest degree of voluntary *consent*. Such a diffuse structure may well be the ecclesiastical wave of the future in the modern world, resembling the simplicity of Burkart's "denominational coalition." Yet, would this model provide enough cohesion for groups which lack the Jews' historic identification and struggles as a people? Seemingly, in most groups, the role of formal ideology would have to be upgraded in importance, if there is to be a balance between the imperatives of cohesion and adaptation.

Notes

1. Burkart's schema seems compatible with Smith's recent suggestion of three stages of denominational growth: (1) initially, the founding of promotion-type mission societies on the 19th century American frontier as more than a loose coalition of local congregations or their representatives; (2) later, the integration of such independent, local

mission groups into single, interdenominational associations; (3) finally, the combining of such task-oriented mission associations or agencies with a "convention" or church government structure into a single, formal denomination-federation. See Elwyn A. Smith, "The Forming of a Modern American Denomination," pp. 111-113, in Russell E. Richey, ed., *Denominationalism* (Nashville: Abingdon, 1977).

2. Paul M. Harrison, *Authority and Power in the Free Church Tradition* (Princeton, Princeton University Press, 1959).

1

Patterns of Protestant Organization

Gary P. Burkart

Contemporary patterns of Protestant organization, while seemingly converging, have emerged out of a complex interplay of ideological[1], polity-related (organizational), and environmental-situational factors. This is the major thesis of this chapter.

A great error would be committed in seeing Protestant organization as all of one color. Glock and Stark[2] have revealed the divergent nature of religiosity among members of various Protestant denominations and have warned us against the futility of making gross comparisons between religious traditions such as a one-lump "Protestantism" or Catholicism or Judaism. A cursory study of patterns of Protestant organization would seem to warrant similar cautions.

We have chosen to elaborate this organizational diversity in terms of the role of various types of religious ideologies adopted, following a suggestion of Wilson[3] that certain types of ideologies have greater or lesser implications for organizational development. We have found it productive to analyze the dynamic interplay of religious ideology (theology, ethics, worldviews), ecclesiastical organization (polity or structure), and environment (situation), for in so doing we discover a richness of form and expression not otherwise possible. Our approach could be considered "dialetic" in the sense that ideology and application in structure (praxis) mutually influence each other.

We will proceed to describe patterns of Protestant organization in terms of their original ideological purposes, changes in these purposes, the varying conceptions of legitimate authority patterns, and the factors that have led to bureaucratic growth and development (i.e., the erection of a far-flung organization with numerous positions and sub-groups guided by a system of rules.) Not all Protestant groups are found to have become bureaucratized in a similar fashion. Likewise, an approach that keeps central the interplay between purpose, structure, and situation helps to alert us to those cases where Protestantism has *not* developed along bureaucratic paths.

We have attempted to keep our analysis open to those cases where purpose and situation have become incongruous, out of phase, or even contradictory. As such we can account for organizational tension, conflict and/or schism (see also Chapter 9, which deals specifically with this subject).

Finally, the use of a developmental approach allows us not only to see the depth and breadth of change within the divergent approaches to Protestant organization, but gives us a basis upon which we can extrapolate future organizational developments. Protestant religious development must always be seen as dynamic and changing, as is the larger structural and cultural milieu of American life.

Religious groups, as other groups, face organizational dilemmas such as centralization vs. decentralization of decision making, adaptation vs. cohesion, acceptance vs. rejection of social change—either within denominations, or between them, or between them and other organizations. Whereas in one period the growth of non-local organization may take precedence, in another (today) there may develop a *decline in national* denominational power *in favor of subdenominational and local* units.

The organization of this chapter is in two parts: (1) a theoretical presentation of general types of organization found in Protestantism at large; and (2) selected case studies of Protestant groups which, by means of a developmental and historical approach, illustrate concretely these divergent patterns. The first part is necessary to make sense out of the numerous types of organization that have developed in Protestantdom; the second, to supply historical data to test the accuracy of this theoretical formulation.

THE GROWTH OF DIVERGENT RELIGIOUS IDEOLOGIES

Theoretical Sources of Religious Ideologies

While not suggesting that religious organization is always the product of ideational dictates, we have nonetheless started our analysis with the nature of religious ideologies and their implications for organizational development. Religious ideologies are seen as arising out of the various ways in which religious groups seek reduction in the tension inherent between a religious system and the world (cf. Weber[4] and Gerth and Mills[5]). Weber's four solutions to the "problem of theodicy" (i.e., the seeming contradiction of evil in the world "permitted" by an all-good God), namely the messianic, transmigration of souls, dualism, and predestination, are recast in light of Judith Willer's[6] suggestions that Weber failed to offer a clarification as to *why* theodicy is a *problem*. It is her belief, in light of the theory of knowledge that she develops, that the theodicy problem arises because of a contradiction in the fact that, in a fully rationalized religious system, the *theology* would posit that God is omnipotent and thus *man* is *powerless*; but the *ethics* would conclude that *man can act* (he has some power.) Thus, the theodicy problem is seen theoretically as a problem of contradiction between religious theology and ethics.

Theodicy and Religious-Worldly Tensions

Logically, the list found under Figure 1 would appear to exhaust the possible "solutions" to the problem of the religious-world tension and theodicy.

In Figure 1, the solutions to theodicy proposed by Weber and the logical possibilities of the present writer (found under the figure) are subsumed under the framework suggested by Willer; namely, that the theological component of the religious system is either dominant and the ethical component subordinate, or the opposite is true. Secularism as an additional ideology is suggested as occurring when both the theology and ethics become subordinated. The numbers in the cells refer to the logical possibilities found in Figure 1.

Solution #8 is the *dualistic* resolution suggested by Weber; likewise, #7 is the *transmigration of souls* resolution; and finally, solution #6 is the *predestination* solution. Solution #5 we have chosen to call the *secularization* solution, since it involves a deemphasis of both theology and ethics. It cannot be called a religious solution to tension between the world and religion because it subordinates both religious theology and ethics. Solutions #1-4 can be seen as sub-types of Weber's *messianic* resolution to the theodicy-world tension problem. The works of Bryan Wilson[7] also suggest various sub-types of the Messianic ideology: the *conversionist*[8] (sees the world as evil and wants to change man and thus the world will change accordingly); the *adventist* (views the world as evil and through an alliance of man with God, the world will be overthrown); the *introversionist* (wishes to escape the world by turning inward to the development of the self through the inspiration of the Holy Spirit); the *reformist* (seeks to use religious principles to reform the evil world, not to

FIGURE 1

CLASSIFICATION OF LOGICALLY POSSIBLE RELATIONS BETWEEN
THEOLOGICAL AND ETHICAL EMPHASES ACCORDING TO WILLER

		THEOLOGY	
		DOMINANT	SUBORDINATE
ETHICS	Dominant	Dualism (#8)	Messianism (#1-4) Transmigration of Souls (#7)
	Subordinate	Predestination (#6)	Secularization (#5)

LIST OF TYPE SOLUTIONS

1. Converting the entire world to the religious system of knowledge so that the world would reflect or be a mirror image of the religious conception of the world (Conversionist).

2. Forming an alliance between God and man so that the "world" could be overthrown and God's Kingdom could be established here on earth (Adventist).

3. Isolating himself from the world and acting in a religious manner (Introversionist).

4. Altering all or parts of society not in accord with the religious view of the world, so that gradually the world would take on a religious nature (Reformist, Utopian).

5. Bringing the thought and action systems of individuals more into accord with the principles upon which the world operates (Secularist).

6. Believing that God is unknowable and all-powerful and has chosen certain members for salvation, thus making action in the world acceptable (Predestinationist).

7. Adopting the belief that one could be released from tension at some future date by actions here in this world (Transmigrationist).

8. Believing that there are or have been evil forces at work in the world, thus man's worldly activities can be directed and guided with the saving help (grace) of the good force (God) (Dualist).

overthrow it); and the *utopian* (which seeks a radical reconstruction of the world, by man, based upon religious principles). Wilson's *manipulationist* type (emphasizes salvation in this world through use of special or esoteric knowledge) has been subsumed under our secularistic ideology, since this group uses quasi-religious means to accomplish secular ends and thus appears not to be a religious means of tension reduction as are his other types.[9]

Religious Ideologies and Organizational Development

Elaborating upon the suggestion of Johnson[10], certain forms of organizational development seem more appropriate to certain ideologies than to others. Certain religious ideologies logically imply differing models of organizational *structure*.[11] Figure 2 illustrates, in summary fashion, the various logical implications for organization deriving from each distinct type of ideology. These are discussed next.

Implied in the *dualistic* resolution to theodicy is a tendency toward *organizational elaboration*. Since the redemption of man is seen as a finished work, what is needed is an organization that can *dispense* these redemptive powers, such as remission of sins and the imparting of sanctification through grace. The *predestinationist* type, on the other hand, implies *little* organizational elaboration, since God is viewed as completely sovereign and no system of sacraments, hierarchy, or organization can change God's plan. The *messianic* type must first be divided into four sub-types, as each has differing implications for organizational elaboration. The *conversionist* type is most likely to lead to elaboration and eventual bureaucratization, since it implies action in the world to convert individuals to the religious message. The *adventist* type emphasizes the impending return of God (Christ) to earth, and its overthrow; thus, an elaborate organization is either *not needed* or is superfluous, since it is seen as imperfect and temporary in nature. The *reformist, utopian*, and *introversionist* types have in common the desire to escape the world in order to reduce tension by either partially or totally changing society, or by changing the inner life of the individual. Since most of these groups rarely get beyond the stage of constructing colonies that are models of their version of the perfect world, the implications for organization are those of community-building. The *manipulationist* and *secularistic* resolutions have implications for organizational elaboration, since their knowledge and action systems are more in accord with that of the world, and thus they are more open to organizational development modeled upon pragmatic notions of accommodation.

TYPES OF PROTESTANT ORGANIZATION

Types of Interorganizational Contexts

Using the suggestion of Warren[12] that organizations may interact in various kinds of contexts in the decision-making process, we will borrow

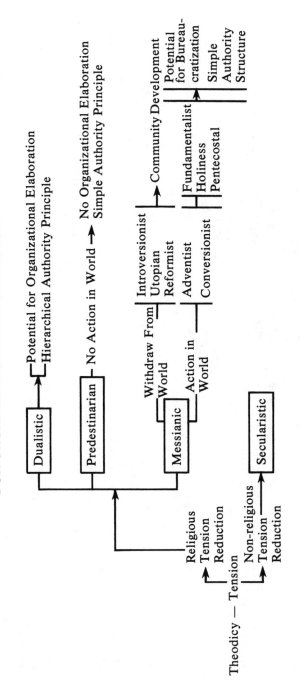

FIGURE 2
SUMMARY SKETCH OF POTENTIAL IMPLICATIONS OF IDEOLOGY
FOR ORGANIZATIONAL DEVELOPMENT

FIGURE 3
WARREN'S TYPES OF ORGANIZATIONAL CONTEXTS

Dimension	Type of Context			
	Unitary	Federative	Coalition	Social Choice
Relation of units to an inclusive goal	Units organized for achievement of inclusive goals	Units with disparate goals, but some formal organization for inclusive goals	Units with disparate goals, but informal collaboration for inclusive goals	No inclusive goals
Locus of inclusive decision making	At top of inclusive structure	At top of inclusive structure, subject to unit ratification	In interaction of units without a formal inclusive structure	Within units
Locus of authority	At top of hierarchy of inclusive structure	Primarily at unit level	Exclusively at unit level	Exclusively at unit level
Structural provision for division of labor	Units structured for division of labor within inclusive organization	Units structured autonomously, may agree to a division of labor, which may affect their structure	Units structured autonomously, may agree to ad-hoc division of labor, without restructuring	No formally structured division of labor within an inclusive context
Commitment to a leadership sub-system	Norms of high commitment	Norms of moderate commitment	Commitment only to unit leaders	Commitment only to unit leaders
Prescribed collectivity-orientation of units	High	Moderate	Minimal	Little or none

Reprinted from "The Interorganizational Field As a Focus for Investigation," by Roland L. Warren, published in *Administrative Science Quarterly* (vol. 12, no. 3, p. 406), by permission of *The Administrative Science Quarterly*. Copyright © 1978 Cornell University. All rights reserved.

his typology for our work as it appears useful in describing how *parts* of religious denominations may relate *to* other *parts* of the same denomination.

Four types of inter-organizational contexts are derived, based upon six criteria. These criteria are (1) the relation of units to an inclusive goal, (2) the locus of inclusive decision-making, (3) the locus of authority, (4) the structural provision for division of labor, (5) the commitment to a leadership sub-system, and (6) the prescribed collectivity orientation of units. The four types of organizational contexts are (1) *unitary*, (2)*federative*, (3)*coalitional*, and (4)*social choice*. Figure 3 indicates the variation found in these types along the six dimensions. These types are artificially simplified; actual cases of organizations would vary from one extreme to the other as a matter of degree.

Interorganizational Contexts and Vertical Structure Control

It can be seen that Warren is describing in another context (community decision organization) the concept of *vertical structural control*. That is, religious organization may be described in terms of the degree of integration between the upper and lower units of the total organization. The unitary type would seem to apply most readily to a group such as the international Roman Catholic Church and would not accurately describe most contemporary Protestant denominations. On the other hand, the social choice context seems to be nothing more than uncoordinated cooperation and probably too informal to describe any distinct type of Protestant organization. However, the *coalitional* and *federative* types do seem instructive in analyzing Protestant organization.

Coalitions and federations thus are, more or less, diffuse forms of cooperation, with some religious coalitions having inherent within them (for ideological reasons discussed above) the possibility of *development into federations*. Likewise, taking the caution of Warren that these types are not to be thought of as all-or-none but as continuous, it would appear that some religious groups having *federative* structure may be more centralized or less centralized (i.e., possess *degrees* of vertical structural control.) To put our argument differently, Warren's *coalitional* type possesses *no* degree of *vertical* structural *control*, since there is no higher level unit. The *federative* types possess *moderate to high vertical* structural *control*; and the *unitary* type, theoretically, possesses *complete vertical* structural *control* over all lower units.

Religious Organization and Authority

The nature of the relationship between the various levels and units of a religious group brings into analytic focus the crucial organizational variable of *authority*. Paul Harrison's work with the then American Baptist Convention (1959)[13] led him to develop several, additional types of authority not found in Max Weber's work.[14] The collation of types in

Figure 4 incorporates both Weber's as well as Harrison's types. Likewise, the expected pattern of authority that would exist in either coalition or federation is included. Each is to be thought of as an idealized or simplified type and thus not to be expected exactly in reality. Each will be described in the next section.

FIGURE 4
COLLATION OF TYPES OF ORGANIZATIONAL FORM AND AUTHORITY

		Democratic	Authoritarian
TYPE OF	Coalition	Quasi-Charismatic & Mimetric-Traditional	Charismatic
ORGANI-ZATIONAL FORM	Federation	Rational-Pragmatic & Quasi-Charismatic	Rational-Legal

Types of Authority and Interorganizational Context

This cross-relating of organizational form with authority type leads to four theoretically distinct types of religious organizations: (1) The *Authoritarian Coalition* is the small, autonomous, homogeneous, undifferentiated, and non-formalized group headed by a charismatic leader (possibly a prophet, strong man, or religious founder). (2) The *Democratic Coalition* is structurally like the authoritarian coalition, but the leadership pattern is characterized by an incomplete institutionalization (legitimization) of power into authority. Quasi-charismatic authority exists when leaders must resort to a type of leadership based upon strong personalities; whereas, mimetic-traditional authority is found as an uninstitutionalized type of traditional authority. It is speculated that this group may resolve these contradictions in types of leadership by developing democratic control. In both the case of the authoritarian and the democratic coalition, the mode of authority is unstable, and power is insufficiently institutionalized. (3) The *Authoritative Federation* appears to be a form of bureaucracy that Weber[15] spoke of in his ideal type; however, the federative form is basically *voluntary* (since American denominations are a type of voluntary association) and so cannot be seen as being as truly bureaucratized as governmental, military, and corporate structures or as demanding of unquestioning obedience. There is no problem of insufficient institutionalization of power, since power is recognized as legitimate authority and so coming from the acceptance of a system of rules by the group's members (i.e., Weber's rational-legal type). For this reason, we can label this type "authoritative" since it accepts the authority of its upper units, even though it rests ultimately upon individual consent. (4) The *Democratic Federation* structurally resembles the authoritative federation but has not sufficiently institutionalized power into authority. The leaders of this group must resort to a combination of rational-pragmatic (making decisions based upon day-to-day operational needs) and quasi-charismatic authority (cf. Harrison[16] for the various non-Weberian types of authority). As such, the group's structure and authority principle are out of balance, and the group is likely to face conflicts.

Organizational Change

Change of religious groups from one type of organization to another is usually a slow process of adjustment by increments. As the operating environment of the group changes, pressures are placed upon the group to routinize both its developing body of knowledge and its patterns of behavior. Internal changes, such as increases in size and diversity of the membership and in task specialization,[17] coupled with shifts in environmental relations (degree of openness to the surrounding culture and society), propel the group to make routine its knowledge, accepting a higher degree of *formalization* (setting up rules, regulations, traditions), and to routinize its behavior by accepting a higher degree of *structural differentiation* (the creation of offices, positions, committees, agencies, etc.). The process of *structural control* is a process in which the elements of this growing structure are integrated by a system of formalized rules and procedures.

Bureaucratization and Types of Horizontal Structural Control

Bureaucratization in the form of increasing *horizontal structural control* (i.e., the integration of offices, committees, and agencies at the *same* level of operation into one policy-making, judicial, and administrative unit) may take place in distinct fashions and in various stages. Involved in each type, as well as in its various stages, are a series of decisions that involve two elements: (1) the option for taking more action in the world, and consequently more bureaucratization; and (2) maintenance of the ideology in its pristine or near pristine form. Decisions that are made in the direction of increasing bureaucratization may be interpreted by certain elements of the group as dilution or abandonment of the group's ideology or purpose. Such beliefs may lead to schisms from the mother group.

Three types of bureaucratization in the form of horizontal structural control (integration of units at the *same* level, e.g., district or national) are possible: (1) the development of a *cooptative structure*, that is, one in which action in the world is carried out, not via the erection of a denominational structure but by the use of secular agencies (such as printing presses, radio and TV stations) and non-denominational missionary societies, or via the combined efforts of several local congregations. As such, the group may act *in* the world but maintain, in fact, its simple authority structure and simple, local, structural arrangement. In terms of vertical structural control, this type can be said to be *coalitional*.

(2) A second avenue of bureaucratization lies in the erection of a *national convention* structure and a *separate, autonomous agency structure* (usually created and run by laymen.) This duality initially appears to allow the group to act in the world and maintain an authority structure and ideology that is simple and in line with its notions of authority. This solution is prone not only to further bureaucratic development but ideological conflict or abandonment at some time in the future. Gradually, as the tasks of the religious group are elaborated, more and more autonomous agencies arise, many seeking resources from the same people and having overlapping programs. A question as to the function of the national convention structure is likely to arise at some point in this development. The "convention" is the only body that can speak for the entire denominational structure that is emerging. The group may eventually reach a decision to seek closer cooperation with these autonomous agencies. If such a decision is reached, it may lead to schisms within the group by those opposing such a move; and it is likely to represent a loosening of the original ideology, as the group is now recognizing the validity of a *structure "between* man and his God." As further organizational pressures toward program coordination, budgeting, long-range planning, efficiency and effectiveness arise, the group may eventually reach a decision point which involves the abolition of the autonomous nature of the agencies and the subordination of them *under the convention* as administrative branches. At this point again, schisms may result, and certainly the group must face the fact that its original ideology has been abandoned (assuming that structural form has been an ideological matter). The group during this period can be said to have moved *from democratic federation*, in which the authority of the group at the top was not recognized, *to authoritative federation*, in which rational-legal authority is bestowed upon such a body. In a similar fashion, the group has moved *from a moderately decentralized* federative structure *to a moderately centralized federative structure*.

(3) A third form of bureaucratization may take place when the group is in possession of an ideology which legitimizes an intermediary body (or set of positions) between the individual (or congregation) and God. This type we may label the *Convention/Agency Structure*. The development

of this form largely represents the growth of agencies *within* the convention structure to meet the needs of the ever-increasing task specialization (e.g., in evangelism, worker pensions, foreign missions, etc.).[18] It must be pointed out that two varieties of this form exist: (a) a group that accepts the principle of *horizontal* structural control, that is, integration of convention and agencies at the top *but* with only *little* to moderate degree of *vertical* structural control (i.e., integration of national convention/agency structure with lower level units via a hierarchical pattern); and (b) a group that accepts the legitimacy of *both horizontal and vertical* structural controls. Schisms are possible in both groups if certain elements feel that there is either too much horizontal or vertical structural control. Both groups have bestowed rational-legal authority (legitimization) at the *top*. Thus, we can say that two types of federations exist: one we can label *moderately centralized federalism*; the other *grossly centralized federalism*.

As bureaucratization increases, there may be a tendency for ideology to secularize. Although this is not inevitable, it may take the form of *goal displacement* in which organizational maintenance comes to be more the aim of the group than its spiritual purpose or message. Another kind of goal shift may come via an emphasis upon *social action*,[19] which opens the group up to its environment and places the group actively in the position of advocating and seeking basic social, economic, and political changes in the non-church environment. The latter may also be a source of bureaucratization by calling for substantial outlays of monies that must be collected from the sub-national units. Since denominational headquarters are largely dependent upon local funding, and since action projects may involve the denomination in sponsoring activities "of dubious religious value" to some, the denomination may be embarking upon a period of instability and conflict.[20] If funds are not forthcoming, the lower units of the denomination may regain some lost autonomy and decision making. If severe enough, this could lead to a shrinkage of upper denominational programs, staff, and structures (cf. Johnson's treatment in Chapter 10), followed by a concomitant decentralization. If the ideology underlying adoption of social action is not firmly grounded in theological and ethical principles, it may resolve into a non-religious means of tension reduction by an acceptance of the *world* at the expense of the *religious*. Figure 5 illustrates these various types of bureaucratization in terms of coalitional and federative types as well as the three types of development of horizontal structural control. The points of potential schismatic developments are also demonstrated. This figure is coded with numbers and letters which will be used to illustrate the various historical pathways Protestant groups have taken. These case studies follow.

FIGURE 5
VARIOUS FORMS OF RELIGIOUS BUREAUCRATIC DEVELOPMENT

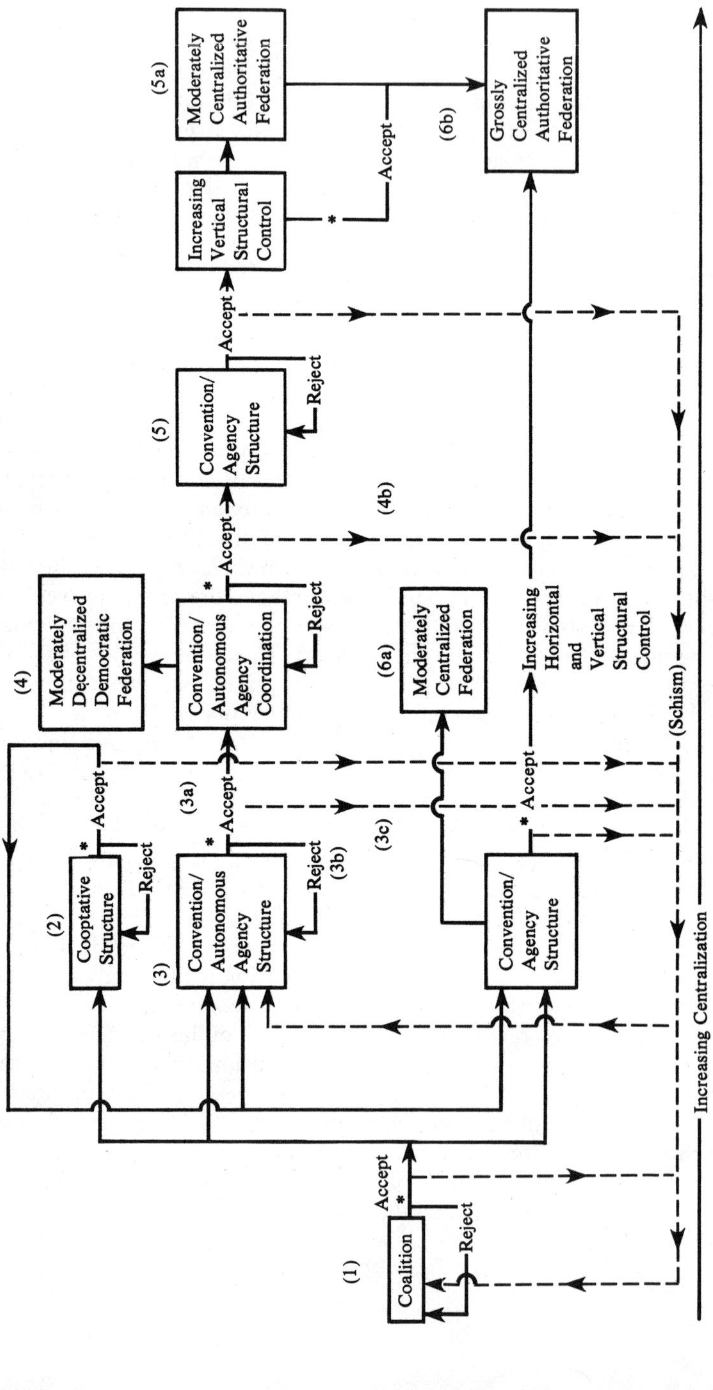

*Decision-making point

CASE STUDIES OF TYPES OF
PROTESTANT ORGANIZATION

The following case studies have been selected because it is felt that they illustrate most of the theoretical types of organization (and ideology) that we have outlined above. We will begin these case studies with the simplest type for sake of illustration and follow with the more complex.

THE RELIGIOUS COALITION

The Children of God

The Children of God arose in the late 1960s as a product of a revitalization movement within American religion. This particular branch of the "Jesus Movement" was founded under the influence of a charismatic leader-prophet, Berg, who proclaimed a new religious ideology to the street people of Southern California. Documentation of the leadership of Berg and his family in the founding and spread of what are today numerous colonies, is found in McFadden[21] and Enroth, et al.[22] Point "(1)" in Figure 5 illustrates the extent of development of this group.

The ideology that Berg promulgated is primarily *conversionist*, with strong emphases upon *fundamentalism, pentecostalism*, and *adventism*. This combination of types of conversionist ideologies and adventism is rare in religious history. These strong conversionist and adventist ideologies assume two main elements: (1) complete assurance of the saving power of Christ, and (2) the depravity of man and consequently the abnegation of the world. This extreme emphasis upon the saving power of Christ and the depravity of man and the world leads to an inherent tension between the religious message (purpose) and the world. This tension is religiously reduced, however, by a strong emphasis upon *both* conversionist and adventist ideologies; first, by positing that all men (and thus the world) may be converted to the salvation knowledge of the group; and second, that God is about to return to earth to reform it in His image. These basic ideological tenets have several organizational implications. The group maintains a relative autonomy from the world in the sense that it is anti-intellectual, anti-cultural, anti-church, anti-social, and anti-historical. Contacts maintained with the world consist only of those necessary for "witnessing" (disseminating the ideology).

Because of the newness of this group and the charismatic nature of its origins, the Children of God has assumed an *authoritarian,* legitimizing principle. As the charismatic influences of the Bergs wane, a structure of authoritarian eldership has taken its place. The elder of each colony is supreme in both religious and secular matters. Insofar as ideology stresses the importance of communal life, the position of authority of the elder is supported. The inherent instability of this type of leadership pattern has long been noted, and the Children of God have not been spared such instability.

The adventist ideology acts to inhibit too much action, including bureaucratization, in the world. The development of an organization simple in differentiation and formalization is consistent with this. The adoption of a communal pattern of organization may be explained by the contradictory dictates of an adventist and conversionist ideological mixture. No formal organization exists to carry out the functions of this group; however, informal means have been devised to create some communication and interaction between the various colonies: an extensive network of ham-operated radios exists; the original Berg family members periodically visit the colonies as moral and secular guardians; and the group prints various tracts and newspapers. Insistence upon communal life militates, at present, against bureaucratization. (Cf. Appendix A for a sketch of the emerging organization of this group).

This group has not yet faced a decision to adopt one of the alternate approaches to bureaucratization more common to groups with conversionist ideologies. It is young and in its formative stage. The Children of God remains an authoritarian coalition simple in structure, simple in authority, and unrationalized in ideology. The insistence upon a communal mode of organization makes predictions for bureaucratization and institutionalization of ideology difficult, since most such communal groups have possessed introversionist, utopian, or reformist ideologies. If the group survives, it may eventually face the crucial decision to elaborate its structure to meet the imperatives stemming from its conversionist ideology.

THE COALITION WITH A COOPTATIVE STRUCTURE

The Churches of Christ

The Churches of Christ arose via schism from the bureaucratizing Disciples of Christ (Christian) in the late 19th century. While a lack of unity existed in the Disciples during most of the 19th century, an official schism was not admitted until 1906.[23] Pathway 1 to 2 in Figure 5 describes the development of this group into a "coalition with a cooptative structure."

The basic ideological premise common to both the Disciples of Christ and the Churches of Christ was that the church should include *nothing* in the way of worship, organization, or belief *not explicitly found* in the New Testament. As the Disciples of Christ began to elaborate their structure in the 19th century, three key departures from this ideological premise materialized in the minds of those Disciples who broke away from their church. The Disciples allowed the following to develop: (1) pastorate (professionalized ministry); (2) use of instrumental music in worship; and (3) formation of national autonomous agencies to fulfill missionary and educational functions. In open defiance of these three developments, the Churches of Christ came into existence as a strongly fundamentalist body with a conversionist ideology. Preaching, converting, and teaching the Bible were and are the main church activities. The adoption of a strict conversionist ideology has had consequences for the ideological options available to the group. One logical consequence of this ideology is tension with the world, seen in fairly complete avoidance of external groups both religious and secular. The consequences for authority principles, structure, and organizational proliferation are most interesting. Internal conflict is one inherent possibility coming from the adoption of a conversionist ideology, since this would force the group to act in the world and thus formalize procedure, while nonetheless trying to maintain a simple structure and authority principle.

The Churches of Christ thus far has largely avoided such conflict (1975 membership was approximately 2,400,000), even though it is nonetheless fulfilling its ideological imperative to act in the world. First, we will examine its somewhat unique method of action fulfillment; and second, how this has been done without compromising its authority principle. The Churches of Christ has adopted what we have chosen to label a "cooptative structure" for development of resources devoted to action in the world, following from deeply rooted ideological bases. The Churches of Christ maintains that *it has no organization above* the local *congregation*; yet it has a far-flung program that is conducted in a cooptative fashion.

Two approaches are used. The first involves local congregations funneling monies into some particular local Church of Christ congregation enabling the eldership of that congregation to perform some nonlocal function. For example, the Highlands Church of Christ in Abilene, Texas, employs a staff and sponsors a very large radio program, "The Herald of Truth", using the services of hundreds of radio stations and expending large sums of money. Similarly, the eldership of the Broadway Church of Christ, Lubbock, Texas, annually raises and spends hundreds of thousands of dollars for directly employing a large staff in foreign mission work. *No separate* denominational *agency* is erected in either case.

A second form of cooptative structure is use of *independent agencies* or organizations to fulfill church functions. This body uses the services of several, non-denominational, worldwide missionary agencies to pursue a vigorous overseas missionary program in some sixty-five countries. In addition, major church periodicals are printed and disseminated by church-related but privately owned and controlled agencies. Since official status for these organizations is lacking, the Churches can claim to have *erected no agencies* for denominational activities. The Gospel Press of Dallas, Texas, is supported by the voluntary contributions from individual church members throughout the country, but the Churches do not formally own or control it. To further development of its ideological program, the Churches of Christ carries on home and foreign missions, publications and education, as well as some personal support functions (homes for orphans, the aged) without erection of a church bureaucracy. It has continued this type of cooptative solution of its action imperatives without construction of complicated organizational machinery. It has likewise maintained its simple authority principle as well as its fundamental conversionist stance.

Since no formal "ecclesiastical" organization exists above the local congregation, whatever cooptative structure that does exist serves the local congregation without being able to dictate policy and program to these congregations. Ultimately, authority resides in the local congregations.[24]

While something like a semi-professionalized ministry has developed in the Churches of Christ, authority is largely of a democratic nature, residing immediately in the hands of the local elected elderships and ultimately in the bodies of the congregational members-at-large. Authority exists as a form of representative democracy where the eldership directly guides the congregation in spiritual and temporal matters, with the people maintaining a voice and a veto. Consequently, the Churches of Christ has not experienced the type of strain that has developed in denominations which have elaborate organizational structures but have not sufficiently legitimized their existence (e.g., as in the former American Baptist Convention). The leadership of the Churches of Christ, however, could be described as "unstable" (in Harrison's sense) in that it is characterized by both mimetic-traditional and quasi-charismatic types of authority. The rise of a semi-professional ministry attests to the pressures to adopt a traditional mode of leadership. While technically schism is not possible in such a non-bureaucratized group, unity is made more difficult because of the quasi-charismatic style of certain Churches of Christ leaders. The leadership as a whole have vacillated between mimetic-traditional and quasi-charismatic modes of authority, both of which are unstable. However, the basic authority principle (no intermediary between God and the individual) has not been compromised; similarly with the strong conversionist ideology. The Churches of Christ today remains a *democratic coalition with a cooptative structure*. It has not yet reached the point where it believes that such a structure results in ineffective church mission. The possibility for other forms of bureaucratization exists in the future, however. (Cf. Appendix B for an organizational chart of the Churches of Christ).

MODERATELY CENTRALIZED FEDERALISM

Christian Church (Disciples of Christ)

The Disciples represents the first, large, indigenous denomination to arise on the American continent. They spread rapidly in what has been called the Second Great Awakening period shortly after the turn of the 19th century. The development of the Disciples from a simple frontier group to a complex 20th century religious organization will be traced.[25]

The Disciples originated from numerous "revitalization" movements within the Methodist, Baptist, and Presbyterian denominations. One branch of this general revitalization movement took the name "Christian", while the other adopted the name "Disciples." A reconciliation of these two movements occurred in the early 1830s led during its formative years by the charismatic Alexander Campbell.

The central focus of the Disciples' movement was a rejection of everything not expressly stated in the New Testament. They adopted a basically Biblical stand which emphasized the possibility for conversion of all men to Christ and salvation. The Disciples ideology, at first, was a reaction to the "ecclesiasticism" and "dogmatism" they believed had developed in groups transplanted to America from Europe. In this sense, the Disciples was a revitalization movement which sought to restore organizational and ideological simplicity in religion. In addition to a conversionist ideological orientation, the Disciples adopted a stance strongly in favor of the *dissolution of all denominations* and the emergence of *one* Christian body. Their intention was to begin a unified Christianity and not found another denomination. The essential tenets of Disciples' ideology then were conversionist, anti-ecclesiastic, anti-dogmatic, and pro-ecumenical.

Growing out of these ideological premises were implications for authority and organizational structure. The Disciples strongly maintained that no authority could exist between God and the individual (following naturally from their vehement anti-ecclesiasticism and anti-dogmatism). While Alexander Campbell initially took a stand against any non-local, organizational proliferation, he reversed his opinion in his own lifetime. Today, the Disciples have not only adopted a bureaucratic structure and abandoned their simple authority principle and structure, but they claim that even their "founding father" was not opposed to non-local organization. Regardless of this later development, the Disciples first arose as a democratic coalition, simple in structure and strong in conversionist ideology (cf. point #1, Figure 5).

Inherent in Disciples ideology was a potential conflict between a principle of simple authority and an ideological pressure to expand and spread the conversionist ideology, goals which implied action in the world. As early as 1845, the American Christian Bible Society and the

American Christian Tract Society were formed, both lay-founded and lay-dominated. Forces promoting national unity, cooperation, and communication between various Disciples congregations impelled them to adopt a national convention structure in 1849. This critical decision point in the life of the Disciples movement put into action forces which later resulted in a schismatic rupture of Disciple brotherhood. The forces opposing the dangers of ecclesiasticism lost what for them was a crucial battle. The convention, however, was limited to only home and foreign missionary activities. Attempts to attach other functions failed, as other autonomous lay agencies arose and died in attempts to create a national response of the action imperative deriving from a conversionist ideology. By the middle of the 19th century, the Disciples had chosen action in the world, but because of ideological constraint against ecclesiastical organization, they adopted a *convention/autonomous agency structure* (cf. pathway 1 to 3, Figure 5).

The Disciples reached another critical decision point in 1869, when it failed to implement the Louisville Plan, which would have created not only a *horizontal* integration of agencies at the national level, but also a *vertical* integration between convention and state and district conventions (cf. pathway 3 to 3b in Figure 5). The Disciples were not yet ready to make such a radical departure from their ideological principles. The remainder of the 19th century and the early part of the 20th saw the erection of an autonomous agency structure which carried out its action functions independent of the national convention. During this period, the Christian Women's Board of Missions, the Foreign Christian Missionary Society, the Board of Church Extension, the National Benevolent Association, the Board of Temperance and Social Welfare, and the Association for the Promotion of Christian Unity were founded. The convention remained largely a popular-style convention without a representative delegate assembly.

This proliferation of autonomous agencies brought a good deal of overlapping of function and competition for resources. An attempt to create a *unified agency structure* was successful in 1920, with the erection of the United Christian Missionary Society, which eventually came to include most of the boards that had developed before this period. This unified agency did not, however, solve the growing problem of total convention/autonomous agency coordination, nor did it adequately define the role of the national convention in the life of the denomination as a whole. The 1950s witnessed the emergence of a new critical decision point in Disciples' denominational life. During these years the decision was made to seek greater coordination (if not structural control) between the autonomous agencies and the national convention (cf. pathway 3, 3a, and 4 in Figure 5). A Commission on Budgets and Promotional Relations was formed to create a unified budget; the National Church Program

Coordinating Council was formed to unify the program of the total denomination; the Council of Agencies was created to make long-range plans for the denomination; a Home and State Missions Planning Council was formed to coordinate mission activity, and finally, a Curriculum and Program Council and Christian Education Assembly were created to coordinate educational and curricular concerns. The 1950s and 1960s saw much debate over the issue of "coordination" (the approach actually adopted) vs. "unification." Finally in 1968, the Disciples reached a most crucial decision point with the adoption of a *convention/agency* structure (cf. pathway 4, 5, and 5a in Figure 5). Horizontal structural control was created by abolishing the autonomous agencies and making them administrative arms of the National Convention. The National Convention itself became a representative, delegate body during this period. The Disciples are today working in the direction of greater coordination of effort between National Convention and the state, district, and local levels (approximate 1975 membership, 1,300,000). A greater degree of vertical structural control seems to be emerging. The Disciples still see their national body as largely advisory, but they have also recognized centralization and bureaucratization. (Cf. Appendix C for an organizational chart of the Christian Church's national unit).

This trend toward bureaucratization has been accompanied by three parallel developments. (1) The first is a gradual modification of the authority ideology from one that recognized no structure between God and man to one that now views the constituent parts of the denomination (at whatever level) as authoritative parts of the whole church. These developments have seen the *Disciples move from a radically democratic federative structure to an authoritative federative structure.* (2) Likewise, modifications in the ethical ideology have occurred. While the early Disciples were one of the strongest conversionist, evangelical groups on the American frontier, they have today developed a great interest in ecumenism and social action. Disciples are today involved in numerous programs not only of a social "welfare" but also of a social "reform" nature.

(3) Two major schisms occurred when the Disciples made crucial decisions to create further bureaucratization and centralization. A group of Disciples never accepted the convention/autonomous agency structure adopted in 1849 and greatly elaborated in the last half of the century. This group officially remained within the context of the Disciple brotherhood until 1906, at which time they became officially known as the "Churches of Christ" (cf. the case study of this group earlier in this chapter). The increasing coordination of convention and autonomous agency and the "abandonment" of the evangelistic spirit in favor of a social action perspective produced a second schism in the 1950s. The

schismatic group adopted a conservative, fundamentalistic ideology and a coalitional structure. It has come to be called "Churches of Christ II." These two schisms were a product of crucial decisions made by the Disciples which bureaucratized and altered their previous ideological and authority principles. These developments represented to some a weakening of the original religion-world tension. On the other hand, the Churches of Christ and the Churches of Christ II adopted ideological and organizational forms which maintain or reconstruct religious-world tension inherent in the theodicy problem referred to earlier.

The American Baptist Churches, U.S.A.

Baptists are a European group transplanted to America. Emerging out of English Puritanism, Independency, and Congregationalism, two variant ideological strains came to influence American Baptists, often called Calvinism and Arminianism.[26] For our purposes, we can ideologically label Calvinism as "predestinarian" and Arminianism as "conversionist." Since Calvinism maintained that grace was given only to certain individuals elected by God, only those would be saved while all the others were to be damned. The Arminian interpretation was more supportive of the notion that grace was free to all and thus all could achieve salvation. This ideological stance conforms nicely with our theoretical conception of the conversionist type of ideology. American Baptists were permeated with both ideologies, but predominantly with the Calvinistic-predestinarian variety. Consequently, the American Baptist movement was not disposed ideologically to develop a complex organizational structure. While Baptists have gradually modified their strict predestinarian view, the group has, nonetheless, impeded the growth of an authority principle which recognizes the legitimacy of an intermediary between God and man. This does not mean that Baptists have been all of one color. There have existed Arminian and Calvinistic Baptists in varying degrees. However, the American Baptist movement at its founding embodied a Calvinistic, predestinarian ideology which was to modify itself under the democratic influences of American culture and gradually abandon its predestinarian opposition to organizational elaboration. The American Baptist fellowship in its formative years of development was basically a coalition, simple in organization and basically predestinarian in orientation, but eventually recognizing associations of local congregations for purposes of "guidance and mutual edification" (cf. point 1 in Figure 5).

It took American Baptists nearly one hundred years to create a national structure. Previous to this critical decision, Baptists carried out their mission either through relatively small associations of local congregations, or through autonomous, lay-created state and national agencies. With the creation of a "national convention" of Baptists in

1814, American Baptists made the decision to carry on religious activity through a convention/autonomous agency structure. While attempts were made to turn the convention into a centralized body to guide all denominational life, these attempts failed, as Baptists chose to create autonomous agencies to carry on the national life of the growing denomination. In 1824, a General Tract and Sunday School Society was formed. Other agencies followed: in 1832, the American Baptist Home Mission Society; in 1837, the American and Foreign Bible Society; in 1888, an American Baptist Education Society; in 1911, the American Board of Ministers' and Missionaries' Benefits. Thus, by the turn of the century, autonomous agencies had been formed to carry on evangelism and pension functions (cf. path 1, 3, 3b in Figure 5).

Since the Southern Baptists had broken away from the "American Baptist fellowship" in the 1840s, the Northern Baptists, in 1907, founded their own convention. The "Northern Baptist Convention" came into existence still publicly speaking of a loose convention/autonomous agency structure that had heretofore existed in the North. The decades between 1910 and 1950, however, saw the *merging of* the national *convention* structure (which could review the work of the autonomous boards, approve agency budgets, and provide for a Council and committee to act on behalf of the Convention between sessions) *and* the "autonomous" *agencies*. The Convention also developed structures to seek coordination and cooperation with the autonomous agencies which carried on most of the denominational activities. These developments were to prepare the way for the decision in the 1950s to seek closer coordination of purpose and planning between the Convention and the agencies. By the 1960s, boards providing for interlocking of the agencies and General Council boards of the Convention were created. Members of the agency boards were included in various committees of the General Council for purposes of coordinating programs, policy-making and long-range planning (Cf. path 3, 3a, and 4 in Figure 5).

The American Baptist Convention (formerly Northern Baptist Convention) in 1973 renamed the agencies, now referring to them as "divisions" of the convention structure (cf. path 4, 5, and 5a in Figure 5). Moreover, changes in the nature of delegate choice were made in order to integrate state and local conventions as far as possible. Thus, organizational need for comprehensive control over the activities of the denomination created an atmosphere favorable to the emergence of more vertical structural integration in the following years (approximate 1975 membership was 1,579,000). Ironically, while becoming more integrated, the denomination at this time adopted a more plural and seemingly less monolithic name, "American Baptist Churches, U.S.A." (Cf. Appendix D for an organization chart of the national unit of this group).

Needless to say, the emergence of a horizontally centralized national organization among American Baptists has been long in coming, growing out of more than 250 years of American history. As crucial decisions to bureaucratize and centralize were made, other developments in Baptist life have occurred. First, the authority principle has changed. Originally, Baptists were staunch supporters of local autonomy and democratic congregationalism. The development of an elaborate national structure placed pressures upon Baptists to abandon their ideology of no interference between the individual and his God. Baptists have become bureaucratized, at first, outside the Convention and now within it. This has placed strain upon their authority principle, and today American Baptists are compelled to recognize the authority of the national convention. The former legitimizing principle has been modified to recognize the authority of the church as a whole. Baptists still insist upon the autonomy of the local congregation, but organizational realities seem to deny this. American Baptists have progressed from a radically democratic coalition to a radically democratic federation and finally today to a moderately centralized authoritative federation (Cf. paths 1, 3, 3a, 4, 5, and 5a in Figure 5).

In addition, the ethical ideology of American Baptists has undergone considerable modification. Beginning as predestinarian (Calvinistic), the elitist ideology has been eroded by years of exposure to American democracy and individualism. The adoption of an Arminian (conversionist) ideology was demonstrated in the merger in 1911 of the American Baptists and the Free Will Baptists (Arminian). With the decay of strict Calvinism as a general normative support, American Baptists were split in the 19th and 20th centuries by the main theological currents of the day: pietism, revivalism, conservatism, liberalism, and fundamentalism. American Baptists today have begun to adopt a social action ideology.[27]

The loosening of ideological purity and the adoption of bureaucratic forms have produced schisms within the American Baptists. While the breaking away of the Southern Baptists in the 1840s was precipitated by the slavery issue, it also arose out of organizational problems, particularly the lack of attention to the needs of Southerners. The Southern Baptists founded their own convention and created *from the beginning* a *centralized convention/agency structure* (cf. path 3c to 6 in Figure 5). As American Baptists were tightening coordination between their convention and the autonomous agencies, and while they were adopting more liberal and less fundamentalistic ideologies, several schisms were produced. In 1933, the General Association of Regular Baptists broke away, adopting a minimum of organization and a Calvinistic ideology. Similarly, in 1947, the Conservative Baptist Association was formed as the result of disputes over the same theological and organizational issues (cf. path 4b to 1, Figure 5).

In two hundred and fifty years, American Baptists have *moved from a simple democratic coalitional structure to an authoritative federative structure*.

The Assemblies of God

The Assemblies of God arose out of a period of religious revival in the early years of the 20th century. There was a need felt on the part of many in traditional denominations to return to primitive Christianity and to turn away from creedal churches and denominations. This revival came accompanied with the experience of speaking in tongues, and thus the Pentecostal movement was formed and spread rapidly.[28]

The Assemblies of God ideology, while giving predominance to the pentecostal position, is largely a conversionist ideology. There is a strong emphasis on conversion and salvation, with overtones of holiness ideology as first developed in the Methodist movement and later in other holiness groups. Its experience of the infusion of the Holy Spirit and the manifestation of the Holy Spirit in speaking in tongues, prophesying, and interpretation of tongues made this group ideologically new to the religious environment of America at that time. Although the group espouses adventist notions, *conversionist* ideologies are predominant. Emphasis upon action in the world coming from conversionistic ideology has presented the Assemblies of God with the same dilemma faced by other more institutionalized conversionist groups; namely, the potential conflict between the need for action and subsequent bureaucratization and the ideological inclination to maintain a simple God-to-man authority relationship.

The need for action in the world led the Assemblies of God to adopt a national structure, in 1914, at the founding convention of this group. The type of action structure adopted by the Assemblies of God was the *convention/agency structure* (cf. path 1 to 6 in Figure 5). While some thought that any structure would impede the free flowing of the Holy Spirit among individuals, those seeing a need to spread the message and to make converts triumphed. The initial activities of the convention consisted mostly of giving support to independent activities already in existence, such as publishing and missionary activities. However, by 1919, the Gospel Publishing House of the Assemblies of God was established. In 1922, the convention established the Central Bible Institute as a "seminary" for Assemblies of God ministers. During these early decades, missionary agencies were formed to carry the pentecostal position abroad as well as at home. In 1935, the Assemblies of God convention established the Sunday School Department to coordinate and unify the church's Sunday School program; by 1941, a Youth Department also was established. By the 1960s an organizational structure had emerged which included agencies for *all* the above functions in addition to pension, benevolence, and public relations activities.

During this period, program planning and coordination between the various national activities was assumed by a General Presbytery which was empowered to act on behalf of the convention between sessions. In 1971, a restructuring of the national convention offices and agencies was proposed and then enacted in subsequent years. These organizational changes were adopted to create more effective and less overlapping functions and agencies (cf. pathway 6 to 6a in Figure 5).

In some fifty years, structurally the Assemblies of God went *from a simple coalition to a moderately centralized federation*, necessitating change in ideological posture as well. Formed in the 20th century, the Assemblies of God was far removed from the localism of the 18th and 19th century American experience. The Assemblies of God has implemented a very rapid increase of horizontal structural control in a convention/agency structure (cf. Appendix E for an organizational chart of the national unit of this group). What took the American Baptists two hundred and fifty years to accomplish, the Assemblies of God accomplished in only *fifty* (approximate 1975 membership was 785,000). One may speculate as to the reasons for such a rapid increase in centralization. While the Assemblies of God espouses congregational control, it likewise sees each individual and congregation as integral parts of the General Assembly and the church-as-a-whole. Members conceive of themselves as a corporate body. This group has not instituted the degree of vertical structural control found in groups such as the Lutherans or the Methodists, but the creation of a tightly-knit, national organization is likely to increase pressures upon the group to adopt more control over regional and local units in order to support and implement its national program of action.

Issues of authority seem not to be as predominant in this group as we have found them to be in others. Perhaps its historical distance from the fragmented type of ecclesiastical control present when the frontier denominations were initially founded, plus the general bureaucratization and deindividualization of American life, have contributed to the Assemblies' acceptance of horizontal integration.

This group has yet to experience schism. The increases in horizontal structural control and the emergence of vertical structural control could create an atmosphere in which schism might occur. While the group has witnessed institutionalization of its pentecostal ideology in the form of guidelines as to the proper time, place, and function of the "tongues" experience, it has largely retained its religious fervor. If bureaucratization leads to further action in the world, the conditions leading to a schism may develop.

GROSSLY CENTRALIZED FEDERALISM

The Lutheran Church in America

Lutheranism began as a revitalization movement in the Roman Catholic Church and drew its strength from the charismatic leadership of Martin Luther.[29] Its immediate development out of the Roman Catholic Church led to a nationalist church mode of organization and an ideology which became buttressed with doctrine and espousing a strong insistence that "faith alone" could bring salvation.

American Lutheranism was free to develop organizational forms as instrumental to its ideological position, since type of form was an adiaphoron in Lutheran theology, and also since in America it was freed from the control of a national church. Lutheran denominations began with an ideology that was essentially "dualistic" in the sense defined earlier in connection with reduction of ideological tension inherent in the theodicy problem. The church retained the Catholic notion of a body which had authority to dispense salvific grace. While Lutheranism deemphasized the legalism of the Catholic Church, it maintained an ideological position as the dispenser of sacramental grace which comes only from the saving powers of Christ's conquest over the devil.

This dualistic ideology predisposed Lutheran bodies to accept the legitimacy of supra-local organization as a valid structure generally to provide administrative supervision over the ministry of Word and sacraments and to provide administrative and financial support for education, missions, publications, and professional functionary support. Nothing in their ideology *specified the exact nature of* the *organization* of the church as long as the Word and sacraments were dispensed. While the Lutherans began with coalitional structures in America, they quickly developed non-local organizational forms which assumed authority over their constituent bodies.

The plural nature of Lutheran groups, stemming from diverse language and cultural groups and differing periods of Lutheran migration to America, makes an effort at precise discussion of organizational and ideological development hazardous. We will attempt here only to trace those strands of Lutheranism that have resulted today in the Lutheran Church in America and some of the history of the present American Lutheran Church. These two bodies and the Lutheran Church-Missouri Synod enroll the overwhelming majority of American Lutherans. The decision to organize a body which incorporated numerous Lutheran "synods" (regional units) came as early as 1820. Prior to this date, numerous independent, regional synods were formed. The founding of the General Synod in 1820 represented the centralization of control over such synods into a *general synod* (cf. path 1 to 6 in Figure 5).

The centralization of the General Synod (coupled with the rise of the more conservative General Council) was in reaction to "Americanizing" (low church) tendencies of the General Synod; and the advent of the Civil War left American Lutheranism divided into three great synods: The General Synod, The General Council, and the United Synod of the South. The two latter were both less centralized than the former. By 1918, these three groups had compromised enough on ideological and organizational positions that a merger was effected, resulting in the United Lutheran Church in America. The creation of the ULCA in 1918 saw the concentration of powers into a council within the national convention which had judicial, legislative, and administrative authority over the various agencies. The ULCA was joined in 1962 by the Augustana Synod (1860), the American Evangelical Lutheran Church (1871), the Suomi Synod (1898) in the creation of the Lutheran Church in America. The LCA represents a vast increase in the degree of centralization of power and the emergence of a *horizontal* structural control over agencies that had been developing in the constituent agencies of the merged bodies. With the creation of the LCA in 1962 (approximate membership 3,000,000 in 1975), the executive and legislative powers of this body were further enhanced. By the early 1970s, the Lutheran Church in America proposed and adopted a tightly-knit national organization and constituent offices (cf. pathways 6 to 6b in Figure 5).

The history of the American Lutheran Church is very similar (1975 membership approximately 2,438,000), differing only in the sense that the merged body that was created in 1960 is more vertically centralized than is the LCA. The American Lutheran Church and the Lutheran Church in America represent bodies that from inception accepted the need for action in the world to bring faith and grace to men. While not as evangelistic as certain other conversionist groups, Lutherans have bureaucratized to meet the ever-increasing degrees of action in the world. While the acceptance of a single, centralized national Lutheran body has not yet developed to date, the creation of mergers of various synods throughout their American history has attested to an ever-increasing degree of both horizontal and vertical structural integration. The Lutheran churches have generally begun with convention-agency structures which have either created their own agencies or have incorporated agencies formed outside the convention's auspices. The ALC and the LCA differ today primarily in the extent of vertical integration. The ALC conceives of its constituent synods ("districts") as administrative branches, whereas the LCA allows these synods more autonomy. While some Lutheran groups have objected to this degree of centralization, these two major groups of Lutherans have pursued a general course of acceptance of and even increase in such authority.

These organizational developments have had concomitant ideological developments. (Cf. Appendices F and G for organizational charts of the national units of the LCA and the ALC. For a discussion of the structure of the Lutheran Church-Missouri Synod, especially in relation to the recent doctrinal-organizational crisis, see Chapter 9).

Luther's belief that the organizational aspect of the church was human and thus subject to error, his adherence to the fact that scripturally there was no justification for any particular type of church form, and his emphasis upon the priesthood of all believers—all meant that *Lutheran church structure* in America (freed from its national character) *could develop* largely *out of expediency, not from ideological dictates*. As the mission of the church grew, little resistance arose to the development of concomitant organization. Accepting the ideology that Christ committed the ministry of the means of grace to the congregations collectively, Lutheran bodies generally accept the belief in their own collective authority and power to dispense such grace. Thus, the *local congregation* is viewed as *only one manifestation* of the larger church.

Lutheran ideology has frequently been permeated with a pietistic overtone which appeals more to the "heart" than to the "head." The existence of the frontier and the democratic individualism of America placed strains on the more orthodox, creedal nature of Lutheran ideology. However, the temptation to adopt a narrowly conversionistic stance has largely been resisted. With the possible exception of the Lutheran Church-Missouri Synod, Lutheran ideology in recent years has undergone a subtle shift in emphasis from an orthodox, creedal response (which would bring the Word to the individual so that he might find faith in Christ) to an outlook which recognizes a role for churches to assist church members and governments in *defining* public *social policies* for national social problems. This stance has been especially true for the LCA. Such a concern is new to Lutherans, but a commitment to start in this direction has been made.[30] If Lutherans have been considered somewhat conservative in the past, this shift in ideological focus could lead to a change in these bodies' images and programs. The three major Lutheran sub-groups since 1967 work together in a federated service agency, the Lutheran Council in the U.S.A.

The adoption of more centralized modes of organization and deviations from ideological "purity" have created schisms among the Lutherans. We have already noted the defection of the United Synod of the South in 1863 and the General Council in 1867 from the General Lutheran Synod. Three other schisms have occurred in the constituent bodies that made up the ALC and the LCA. The National Evangelical Lutheran Church was formed in 1898 by a defection from the Suomi Synod, a partner in the merger creating the LCA. This schism came about because of the desire of this body to return to a congregational-coalitional type of structure. Likewise, the Lutheran Free Church broke away from the United Norwegian Synod in 1897, seeking a congregational-coalitional form of organization. The Evangelical Lutheran Synod was formed in 1917 as a reaction to what it believed was an ideological compromise that occurred when the Evangelical Lutheran Church was created by merging the Hauge, Norwegian, and United Norwegian Synods in 1917. It retained a convention/agency structure but reinstituted what it believed was an uncompromised Lutheran ideology. These schisms have been responses, at least in part, to the adoption of decisions in the mother groups to bureaucratize and centralize their structure and/or alter preexisting ideological positions. As schismatic groups arose, they increased religious tension with the world around them.

The United Methodist Church

Methodism began as a revitalization movement within the Church of England under the guidance of John Wesley and George Whitfield. The basic initial ideological and organizational forms of English Methodism were adopted by American Methodists. We shall trace the complex historical development of Methodism *from* an essentially *coalitional religious movement to* a contemporary *federative structure with* a degree of *centralization* found in few Protestant churches.[31]

The ideology that American Methodists inherited from John Wesley's movement to reform the Church of England gave primacy to experience as valid religious activity. It likewise gave strong emphasis to four major concerns: (1) universal redemption, (2) justification, (3) regeneration, and (4) holiness. The overwhelming thrust of Methodist ideology has been its extreme Arminianism (conversionist ideology). There was to be "free grace" for all. Justification meant the forgiveness of sinners by God, while regeneration was believed to be the removal of the power of sin over the life of the individual. The concept of holiness involved the notion that the power of grace is so complete that perfect love can govern both the heart and life of man. American Methodists were, at their beginning, a *thoroughly conversionist* association of believers. We have already noted that such an ideology is conducive to action *in* the world. We have also noted that in other groups this conversionist ideology was accompanied by an authority ideology that prohibited the erection of any structure between man and God. The Methodists began with a different principle of authority and have retained this initial premise. Growing out of the hierarchical and episcopal Church of England, Wesley became a dominant figure in the organizational aspects of his revitalization movement. Consequently, he could assume the role of bishop or general superintendent of the various "societies" (congregations) that were formed. The formal split with the Church of England and the independence of American Methodists from their English counterparts compelled Wesley to ordain bishops to rule over the rapidly growing Methodists in the recently independent American colonies. Thus, the episcopal principle was continued in American Methodism. While Methodism began as a simple coalitional structure (i.e., various "circuits" were made up of several local "societies" served by an itinerant minister), it had inherent in its ideology the potential for organizational elaboration coming from its strong conversionist ideology and its acceptance of a centralized principle of authority.

By the time Methodists decided that some national organization for activity was necessary, the basic *vertical structure* of Methodism was already in existence. This consisted of local Quarterly Conferences, held four times annually in each circuit and presided over by an elder; Annual Conferences, formed to divide the country into geographic regions and supervised by bishops (general superintendents); and the National General Conference formed in 1792 as the general legislative body of the new church and held every four years. Shortly thereafter, a House (later Council) of Bishops was also formed.

These developments saw the rise of a *dual* mode of organization, the conference system on the one hand and the episcopacy on the other. In the 19th century, a third structure within Methodism, the "society" structure, was also developed. Thus, Methodism adopted a *convention/ agency structure with an episcopacy* (Cf. pathway 1 to 6 in Figure 5). This agency structure arose initially out of lay interest in the activity of the church, although laymen were excluded from conference structure until the end of the 19th century. As lay-staffed agencies were formed, they were gradually assimilated into the convention-episcopacy structures. A publishing agency was formed in 1789; the Missionary and Bible Society was formed in 1819; the Methodist Sunday School Union in 1827; and the Church Extension Society in 1864. By the third quarter of the 19th century, these boards had been brought under the auspices of the convention. Gradually, other agencies were added as needs for action arose. The Methodist Church was formed in 1939 out of three groups: the original Methodist Episcopal Church, the Methodist Episcopal Church-South, and the Methodist Protestant Church. This led to an amalgamation of agencies, but by the 1950s a need for greater coordination and restructuring of the entire agency system was expressed. By this time the Methodist church (1950 membership was approximately nine million members) had consummated a merger with the much smaller Evangelical United Brethren Church to form the United Methodist Church in 1968 (1970 membership approximately 10,500,000). This series of mergers created rapid amalgamations of agencies and consequent overlappping of functions and purposes. To coordinate the work of these numerous commissions, boards, and agencies, the General Conference of the United Methodist Church created two bodies, the

Program Council and the Council of Secretaries to review and coordinate the work and planning of these bodies. (Cf. pathway 6 to 6b in Figure 5; likewise, see Appendix H for an organizational chart of the national unit of this group.)

We may note the following concomitant developments in Methodist ideology:

1. Little modification of the original authority ideology has taken place in United Methodism. Methodists *began* with a principle conducive to a *high* degree of *vertical* structural *control* and have *maintained* that principle; they have kept and strengthened the role of the episcopacy. The bureaucratization of Methodism has taken place chiefly through the elaboration of the agency structure and concomitant attempts to create a unified convention-agency-conference program. While schisms have resulted from the adoption of such an authority ideology, the mainstream of United Methodism has consistently upheld such an authoritarian ideology and structure. Methodists term themselves a "connectionalist" denomination.

2. The penetration of Methodism into secular society has resulted in the modification of its ideology. Chiles[32] contends that the three central foci of Methodist ideology have been revelation, a concept of sinful man, and free grace. It is Chiles' contention that reason has come to dominate the place formerly held by revelation. Rationalism is called upon to "verify" the truths of the Scriptures. The original Wesleyan concept of man totally depraved and sinful by nature has been modified to a position that maintains that sin is no longer presupposed as a flaw in character of man's nature but merely the act of voluntary violation of known obligations. In a similar fashion, the doctrine of free grace has been replaced by a notion of free will. Whereas originally grace was seen as free to all as the indispensable means of salvation given by God to man, the newer conception sees man as the instigator of repentance and faith. These are no longer God's gifts to man; consequently, salvation has come to be the result of man's effort to moralize and spiritualize his life.

In general, this ideological shift represents an encroachment upon the sovereignty of God and the ascendancy of the power of man. While there has been a renewal of interest in original, Wesleyan Methodist ideology in recent years, today the United Methodist church has adopted a thorough commitment to social action, a stance which shifts the emphasis *from* saving the *individual to* modifying or "saving" a *society* by reforming it.

3. The centralization of authority in Methodist experience and the weakening of the original Wesleyan ideological premises, in part, has led to numerous schisms and realignments as these organizational and ideological shifts have occurred.[33] In each of these schisms, issues of ideological abandonment or the creation of non-legitimate bureaucratic

structures compelled groups to break ties with the mother group and to reestablish a religious tension through reconstruction of religious ideologies and authority principles based upon simple religious conceptions.

CONCLUSIONS

This investigation of types of Protestant organization has revealed that Protestantdom has *not* worked from *one* basic organizational *model* and that its variegated histories are replete with organizational growth, development, and change in types.

We have hypothesized that organizational development is accounted for, in part, by the divergent ideological outlooks Protestant groups have developed toward basic tasks and worldly involvement. This approach recognizes, however, the importance of such non-ideological factors as the religious and non-religious environments in which religious groups arise and are nurtured. The importance of variables such as size, autonomy, heterogeneity, and task specialization has been recognized. Also of significance is the growth of ideological-organizational imbalance or incongruence, often followed by attempts of groups to adopt or regain organizational stability and/or "purity", and to reduce conflict and inconsistency. The phenomenon of "power" and "politics" has probably also been insufficiently emphasized here, less so than has actually been the case.

The distinction between vertical and horizontal structural control is an empirically useful set of concepts in delineating types of Protestant organization, as our case studies have revealed. The phases within an organization related to *horizontal* structural control reveal much to us about the varying and divergent processes of religious bureaucratization. The varying degrees of *vertical* structural control (the integration of lower units with upper organizational units) reveal a diversity of types of organization whether they be coalitions or federations, moderately centralized or grossly centralized.

In the final analysis, we must admit to a *pluralism* of Protestant organizational models, just as we witness a pluralism in the larger religious environment of American Protestant, Catholic, and Jewish institutional and cultural modes.

This theoretical and empirical investigation of American Protestant organization seems to suggest the following considerations for those intimately involved with denominational life, decision making, management, and planning:

1. American Protestantism is both ideologically and organizationally divergent in form, and thus statements of program, plan, implementation and evaluation must be closely analyzed in terms of these divergent types of ideology and organization. Each has differing problems and potentials.

The on and off history of the Consultation on Church Union (COCU) has attested to this caution.

2. Organizational decision making must keep central both the history of ideological development, which tends to function as a denominational "self-image," its change or resistance to change, as well as purely organizational and environmental exigencies such as the degree of vertical and horizontal structural control permitted by the group; also increasing size and diversity of membership; and the degree to which the denominational structure is open to elements in its external environment. What may make *organizational* sense (e.g., denominational growth, fiscal efficiency, or tactical effectiveness) may *not* make *ideological* sense (in spite of actual deviations in practice from such a self-image). Organization and purpose may be contradictory, conflicting, and changing in opposing directions; or they may mutually support each other.

3. While there is a tendency for religious groups to secularize to some degree as they develop vertical and horizontal structural control mechanisms, the various units within the interorganizational context may, in fact, be working at cross-purposes. This is possible not only because few organizations are completely integrated, but particularly so in Protestant religious groups because so many have traditionally deemed the *local* units as the most important. Furthermore, since religion in America is voluntary, *upper* level units are to a considerable degree *dependent upon* cooperation at the *lower* level in providing operating funds. Thus, upper level units must keep a vigilant ear to all levels of their denominational operations. Likewise, because few religious organizations are tightly integrated, upper level units may be able to pursue and implement policies and programs that are somewhat incongruent with the purposes, goals, and ideological stances of their constituent units (e.g., NCCC being more liberal than the grass roots). Because most Protestant organizations lack a tightly unified structure and have histories of congregational control, denominations are constantly faced with the problems of coordination, being at cross-purposes, or ideological and organizational imbalance. Our case histories would tend to warrant the original, theoretical assumption that religious ideology (purpose) and religious organization (praxis) stand *in a dialectical relation* to one another. Ideology functions to create an image for the denomination to develop within, but religious ideologies are nurtured, changed, or ignored in light of environmental and organizational influences. Thus, we see the wisdom of much religious thought and the insight of Max Weber that religion and the world stand *in* a relationship of *tension* one with another. If religion remains at the ideological level alone, it is ineffective in reaching its purpose; on the other hand, if religion becomes too involved in the world, it may lose its purpose or meaning for existence.

Appendix

A. CHILDREN OF GOD

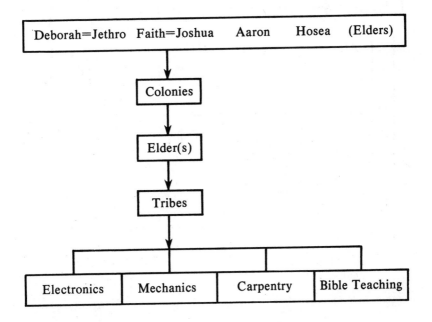

B. CHURCHES OF CHRIST

Local Congregation

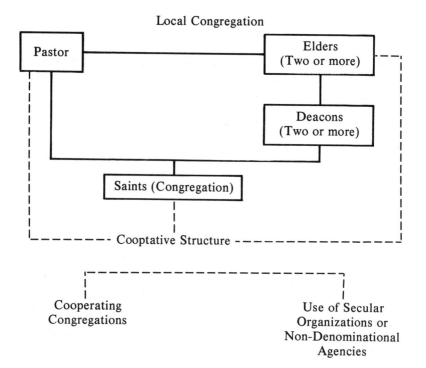

APPENDIX C

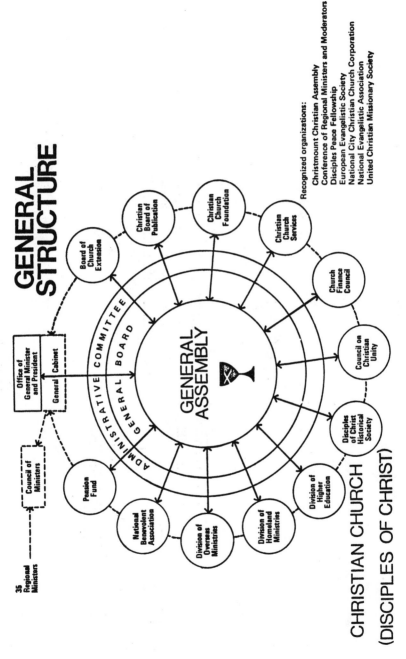

GENERAL STRUCTURE

CHRISTIAN CHURCH (DISCIPLES OF CHRIST)

APPENDIX D

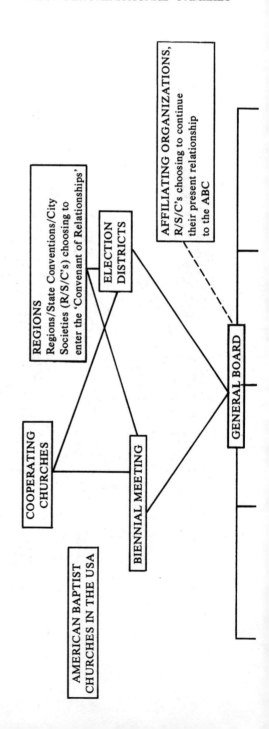

AMERICAN BAPTIST CHURCHES IN THE USA

COOPERATING CHURCHES

BIENNIAL MEETING

REGIONS
Regions/State Conventions/City Societies (R/S/C's) choosing to enter the 'Convenant of Relationships'

ELECTION DISTRICTS

AFFILIATING ORGANIZATIONS, R/S/C's choosing to continue their present relationship to the ABC

GENERAL BOARD

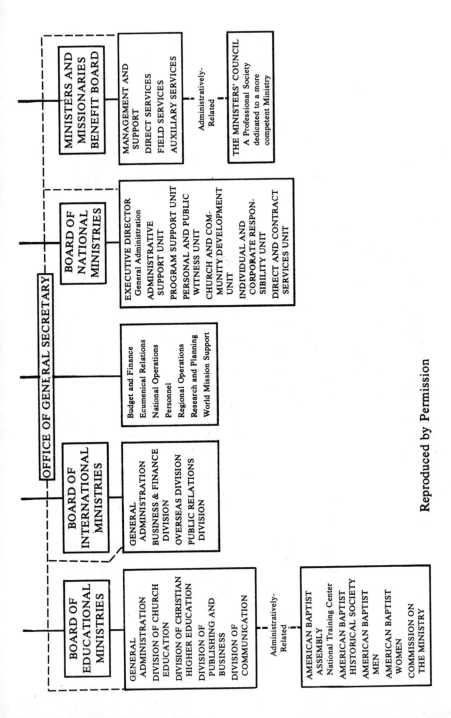

Reproduced by Permission

APPENDIX E
THE ASSEMBLIES OF GOD

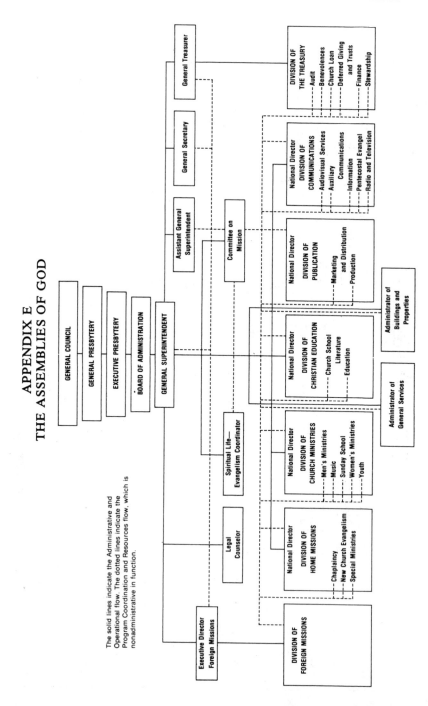

The solid lines indicate the Administrative and Operational flow. The dotted lines indicate the Program Coordination and Resources flow, which is nonadministrative in function.

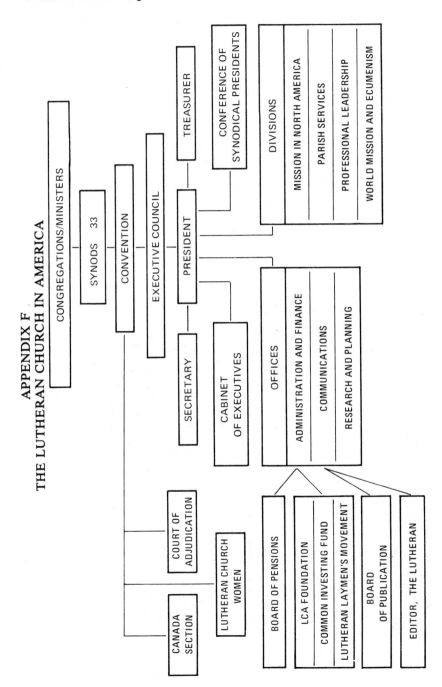

APPENDIX F
THE LUTHERAN CHURCH IN AMERICA

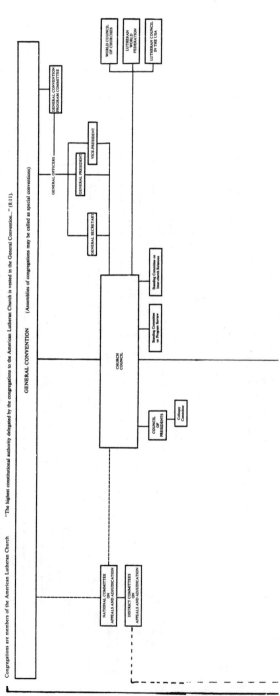

APPENDIX G
FUNCTIONAL RELATIONSHIP BETWEEN UNITS IN THE AMERICAN LUTHERAN CHURCH

Congregations are members of the American Lutheran Church   "The highest constitutional authority delegated by the congregations to the American Lutheran Church is vested in the General Convention..." (8.11).

GENERAL CONVENTION   (Assemblies of congregations may be called as special conventions)

GENERAL OFFICERS

VICE-PRESIDENT

GENERAL PRESIDENT

GENERAL SECRETARY

GENERAL CONVENTION PROGRAM COMMITTEE

WORLD COUNCIL OF CHURCHES

LUTHERAN WORLD FEDERATION

LUTHERAN COUNCIL IN THE U.S.A.

CHURCH COUNCIL

Standing Committee on Inter-church Relations

Standing Committee on Program Review

COUNCIL OF PRESIDENTS

Colloquy Committee

NATIONAL COMMITTEE ON APPEALS AND ADJUDICATION

DISTRICT COMMITTEES ON APPEALS AND ADJUDICATION

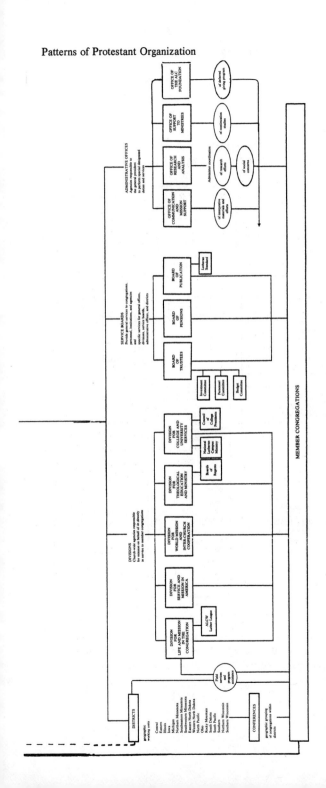

APPENDIX H
General Agency Structure of the United Methodist Church, 1977-80

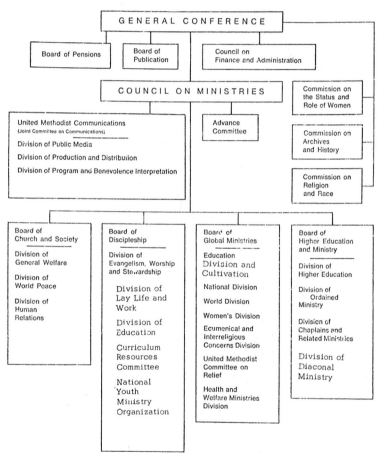

Quadrennial commissions authorized by the General Conference include
Continuing Commission on the Black Colleges and Study Commission on
the Episcopacy and the District Superintendency.

Notes

Thanks to Winthrop Hudson, Professor of Church History, The University of Rochester; David Willer, Professor of Sociology, University of Kansas; the Editor; and my sociology of religion classes for their critical readings and/or comments on a preliminary draft of this chapter.

1. Ideology as used in this chapter refers to the theological, ethical, and worldview systems of religious groups.

2. Charles Y. Glock and Rodney Stark, *American Piety: The Nature of Religious Commitment* (Berkeley: University of California press, 1965).

3. Bryan Wilson, "An Analysis of Sect Development," *American Sociological Review*, 24, 1, 1959; *Patterns of Sectarianism* (London: Heinemenn, 1967); *Religious Sects: A Sociological Study* (London: Weidenfeld and Nicolson, 1970).

4. Max Weber, *The Sociology of Religion*. Translated by Ephraim Fischoff (Boston: Beacon Press, 1922 and 1963), pp. 138-139.

5. H. Gerth and C. Wright Mills, "Religious Rejections of the World and Their Direction," *From Max Weber: Essays in Sociology* (New York: Oxford University Press, 1958), pp. 325-326.

6. Judith Willer, *The Social Determination of Knowledge* (Englewood Cliffs, N.J.: Prentice-Hall, 1971), p.64.

7. Bryan Wilson, "An Analysis of Sect Development," *Patterns of Sectarianism; Religious Sects: A Sociological Study* (see note 3 above).

8. This type may be seen as having three sub-types: the *fundamentalist* (emphasizes the conversion experience and a Biblical literacy), the *holiness* (seeks a second blessing or sanctification beyond conversion, and the *pentecostal* (seeks a third blessing in the form of the fusion and gifts of the Holy Spirit.

9. It seems clear that Wilson's types correspond in part to our hypothesized types of tension resolution. Our type 1 is Wilson's conversionist; type 2 is the adventist; type 3 is the introversionist; type 4 is the reformist and utopian.

10. Benton Johnson, "On Church and Sect," *American Sociological Review*, 28 (August 1963).

11. The transmigration of souls ideology is not considered here as it is not a part of Protestant or Christian tradition.

12. Roland Warren, "The Interorganizational Field As A Focus For Investigation," in Merlin B. Brinkerhoff and Phillip R. Kunz (eds.), *Complex Organizations and Their Environments* (Dubuque: Wm. C. Brown, 1972), pp. 313-318.

13. Paul Harrison, *Authority and Power in the Free Church Tradition: A Social Case Study of the American Baptist Convention* (Princeton: Princeton University Press, 1959).

14. Max Weber, *The Theory of Social and Economic Organization* (New York: The Free Press, 1958).

15. Max Weber, *The Protestant Ethic and the Spirit of Capitalism* (New York: Charles Scribner's Sons, 1947), pp. 329-340.

16. Paul Harrison, *Authority and Power in the Free Church Tradition: A Social Case Study of the American Baptist Convention* (Princeton: Princeton University Press, 1959), p. 213.

17. Task specialization seems to take a somewhat consistent course of development. First, tasks centering around ideological dissemination such as home and foreign missions, publication, Sunday School, education and laity work evolve. Secondly, the tasks of maintaining the functionaries of the growing organization develop in the form of pension and insurance tasks. Thirdly, tasks related to environmental relations such as benevolence, public relations, social action, and Christian unity emerge.

18. See Gibson Winter, *Religious Identity: The Formal Organization and Informal Power Structure of the Major Faiths in the U.S. Today* (New York: Macmillan Co., 1968), for a more detailed account of agency development in American religious organizations.

19. While not wishing to take sides in the "social action" controversy in contemporary religious life and while not implying that social action amounts to secularization, if it leads to a deemphasis upon theological and theologically based ethical concerns, it would fit our definition of secularization introduced earlier in this chapter.

20. Cf. Dean Hoge's *Division in the Protestant House* (Philadelphia: Westminister, 1976), for details of lay, Presbyterian reaction to the United Presbyterian Church's social action program.

21. Michael McFadden, *The Jesus Revolution* (New York: Harper and Row, 1972).

22. Ronald M. Enroth, Edward E. Ericson, Jr., and C. Breckinridge Peters, *The Jesus People* (Grand Rapids: William Eerdman's, 1972).

23. Materials to develop the historical and empirical case study for the Churches of Christ have been taken from Frank S. Mead, *Handbook of Denominations in the United States* (New York: Abingdon Press, 1961); A. T. Degroot, *Disciple Thought: A History* (Fort Worth: Texas Christian University, 1965); Oliver Reed Whitley, *Trumpet Call of Reformation* (St. Louis: The Bethany Press, 1959); Winifred Ernest Garrison and Alfred T. DeGroot, *The Disciples of Christ: A History* (St. Louis: The Bethany Press, 1958); Gary P. Burkart, "An Expanded Typology of Religious Group Organization: A Model for Systems of Knowledge and Social Structure," unpublished M.A. thesis in sociology,

University of Kansas, 1971; and "A Model for Religious Group Organization and Ideology Applied to Selected Case Studies," unpublished Ph.D. dissertation in sociology, University of Kansas, 1974.

24. It should be realized that most of the material for these case studies reflects the official image projected by these groups or, as the sociologist would prefer, the "formal structure" and pattern and not the actual, operating patterns (the "informal structure"). This comment is perhaps most relevant in those groups that have not legitimated authority at the top. The whole point of Harrison's study of the American Baptist Church was to show that sometimes greater power can be exercised in the absence of formalized authority. That individual congregations in the Churches of Christ appear to be replicas of each other is probably no accident. Informal control in these types of organizations is often more effective than formal control. Likewise, the actual operating situations of other groups that follow in this chapter are likely to deviate from the group "image" that is officially projected.

25. Christian development will be traced with the aid of the following, A. T. DeGroot, *Disciple Thought: A History* (Fort Worth: Texas Christian University, 1965); Oliver Reed Whitley, *Trumpet Call of Reformation* (St. Louis: The Bethany Press, 1959); Loren E. Lair, *The Christian Churches and Their Work* (St. Louis: The Bethany Press, 1963), W.E. Garrison and Alfred T. DeGroot, *The Disciples of Christ: A History* (St. Louis: The Bethany Press, 1958); *Provisional Design: General Rules and Policies of the Christian Church*, 1972; *Yearbook and Directory of the Christian Church*, 1972; *Not the Only Christians, But Christians Only*, 1972; William B. Blakemore, ed., *The Revival of the Churches*, Vol. III (St. Louis: The Bethany Press, 1963); Ralph G. Wilburn, *The Reconstruction of Theology*, Vol. II (St. Louis: The Bethany Press, 1963).

26. The following sources were used to construct the case study on the American Baptists: *Some Notes on Organizational Development in the American Baptist Convention and Its Antecedents* (American Baptist Publication Society, 1969); *The American Baptist Churches in the U.S.A.* (The American Baptist Publication Society, 1973); Charles L. White, *A Century of Faith* (Philadelphia: The Judson Press, 1932); Orbett, *A History of the Baptists* (1963); William W. Sweet, *American Culture and Religions* (Dallas: Southern Methodist University Press, 1951); *By-Laws and Acts of Incorporation of the American Baptist Churches, U.S.A.* (Board of Educational Ministries, American Baptist Churches, 1973).

27. This last statement is not to suggest that Baptists have not been involved in reform movements as they have. Such undertakings as support for the American Revolution, the Anti-Slavery Campaign, the fight for prohibition, and the leadership found in the "social gospel" movement indicate this to be so.

28. The following authors and sources were used to develop the case study on the Assemblies of God: *Who We Are and What We Believe*, Assemblies of God (Gospel Publishing House, 1972); *In the Last Days: An Early History of the Assemblies of God*. Assemblies of God (Public Relations Department, 1970); *Statement of Fundamental Truths*, Assemblies of God (The Gospel Publishing House, 1973); *Introducing the Assemblies of God*. Assemblies of God (Gospel Publishing House, 1972); Thomas F. Zimmerman, *The Pentecostal Position* (The Gospel Publishing House, 1973); *Meet the Assemblies of God*, Assemblies of God (Public Relations Department, 1973); *The Biennial Report, 1971-1973*, Assemblies of God (Gospel Publishing House, 1973); Jessyca Russell Gaver, *Pentecostalism* (New York: Award Books, 1971).

29. The case study on Lutherans was constructed with the use of the following: Carl Meyer, ed., *Moving Frontiers: Readings in the History of the Lutheran Church-Missouri Synod* (Saint Louis: Concordia Publishing House, 1964); Altman K. Swihart, *Luther and the Lutheran Church: 1482-1960* (London: Peter Owen Ltd., 1960); Henry E. Jacobs, A History of the Evangelical Lutheran Church in the United States (New York: Charles Scribner's Sons, 1893); "Introducing the Family: The United American Lutheran Church," *The Lutheran Standard*, January 3, 1961; "Introducing the Family: The Evangelical Lutheran Church," *The Lutheran Standard*, January 17, 1961; *Preliminary Report of the Commission on Function and Structure*, Board of Publication (Lutheran Church in America, 1971); *Toward Greater Effectiveness for Mission: A Proposal for New Structures in the National Offices of the American Lutheran Church*, The Board of Publication (The American Lutheran Church, 1972); *Handbook of the American Lutheran Church*, Board of Publication (The American Lutheran Church, 1972); *Lutherans Believe* (The Lutheran Council of Greater Chicago, 1961); *Basis for Lutheran Social Action*, Commission of Research and Social Action (The American Lutheran Church, 1965); *Handbook of the Lutheran Church in America*, Board of Publication (The Lutheran Church in America, 1972); *Our Approach To Social Involvement*, Commission on Research and Social Action (The American Lutheran Church, 1968).

30. Cf. *Basis for Lutheran Social Action,* Commission of Research and Social Action (The American Lutheran Church, 1965); and *Our Approach to Social Involvement*, Commission on Research and Social Action (The American Lutheran Church, 1968).

31. The case study on the United Methodist Church was made possible with the aid of the following sources, Robert Currie, Methodism Divided: *A Study in the Sociology of Ecumenicalism* (London: Faber and Faber, 1968); Rupert E. Davies, *Methodism* (London: The Epworth Press, 1963); J. M. Buckley, *A History of Methodists in the United*

States (New York: Charles Scribner's Sons, 1899); Wade C. Barclay, *Early American Methodism: 1769-1844* (New York: The Board of Missions and Church extension of the Methodist Church, 1950); William W. Sweet, *Religions on the American Frontier, 1783-1840: The Methodists*, Vol. IV (Chicago: The University of Chicago Press, 1946); Nolan B. Harmon, *The Organization of the Methodist Church: Historical Development and Present Working Structure* (Nashville: The Methodist Publishing House, 1962); *The Book of Discipline of the United Methodist Church* (Nashville: The Methodist Publishing House, 1972); Emory S. Bucke, ed., *The History of American Methodism*, Volumes I, II, and III (New York: Abingdon Press, 1965); Robert E. Chiles, *Theological Transition in American Methodism: 1790-1935* (New York: Abingdon Press, 1965); Henry D. Rack, *The Future of John Wesley's Methodism* (London: The Lutterworth Press, 1965).

32. Robert E. Chiles, *Theological Transition in American Methodism: 1790-1935* (New York: Abingdon Press, 1965).

33. The following are the major schisms in Methodist history in America. The Christians (Methodists) were the first to break away in 1790, since they never accepted the principle of a centralized organization. The Wesleyan Methodists broke away in 1843 because of their desire for a less centralized organization. The Methodist Episcopal Church-South split off in 1844 over issues of slavery and organizational distribution of power. The Methodist Protestant Church (1830) was formed to allow lay representation in the conference structure. The original Methodist Episcopal Church merged with two other groups as stated to form the Methodist Church. The Congregational Methodists broke with the Methodist Episcopal Church-South in 1852 to establish a congregational-coalition type of structure. The Reformed Methodists formed their own group in 1814 out of a belief that the mother group had abandoned its ideological purity and was becoming too centralized. The Free Methodists broke away from the Methodist Episcopal Church in 1860 to restore emphasis upon holiness. Ideological reasons led to the formation of the Southern Methodist Church in 1939 at the time that the Methodist Church-South merged to form the Methodist Church. Likewise, the Fundamental Methodists organized in 1942 out of a sense of ideological and organizational abandonment by the merger of 1939. The Evangelical Methodists came into existence in 1946 to combat what they believed were modernistic ideas and too much centralization developing in the new Methodist Church.

2

Roman Catholic Organization Since Vatican II

Gertrud Kim, O.S.B.

THE SECOND VATICAN COUNCIL: PRECIPITANT OF CHANGE

Any contemporary discussion of the Roman Catholic Church (RCC) must begin with the Second Vatican Council, a historical watershed in the modern history of Roman Catholicism. Within the RCC, such an "ecumenical council" is convened by a call from the Pope, who presides at its sessions and confirms its decrees. Subject to this essential dependence on the Pope, a council has supreme power over the entire Church in the world. Of twenty-one such ecumenical councils, the most recent one, the Second Vatican Council, was opened by Pope John XXIII on October 11, 1962, and continued after his death and the election of Pope Paul VI (on June 21, 1963), finally closing on December 8, 1965. As the RCC appeared to have become a "museum full of ancient artifacts," Pope John wished the Council to serve as an *aggiornamento*, a way of bringing the RCC "up-to-date where required," in order to spread its message "to all men throughout the world."[1]

The significance of the Council is not limited to the RCC. Pope John's historic role supports the assertion that *rationality and charisma can converge* and that charisma may be found at the *center* as well as at the periphery of the institutional fabric in question. The Council testified to the power of radicalization from within as well as challenge from without.[2] The last fifteen years of the post-Vatican RCC call into question the Marxian view of the function of religion and offer evidence of the Weberian thesis of the "transformative capacity of religion."[3]

More than a decade has now passed since John XXIII "opened the windows" of the RCC. Where has the RCC come from? Where is it going? The present chapter examines changes formally introduced by the Council, actual implementation or non-implementation of those changes, consequences of implementing and/or not implementing those official changes, and a few ways of dealing with those possible consequences. Included in this chapter is also an attempt to depict the RCC both as a whole and also as it is in the denominational society of the United States; for structure and process, parts and whole, and past, present, and future are mutually interdependent and inseparable.

THE ROMAN CATHOLIC CHURCH

Characteristics of the RCC

Religious denominations in most countries today exist as voluntary, complex organizations in a pluralistic marketplace; they face similar problems and similar dilemmas. Among them, convergence is evident both in structure and in function.[4] Yet, religious denominations differ not only from other voluntary organizations but also *among themselves*. Both convergence and divergence are sociological realities to be recognized. If not in matter, at least in degree, a number of characteristics set the RCC apart from other denominations, and these characteristics need to be understood. For present purposes, three differences are briefly identified.

1. Scope: Time and Space—Eldest, Longest, Most Inclusive

Among Christian denominations the RCC is the eldest. The impact of age on organizations as on human beings is varied and of great significance. First, organizational inventions of a particular time depend on the entire fabric of the period. Thus, the "secular" organizational models prevalent at a given time ordinarily influence the development of other (e.g., religious) organizations in existence at that time as well.[5] Second, as the "liabilities of newness" are lessened only through the passing of time, organizations need time, often a long period of time, to develop into efficiently working systems. Third, if a given organization survives the liabilities of newness, it then takes on qualities of familiarity, competence, and sacredness. At this point, there may emerge an "organizational man" focus whereby the life orientation of participants centers in the organization so that loyalty to the organization becomes taken-for-granted beyond question.[6]

The positive impacts of age can be continuous, however, only if the organization functions in a "placid" environment. In a "turbulent" environment, the age of an organization and its capacity for effectiveness and efficiency may be curvilinearly, if not negatively, related. The dominant organizational structures of Western, Medieval, feudal society, for example, are not only outdated but may be ineffective in contemporary, post-industrial society. While some members may still be committed to an organization partly because of their "trained incapacity," others find themselves alienated. The organization as a whole suffers from what sociologists call "dilemmas of institutionalization." Furthermore, attempt to promote change in such an organization is resisted and frequently results in the formation of *parallel substructures* which, in turn, create incongruence in organizational structure and functions and diminish cooperation and coordination within.

For the RCC, its agedness is thus not an unmixed blessing. In many contemporary societies, for instance, its *ascriptive* orientation conflicts with that of *achievement*, and the *monarchical* pattern of authority with that of *democracy*. In short, as "arrangements that worked well at one time turn out to be institutional fixtures of negative significance in another," the RCC today suffers from "strategic decisions made long ago amidst the historical and social contexts which have since dramatically changed."[7]

Therefore, if the RCC of today does not want to be a prisoner of history and a victim of its own structures, it needs to review its "old familiar concepts" and strip off its non-essential, historical accretions.[8] But the process of sociological reconstruction is always delicate and often dangerous, especially when it comes to religious systems. First, there are people whose *faith* resides not only in the immutable "essence" but also *in the historical "accidents."* Thus, *any change* at all *may generate a climate where the entire institution is seen as problematic.* Second, there are those whose vested interests and trained incapacity bind them to the traditional establishment. Third, functionaries in religious (as other) organizations frequently have no clear vision of new and more viable alternatives. Finally, and most importantly, in the RCC there is yet no agreement as to *which* elements constitute the *permanent essence and which* do *not.*[9] Given these conditions, it is a real surprise to observe the new directions the RCC has taken in recent years.

The RCC is not only a Christian denomination with the oldest roots, but it is also the *largest* in its national and societal coverage. Having the practice of inclusive membership and the ambition to be a "universal church," this Church moved into ever new frontiers so that today it is an *international*, religious system *transcending political and societal boundaries*. Because the RCC is an international system, it has witnessed the Rhine flowing into the Tiber, most clearly during the Council, and the Amazon flowing into the Rhine, Tiber, and Mississippi.[10] There has also been sharing of both monetary-material and personnel resources on a global basis.[11] Also, since the RCC is international, it may be *less* likely to become a prisoner of a *particular, national membership base* and a given societal environment.

On the other hand again, being international is not an unmixed blessing. With too high an international heterogeneity and diversity, the RCC finds it difficult to present a unified front to the outside and maintain internal cohesion. There are important differences in the religious needs of people in different continents and cultures as well as differences among various social groups—e.g., men vs. women, old vs. young, those raised in a faith vs. converts from another religious tradition or from no religion at all, those who view their religious-denominational affiliation as secondary, reinforcing their other commitments in secular society vs. those who see their religion as primary with all else paling beside it. Therefore, the RCC should also find it difficult to meet the diverse needs of its variegated membership.[12]

Both its long history and wide presence set the RCC apart from other Christian denominations. Moreover, organizational age and geographic coverage interact to produce other effects most critical of which seems to be its aid toward solving the "plausibility" problem in the pluralistic and relativized world of today. As religion is socially constructed and socially maintained, the plausibility of a religious system and the feasibility of religious life would increase as historically and contemporaneously the number and types of people who subscribe to it increase. Such an aid is especially invaluable to the contemporary marketplace where populism dominates.[13] At the same time, if such an aid elevates historical accidents to the state of "eternal essence" as well, the *adaptive* capacity of the RCC may be diminished. In short, the scope of the RCC, historic and contemporary, endows it with various attributes not shared by other Christian denominations in the United States.

2. Organizational Structure of the RCC

The contemporary RCC also differs from other denominations in regard to its structure. Although no existing structure conforms to any ideal type, compared to other denominations the RCC is *more corporate than federated* in its governmental form, and its *polity* is *episcopal* rather than either presbyterian or congregational. In its formal structure, the RCC is highly centralized by virtue of policy decisions by the Holy See.[14]

Since the RCC is a hierarchically organized corporate entity, *a given national church has no life of its own but exists as a subunit* within the entire international system. With the RCC, the term "national church" itself is a misnomer, for there *is no national church*. As the relation between the inclusive decision-making structure of the Vatican and all subunits within it is unitary, the *final authority* over the unit rests *at the top*; all national and/or specialized units are formally organized in a division of labor to achieve system-wide goals, and they are expected to orient themselves toward the well-being of the "parent" rather than toward their own, respective subgoals.[15]

On a more local (i.e., diocesan and parochial) level, the episcopal form of polity sets the tone for the relationship between the local clergyman and his people by making a pastor's appointment dependent upon episcopal choice and by subjecting him to episcopal discipline. The priest must first be socially recognized as priest before he can so function, and such recognition is possible only if the individual cleric affiliates himself to a bishop—an affiliation formally controlled through a system of role induction and socialization of identity. The structure of the RCC is such that priests are constantly reminded of their irrevocable loyalty to their particular bishop, who may at any time directly control their pastoral destiny. As the clergy are under the direct control of the episcopal authority, the laity in the RCC have *little official authority* over their local congregation or their clergy, *although* they may have much, actual, *informal power*. However, as authority without power is a rubber stamp, *power without legitimacy is precarious*, and more so in the RCC because it is a normative organization.

The RCC can do little about the consequences of its longevity; it chooses to pay the price of its international coverage. Since the time of the Council, the contemporary RCC is leaning in the direction of evaluation and reconstruction of its structures. Of many issues related to structure, only two are chosen for brief consideration. First, because the RCC is hierarchically organized, formally *accountability* within it is always *upward*—pastors are accountable to their bishop and bishops are accountable to the Pope—and rewards for performance (negative and positive) are not dependent on the evaluation by the "lower-archy." Therefore, compared to their counterparts in other denominations, *religious professionals in the RCC are freer from local and lay pressures*, and such freedom facilitates the pursuit of ideals and goals even when the laity disagree with them. In those pursuits, religious professionals in the RCC (occasionally supported by certain sociologists) see their pursuits as prescribed in the teachings of the Gospel and their "right and obligation" to "challenge" the "comfort"-seeking laity.[16] Theological issues aside, however, if pursuit of "challenge" or the prophetic role of religion ignores "comfort" or the "priestly" function, yet if the laity nonetheless seek "comfort" from their religion, then organizational "transcendence" (i.e., freedom of an organization from the demands of its members for the pursuit of its mission goals) may not actually be any better than organizational vulnerability. The laity's *lack of authority* does *not* mean *lack of power*. In a pluralistic society, unsatisfied needs lead members of voluntary associations to search for new ways, religious and/or non-religious, for meeting those needs. Though Catholic laity generally lack formal political power, besides their "financial weapon", i.e., withholding contributions, they can have their last say in completely withdrawing from church participation. Furthermore, who is going to say that "professional" religion is truer than "lay" religion? Does not a seminarian lose a certain kind of "faith" while he is converted to the more professional type of faith of his seminary faculty? Most importantly, with the post-Vatican conception of the church as "the people of God," the RCC may *no longer be able to legitimate* the existing distribution and exercise of power and *authority* proceeding *from top down.*

Second, whereas good and rational decisions generally but more so today require accurate and relevant information, the severest problem of the RCC today appears to be the *lack of upward flow of information* due to the way it is organized and operates. In large organizations, top decision makers depend on the "middle-" and "lower-archy" for implementing or non-implementing their decisions. Such implementation is likely not only when the decision itself is wise, but more so when it is *wisely made*. As a case in point, the controversial "Humanae Vitae" encyclical on birth control became an indicator of system failure, *not only because of its content, but also* because of *the way it came into being*.[17] Similarly, the U.S. bishops debated for many years on the manner of receiving the consecrated host, while their people had already decided on the manner they thought appropriate for such an event.

Of course, no organization can make every decision on the basis of empirical considerations, public opinion, or democratic participation. Neither is organizational efficiency an end in itself. Nevertheless, with all its benefits and costs, a unitary, corporate, episcopal structure differentiates the RCC of today from other contemporary denominations in the United States.

3. Functionaries in the RCC

Historically, celibacy for religious professionals in the RCC developed at various times and for various reasons, theological and practical.[18] Today, *sacerdotal celibacy differentiates the RCC* and its functionaries from other Christian denominations and their functionaries. Historically, celibacy provided a mechanism for maintaining wealth in the Church, prevented familial intrusion into its polity, reduced the claims of competing roles and status positions upon its functionaries, and generated and channeled the entire energy and attention of its personnel to works of mission. Nevertheless, today, the question of obligatory celibacy is being openly debated. In 1970, an NORC study on Roman Catholic priests in the United States reported that "more than half the priests are at least somewhat in favor of the change, and approximately three-fifths expect the change." On the other hand, there is little evidence that the RCC would change its policy, as in the same year only 11% of U.S. Bishops either "strongly or somewhat agreed" that clerical celibacy should be a matter of personal choice for diocesan priests; furthermore, the Vatican continues its insistence on celibacy. Even if the policy were to change, the essential nature of its functionaries would probably remain the same for some time yet, as only about one-fifth of priests in 1970 admitted to any possibility of marriage for themselves.[19] There may be other characteristics which the RCC prescribes for its priesthood, but none appears so peculiar and so paramount as the question of celibacy. Therefore, understanding of this issue is critical in understanding this Church and its functionaries.

Interaction Effects

As no social fact either exists or operates in a vacuum, examination of a given social fact in isolation is not adequate for sociological curiosity. Because the RCC is both international and corporate-unitary, it differs from, e.g., the World Council of Churches, an international but federated organization of churches. Because the RCC is international and its clergy are celibate, it *can control* the *distribution* and location *of its priests*. Because the RCC is a unitary structure and its clergy are free of familial privileges and obligations, *it can call into question as well as provide legitimacy for civil authorities and can both challenge and comfort its people*. More concretely, e.g., the post-Vatican II church-state conflict in Paraguay was facilitated because the RCC is an international corporation whose functionaries lack local roots and familial relations and identify rather with the parent organization.[20] Because the RCC is not bound by a given nation-state, it appointed "a leftist bishop" as Archbishop of Asuncion, and its national bishops' conference elected "a critical young rural bishop" to be president of the conference. Priests in Paraguay accepted the post-Vatican ideologies, and international religious orders provided material and personnel resources for the struggle. The RCC in Paraguay is not a deviant case. Though variant in relative scale, intensity, and power, similar ferment has been almost ubiquitous in many third-world nations. Also it may be that, in the United States, so-called "Americanism" was *not* to dominate the RCC in the New World, not only because immigrant Catholics were loyal to Vatican but also because the RCC was an international establishment and its functionaries lacked local roots.

In conclusion, the RCC as a religious denomination shares many characteristics with other denominations; it is also unique—similarity does not mean identity. Of the many characteristics of the RCC, the most particular are its *long history, unitary-corporate structure, and celibate functionaries*. Finally, the RCC is an "interaction effect" of its commonalities and peculiarities.

The RCC in the Last Quarter of the Twentieth Century

The Swiss guards at the Vatican palace have amused many popes, for sure; many popes also have been entangled in the maze of the contemporary organization of the Church. At the same time, the RCC has survived the test of history. The pre-Vatican RCC was once evaluated as "excellent" in its management functions and structures; even today, if "organization of communities of faith have to be evaluated in terms of their adequacy to defend and/or extend the faith without substituting their organizational activities for the central task," "the Catholic hierarchical structure seems most adequate to keep its organizational elaboration in line with the task of faith."[21] The RCC is once again *changing* itself *from* what was appropriate for the *garrison Church of the Counter-Reformation to* the *open Church of the ecumenical age*. But at this point, it is uncertain how much has to be destroyed by revolution before the barriers to organic and evolutionary growth are removed. On the whole, then, the RCC is for "constant improvement, so that the structured organization will be an ever more impressive sign of the invisible reality."[22]

Figure 1 depicts the formal structure of the RCC in the last quarter of the twentieth century. The hierarchy, as the supreme governing body of the Church, consists of the Roman Pontiff and the bishops.[23] As the supreme head, the Pope has primary jurisdiction over the entire RCC; the bishops, in subordination to the Pope, have ordinary jurisdiction and authority for the affairs of their dioceses. Assisting the Pope and acting in his name in the central government and administration of the Church are the sacred College of Cardinals and other officials of the Roman Curia. Cardinals are chosen by the Pope and collectively form the sacred College of Cardinals, a kind of self-perpetuating oligarchy. In 1978, there were 125 cardinals (32 Italian, 12 American), with 115 eligible (being aged 80 or under) to elect a new Pope. Although Italians still constitute the largest grouping in Vatican City and the Roman Curia, there has been a substantial internationalization. The number of non-Italians in the Curia increased from 570 to more than 1,400, a rise of 145%, while the number of Italians increased from 750 to 850, a rise of only 14% during the same period, from 1961 to 1970.[24] Above all, after 456 years of rule by Italians, the RCC in 1978 elected a *non*-Italian, Karol Wojtyla of Poland, as Pope John Paul II.

An *ecumenical council*, an assembly of the bishops of the entire RCC, is convened by the Pope, who presides at its sessions and confirms its

FIGURE 1
ORGANIZATION OF THE ROMAN CATHOLIC CHURCH

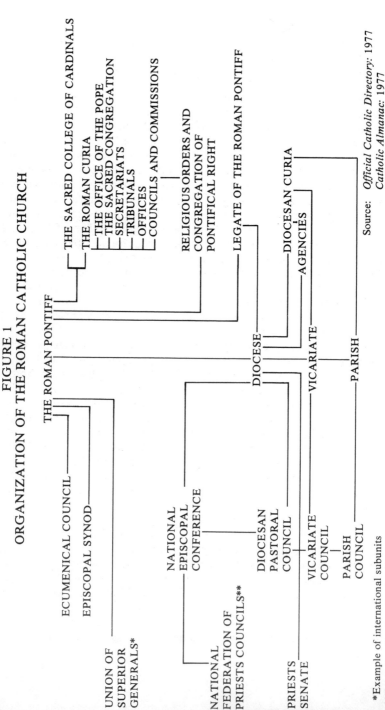

Source: *Official Catholic Directory: 1977*
Catholic Almanac: 1977
Canon Law: A Text and Commentary

*Example of international subunits
**Example of national subunits

FIGURE 1A
DIOCESAN AND PARISH ORGANIZATION

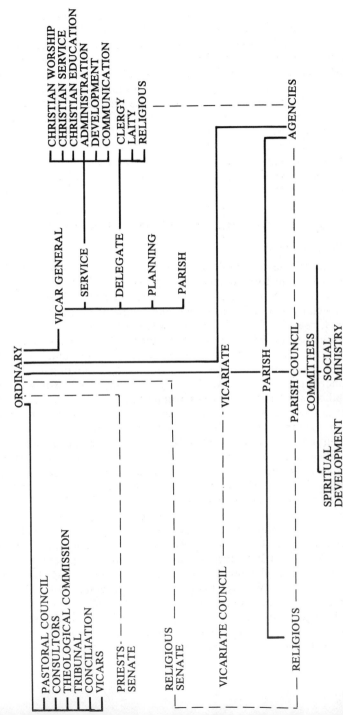

SOURCE: This is based on *Directives and Guidelines for Parish Councils* (Archdiocese of Detroit: Vicar for Parishes Office, No date: Revised Edition) and a chart provided by Parish Council Service, Archdiocese of Chicago, in April, 1977.

decrees. Subject to the essential dependence on the Pope, the council has supreme power over the entire RCC. The *synod of bishops* was chartered by Pope Paul in 1965 and consists of elected representatives of *national conferences of bishops*. Like the ecumenical council, the synod of bishops is subject to the Pope, who has authority to call it into session, to assign its agenda, and to give its members deliberate as well as advisory power. Since 1965, there have been five such "synods," including the synod of September, 1977.[25] On the international level, the office of the *Pope*, the sacred *College of the Cardinals*, the *Roman Curia*, the *ecumenical council, and* the *synod of bishops* constitute the formal and *permanent* units of the *organization of the RCC*. In this international system, the RCC in the United States exists as a relatively vital and loyal subunit.

THE RCC IN THE UNITED STATES

Historical Start

The RCC in the United States is what it is today precisely because of its distinct history in this country. Though Catholic explorers had traversed much of the country and missionaries had done much work (especially among Indians) from the beginning of the New World, the mainstream of Catholic history was started only at the end of the Revolutionary War with the establishment of the Diocese of Baltimore. By then, the nation had become solidly Protestant, as Catholics constituted only 1% of the total population, although part of the early American establishment. The day of peaceful coexistence between Catholics and Protestants was over by 1820, when Catholic immigrants swept over the American shore, and the societal context presented the "immigrant religion" with "the dilemma of becoming American enough to survive in the new society and remaining Catholic enough to maintain its allegiance to the world-wide Catholic faith." The history of the RCC became a struggle between the "Americanizers" and the "Anti-Americanizers."[26] To defend itself from the hostile society, the RCC established a host of social organizations, so that within the Catholic-ethnic "ghetto," the Church was literally all-encompassing. If there had been no external threats, conflicts between ethnic groups within the Church might have resulted in some permanent splits. Throughout the entire history of the RCC in the United States, the dominant ethnic group has been the Irish, who have had all the advantages vis-a-vis other Catholic nationality groups. Even today, the power structure of the RCC in the United States still continues to be largely Irish.

Though human history rarely makes an abrupt turn, the history of the RCC in the United States did make such a turn with the birth of John F. Kennedy and his generation. As its people became thoroughly Americanized, the RCC had to leave its immigrant religious ghetto. As nativism collapsed, the Church became autochthonous but lost the internal cohesion engendered by an external enemy and had to confront the laity for whom it was not yet ready. Furthermore, risks and opportunities of the historic turn were literally compounded as they intersected with the ferment of the Vatican II era. In this double process of change, the RCC in the United States stands at a crossroads of historic importance.

Recent Trends in the U.S. RCC

Like many social phenomena, institutional vitality is complex. The problem of such vitality is even greater when it concerns organized religion. Given the lack of direct measures of the vitality of the RCC in the United States, data on selected elements over the last quarter of the century are presented. To be sure, trend data are not directly concerned with vitality but with changes over time.[27] Examining trends among members, clergy, and various organizational units in the system should indirectly reveal levels of past performance, the present level compared to the past, and performance trends for the future.

Membership. Whereas Catholics constituted only 1% of the U.S. population in the eighteenth century, mainly as a result of immigration and natural increase, Catholics grew to over 15% by the 1920s and to 25% by the late 1950s.[28] But since then, the RCC itself and most surveys report little change in membership figures. On the other hand, very recently, Greeley and his colleagues at the National Opinion Research Center reported large defections from the Church among the young as compared with the past. Also over the ten-year period from 1963 to 1974, declining were weekly mass attendance, monthly confessions, visits to the church to pray at least once a week, daily private prayer, making retreats and days of recollection, reading Catholic magazines or newspapers, and having religious conversations with priests. On the other hand, Greeley and colleagues reported that receiving weekly communion doubled in the same interval. New developments also emerged—charismatic prayer meetings, informal home liturgies, and various religious discussion groups. Perhaps an even clearer sign of spiritual health may be found in the fact that "young people are more likely now than they were in 1963 to say that they go to mass to worship God," rather than "not to sin" or "not to offend" their parents.[29]

Despite a recent decline in respect for leaders in the United States as a whole, Catholics still respect their ecclesiastical leaders, at least more than they do recent U.S. presidents. But Catholic people have also noted the diminishing quality of Sunday sermons and rejected their Church's teachings on certain matters (e.g., sexual morality, certain liturgical restrictions). They have also become uncertain about some of the tenets of their faith and have expressed a lack of confidence in their capacity to hand on their religious values to their children.

While U.S. Catholics have changed over the ten-year interval since Vatican II, such changes have actually been going on over a much longer period. Table 1 presents weekly church attendance for the period between 1952 and 1978 with thirteen time-points of observation. While survey data on weekly church attendance may mean little, they are the only available data for the period with multiple observations.

First, it is clear that weekly church attendance was at its height in the early 1960s and since then has consistently been in decline.[30] In the opening year of the Council, 1962, 75% of Catholics in the United States reported weekly church attendance; but in 1964, even before it was over, only 66% were attending church weekly—a 9% decline in two years. In the year of the encyclical "Humanae Vitae" in 1968, 63% of Catholics attended weekly, but by 1972, only 53% did so, another 10% decline in four years. In the next four years, there was still another 10% decline. Although there was a 7% increase in 1977 over 1976, there was a 2% decrease in 1978 over 1977. Also, although the rate of decline has decreased since the Vatican II, the general trend of Catholic church attendance has been consistently downward. Given these facts, the search for explanation may be endless.

First, Table 1 eliminates possible explanation by something from the larger society, *since over the same time period Protestants* maintained a *similar level* of attendance. Second, the Kennedy era of the early 1960s was accompanied by high church attendance, and it may be speculated that the President's example may have raised the attendance of his co-religionists. Third, the Second Vatican Council may have signaled the end of "Sunday mass religiosity" for some. For such, "once it became legitimate to eat meat on Friday," it was easy "to consider themselves to be free from all religious and ecclesiastical obligations. If you turn the altar around and put mass into English, anything goes."[31] But once the Council weeded out that type of Catholic, the decline was less than 1% per year until 1968. Fourth, it may also be speculated that the unpopular encyclical "Humanae Vitae" may have driven out another type of Catholic between 1968 and 1972, effects of which are still continuing. On the other hand, it is difficult to attribute continuing decline in church attendance to a *single decision* made several years ago. Rather, does not the new organizational norm for weekly church attendance among American Christians simply seem to lie between 35% and 40% (unless there is effective social engineering to raise it)? If so, it could again be expected that the complete Americanization of immigrant Catholics by the early 1970s would be accompanied by concomitant changes in religious beliefs and practices as well. If this is true, we may further ask: would it have been possible to have predicted and taken certain steps to have controlled this change in a desired direction however defined?

TABLE 1
WEEKLY CHURCH ATTENDANCE OF U.S. ROMAN
CATHOLICS AND PROTESTANTS: 1952-1978 (per cent)

Year of Survey	Catholic Attendance				Protestant Attendance		
	SRC*	NORC GSS	NORC Greeley	Gallup	SRC*	NORC GSS	Gallup
1952	64%				32%		
1956	71				34		
1960	76				37		
1962	75				39		
1963			71%				
1964	66				39		
1965				67%			38%
1966				68			38
1967				66			38
1968	63			65	33		39
1969				63			38
1970				60			37
1971				57			38
1972	53	61		56	36	38%	37
1973		48		55		36	37
1974		50	50	55		36	37
1975		46				37	
1976		43				36	
1977		50				34	
1978		48				34	

* Whites only; figures for 1960, 1964, and 1968 have been deweighted by ((Raw N/Weighted N) * (1/(1+Variance of the original weight))* Original Weight).

Sources: SRC: Election Studies by Survey Research Center, University of Michigan.

NORC-GSS: General Social Survey by National Opinion Center, University of Chicago.

NORC-Greeley: *Catholic Schools in a Declining Church,* by Andrew M. Greeley, William McCready, and Kathleen McCourt.

Gallup data: Table 5.19: "Weekly Church Attendance for Catholics and Protestants 1965-1974," cited in Greeley, McCready, and McCourt, p. 150

Clergy. With its sacerdotal-sacramental system, the RCC is completely dependent on its clergy. Although there have been changes in the image of the priesthood and Catholics may not respect their clergy as they once did, *the laity still expect* their *clergy to provide leadership* in interpreting human experience in the light of transcendent symbols, to *challenge* their complacency, and to promote the expression of *spiritual sensibilities* from within their lives.[32]

In 1970, NORC found that Catholic priests in the United States were high in personal morale, liberal on certain social and racial matters, and quite mature in their emotional growth. They accepted the bishop as the principal leader and decision maker in the diocese, supported ecumenism, worked long hours, had close friends, and found "home" where they resided. They also prayed regularly, reported frequent religious experiences of union with God or Christ, and accepted the basic religious values of the Church. Above all, "A large majority of the clergy say that, if they had the choice to make again, they would enter the priesthood." NORC also found *many differences between priests and bishops* on matters of ecclesiastical structure and distribution and exercise of decision-making power, sexual morality, and many other topics. The majority of the priests did not accept the present position on obligatory celibacy even though they valued celibacy and probably would not marry even if celibacy became optional. Priests did not enjoy a high degree of self-actualization and psychological well-being, with associate pastors especially suffering from low job satisfaction and inadequate relationships with colleagues. Above all, "there has been a considerable decline in enthusiasm for vocational recruiting, a phenomenon that may be far more serious than the resignation rate."[33] At present, there are no data comparable to these NORC findings for 1970.

Table 2 presents the number of priests in the United States between 1920 and 1977, along with the number of male and female religious and seminarians in the same period. First, it is clear that, over a forty-seven year period from 1920 to 1967, the number of priests grew 185% or about 4% annually. But *since 1967,* there has been an *8% decline,* or just under 1% annually over the past ten years. Second, within the priesthood, the pattern (or time) of growth differs for religious vs. diocesan priests. Third, the decline in the number of priests will likely continue for some time to come as the number of seminarians continues to decline and the number of resignation from priesthood rises. In 1985, it is predicted that the RCC in the U.S. could easily be staffed with one-fourth fewer priests than it was two decades ago.[34]

As stated repeatedly, there is no question as to the centrality of the priesthood within Roman Catholicism. At the same time, throughout the history, both male and female "religious" (i.e., those in religious orders) have *played critical roles* in the Church and for its people. Sociologically speaking, Catholicism in the U.S. would have been something other than what it is today if it had not had its religious, especially, the female religious.[35] Among female religious, the long period of numerical growth stopped in 1966; among male religious, in 1967. Once begun, the rate of *decline among female* religious has been *much greater than among male* religious. Though there are no national statistics on religious vocations, it would not be a surprise if they are not as numerous as they once were up until the early 1960s.

At present, there is almost universal agreement about continuing numerical decline among priests and religious. Some see signs of a leveling off; for others such an end is still far off. Some see a rise in quality as quantity declines; others see decline in both quality and quantity. "With the number of priests dwindling, lay people are having to assume greater responsibility out of sheer necessity."[36] Some welcome this change; others lament it.

Hierarchy-agency. As elsewhere, the dualistic character of the RCC in the U.S. is seen in its *hierarchy-agency structure*. To perform its priestly, pastoral, and prophetic functions, the RCC in the U.S. from the beginning developed many activities and organizations such as charities, schools, hospitals, and cemeteries administered largely by clerical functionaries and related to the bishop's office through priest-directors or chaplains.[37] Through these agencies, the RCC not only became "pervasive" (i.e., set norms for many activities inside and outside itself) but also literally embraced its people and thereby maintained an effective plausibility structure over against the Protestant world.[38] For many Catholics, "being Catholic" encapsulated their lives, and their *religion* involved a *complete style of life*. Table 3 presents trends on a few selected functional agencies, with data on the hierarchical structure of the RCC.

In 1978, there were about fifty million Catholics in the United States. For the RCC in the United States, the top unit is the *archdiocese,* of which currently there are 32. Under the 32 archdioceses are 138 *dioceses,* and within the 32 archdioceses and 135 dioceses there are 18,625 *parishes* and 4,088 *missions*. Although 10 new dioceses came into being in the 1970s, the number of *seminaries* declined drastically since the 1960s.[39]

While the Catholic population increased about 77% over the last 25 years or so, the number of *schools* has remained virtually constant or declined. Although there were 238 Catholic colleges and universities in 1977, over the preceding fifteen years or so 51 colleges and universities closed their doors. Over 800 high schools and 2,000 elementary schools also closed their doors since the 1960s. If the importance of early socialization and observations of positive effects of Catholic education cannot be disregarded, those concerned with the future of the RCC

TABLE 2
NUMBER OF PRIESTS, RELIGIOUS, AND SEMINARIANS IN THE UNITED STATES 1920-1978

Year	Diocesan Priests	Religious Priests	Diocesan Seminarians	Religious Seminarians	Religious Sisters	Religious Brothers
1920	15,389	5,630	+	+	+	+
1930	18,873	8,052	+	+	+	+
1940	22,450	11,462	+	+	+	+
1950	26,583	16,387	12,464	13,158	147,310	7,377
1960	32,569	21,227	20,278	19,618	168,527	10,473
1965	35,925	22,707	26,672	22,230	179,954	12,271
1966	36,419	22,774	26,184	21,862	181,421	12,255
1967	36,871	23,021	24,293	21,086	176,671	12,539
1968	37,453	22,350	22,234	17,604	176,341	12,261
1969	37,454	22,166	19,573	14,417	167,167	11,755
1970	37,272	21,920	17,230	11,589	160,931	11,623
1971	37,020	21,141	14,987	10,723	153,645	10,156
1972	36,727	20,694	13,554	9,409	146,914	9,740
1973	36,223	20,746	12,925	8,855	143,054	9,201
1974	36,058	20,654	11,765	7,583	139,963	9,233
1975	35,808*	19,881*	11,223	6,579	135,225	8,625
1976	35,982*	19,711*	11,015	6,232	130,995	8,563
1977	35,711*	19,436*	10,344	5,599	130,804	8,745
1978	35,600*	19,889*	9,560	5,438	129,391	8,460

+ Indicates no data are available. Information on the total number of U. S. seminarians (both diocesan and religious) is available, however. In 1920 the total number of U. S. seminarians was 8,944; in 1930, 16,300; in 1940, 17,087.

TABLE 2 CONTINUED

* These figures are derived from *The Official Catholic Directory 1975-1978* and *The Catholic Almanac 1976-1979.* *The Official Catholic Directory* excluded U.S. priests in mission countries up to 1974 and started to include U.S. priests in mission countries from 1975 on (see *The Catholic Almanac 1976*). Therefore, in order to make figures comparable over the years, U.S. priests in mission countries in 1975-1978 are excluded. The number of priests reported in *The Official Catholic Directory 1975-1978* are the following.

Year	1975	1976	1977	1978
Diocesan Priests	36,005	36,175	35,904	35,766
Religious Priests	22,904	22,672	22,397	22,719

Source: *The Official Catholic Directory: 1920-1978* (New York: P.J. Kenedy and Sons). *The Catholic Almanac: 1976-1979* (Huntington, Indiana: Our Sunday Visitor).

Reprinted by permission of P.J. Kenedy and Sons.

TABLE 3
NUMERICAL TRENDS FOR ORGANIZATIONAL UNITS AND TEACHERS OF
THE ROMAN CATHOLIC CHURCH IN THE UNITED STATES, 1950 to 1978

UNIT	Year						
	1950	1960	1970	1975	1976	1977	1978
Catholic Population	27,766,141	40,871,302	47,872,089	48,701,835	48,881,872	49,325,752	49,836,176
Archdioceses	23	27	31	32	32	32	32
Dioceses	102	109	125	132	135	135	138
Parishes	15,292	16,896	18,224	18,515	18,531	18,572	18,625
Missions	4,927	4,860	4,262	3,760	4,007	3,894	4,088
Seminaries	388	525	501	373	371	387	376
Colleges and Universities	225	265	292	251	245	241	238
High Schools	2,382	2,433	2,082	1,676	1,616	1,601	1,572
Elementary Schools	8,502	10,372	9,947	8,539	8,484	8,375	8,299
Schools for nurses	367	347	260	141	135	131	124
Orphanages	352	279	217	209	205	219	204
Homes for the aged	254	326	419	463	458	461	486
Hospitals	849	945	902	761	750	730	728
Teachers (F. T.)	106,777	160,447	199,468	171,797	171,700	167,836	170,987
Priests	7,436	10,890	9,958	6,974	6,374	6,009	6,402
Sisters	82,048	98,471	85,616	56,050	52,957	50,121	46,670
Laity	13,477	45,506	98,001	104,827	108,502	107,856	114,188

Source: *Official Catholic Directory: 1950–1978* (General Summary Statistics).
Reprinted by Permission of P.J. Kenedy and Sons.

should look for some "functional equivalents" of Catholic education.[40] Similarly, the number of orphanages and hospitals has declined, but homes for aged grew from 254 in 1950 to 486 in 1978.

The lower part of Table 3 reports the number of full-time teachers in Catholic schools with their ecclesiastical statuses. As important as the number of organizations are the *personnel* themselves. In regard to Catholic school personnel, the most significant change has been in relation to ecclesiastical status. Whereas only 13% of teachers in Catholic schools were lay in 1950, in 1978 laity constituted about 67% of the teachers. Compared to 1960, today there are about 5,000 fewer priests and 48,000 fewer female religious teaching in Catholic schools. Most of the consequences of this change are not yet known. But the decline of religious personnel in Catholic schools definitely means higher costs, as Catholic schools have paid their teaching religious only a small fraction of lay salaries. Increase in the number of lay teachers (many of whom may not even be Catholic) may also mean less control over schools by the RCC and its hierarchy.

Though no hard data are available, similar phenomena seem to have taken place in many other *agencies* in the Church. Today, even casual observers notice how few female religious work in Catholic hospitals, whereas until a few years ago many were almost completely staffed by them. Again the change means *higher costs and less control* over the hospitals by the RCC and the religious communities which may nominally own the hospitals. Furthermore, once a Catholic hospital is administered by an "outsider," the religious working there become "employees." If "detotalization" of the religious was started by the Council, the process is completed by structural changes in their work and maintained by the new structures of work and life.[41] Again, the consequences of these changes are not yet known; but they will indeed be profound.

WORLD-U.S.A. COMPARISONS

As the RCC is a world system, it is important to note how the Church in a given country stands in relation to the entire system. Table 4 presents some "comparable" data. First, in 1976 there were over 700 million Catholics in the world, constituting 18% of the world population, with U.S. Catholics constituting almost 7% of the world Catholic population. Second, the number of archdioceses and dioceses are proportionate to the Catholic population in the U.S. In 1976, U.S. Catholics constituted 6.9% of Catholics in the world, and U.S. archdioceses and dioceses were 6.6% and 7.6% of all such structures worldwide. Also over the ten-year period, growth in number of U.S. archdioceses and dioceses were comparable to that in the entire Church. Third, over the last ten years, the

TABLE 4

SELECTIVE COMPARISONS BETWEEN THE WORLD-WIDE ROMAN CATHOLIC CHURCH AND THE CATHOLIC CHURCH IN THE UNITED STATES: 1966 and 1976

Personnel Category	Number World-wide		Number in U.S.A.		% U.S.A. of World Total		% Change in decade	
	1966	1976	1966	1976	1966	1976	World-Wide	U.S.A.
Catholic Population	590,645,714	705,711,680	46,246,175	48,881,872	7.8	6.9	19.5	5.7
Archdioceses	444	484	29	32	6.5	6.6	9.0	10.3
Dioceses	1,563	1,765	121	135	7.7	7.6	12.9	11.6
Cardinals	97	136	5	12	5.2	8.8	40.2	140.0
Archbishops	421	398	30	58	7.1	14.6	−5.5	93.3
Bishops	2,107	2,359	217	338	10.5	14.3	13.9	55.8
Priests +								
Diocesan	291,381	269,443	36,419	35,982	12.5	13.4	−7.5	−1.2
Religious	143,040	149,574	22,774	19,711	15.9	13.2	4.6	−13.4
Total	434,421	419,017	59,193	55,693	13.6	13.3	−3.5	−5.9
Seminarians	105,010	52,960	40,046	17,247	38.1	32.6	−49.6	−56.9
Religious								
Men	189,892	214,121	12,255	8,563	6.5	4.0	12.8	−30.1
Women	1,060,680	977,608	181,421	130,995	17.1	13.1	−7.8	−27.8

+ Figures of U.S. priests in 1976 have been adjusted. See notes to Table 2.

Source: Catholic Almanac, 1967 and 1977.

number of cardinals, archbishops, and bishops appointed to the U.S. increased much more than for the Church-in-general. Fourth, for 1966 and 1976, about 13% of all priests in the Church were from the U.S.A. It may also be noted that, although the number of priests declined for the entire RCC and for the United States, *religious priests in general have grown* in numbers *while* religious priests in *U.S.* have greatly *declined*. Fifth, there has been a general *decline in* the number of *seminarians*, but the decline is much *greater in the United States* than in general. Still, seminarians of the U.S.A. constitute one third of all the seminarians throughout the world. Six, whereas male religious in general grew about 13% between 1966 and 1976, U.S. male religious declined about 30% over the same period. While female religious lost about 8% of their members on a world basis in the last ten years, the decline among U.S. female religious was 27%. In sum, over the last ten years, compared to the entire church, the "lower-archy" of the RCC in the United States declined greatly in numbers, while the "higher-archy" grew much, at least numerically, with the Catholic population remaining relatively stable. On the whole, then, an *inverse relation* appears *between hierarchical status and the rate of decline*, although the stability of Catholic population in general disturbs such a relation. In the post-Vatican Church, therefore, there may have developed "a spurious sense of control" at the top, while the lower levels decided their own course of action independently of the hierarchy.[42]

CHANGES THROUGH THE SECOND VATICAN COUNCIL

Changes in "Meanings"

So complex and extensive have been the work and results of the Council! At the same time, over-simply stated, there is a consensus that the *most critical change* introduced by the Council has been *on the level of meaning rather than structure*. This change on the level of meaning has been variously conceptualized, ranging, e.g., from being labeled simply as "redefinition of the situation" or "reinterpretation of basic truths," over to "a radical shift within the Roman Catholic system of signification" or a "shift in foundational perspective;" also as "paradigm shifts," "transmythologization," "the differential definition of the function of power in the church," "changes in the theology of the church," "socio-cultural change," and "religious reform."[43] Among changes introduced or legitimated through the Council, important are a *changed conception of "God"* plus concomitant changes in the meaning of "the *Church*," the "ideal" distribution and exercise of *authority* in the Church, and in the "ideal" *relationship of* its *members* to God and to the Church. On the other hand, the Council *little changed* the *structure* of the Church, probably because the implications of the new meanings were not yet adequately foreseen by the policy makers and because existing structures have greater survival power (as is true in general).

In an important sense, the Council may be seen as a *struggle between two systems of meaning*; there was no unequivocal victory for either side. Although the Council members who internalized the new meaning system attempted to modify the existing structures and introduce new structures according to the mandate of the new meanings, structural changes effected by the Council in reality *changed* very *little of the formal organization* of the RCC. This observation should become clear as the Conciliar changes on the structural level are further examined. But, before looking at changes on the level of structure, it may be in order briefly to reflect on a few of the new meanings and their implications.[44] Associated with the two meaning systems are two "models" for thinking about the deity and also *two models of "church."*

Although the RCC conception of the divine has included *both* transcendence and immanence, the meaning system dominant *prior to the Council* saw *God*, above all, as being *transcendent* and His action in the world proceeding from His timeless knowledge and unfailing will, which guide humanity to the ultimate end of His eternal design; whereas the *new* emerging system of *meaning* conceives of *God* as not only present in but also *acting through human history* and as giving meaning and significance to individual and collective struggles and activities of the whole humanity.

More importantly now for our purposes are the two correlated models for "church." Associated with the idea of a *transcendent* God is a conception of the church as a visible society, hierarchically structured, whose mission is the salvation of souls objectively accomplished through the preaching of the Word and the administration of the sacraments. In this idealized conception of church, the organization should place decisions and power in the hands of a small group of persons assuming an uncontested authority. In this church, institutional cohesion is based on a system of authority, conceived in a vertical way and legitimized by a special divine assistance so that *authority* becomes as a *key value*. For the *immanent* God, the church is concerned with the world-at-large, *open* to its societal environment and intent on building up human solidarity. Above all, according to this model, *the church is the "people of God."* In this church, authority and power is for service, and institutional cohesion would be built on a real participation on the part of its members on every level. With collegiality, there is "subsidiarity" or *sharing* and delegation *of power*. With the principle of collegiality and subsidiarity, there is co-responsibility.

Changes in Structure

Though some have insisted that the RCC is organized in contradiction to its meaning system, given these changes on the level of meaning, certain structural changes were inevitable. In contrast to the pre-Vatican Church, today there are (1) an episcopal synod, (2) national and regional conferences of bishops, (3) pastoral councils on national, regional, diocesan, and parish levels, (4) presbyterial senates, and (5) parish councils. These organizational units are introduced and/or reintroduced into the RCC according to the inherent mandate of the new meaning system, and they will have impact for the future RCC. As each unit is examined even briefly, it becomes clear that these units have *not directly changed the formal structure* of the RCC.

On the highest level, according to the ideal of "collegiality"—the idea that the bishops of the world form a team with the Pope in authority and responsibility—the Council established the *Episcopal Synod*. According to the *motu proprio* of the Synod promulgated in 1965, the Episcopal Synod is an advisory body and would have deliberative power only when such power is conferred upon it by the Pope, who would in such cases confirm the decisions of the Synod. As with other new units, the Synod is a group of individuals whose main function is to advise rather than to decide. Also as with all other new units, the Synod had its functional equivalent, the College of Cardinals, in the pre- and post-Vatican Church.[45]

On the national level, the conciliar decree, *Christus Dominus*, made the *national or regional conference of bishops* into a quasi-judicial canonical entity for the purpose of fostering the Church's mission by providing the bishops of each country or region with an opportunity to exchange views and insights into various matters and to exercise in a joint manner their pastoral office. Being composed of every bishop, residential and titular, each conference has the right to initiate actions that are juridically binding on all bishops of the territory. At the same time as a rule, however, the national decisions must be ratified and implemented by *each* bishop, as each bishop is formally under the direct authority of the Pope. In the pre-Vatican Church, many national conferences of bishops were in existence; if they were not, there was a plenary council whose composition and function differed little from a national conference of bishops in the post-Vatican church. Thus, again, establishing or legitimizing the national conference of bishops changed little of the *formal* structure of the RCC.[46]

On the diocesan level, Pope Paul promulgated "Ecclesiae Sanctae" in 1966, which included the norms for the establishment and operation of a *senate of priests* within each diocese or group of dioceses. According to the *motu proprio*, though the senate should and can give advice to the bishop, it has "a merely consultative voice," leaving the decision-making power and authority of the bishop intact.[47] The pre-Vatican Church's functional equivalent of the presbyteral senate was the cathedral chapter, administrative council, or the board of diocesan consultors. In pastoral councils, representatives of all the people in the RCC could come together to form an advisory body to the "ordinary" (bishop) of the diocese or to the pastor of the parish.[48] Again, such a council on whatever level is only an advisory rather than decision-making body. Almost identical in composition and purpose with the diocesan pastoral council was the former diocesan synod; and the *parish council* of today is not much different from many parish committees of yesterday.[49]

Thus, on the whole, three features uniformly characterize all the new organizational units introduced by the Council. First, *all units are advisory* bodies despite the fact that the principle of subsidiarity prescribes that decisions be entrusted to the body on the lowest appropriate level and not be usurped by a higher authority.[50] Second, as would have been predicted on the basis of responses to change efforts observed in other organizations, the efforts of those committed to the *new meanings* but weak in power and authority *resulted in* the formation of *parallel duplicative units* rather than modifying or eliminating the existing functionally equivalent units, often a less practical and more difficult task than forming a new unit. Because of these two features— their advisory character and non-exclusive domain—the establishment of the new units has probably little directly changed the formal structure of the RCC. This, of course, does not deny that these new units have already had and are likely in the future to have much impact, to be sure. The third feature shared by all the new units is the fact that *they are constituted as groups rather than as individuals*. This committee-character of the new units has had and will have foreseeable conse-quences in the future. In a group, both accountability and responsibility may be diffuse; but, precisely because of that fact, *groups can be bolder* in their proposals, *more assertive* in their pursuits, and have less fear of reprisals.

Unless changes are implemented on local levels, i.e., of dioceses and parishes, they remain dead letters. But presently there are no systema-tically collected data on the subject. Of the many problems involved in using official statistics and directories, two may be noted as a precau-tionary gesture. The first problem involved in literally counting a given new organizational unit, e.g., in a directory, is that various names are used for a given unit. For example, a group of priests who represent "the body of priests and who by their counsel can effectively assist the bishop in the government of the diocese" is called by various names, such as "senate of priests," "priests' senate," "presbyteral senate," "council of priests," and some other names.[51] Second, because most of the new units depend on either the particular bishop or the pastor for formation and continuation, they may be dissolved at anytime. For example, the Bishop of Evansville recently (1976) suspended the seven-year-old diocesan pastoral council there.[52] Although the Archbishop of Boston "strongly exhorted" the establishment of a parish council in every parish of the

Archdiocese in 1973, the pastor of Thomas Aquinas parish abolished his parish council in 1975. In Good Shepherd parish in Arlington, Virginia, a parish council was born, died in 1974, and was reborn the next year. Thus, data are scarce and such as exist may not reflect the whole reality. Generally, however, the degree of implementation across the U.S. varies widely as result of the "permissive" and "non-legislative" character of the Vatican Council documents.

Extent of Implementation

The U.S. episcopal conference, the National Conference of Catholic Bishops, became a canonical body when its statutes were approved by the Holy See in 1970. By that year, there were already 26 episcopal conferences whose statutes had been approved by the Holy See. Notwithstanding, already by the late 1800s, the American archbishops and later the whole American hierarchy had begun to meet on an annual basis as a collegial body.[53]

In 1976, ten years since the *motu proprio* on the senate of priests and pastoral council, according to the *Official Catholic Directory* 109 of 158 Roman-rite dioceses and archdioceses (69%) had a senate of priests, and 51 Roman-rite dioceses and archdioceses (32%) had a pastoral council. On the other hand, in 1970, there appeared an unreferenced report of 82 of 154 dioceses and archdioceses having a diocesan pastoral council. In 1974, another report stated that there were 83 dioceses/archdioceses with a pastoral council. A survey of the parish councils taken in 1974 found that 72% (13,327) of 18,433 parishes had "councils of some form or another."[54] Of course, these data may be quite unreliable. More importantly, the question of number may be less important than the quality of performance of existing units.

According to the 1974 survey of the parish councils by the National Council of Catholic Laity, "parish councils have been most successful in the Midwest and in medium and small-medium dioceses." Large dioceses showed the poorest record: "only 12 per cent of the parishes in Los Angeles, for example, had parish councils as of June, 1974; 30 percent in Cleveland, 33 percent in Chicago, 35 percent in Boston, and so forth—all against the national average of 72.2 percent."[55] Also, a study on the emergence of clergy personnel boards between 1962 and 1972 found that "a high median family income in the area, location in the South, an elderly non-Irish bishop from a low social class background, and a small proportion of Irish clergy all exert a positive direct effect on personnel board innovation."[56]

The writer has collated data on the impact of the size of diocese (total number of priests, diocesan and religious), number of dioceses in the state, and geographic location of the dioceses upon the implementation of diocesan pastoral councils and senates of priests for the year 1976.[57]

First, just as in the case of parish councils, the rate of introducing diocesan pastoral councils was high among dioceses (36%) medium-sized in number of priests. But unlike the case of parish councils, more large dioceses (although below average—32%) introduced pastoral councils than did the very small dioceses. Thus, in terms of pastoral councils on both diocesan and parish levels, *medium-sized dioceses* were *more* likely to have *implemented* the change. On the other hand, there seems to be a direct relationship between size of the diocese and the likelihood of the diocese to have a senate of priests. While less than half (44%) the small dioceses had senates of priests, about three-fourths of the medium-sized and more than four-fifths of the large-sized dioceses had senates of priests in 1976. Thus, on the whole, the number of priests in a given diocese has some noticeable effect on implementing the Council decrees and papal directives on senates of priests and pastoral councils on the diocesan level.

Second, the number of dioceses in the state where a given diocese is located also seems to have some impact on implementing change. First, dioceses located in a state where there are four or more dioceses were most likely to have diocesan pastoral councils (39%); while a lone diocese in a state was more likely to have a diocesan pastoral council (31%) than dioceses in a state where there were two (25%) or three (24%) dioceses. Second, by 1976, all lone dioceses had a senate of priests, while about two-thirds of multiple (4 or more) dioceses and about three-fifths of dioceses with one or two other dioceses in the state had a senate of priests in the same year. The rate of implementing change seems to be higher when a diocese is alone in a state or with three or more other dioceses in the same state.

Third, whereas parish councils seem to flourish in the Midwest and personnel boards in the South, diocesan pastoral councils are more likely to be found in Mid-Atlantic and North Central states (45% and 44%). Dioceses in the Pacific (6%), East South Central (12%), and New England (18%) regions were least likely to have established diocesan pastoral councils by 1976. Thus, there seems to be regional variation to diocesan pastoral councils. At the same time, regional differences seem to be smaller for priests' senates, except for the Northeastern states. In the Northeast, while 90% of dioceses in New England have a senate of priests, only 45% of dioceses in Mid-Atlantic states have one.

Lastly, is the tendency to implement change selective or indiscriminate? Is it more likely for a diocese to have both a pastoral council and a senate of priests than to have either a pastoral council or a senate of priests than both?

Although there may be some tendency for a diocese to have both a pastoral council and a senate of priests, the tendency is too small to be real. While 69% of all dioceses have a senate of priests, only 72% of dioceses with a pastoral council have a senate of priests. Also whereas 32% of all dioceses have a pastoral council, only 34% of dioceses with a senate of priests have a pastoral council. For the pastoral council and the priests' senate, at least, implementation seems to be quite "random" in being neither selective nor indiscriminate. Still, there may be some selectivity, as dioceses in New England are much more likely to have a senate of priests (91%) but far less likely to have a pastoral council (18%); dioceses in the Mid-Atlantic region are far above average in having a pastoral council (45%), but far below in having a senate of priests (45%). There may also be some indiscriminate implementation or non-implementation of change as dioceses in the Pacific region are far less likely to have either a senate of priests (56%) or a pastoral council (6%) than dioceses in other regions in the United States. It may also be of some interest to note that, contrary to the widely accepted belief in the power of the bishop (or pastor) in a diocese, the actual *rate of change in a diocese or parish may be a function of many variables beyond the personal control* and individualistic characteristics *of* the *ordinary* of the diocese *or* the *pastor* of the parish. However hierarchical the Church may be, in reality the theory of "great man" is also limited even in that Church.[58]

Of course, many other important changes have occurred in the RCC since the Council, but only a few of them have been examined because of lack of data and space. Changes are continuous; *changes beget changes*. New meanings introduced and/or legitimized through the Council begin to permeate the RCC and the lives of its people. Even if the new structures are only consulative and must coexist with other parallel units, the new organizational units established since the Council will definitely not vegetate. In a word, much more change is predicted both "in" and "of" the Church. Possible future changes are the concern in the following section. These changes are seen as consequences of past changes.

FUTURE CONSEQUENCES OF THE SECOND VATICAN COUNCIL

Institutionalization of "Change"

The significance of an event is imposed by the observer upon the object, neutral in itself. Given a sociological frame of reference, the *Second Vatican Council* can be said not only to have made many changes but, more importantly, to have *institutionalized the very process of change itself.* Therefore, for the RCC in the long run it may be contended that this institutionalization of change, rather than merely the number and the extent of changes themselves, must receive attention. As history testifies, the RCC has never been static. Previously, when the

RCC made changes, it legitimated its moves by its recourse to "ultimate truth," to be preserved at any cost and to be taught in every way. But with the conceptual foundations of the Church shaken and the validity and adequacy of the assumptive systems used to understand reality questioned, the RCC may seem to be glorifying change itself as a divinely ordained process, or at least as the only viable way of approaching reality. Thus, change may be valued because it is change. Also, the implementation of many post-Vatican II changes required a basic conceptual redefinition of change, and the RCC systematically had to foster a new conception of reality and change, not only for its functionaries but also for its grassroots as the first phases in the process of *aggiornamento*.

But if security under the "perfect" and, therefore, "unchangeable mother church" had its inherent problems, the search for the ever-new in the post-Vatican II Church involves no less a danger for the RCC. "Making a theological virtue out of necessity" produced another theological "vice" that the Church would have to suffer from for many years to come. If religion is to include "an enduring set of distinctive beliefs about the ultimate nature of reality," *permanence* has also to be some part of religion itself. Furthermore, the contemporary people of "homeless mind" may rightly expect the Church to serve as an anchorage for their endless and, often, directionless "floating." Second, once the institutionalization of change has taken place on the levels of both conception and practice, it also tends to undermine the faith of those whose belief is based on the apparent permanence of the Church as well as the vested interests of the office-holders trained to work within the existing establishment. Since the present Church seems to be able neither to differentiate the unchangeables from the changeables nor to present the whys for its indecision, a *general climate* of opinion may tend to *emerge which regards the entire religion as problematic.* If the *aggiornamento* of the Council stripped off the historical accretions of the institution, it may also have shaken the foundations of the entire edifice itself.[59]

Politicization

A second important consequence of the Council and its subsequent change appears to be *politicization or* rather the *legitimation of politics* within the RCC. As "politics" are ways of allocating resources in order to bring about some desired end, they have certainly been an integral part of the RCC throughout its history. But, whereas the pre-Vatican RCC tried to obscure the political reality of its operations, the post-Vatican RCC can neither ignore its being a political institution nor seek immunity from further politicization. First, even if the public did not understand the meaning of the phrase, "the Rhine Flows into the Tiber," reports of what had happened both inside and outside the Council halls made apparent the power of human political hands for the destiny of the RCC. Even with the Vatican skill of "secret management," it has become clear that the act of voting is the final stage and symbolic ritual of all political processes. Acquisition of "cynical knowledge" on local levels, i.e., diocesan and parochial, has been also evidenced, particularly, in the United States.[60] At this point, some assert that members of the RCC must know this fact, try to utilize this tool for the Church, and direct the subtleties of political maneuverings in an effort to protect the Church from political savagery—from within, of course, as well as from without. Also the fact that the new organizational units introduced by the Council—the Episcopal Synod, National Conference of Bishops, senates of priests, diocesan pastoral councils, and parish councils—have no formal organizational authority necessitates that those units *resort to informal tactics of power*. In other words, the *Council created organizational units whose operation depends on politics rather than on administration*. The contemporary Church, therefore, has not only politically more cognizant members and campaigners for the politicization but also contains formally incipient structures for the political operations. These structures are also a "school" for training future political leaders and an arena for development of future political coalitions.[61]

As in the case of institutionalization of change, the post-Vatican II politicization of the Church presents a number of problems and dangers as well as new opportunities. First, the more politicized an organization is, the *more resources* will have to be spent *for internal politics* and rivalry rather *than* for performance of organizational *programs*. Second, if the amount of political activity and hierarchical rank within the organization are positively correlated, the hierarchy will have to devote their efforts to politics and, in that situation, there is the danger that the Church will be left to guidance by the "lower-archy" and the bureaucratic functionaries. If organizational rank and organizational commitment are also positively related, the risk involved in leaving the Church to the works of the "lower-archy" may be great.[62] Third, as the operations of power are precarious and unpredictable, an RCC guided by power more than by authority may suffer from insecurity and from a programmatic short-range approach to organizational maintenance and development.[63] Fourth, if internal competition and conflicts arise, the problem of inadequate integration may paralyze the Church when it needs to attend other tasks. Finally, as a religious organization, the Church needs *personnel* who are *not only politically but also spiritually "wise."* When the two qualities are not combined, there is the danger that the spiritually wise have less chance to guide the Church because they would tend not to be placed in strategically important positions in the

RCC. If the desires of the rank and file members, the parishioners, are important, the RCC cannot afford to have solely "political" leader types, at least at present and in the United States.[64] On the other hand, at the same time that *politicization* leaves much of the work in the hands of the lower-archy, it would automatically *facilitate* the implementation of the principles of *collegiality, co-responsibility, and subsidiarity*. It would also facilitate the *upward flow of information* for the hierarchy and better decision making and policy implementation at the lower level of the Church. Also it may be that in the Church, unlike in other organizations, *commitment* may be quite evenly distributed or evenly *inversely distributed in relation to hierarchical rank*. In that case, there would be no reason to lament "the eclipse of episcopacy" or pastors "becoming an endangered species."[65]

Voluntary Proliferation

A third important consequence and development since the Council is the *continuing proliferation of new voluntary associations*. First, both institutionalization of change and politicization *require organization*, as organization is one of the mechanisms for achieving change through political processes. Second, as one organization emerges to achieve certain ends, another tends to emerge in order *to counteract* and prevent *the first* organization from achieving its ends or performing certain functions in the Church. This process at present seems to result from ideological and conceptual polarization in the RCC. The Confraternity of Catholic Clergy, e.g., was formed to combat democratization via post-Vatican II-born organizations such as diocesan pastoral councils, personnel boards, priests' senates, and other diocesan-centered agencies. Similarly, among women religious, the National Assembly of Women Religious, the Leadership Conference of Women Religious, and the Consortium Perfectae Caritatis often work at cross-purposes.[66] Third, in the post-Vatican Church, organizations, especially *non-official and non-legitimate* ones, have *come into being as* the *official and legitimate* ones *fail* to be formed or fail to perform certain functions. For example, many associations of priests, non-official and non-legitimate, have been formed when the ordinary (bishop) does not allow the formation of a senate of priests, official and legitimate; and/or the senates which *are* formed are seen as *coopted by the ordinary and* thereby *failing* to perform their proper roles for their constituents and for the Church.[67] Fourth, as the senates of priests, pastoral councils, and parish councils are basically geared to the *local* level, the formation of *national* organizations follows predictably. The National Federation of Priests' Councils in 1976 consisted of 86 official senates of priests, 19 unofficial "associations" of priests, and 9 religious orders of men. It has sought, since its formation in 1968, "to promote the betterment of the priests in the U.S.—in their personal spirituality and in their ministry." As the formation of a senate of priests in a diocese *allows priests to interact* with their bishop *as a group* rather than only as individuals, the formation of the National Federation of Priests Councils also *allows senates and associations* of priests *to interact* with the bishops and their National Conference *as a group*. The NFPC also provides the means for exchange of information, experience, and other resources. The NFPC also provides a comparative reference framework which may lead progressive bishops and dioceses and so assist in setting the tone for the whole national church.[69] Other national organizations such as the National Association of Laymen, National Conference of Diocesan Parish Council Personnel, National Association of Resigned/Married Priests, Priests Associated for Religious, Educational, and Social Rights, and many others perform functions similar to those of the NFPC.

There can be no question of the fact that organization is one of the best tools man ever discovered. Through organizations man transcends himself and achieves something beyond his individual reach. At the same time, proliferation of too many organizations may mean waste of human resources spent in tending instead of using them. Second, from the point of view of the larger organization, the RCC, these new organizations are *subunits* whose works and aspirations *must be channeled and coordinated*. Thus, the parent organization, the RCC, may need to establish another unit for that purpose, similar to the often observed "committee on committees." Such a process leads, in turn, to further complexity so that "complexity begets complexity." Third, since many of the new associations are "protest" units within the Church, they *need to be integrated with the whole* and with other subunits. Once a nonconforming enclave has been formed, mild checks are no longer sufficient to contain it, and use of control techniques such as condemnation, avoidance, and expulsion can lead to conditions of internal polarization and loss of resources. Protest enclaves also often thrive on such "persecutions." Conversely, the parent organization may attempt to *absorb* the nonconforming enclave *by converting it into* a new, *legitimate* subunit. Through such conversion, the nonconforming enclave obtains a legitimate outlet for its nonconformity, and the parent organization receives the services of an energetic and devoted group. In the past, this has frequently been the source of new religious orders (see Chapter 4). The process of protest absorption also allows for the gradual legitimation and preservation of innovation, which may be a highly creative contribution in an age when change is valued simply because it *is* change. But if this absorption becomes—or "is seen" to have become—*cooptation*, there may emerge another "protest" unit to preserve the original purity against the coopted and therefore "compromised" unit. Then, the problem may be how to convert the protest unit in such a way to contribute to the inclusive organizational goals and to allow it to pursue its original impetus.[70]

Change Begetting Change

Finally, institutionalization of change, politicization, and proliferation of organizational units will lead to further change. Most importantly, the imperative of compatibility within structure, within meaning, and between structure and meaning will generate much change. Even though lack of correspondence between meaning and structure exists in most social realities, *ideals* which are *not achieved* are *neither unimportant nor ineffective*. They endure as perennial challenges to the existing structure and thus continue to influence the shape of actual patterns and practices.[71] Also meaning may lag behind the development of structure, but it can also lead the structure to a new stage in its history. Thus, until a certain degree of symmetry is achieved between the way Catholicism conceives of its God, its Church, its people, and the way it organizes and conducts itself, there will be change. Of course, the process of convergence between structure and meaning may be thwarted by those in high positions in the existing structure as well as by many other variables inside and outside the Church. Perfect convergence will probably never be possible, not only because both structure and meaning change as response to each other but also because of their own internal dynamics and their differential interaction with different external forces in the larger society.

In sum, then, institutionalization of change, politicization, and proliferation of organizational units are some of the consequences of the Second Vatican Council; they are still in progress; and these three processes will lead the RCC toward further changes. There are other conditions of the RCC which need much attention and sociological engineering, as well as faithful prayers. On the whole, the RCC in the United States may be "healthier" than the RCC in many other countries; even so, with its many resources it also has many problems and uncertainties.

ORGANIZATIONAL IMPERATIVES OF THE RCC IN THE UNITED STATES

Not only because the RCC defines itself as "the people of God" but also because it is a voluntary association in a pluralistic, "denominational society," it must attend to the needs of its constituents on every level. Of many questions confronting the RCC today, from its own perspective most important is the question of *how* to *assure* "the *continued acceptance of, and fidelity to, the basic elements of the church's creed, cult, and code by members...*"[72]

Clearly, any attempt to deal with the question involves theological, pastoral, and sociological decisions. First, the RCC must decide what the basic elements of "creed, cult, and codes" are and how they are to be conceptualized theologically and formulated. But given the present polarization in about every aspect and the certain popularity of relativism, situationalism, personalism, and openness even in theological and religious matters, the RCC may find it difficult to make such decisions.[73] Second, once the RCC has made the first decision, it must discover and implement ways of convincingly presenting those basic elements. But at present, as in the case of theological decision (or indecision), the RCC seems unable to satisfy the religious quest of its people. U.S. Catholics report that the quality of sermons is low and that the *kerygmatic, teaching ministry* of the Church *has stopped* for all practical purposes, with sermons and teachings in the Church becoming mainly presentations of background information on such issues as urban poverty, race relations, personal interaction, and psychological fulfillment. Lack of theological development and the eclipse of teaching ministry in the RCC appear most paradoxical in this age of the knowledge explosion.[74] Third, the question of how to assure continued fidelity to the basic tenets is complicated by the contemporary facts of increasing spatial and social mobility, loss of traditional mechanisms of transmitting and maintaining "deviant" religious systems, and a socio-cultural environment characterized by extensive change, complexity, and pluralism. Therefore, as any denomination whose normative beliefs and practices deviate from the societal constitutional norms and ideologies must do, the *RCC must construct social organizations of its own in order to generate and sustain the plausibility of and commitment to its minority ideals* in a general climate of competing ideas and valuations in the dominant culture. Again, because of its internal conflict and uncertainty, its inability to recognize the human facets of faith and religious commitment, and perhaps more importantly the general lack of knowledge of social organization and process, the RCC has not built a world whereby the religious quests of its people are met and fidelity to itself is assured.

Second, although the Council has called for greater participation by the laity, it has changed little in its sacramental and organizational dependence on its priesthood. On the other hand, the RCC in the United States as well as in the entire world experiences continued decline in the number of priests; an end to this decline is not in sight, as the decline in the number of seminarians also continues. Not only do priests leave their priesthood; those *remaining* in the priesthood *do not actively recruit* new members as they used to do before the Council; and post-Vatican II Catholics are now less likely to be pleased to see a son becoming a priest.[75] If the RCC defines the declining number of priests as a problem, there are three ways of dealing with the problem; first, the RCC may choose to eliminate the distinction between laity and priesthood on the basis of order so that present priestly functions can be performed by anyone; second, the RCC may, of course, recruit new members into the priesthood and maintain those already in it; third, it may utilize differently whatever number of priests it has and will have. Presently, the first option is theologically untenable and politically unattainable. The second option is simply empirically unrealistic, not only in the United States but also in most parts of the world, since religious organizations have few resources to attract recruits *unless* they are *already* normatively *motivated*. Moreover, today's world-at-large is, at most, not supportive of religious careers. Thus, for the RCC, *better utilization of priests it already has is* not an option but an *imperative*, at least, at present.

Repeatedly, studies have shown that priests are constantly afflicted by multiple roles and the need to be devoted to roles least prepared for and least liked. The requirement of specificity of the administrator and diffuseness of the priest role cannot be maximally satisfied at the same time. Even young priests, despite media publicity of the crisis, appear to be committed to the specialized duties associated with priesthood.[76] Moreover, many Catholics dislike their priests spending a disproportionate amount of time on non-traditional roles and prefer to have them devote themselves to preaching and other priestly functions.[77] Although some Catholics welcome various specialized services from their priests, others see such services as outside the domain of priesthood and as something in the professional domain of the psychiatrist, the lawyer, or the physician.[78] (For more on this, see Chapter 8). The Council recommended that the laity contribute to the functioning of the RCC. Rather than trying to be all things, it may be time for the "foot" to be a "foot," not a "hand." The long societal history of structural differentiation and role specialization testifies to the *importance of the principle of limited spheres of competence and the necessity of specialization.*[79] If the RCC chooses the third option to deal with the shortage of priests, the very shortage would be not a problem but a blessing, for it would facilitate the realization of the principles of collegiality, since hierarchical status would become less significant; of shared responsibility, as both laity and priests would have important and unique tasks to perform; and of subsidiarity, as both laity and priests would have proper authority commensurate to their responsibility. Again, for the RCC to specialize is not only an ideal to pursue but also a necessity!

On the organizational level, the RCC like other denominations is imperfect, departs from its ideals, and carries its "treasure in earthen vessels." The RCC must seek to better the flow of communication upward and downward, facilitate friendship groups, create climate for trust and confidence, provide popular participation in decision-making processes and in selection of leaders, promote both diversity and harmony among various groups, institute mechanisms for evaluation, and maximize openness to growth and development.[81] For the RCC of the future, loyalty must be generated, not simply gathered; its impact must be planned, developed, and aimed with both steady and long-term directedness and also short-range, local variation, and flexibility.[82] In other words, the RCC needs to be better institutionalized. Conscious of all the "dilemmas" of inadequate institutionalization, the RCC must endeavor to build into itself processes for including many circles of disciples gathered about charismatic leaders and for fostering religious fervor, self-expression, self-criticism, and prophecy. Not only is institutionalization inevitable; it is a necessity if any human endeavors, including religious ones, are to have any impact on human existence. The *RCC as a human endeavor must find ways of better institutionalizing itself* if it wants to achieve whatever goals it may have.[83]

Of many questions requiring both theological and practical considerations, only a few have been commented on briefly as they arose throughout this chapter. The questions of how to assure continued commitment to the Catholic religious system, how to deal with the declining number of priests, and what to make better in the organization of the RCC have just been discussed. Still, there are other important questions not yet mentioned at all. None of the specifics of the issues discussed were even suggested. Yet, the general thrust and approach underlying the chapter should indicate what the other issues may be and how they may be dealt with. On the other hand, decisions on specifics are technical in nature and need to be pragmatically viewed and carefully engineered. In short, the RCC needs the services of many specialties.

CONCLUDING DISCUSSION

For science, the term "fact" is pivotal since all science adduces it sooner or later. Yet, as no "facts speak for themselves," there are no given facts apart from one's prior definition. Thus, the process of knowing involves both processes of definition as well as gathering of data. Therefore, for precision, if the reader (and the editor) could have tolerated such cumbersome sentence structures, most of the assertive propositions throughout the chapter should have been transformed into conjectural statements, as the former lack refinement in both systematic collection of data and in conceptualization. If the present chapter can be a stimulus for the development of an antithesis in Hegelian dialectic, it fulfills its first task.

However speculative it has been, the most interesting point emerging from this study is that the *RCC has really changed little in its formal organizational-authority structure, while* it has brought about many truly *revolutionary* changes *in other aspects*. In general, many organizations change structurally to bring about some modifications in the belief-attitudinal systems and behavior patterns of its members; but often, the "old ways" persist in the "new house." For the RCC, the good olden days are gone, even though its official organizational edifice remains intact. Second, it is also clear that, whatever the ferment of the pre-Vatican II RCC might have been, the *Second Vatican Council was the opportunity mechanism for historical change within the RCC and in its relation to the world-at-large*. The Council freed the bishops from their daily vicissitudes and led them to associate among themselves to "compare notes" and with the Roman Curia to learn the intricacies of the "game." Through differential association, decreased association with administrative pressures and increased association with idealistic pursuits, the Council fathers precipitated many changes. Third, as time passes on, it becomes clear that many manifest eufunctions are accompanied by latent dysfunctions. In order to survive in the rapidly changing environment, the RCC *needs to be flexible and adaptive*. At the same time, as a religious organization, it seems to *need* some degree of *permanence and consistency*. Since religious systems purport to strive for the ultimate, complete relativization may deaden the life of religion itself. In the age of tremendous societal change, the RCC may even benefit from a tactful management of its "permanent" elements. Fourth, it may also be recalled that none of the new organizational units has a formally authoritative voice or decision-making power but only a consultative voice or advisory power. If integration and cohesion are continually pursued as values in themselves, unless skillfully managed these new units may become problematic. Also, having no authority, the new units have to be political rather than administrative subunits of the RCC. (See Takayama's perceptive comments on this problem in Chapter 9.)

Even though all that has been said thus far depends on the basic validity of the present study and its theorizings, it may be stated that the RCC is not free of problems and dangers. Even if mankind keeps on asking fundamental religious questions, there is no guarantee that the RCC will be able to convince substantial proportions of the population to accept its answers and frequent its churches. In fact, not even a *Third* Vatican Council would assure such a future for the RCC.[84] So in the final analysis, whatever the present study has observed, there is no way of either discrediting or confirming what a believer thinks of his church. For such a one, "of course. . .Christian hopefulness, if it is worth the name, does not rely on sociological analysis."[85] On the other hand, "No one lights a lamp to put it under a tub; they put it on the lamp-stand where it shines for everyone in the house" (Matt. 5, 15). Therefore, in the Decree on the Media of Social Communication, the Council Fathers wrote, "The Church recognizes that these media. . .contribute to the spread and support of the Kingdom of God," so it is "an inherent right of the Church to have at its disposal and to employ any of these media. . .for the instruction of Christians and all its efforts for the welfare of souls."[86]

Acknowledgments and Notes

Special thanks to Dr. Ross P. Scherer. I have always admired his living faith and intellectual integrity. This chapter owes much for his encouragement, guidance, and support. Above all, his scholarly endeavors have edified me greatly.

Father Ralph Starus of the Office for the Laity in the Archdiocese of Chicago also assisted me graciously, by providing many materials on various councils.

1. Xavier Rynne, *Letters From Vatican City* (New York: Farrar, Straus, 1963), p. 71; Walter M. Abbott (ed.), *The Documents of Vatican II* (New York: P. J. Kenedy and Sons, 1966). Since none of the conciliar documents specified how it was to be implemented, Pope Paul VI has been promulgating sets of *motu proprio*, i.e., norms to guide implementation of decrees of the Council. For this face, see Francis G. Morrisey, "The Role of Canon Law Today," *Chicago Studies* 15 (1976), 242; Also, these norms are being applied on experimental basis and are to be replaced by the Code of Canon Law currently under revision. For this, see Pope Paul VI, *Ecclesiae Sanctae: Implementing Four Council Decrees* (Washington, D.C.: National Catholic Welfare Conference, 1966).

2. Peter L. Berger, "Charisma and Religious Innovation: The Social Location of Israelite Prophecy," *American Sociological Review* 28 (1963): 950; also see E. K. Nottingham, *Religion: A Sociological View* (New York: Random House, 1971), p. 223; Thomas M. Gannon, "In the Eye of the Hurricane: Religious Implication of Contemporary Trends," *Social Compass* 19 (1972): 215.

3. S. N. Eisenstadt, "The Protestant Ethic in an Analytical and Comparative Framework," S. M. Eisenstadt (ed.), *The Protestant Ethic and Modernization* (New York: Basic Books, 1966), p. 10. Eisenstadt defines "transformative capacity" as "the capacity to legitimize, in religious or ideological terms, the development of new motivation, activities, and institutions which were not encompassed by the original impulses and view."

For reasons of changes in Roman Catholicism, see, Peter L. Berger, *The Sacred Canopy: Elements of A Sociological Theory of*

Religion (Garden City: Doubleday, 1969), pp. 117-124; Ivan Vallier, *Catholicism, Social Control, and Modernization in Latin America* (Englewood Cliffs: Prentice-Hall, 1970), p. 17. Mainly, Berger sees inherent forces of change in Roman Catholic theology, especially, in sense of historicity in the conception of God and the polar tension between this worldly and otherworldly tendencies. Vallier sees the main force for changes in the attempt to generate influence.

4. Gibson Winter, *Religious Identity* (New York: Macmillan, 1968); Peter L. Berger, "Religious Institutions," in Neil J. Smelser (ed.), *Sociology: An Introduction* (New York: John Wiley, 1973).

5. Ross P. Scherer, "The Church as a Formal Voluntary Organization," pp. 81-108 in David H. Smith et al. (eds.), *Voluntary Action Research: 1972* (Lexington, Mass.: Lexington Books, 1972).

6. For "liabilities of newness," see Arthur L. Stinchcombe, "Social Structure and Organizations," pp. 146-160 in James G. March (ed.), *Handbook of Organizations* (Chicago: Rand McNally, 1965); For the relationship between organization and its environment, see, F. E. Emery and E. L. Trist, "The Causal Texture of Organizational Environment," *Human Relations* 18 (1965): 21-31. For the formation of parallel substructures in change-resisting organizations, see M. Joseph Smucker and Anton C. Zijderveld, "Structure and Meaning: Implications for the Analysis of Social Change," *The British Journal of Sociology* 21 (1970): 375-389; For "the imperative of compatibility," see Talcott Parsons, *The Social System* (New York: Free Press, 1951), pp. 151-168.

7. Vallier (1970), quotation p. 17, op. cit.; Andrew M. Greeley, *A Future to Hope in: Socio-Religious Speculations* (Garden City: Doubleday, 1968), quotation p. 212.

8. K. R. Bridston, *Church Politics* (New York: The World Publishing Company, 1969).

9. Gannon (1972), op. cit.

10. R. M. Wiltgen, *The Rhine Flows into the Tiber: The Unknown Council* (New York: Hawthorn Books, 1967), p. 287; Vallier (1970), op. cit.

11. Pope Paul continues to emphasize the global dimension of the RCC in his *Evangelii Nuntiandi: On Evangelization in the Modern World* (Washington, D.C.: United States Catholic Conference, 1975). In 1977 there were 6,760 U.S. foreign missionaries, but that figure was 2,895 less than that in 1968. See United States Catholic Mission Council, *Mission Handbook: 1977* (Washington, D.C.: U.S. Catholic Mission Council, no date).

12. N. J. Demerath III and P. E. Hammond, *Religion in Social Context* (New York: Random House, 1969), p. 191.

13. Berger (1969), op. cit.

14. Scherer (1972), op. cit.; William A. Glaser and David L. Sills (eds.), *The Government of Associations: Selections from the Behavioral Science* (Totawa, N.J.: The Bedminster Press, 1966); W. S. Salisbury, *Religion in American Culture: A Sociological Interpretation* (Homewood: Dorsey Press, 1964).

15. Roland L. Warren, "The Interorganizational Field as Focus for Investigation," *Administrative Science Quarterly* 12 (1967): 396-419. For conciliar position on this, see Abbott (1966), op. cit., especially, "Dogmatic Constitution on the Church" and "Decree on the Mission Activity of the Church."

16. William C. McCready, "Spiritual Life in Contemporary American Society," *Chicago Studies* 15 (1976): 13-26; Dean M. Kelley "Why Conservative Churches Are Still Growing," paper presented at the annual meeting of Religious Research Association (Philadelphia, 1976); George Cornell and Douglas Johnson, *Punctured Preconceptions* (New York: Friendship Press, 1972). Only recently, some members of the RCC have come to realize that to treat popular religion as problematic constitutes a problem in its own right and ask, "Why is it that certain practices and persuasions which the people feel to be genuinely religious are dismissed by their pastors as magically superstitious?" As this realization converges with the theological rediscovery of God's people, they hope more adequate pastoral approaches to popular religion would appear. For this discussion, see "Let the People be: 'Popular Religion' and the Religion of the People," *Pro Mundi Vita Bulletin* 61 (1976). Also, in the post-Vatican II RCC, diversity is fostered but not for those who see meaning and relevance in the old; while self-determination is preached, new ways are imposed on everyone regardless of their decision. It seems that, in the name of renewal, certain sectors of the RCC had to suffer "unnecessarily," because of religious ethnocentrism of many. The question of relevance is "relevance to whom." Genuine diversity should *allow old as well as new*; openness to the left as well as right. Of course, empirically who wins is a question of power.

17. Francois Houtart, "Critical Decisions and Institutional Tensions in a Religious Institution: The Case of Vatican II," *Review of Religious Research* 9 (1968): 131-146; Andrew M. Greeley, William C. McCready, and Kathleen McCourt, *Catholic Schools in a Declining Church* (Kansas City: Sheed and Ward, 1976). Houtart sees the encyclical not accepted because the way it was written (style or process) rather than its content, and Greeley et al. see the failure of the encyclical as an indication of failing management in the RCC, whereby effective decision-making is prevented, especially by lack of upward flow of information.

18. For historical development and functions of sacerdotal celibacy, see Lewis A. Coser, *Greedy Institutions: Patterns of Undivided*

Commitment (New York: The Free Press, 1974); Max Weber, *The Sociology of Religion* (Boston: Beacon Press, 1963); Werner Stark, *The Sociology of Religion: A Study of Christendom, Types of Religious Man* (New York: Fordham University Press, 1970); Rosabeth Kanter, *Commitment and Community* (Cambridge: Harvard Press, 1972).

19. National Opinion Research Center, *The Catholic Priest in the United States: Sociological Investigations* (Washington, D.C.: United States Catholic Conference, 1972), pp. 234, 246. The study was under the direction of Andrew M. Greeley and his associates.

20. Kenneth Westhues, "The Established Church as an Agent of Change," *Sociological Analysis* 34 (1973): 106-123; *Mission Intercom*, a newsletter, is full of such incidents.

21. Winter (1968), quotation, pp. 100-101, op. cit.; The pre-Vatican RCC was also evaluated highly, at least, by one study. See, The American Institute of Management, *The Nineteen Centuries of the Roman Catholic Church: Management Audit* (New York: American Institute of Management, 1956, 1960, 1962).

22. Andrew M. Greeley, *The Hesitant Pilgrim: American Catholicism after the Council* (New York: Sheed & Ward), quotation p. xiv.

23. Figure 1 is based on two sources. Our Sunday Visitor, *The Catholic Almanac: 1977* (Huntington: Our Sunday Visitor, 1977); P. J. Kenedy, *The Official Catholic Directory: 1977* (New York: P. J. Kenedy, 1977).

24. Our Sunday Visitor (1977), p. 189, op. cit. In 1977, thirty-six of 136 cardinals are Italians, and five of twelve heads/principal officers of departments of the Roman Curia are Italian; In June, 1977, four cardinals were appointed and two of them were Italian. See, "New Cardinals may Succeed Pope," *Chicago Tribune,* June 3, 1977, p. 18.

25. T. L. Bouscaren et al., *Canon Law: A Text and Commentary* (New York: Bruce Publishing Company, 1963 (1946); Maurice Bonaventure Schepers, *The Church of Christ* (Englewood Cliffs: Prentice-Hall, 1963), p. 76; *Our Sunday Visitor* (1977), p. 186, op. cit.

26. Andrew M. Greeley, *The Catholic Experience* (Garden City: Image Books, 1967). Also see Will Herberg, *Protestant, Catholic, Jew* (New York: Doubleday, 1955).

27. For comparative trends in other denominations, see N.J. Demerath III, "Trends and Anti-trends in Religious Change," pp. 349-445 in E. B. Sheldon and W. E. Moore (eds.), *Indicators of Social Change: Concepts and Measurements* (New York: Russell Sage, 1968); Kelley (1976), op. cit.

28. Andrew M. Greeley, *The Denominational Society: A Sociological Approach to Religion in America* (Glenview: Scott, Foresman, 1972), p. 89.

29. Greeley et al. (1976), op. cit.; McCready (1976), op. cit.

30. Using the Gallup data and their own surveys, Greeley and his associates attribute decline mainly to Humanae Vitae. See, Greeley et al. (1976), op. cit. It is also to be noted that taking the Gallup data only from 1965 on resulted in ignoring decline in church attendance during the Council. Of course, the decline before 1965 cannot be due to the content of Humanae Vitae of 1968.

31. Greeley et al. (1976), p. 107, op. cit.

32. McCready (1976), op. cit.

33. NORC (1972), p. 312, op. cit.

34. Richard A. Schoenherr and Annemette Sorensen, "Organization Structure and Changing Size in U.S. Catholic Dioceses, 1966-1973," unpublished paper (The University of Wisconsin—Madison: Comparative Religious Organization Study, 1975), p. 14.

35. It may be of some interest to note that the NORC priesthood study found that one-fifth of priests and one-third of Bishops were strongly encouraged by woman religious to enter priesthood. See NORC (1972), p. 49, op. cit.

36. William J. Mehok, "Religious Life in Transition: An Analysis of Membership Trends and a Projection to 1982," *CARA Forum for Religious* 1 (1976); Raymond L. Fitz and Lawrence J. Cada, "The Recovery of Religious Life," *Review for Religious* 34 (1975): 690-718; "A Time of Renewal for U.S.," *U.S. News & World Report*, April 11, 1977, quotation, p. 64.

37. Clarence L. Abercrombie III, *The Military Chaplain* (Beverly Hills: Sage Publication, 1977), pp. 138-140; Winter (1968), p. 48, op. cit.

38. Graema Slaman, *Community and Occupation* (London: Cambridge University Press, 1974); Berger (1967), op. cit.

39. Some of the decline in the number of seminaries due to the elimination of minor seminaries since the Second Vatican Council.

40. Greeley et al. (1976), op. cit.

41. For the detotalizing effect of the Vatican II, see Scherer (1972), 90. op. cit. A similar trend is taking place for the seminary education. Now, as more seminarians are educated in regular universities, the RCC should have less control over their religious and organizational "formation." Consequences for such non-exclusive socialization may be great for the system.

42. Winter (1969), p. 64, op. cit.

43. Vallier (1970), pp. 17, 107, op. cit.; Houtart (1968), 314, op. cit.; Rocco Caporale, "The Dynamic of Hierocracy: Processes of Continuity-in-Change of the Roman Catholic System during Vatican II," *Sociological Analysis* 28 (1967): 61; Pierre Hégy, *L'autorité dans le Catholicisme Contemporain, du Syllabus à Vatican II* (Paris: Beauchesne, 1975). The actual quotes are taken from a review by Jean-

Jacques D'Aoust, *Church History* 45 (1976): 122-123. Avery Dulles, *Models of the Church* (Garden City: Doubleday, 1974); Bernard F. Donahue, "Transmythologizing Church Politics," *The American Ecclesiastical Review* 169 (1975): 3-16, 147-163.

44. Houtart (1968), op. cit.; Donahue (1975), op. cit.; Abbot (1966), op. cit.

45. P. Hebbelwaite, *Inside the Synod: Rome, 1967* (New York: Paulist Press, 1978); Morrisey (1976), 234, op. cit.; Bouscaren et al. (1963), op. cit.; The *motu proprio* is included in Pope Paul VI, *Apostolica Sollicitude* (Washington, D.C.: National Catholic Welfare Conference, 1965).

46. Arthur X. Deegan, "Directions in Catholic Organization," paper presented at the annual meeting of the Society for the Scientific Study of Religion and the American Association for the Advancement of Science (Chicago, 1970).

47. Pope Paul VI (1966), op. cit.

48. Abbott (1966), op. cit.; Charles Fecher, "Parish Councils: A Long Way to Go," *Sign* 51 (1972): 27-29; Joseph Bernardine, "The Collegiality of the U.S. Bishops," address at semiannual meeting of Catholic Bishops (Chicago, 1976); Deegan (1970), op. cit.

49. Morrisey (1976), op. cit.

50. Thomas McDonough, "The Parish Council's Role: Louisville Archdiocesan Guideline," *Origin* 5 (1976): 571-579.

51. Pope Paul VI (1966), p. 15, op. cit.; Kenedy (1977), op. cit.; T. P. Ference et al., "Priests and Church: The Professionalization of an Organization," *American Behavioral Scientist* 14 (1971): 507-525.

52. *Our Sunday Visitor* (1976), p. 99, op. cit.; *National Catholic Reporter* (Dec. 5, 1975).

53. *Our Sunday Visitor* (1977), pp. 445-446, op. cit.; Greeley (1967), p. 30, op. cit.

54. Since OCD used various names for both the pastoral council and the senate of priests, and since data are derived by hand-counting the units, much caution is invited in analyzing the data. Also, the quality of statistics in OCD may not be complimented, and objections may be made that the OCD reports the "official" rather than the "real" figures.
    Richard P. McBrien, "Parish Councils—Ten Years Later." paper provided by the Office for the Laity in the Archdiocese of Chicago (1977).

55. Ibid.

56. Robert P. Szafran, "The Occurrence of Structural Innovation within Religious Organizations," unpublished Ph.D. dissertation (University of Wisconsin—Madison, Department of Sociology, 1977).

57. "Senate of priests" includes "senate of priests," "priests' senate," and "presbyteral senate" but excludes "associations" and "councils" of

priests. The latter two designations are usually used for unofficial associations of priests. See, Ference et al. (1971), op. cit.; National Federation of Priests Councils, *Annual Report: Priests/USA* (Chicago: National Office of NFPC, 1976).

58. Increasingly, the laity and the clergy have become assertive in their pursuit, even against the hierarchy. Already in 1968, a number of priests in San Antonio called for the resignation of the Archbishop (Robert E. Lucey), who announced his resignation in 1969. The account is reported by Louis Schneider and Louis Zurcher, "Toward Understanding the Catholic Crisis: Observations on Dissident Priests in Texas," *Journal for the Scientific Study of Religion* 9 (1970): 197-207. Disobedience against the hierarchy among clergy has been also reported in John A. Struzzo, "Professionalism and the Resolution of Authority Conflicts among Catholic Clergy," *Sociological Analysis* 31 (1970): 92-106. The ultimate threat to the organization of the RCC may be resignations by the clergy, as reported by John Seidler, "Priests Resignations in a Lazy Monopoly," paper presented at the annual meeting of Religious Research Association (Philadelphia, 1976).

While the Catholic clergy become assertive in their relations to the bishop, the laity become so in their relations to the clergy and hierarchy. For example, some parishioners of Good Shepherd Parish of Arlington, Virginia were in disagreement with their pastor and bishop with much "success," as reported in *Our Sunday Visitor* (1976, 1977), op. cit.; similar events were reported in the Archdiocese of Chicago in the *Chicago Tribune,* "West Side Church Members Demand Ouster of New Priest," March 25, 1974 (the new priest was later transferred to another parish).

59. Peter L. Berger et al., *The Homeless Mind* (New York: Random House, 1973); See, also Introduction in which Scherer expounds the dilemmas and need for balance among all organizations, especially religious ones.

60. Seymour Lipset, *Political Man* (Garden City: Doubleday, 1963), p. 185; Bridston (1969), p. 9, op. cit.; Greeley (1972), p. 112, op. cit.; Fred H. Goldner, R. Richard Ritti, and Thomas P. Ference, "The Production of Cynical Knowledge in Organizations," *American Sociological Review* 42 (1977): 539-551.

61. Robert Michels, *Political Parties* (New York: Free Press, 1962).

62. A. L. Stinchcombe, *Constructing Social Theories* (New York: Harcourt, Brace & World, 1968).

63. Paul Harrison, *Authority and Power in the Free Church Tradition* (Princeton, Princeton U. Press, 1959).

64. *Chicago Daily News,* "Chicago Catholic Profile of Change," March 2, 4, and 5, 1974.

65. Nelson Logal, address made at the Second Annual Forum of the Confraternity of Catholic Clergy (New York, 1976). Logal sees changes

in the post-Vatican church lead to these results and exhorts participants of CCC to combat those changes.

66. Ibid.; Ference et al. (1971), op. cit.; similar observations were made by Richard Smith, S. J., Department of Theology, Loyola University of Chicago.

67. For example, the case of the Archdiocese of Chicago is reported by Anthony J. Vader, "Professional Clerical Organizations," unpublished paper (Department of Sociology, Loyola University of Chicago, 1976).

68. National Federation of Priests Council (1976), op. cit.

69. Ference et al. (1971), op. cit.

70. Ruth Leeds Love, "The Absorption of Protest," in H. Leavitt and L. Pondy (eds.), *Readings in Managerial Psychology* (Chicago: University of Chicago Press, 1973).

71. Smucker and Zijderveld (1970), op. cit.; Parsons (1951), op. cit.

72. Gannon (1972), 225, op. cit.

73. Terence E. Tierney, "The Resignation of Priests," *Clergy Review* 59 (1974): 767-772; Pro Mundi Vita, "The Catholic Pentecostal Movement: Creative or Divisive Enthusiasm," *Pro Mundi Vita Bulletin* 60 (1976): 3-33; Houtart (1969), op. cit.

74. James A. Beckford, *Religious Organization* (The Hague: Mouton, 1975).

75. NORC (1972), pp. 268-272, op. cit.; Greeley et al. (1976), op. cit.

76. Mary Ellen Reilly, "Perceptions of the Priest Role," *Sociological Analysis* 36 (1975): 355.

77. *Chicago Daily News* (1974), op. cit.

78. Demerath and Hammond (1969), p. 190, op. cit.

79. Vallier (1970) sees the role of priests as a spiritual leader within the local church (rather than as clerical authority in the society) and the main functions of the church (i.e., the RCC) as a socio-religious community from which laymen proceed into society as autonomous Christians. See Vallier (1970), p. 115, op. cit.; on the other hand, the tendency in various denominations has been toward de-differentiation and de-specialization. On this point, see, Richard E. Sykes, "An Appraisal of the Theory of Functional Structural Differentiation of Religious Collectivities," *Journal for the Scientific Study of Religion* 8 (1969): 289-200; Robert Bonn and Ruth T. Doyle, "Secularly Employed Clergymen: A Study in Occupational Role Recomposition," *Journal for the Scientific Study of Religion* 13 (1974): 325-344.

80. Others have proposed different approaches to the problem. For example, Joseph H. Fichter advocates not clinging to the traditional conceptions of the priest's sacerdotal duties and strengthening his "secular" professional training. See Joseph H. Fichter, *Organization Man in the Church* (Cambridge: Schenkman, 1974).

81. Greeley (1968) pp. 206-214, op. cit.

82. Vallier (1970), p. 60, op. cit.

83. Greeley sees Thomas O'Dea's dilemmas of institutionalization as dilemmas due to ineffective institutionalization. Also while, in the post-Vatican RCC, institutionalization of anything is rejected at any cost, Greeley sees (and rightly so) much benefit in institutionalization. See Greeley (1972), pp. 79-85, op. cit.

84. In 1974, Ross P. Scherer (private communication) raised the question of another council, labeled Vatican III, for example, to give the seal of legitimacy to the binding nature of structures set up as "consultative" by Vatican II. In May, 1977, a group of about 70 leading Catholic theologians and social scientists had three days of discussions in one of the first international meetings at the University of Notre Dame to plan for a Third Vatican Council. See *Chicago Tribune* May 28, 1977, p. 18.

85. Andrew M. Greeley, "Andrew M. Greeley Replies to His Critics," *Journal for the Scientific Study of Religion* 13 (1974): 229.

86. Abbott (1966), op. cit.

3

Patterns of Jewish Organization in the United States

Daniel J. Elazar

"Religion" is usually understood to be a subject oriented toward *transcendental* concerns; even the sociology of religion has been mainly concerned with the way in which individuals and groups function in pursuit of the transcendental concerns which interest them, whatever they may be. "Organization" is usually understood to be a subject oriented toward very *immanent* concerns. Indeed, the term is often used as a euphemism for "politics" or "government," both of which deal with the organization and direction of human activity for the most immanent of social concerns, the science or art of founding, shaping, and living in organized (i.e., civil) society. This chapter focuses very little on transcendental concerns or even on the way in which Jews function for overtly transcendental purposes. Rather, it is designed to reflect an understanding of religious organization as "politics" or "government," albeit in a special way. It focuses on the *Jewish community, not* on the Jewish *religion* or even the Jewish religious community as embodied primarily in synagogues or synagogue organizations. In its focus, it follows the traditional Jewish understanding of the Jewish community as an entity, an understanding which has permeated the culture and behavior of Jews so as to be (like all culture) second nature to them, to the point where its articulation within Jewish ranks is usually unnecessary, even after three centuries of deculturization of the Jews of the West, during which time other, particularly Protestant and socialist, notions of "community" and "religion" have made serious inroads into the ways in which Jews define themselves or attempt to describe the nature of Judaism.

If this represents a departure from the conventional approach to the study of denominational organization, it is a justified one. The growing interest in black religious organization as a separate ethno-cultural phenomenon indicates that considerations other than those usually espoused under the rubric "religious" in the United States are finally being brought into focus as part of the study of "religion" in the United States. From a traditional Christian point of view, it would be difficult to argue that "black" Christianity has its own orientation toward the transcendental. At the same time, social scientists would agree that, as an empirically verified matter, blacks have developed their *own* ways of pursuing religious goals, for whatever reasons, ways which include an organizational component and which are now being defined in an increasingly *independent*, ethno-cultural context.

Consequently, from the outset, we are confronted with an understanding of "religious organization" that must be considered a radical departure from the understanding abroad in the Western world only a few years ago. It would not be untoward to say that the *Jews*, functioning in their collective capacity, *have* by their very way of life *been the pioneers* of that understanding in the West. In due time, one may expect that understandings of "white Christianity," in its various divisions and denominations, will reflect an increased appreciation of the ethno-cultural bases which undergird it.

THE SPECIAL CHARACTER OF JEWISH ORGANIZATION

We must therefore begin with the recognition that *Jews do not separate* organization for what might be called *"churchly"* purposes *from* organization for other Jewish *communal* needs, because in Jewish life there is no meaningful line of separation between the two. This situation reflects the basis of Jewish communal organization which is both organic and associational.[1]

The Jewish community is a product of a unique blend of kinship and consent. The blend is already reflected in the Biblical account of its origins: a family of tribes that becomes a nation by consenting to the Covenant.[2] It continues to be reflected in subsequent Biblical narratives. Post-Biblical Jewish history gave the blend new meaning. The fact that Jews are born Jewish puts them in a special position to begin with, one which more often than not has forced them together for self-protection; yet, sufficient opportunities for conversion, assimilation, or the adoption of a posture of simple apathy towards any active effort to maintain Jewish life were almost always available as options. In the modern era, these options have expanded considerably in every respect. Today, they stand at what is probably an all-time high, even though counter-pressures have begun to reemerge.[3]

The Jewish way of life can be understood as a matter of familial solidarity, but it must also be understood in the light of the active will of many Jews to function *as a community*. This has two consequences. The "Jewish community" in the largest sense is defined as all those people born Jews or who have consciously and formally embraced Judaism though born outside the Jewish fold. In this respect, the Jewish community is more like Catholicism than Protestantism in the determination of its membership base. It extends far beyond Catholicism, however, in offering options for participation in the life of the community to those who choose to supplement their *organic* ties by *associational* ones.

In sum, Jews can be fully understood only when they are recognized as members of a covenantal community, linked by a shared destiny and a common pattern of communications, whose essential community of interest and purpose is reflected in a well-nigh complete panoply of organizations. In traditional terms, Judaism itself is essentially a *theopolitical* phenomenon, a means of seeking salvation by constructing God's polity, the proverbial "city upon a hill," through which the covenantal community takes on meaning and fulfills its purpose in the divine scheme of things.[4] While American civilization has influenced Jews to the extent that "being Jewish" is no longer an all-embracing way of life for most members of the Jewish community, nevertheless, the concept of and behavior involved in "being Jewish" remains far more broad-gauged in its scope and reach than the concepts of and behavior involved in "being Catholic" or "being Protestant." Even the phrase, "being Jewish," which is common enough in the language of modern Jewish discourse, is rarely found in Christian discourse. There are distinct ways in which different people "are Catholic" or "are Protestant," but they have to do with denominational and, more importantly, ethnocultural factors which shape the various Catholic and Protestant subcommunities. Traditional discussions of these matters in America have tended to ignore these distinctions and to assume that a certain universalism inheres in "Catholicism" or "Protestantism" that is undiluted by these more "mundane" factors and which is, ipso facto, absent from Judaism. At the very least, the separation of *black religion* in our work today marks a step away from that tradition and toward a greater appreciation of the realities of socioreligious communalism.

In the end, while associational activity provides the motive thrust for the maintenance and continuation of Jewish life, the organic ties persist and tend to be strengthened when the survival of the community seems to be at stake. It seems true, if not particularly scientific, to say that Jews, even very marginal ones, tend to have a "sixth sense" about threats to their security and survival as Jews. Since the Holocaust of World War II, when the Jewish people lost one-third of their total number, this "sense" has been sharpened considerably.

In sum, it is *not simply* association with a *synagogue* that enables a Jew to become part of the organized Jewish community. Affiliation with *any of a whole range of organizations*, ranging from clearly philanthropic groups to "secularist" cultural societies, offers the same option. Consequently, any meaningful discussion of Jewish "religious" organization must include the local federations for Jewish service which deal primarily in welfare, educational, and cultural activities as well as synagogues; Jewish community relations organizations as well as religious schools. In fact, as we will later point out in greater detail, one of the most striking recent developments in the realm of Jewish organization is a *reversal* of the trend toward increasing the role of the synagogue in Jewish life, a trend which had emerged after World War II to become seemingly dominant by 1960, and which has now clearly passed its high point.

The American Jewish community is *built upon an associational base* to a far greater extent than any other in Jewish history. That is to say, not only is there no inescapable compulsion, external or internal, to affiliate with organized Jewry, but there is no automatic way to become a member of the Jewish community. Nor is there even a clear way to affiliate with the community as-a-whole. All connections with organized Jewish life are based on voluntary associations with some particular organization or institution, whether in the form of synagogue membership, contribution to the local Jewish Welfare Fund (generally considered to be an act of joining as well as contributing), or affiliation with B'nai Brith Lodge of Hadassah (the Women's Zionist Organization) chapter.[5]

This associational approach is typically American, a reflection of a social order based on chosen affiliation rather than descent. Americans do not like to think of themselves bound to anything by birth; hence they seek to transform all organic ties into associational ones. Even such organic entities as the family frequently take on an associational character in American Jewish life, viz. the development and spread of the "family club," a formal association of relatives!

Indeed, the usual pattern for affiliated Jews—like that of their fellow-Americans—is one of multiple association with memberships in different kinds of organizations reenforcing one another and creating a network of Jewish ties that binds the individual who chooses to become enmeshed in them more firmly to the community. Without that associational base, there would be no organized Jewish community at all; with it, the Jewish community attains the kind of social status (and even a certain legal status) that enables it to fit well into the larger society of which it is a part.

THE FEDERAL ELEMENT IN
JEWISH ORGANIZATION

The key to Jewish organization lies in its flexibility, and that flexibility is reflected institutionally in the *federal character of Jewish communal organization*. Since its emergence as an "organization" over 3000 years ago, the Jewish community has been organized on federative or federal principles from first to last and has enhanced its survival power by applying them almost instinctively in changing situations. In this respect, it stands in rather sharp contrast to the Roman Catholic Church, the second oldest continuing "organization" in the history of the Western World. The latter is built upon hierarchical principles from the first to last and gains its survival power by their careful and intelligent manipulation. (The contrast may well be instructive and may well provide a point of departure for further research in the realm of the organization of religious communities.)

The original "federal" bargains that created the Jewish people were embodied in the various covenants described in the Bible, culminating in the Covenant of Sinai.[6] Indeed, the very term "federal" is derived from the Latin *foedus* or "covenant" and has its origins in the Biblical experience as it was understood by the Puritans who developed their "federal theology" to deal with the great questions of humanity and the universe.[7] The utilization or application of federal principles, first applied in the federation of the twelve tribes, has undergone numerous permutations in the long course of Jewish history. But today, in an era of *a*traditionalism, it is *one* tradition that is *not* being abandoned by Jews.

The *congregation* is the cornerstone of this federal structure, the first institution to be established when a sufficient number of Jews has gathered in one place to create an organized community (usually, but not necessarily, ten men). Indeed, the terms "congregation" and "community" are *synonymous* in Hebrew (as in German). Jews have come together to form congregations wherever they found themselves. In keeping with the federal principles which underlie Jewish organization, they do so by formally consenting to articles of agreement or charters which bind them together as a community in the manner defined by Jewish law and custom. The term for such articles of congregational-cum-communal agreement used by the Sephardic Jews, *Askamot* (articles of agreement), conveys this meaning exactly.

Only in modern times did "congregation" and "synagogue" tend to become synonymous. While every congregation included provisions for worship (a "synagogue"), it was not likely to begin and end with that function. This was particularly true in the past, though it remains equally true in a somewhat different way today. On the contrary, since Jews do not need institutional arrangements of a synagogical nature to pray, the organization of a congregation was more likely to come about when there was a need to structure the incipient community's social welfare or educational tasks, through establishment of a cemetery, creation of institutionalized mechanism for aiding the poor, or inauguration of a school. The congregation is a very flexible device that can accommodate all those services and more, usually through a system of *hevrot* (fellowships) or committees, drawn from the congregational body as a whole.[8]

As a community expanded, its organization necessarily became more complex, leading to an elaboration of the *hevrah* system or even, particularly in modern times, to the creation of other congregations or organizations within the same locality. Ultimately, they would develop federal or confederal links to one another to create a more elaborate communal structure.

Under the impact of socio-political emanicipation (in Europe), Protestantism (both there and in the United States), and the sheer increase in Jewish population (in both places), this federative process was accelerated leading to the emergence of the modern synagogue as essentially a place of worship although with ancillary functions to perform. Individual synagogues came to embody specific relio-ideological identifications in Judaism—Reform, Orthodox, Conservative. Many of the functions formerly housed within congregations when they were entirely in the hands of volunteers were now "spun off" and restructured in more elaborate ways, becoming professionalized and being given separate organizational bases of their own within the overall community.[9]

Thus, as the decision to be involved in Jewish life became increasingly a voluntary one, the new voluntarism extended itself into the internal life of the Jewish community as well, generating pluralism *even within* previously *free* but relatively homogeneous and monolithic community structures. This pluralism was increased by the breakdown of the traditional reasons for being Jewish and the rise of new and different incentives for Jewish association. It demanded new federal arrangements to achieve a degree of unity within a community larger and far more diverse than any which Jews had confronted in their long history.[10]

The pluralistic federalism that has emerged in the contemporary Jewish community substantially eliminates the neat patterns of communal organization that were frequently to be found in other times, the kind which are easily presented on organization charts. Certainly, the model of a hierarchical organizational structure does not offer an accurate picture of the distribution of powers and responsibilities in the Jewish community today. There is *no* functioning, organizational *pyramid* in Jewish life; no national organization able to issue directives to local affiliates; and no local "judiciary" or "roof" organization able to order others within its "jurisdiction" into line. ("Judicatory" is a Presbyterian term widely adopted to refer to generic, *regional*, ecclesiastical authority structures.) In sum, there is no *central* governing agent in most Jewish communities which serves as the point at which authority, responsibility, and power converge, even at the local level.[11]

The structure of the contemporary Jewish community is best understood as a multi-dimensional matrix that takes the form of a communications network; a set of interacting institutions which, while preserving their own structural integrity and filling their own functional roles, are informed by shared patterns of culture, activated by a shared system or organizations, and governed by shared leadership cadres. The character of the matrix and its communications network varies from community to community. In some cases, the network is connected through a common center which serves as the major (but rarely, if ever, exclusive) channel for communication. In others, the network forms a matrix without any real center, with the lines of communication crisscrossing in all directions. In all cases, the boundaries of the community are revealed only when the pattern of the network is uncovered. The pattern itself stands revealed only when both of its components are—namely, its *institutions* and organizations with their respective roles *and* the way in which *communications* are passing *among them*.

The pattern itself is inevitably a dynamic one. That is to say, there is rarely a fixed division of authority and influence but, rather, one that varies from time to time and usually from issue to issue, with different elements in the matrix taking on different "loads" at different times and relative to different issues. Since the community is a voluntary one, persuasion rather than compulsion, influence rather than power are the only tools available for making and executing policies. This, too, works to strengthen its character as a communications network, since the character, quality, and relevance of what is communicated and the way in which it is communicated frequently determine the extent of the authority and influence of the parties to the communication.[12]

A TYPOLOGY OF COMMUNAL ORGANIZATIONS

Institutions and organizations playing at least four kinds of roles are to be found in every fully functioning and completely organized Jewish community. They are:

1. Government-like institutions, whether "roof" organizations or separate institutions serving discrete functions, that play roles and provide services on all planes (countrywide, local, and—where used—

intermediate) which, under other conditions, would be played, provided, or controlled—predominantly or exclusively—by governmental authorities (for instance, external relations, defense, education, social welfare, and "public"—that is, communal—finance).

2. *Localistic institutions and organizations*, that provide a means for attaching people to Jewish life on the basis of their most immediate and personal interests and needs.

3. *General purpose, mass-based organizations*, operating on all planes, that function to (a) articulate community values, attitudes, and policies; (b) provide the energy and motive force for crystallizing the communal consensus that grows out of those values, attitudes and policies; and (c) maintain institutional channels of communication between the community's leaders and "actives" ("cosmopolitans") and the broad base of the affiliated Jewish population ("locals"), for dealing with the problems and tasks facing the community in the light of the consensus.

4. *Special interest organizations*, which, by serving specialized interests in the community on all planes, function to mobilize concern and support for the various programs conducted by or for the community and to apply pressure for their expansion, modification, and improvement.

The first two of the preceding types are essentially embodied in the institutions which form the structural foundations of the community, and the last two essentially in organizations which function to activate the institutional structure and give it life.

Institutions of the first (quasi-governmental) type are easily identifiable in most communities. They include the Jewish federations mentioned above and those institutions and organizations dedicated to serving community-wide needs that are associated with them. In a typical local community, they will include a Jewish Community Center, a central agency for Jewish education, a Jewish community relations council, various social welfare institutions to deal with problems ranging from adoption to aging, a Jewish hospital, a welfare fund, and various cultural societies claiming community-wide appeal.

The most important localistic institutions are the synagogues which, by their very nature, are geared to be relatively intimate associations of compatible people. Even the very large American synagogues that lose their sense of intimacy remain "localistic" institutions in this sense, within the overall community context. The most important localistic organizations other than synagogues are lodges, family clubs, *landsmanschaften* (associations of immigrants from the same town in the "old country"), occasional "secular" societies that function as synagogue surrogates for those who actively proclaim their non-belief.

In the United States, B'nai Brith and Hadassah, with lodges or chapters in virtually every organized Jewish community from Maine to

Alaska, come closest to performing the functions of organizations in the third (general, mass-based) category. They are supplemented by a number of smaller countrywide organizations such as the American Jewish Committee, American Jewish Congress, National Council for Jewish Women and the various Zionist groups (of which Hadassah is formally one) recently united as the American Zionist Federations.

While the special interest organizations are best identified on a local basis, there are some common patterns countrywide. Certainly the various groupings of synagogues with their men's clubs, sisterhoods, and youth groups represent the major example in this category. In addition, local groups abound which serve and support such diverse interests as Jewish institutions of higher learning, Jewish-sponsored hospitals and medical centers, vocational training programs for Jews in other countries, and a variety of Jewish cultural institutions.

It is conceivable that, in the smaller Jewish communities, the four kinds of roles may be compressed within fewer institutions and be filled incompletely as a consequence. In any case, the *functions themselves must be institutionalized somehow* in order *for* an organized *community* actually *to exist*. The mapping of any particular community's organizational structure along the lines of this typology will reveal many of the more permanent channels into which the community's communications network is set and also expose the ways in which the channels are used.

DEVELOPMENT OF THE STRUCTURE OF JEWISH ORGANIZATION IN AMERICA[13]

The United States, with some six million Jews contains over half of all the Jews in the diaspora and nearly half of all the Jews in the world today. Historic events combined to make the U.S.A. the first large, fully modern society built from the first on individualistic principles; pluralistic in the full sense of the word; and settled by several significantly different waves of very adventurous Jewish immigrants who shared one common commitment, that of seeking new lives as individuals. This combination prevented the development of sufficient homogeneity to permit the emergence of a neat, unitary, Jewish communal structure. Consequently, every effort to create even so much as a single, nationwide "address" for American Jewry has failed.

The *kehillot* (organized Jewish communities) of other times and climes were all developed for much smaller communities. Since Roman times, probably none exceeded a few hundred thousand population, and most were far smaller than that. The metropolitan areas with the largest Jewish populations in the United States—New York, Los Angeles, Philadelphia, Chicago, Boston, Miami—are themselves larger than all but a handful of countrywide communities that have existed over the long history of the Jewish People.[14]

In the earliest period of Jewish communal life in the United States, the small and relatively homogeneous Jewish population managed to achieve unity on the local plane through a system of local congregations not dissimilar to that presently found in countries like New Zealand (Jewish population: 5,000), whereby the Jews in each city joined together to create one common congregation which provided all the communal services (religious, social, and educational) which they desired, directly or through its *hevrot*. Jews from all parts of the world joined these "community congregations," accepting the ritual and organizational patterns of their Sephardic (i.e., Jews from the Iberian Peninsula) founders as their own. Between 1654 and the end of the eighteenth century, "community" and "congregation" were virtually synonymous terms and were so recognized by Jews and Gentile alike.

The wave of migrants that arrived from Central Europe in the nineteenth century put an end to that kind of unity. A larger and more complex American Jewish community introduced a multiplicity of congregations on the local scene, based on the diverse ritual preferences of their founders and members. The new immigrants from Central Europe wanted their own synagogues, first to preserve their particular orthodox traditions and later to institute Reform. Jewish organizational life was still basically *congregational*, but rudimentary social services and educational institutions at least nominally independent of any congregation began to emerge by mid-century. In fact, even they tended to be dominated by leaders of particular congregations wearing different hats.

From the late 1850s to the early 1880s, the growing American Jewish community experimented with a representative Board of Deputies of American Israelites, modeled after the Board of Deputies of British Jews in the United Kingdom. The experiment was launched with great difficulty and failed almost immediately. Neither it nor its more narrowly based successor, the Union of American Hebrew Congregations (the very name reveals how contemporaries still conceived of Jewish life as concentrated in the *synagogue* and potentially unifiable on a congregational basis), ever came close to achieving universality. The divisions between traditionalists and liberals were already too great for easy accommodation on the religious front.

Whether any similar experiment would have succeeded or not became a moot point when the mass migration from Eastern Europe created the largest and most diverse Jewish community in history, scattered over the largest area ever considered as embracing a single "countrywide community." Even local communities lost whatever features of unity they might have had under the impact of the new immigrants. The new immigrants' own efforts to introduce community structures based on European models failed as fully as the earlier efforts to introduce the Anglo-Jewish model. European rabbis sent to the New World to create orderly religious institutions retreated in disorder, and even such American-generated efforts to adapt European forms such as the New York *kehillah* failed because of American conditions.

At the same time, the new immigrants brought with them, or stimulated by their arrival, the beginnings of a system of Jewish communal life which turned out to be more suited to the American environment; and that, despite appearances to the contrary, has been able to mobilize Jewish energy for the great tasks which have confronted American Jewry. While that system had its origin in the closing years of the nineteenth century, its development is essentially a twentieth-century phenomenon.

The roots of the present system were planted by the Jews already established in the United States at the time of the mass immigration in response to the needs of the new immigrants as they perceived them, as modified by the organizational demands generated by the latter for and by themselves. Their response led to the creation of Jewish organizations of all four previously defined "types": (1) welfare federations, "defense" agencies, congregational "roof" organizations, and seminaries in the first category; (2) Orthodox, Conservative, and Reform synagogues, *landsmanschaften*, and fraternal organizations in the second; (3) organizations such as B'nai Brith (actually expanded from its earlier form), the American Jewish Congress, and the Zionist groups; (4) and a welter of "national" and local groups. At the same time, the connections between these multifarious organizations and groups were minimal, if not simply nonexistent. *No real communications network existed*, on either the countrywide or local planes.

World War I brought the first real steps toward the creation of such a network. The unification of overseas welfare activities under the newly formed Joint Distribution Committee was the first successful effort to link old-line (i.e., "German"), Orthodox, and secularist elements into a common framework. While the War also produced abortive attempts at creating Jewish unity on a mass basis countrywide, in the aftermath of their failure, new efforts were generated on the local plane to link the diverse elements in the community for at least limited welfare and "defense" purposes. During the 1920s, the Welfare federations and community councils, the institutions which embodied these efforts, took root locally and began to coalesce on a countrywide basis.

The demands placed upon the American Jewish community beginning in the late 1930s led to a growing recognition of the need to reconstitute the community's organizational structure, at least to the extent of rationalizing the major interinstitutional relationships and generally tightening the matrix. These efforts at reconstitution received added impetus from the changes in American society as a whole (and the Jews' place in it after 1945). They signaled the abandonment of earlier chimerical efforts to create a more conventional organizational pyramid, in imitation of foreign patterns, which would have been quite out of place, given the character of American society as a whole.

Trends in Jewish Organization after World War II

The aftermath of World War II brought with it an expansion of the trends already noted in Jewish organizational life in the 1930s, only radically intensified as a result of the new conditions of what had become, in effect, the post-Modern world. American Jewry had become the foremost Jewish community in the world, larger than any other functioning Jewish community by far—indeed, ten times larger—than its nearest functioning counterpart. Within it was located the bulk of the wealth which world Jewry could mobilize to undertake the tremendous tasks of relief and reconstruction which confronted it as a result of the Nazi holocaust, tasks which were increasingly to be concentrated in the foundation of the new State of Israel, as the initial demands of postwar relief were satisfied.[15]

At the same time, American Jewry confronted a new situation at home, in which the barriers against full participation in American society rapidly fell away to be replaced by what Will Herberg was to call the "triple melting pot," or the recognition of Judaism and Catholicism, along with Protestantism, as the three "legitimate" American faiths.[16] Finally, the opening of the metropolitan frontier with the resultant suburbanization of America saw the Jews in the vanguard of the movement to the suburbs or, at the very least, out of old neighborhoods to suburban-like areas within the central cities, requiring institutional adaptations to new lifestyles.

All these factors influenced the course of Jewish organizational development between the end of the war and the mid-1960s. In the first place, there emerged some institutions which began to centralize or, at least, properly structure the government-like functions undertaken by the Jewish community. These were generally the organizations that were part of the federation movement. Locally and then nationally through the Council of Jewish Federations and Welfare Funds, the federations gained in strength. The major impetus behind their gain was their *emergence as the dominant fundraisers* in the Jewish community.

Pioneering in "single drive" fundraising in the style of the United Funds, the federations became the powerhouses behind an unprecedented voluntary effort. The exciting tasks of raising funds for post-war relief and the rebuilding of Israel, which captured the imaginations of American Jews as well as the bulk of the money raised from them, stimulated a phenomenal increase in the amount of money contributed for all Jewish communal purposes. The impetus provided by "Israel" redounded to the benefit of *domestic* Jewish needs as well, since the larger sums forthcoming from the coordinated drives were also allocated as to increase their resources too.

The federations did not (and do not) subsidize synagogues or those functions which had come under the synagogues' wing. By common agreement, the latter were left to raise their own funds and also did so with remarkable success. Nevertheless, though large amounts of money were raised for the construction and maintenance of synagogues in the same period, synagogue fundraising had neither the excitement nor the demands for continuity that abetted the annual federation "drives." Their great efforts were necessarily "one shot" affairs, and their annual needs remained relatively limited and seemingly parochial as well.

The substantive quality and the recurring nature of the federations' tasks served to strengthen their hands in other ways as well. They attracted leadership, both voluntary and professional, of the highest caliber available to the Jewish community. In time that leadership, at least partly because of the nature of the tasks which confronted it, *began to see Jewish communal problems as connected* with one another. Federation leaders began to concern themselves with the broad range of Jewish needs, not simply with overseas relief or with the welfare functions that had been traditional to the federations in the pre-World War II period.

By 1960, most of the major Jewish federations were engaged in community planning of some sort, were supporting Jewish educational and cultural programs as well as welfare, defense, and overseas services, and were beginning to think of themselves as the central bodies for Jewish communal endeavor within their respective areas of jurisdiction. Increasingly after 1960, federations began to define the range of their interests *as embracing* virtually *the total Jewish community, excluding only the synagogues* themselves. By the mid-1970s, new relationships between the federations and the synagogues had also began to emerge. At the same time, on the countrywide plane, the Council of Jewish Federations and Welfare Funds began to strengthen its position as well, often providing the impetus for local federations to become involved in one area or another that had previously been defined as outside their purview.[17]

During this period, there was also a sorting out of roles among the previously existing countrywide organizations, many of which had previously aspired to the central role being assumed by the federation movement. Thus, the Zionist organizations, the American Jewish Congress, the American Jewish Committee, and B'nai Brith began to edge away from the tasks of actually providing government-like services and to redefine themselves as the mass-based organizations whose task it was, in effect, to capture the federations or become the motive forces behind them.

The end result of all this was the creation of a *network* of institutions and organizations implicitly based on the principles delineated above. This network functioned best on the *local* plane where the tasks to be carried out were most concrete, the needs apparent, and the resources most easily mobilized. Its capacities were more *limited* on the *countrywide* plane where symbolic issues and matters of personal and organizational prestige often dominated organizational politics, causing interpersonal and interorganizational rivalries that often obscured the real organizational strength of the American Jewish community.

The one set of organizations willing to challenge the federation movement were the three synagogues movement, both in their congregations as discrete movements and in combination as the Synagogue Council of America. The decade of the 1950s was a particularly propitious time for them to assert themselves. The apparent redefinition of Jewishness as an exclusively religious phenomenon, in order to increase its appeal to a new generation of Americanized Jews, obviously strengthened the hands of those who claimed to be the spokesmen for *Judaism as a religion*.

While the federations were expanding their operations at the communitywide level and involving the "cosmopolitans" first and foremost, the synagogues were pioneering the suburban frontier on the most immediately local level and attracting wide support from among the "locals". Since the synagogues were best geared to satisfying the immediately personal needs of their members or potential members, they had a great opportunity to reach out to a new generation seeking institutionalized ways to express their Jewishness, yet largely estranged from the traditions of Jewish observance. Their growing monopoly over the celebration of the Jewish "rites of passage" insured them a steady and even growing clientele.

The synagogues' position was enhanced by the impact of the metropolitan frontier. The Jews who streamed into the great cities during the heyday of the urban frontier settled in neighborhoods where their organic links were as strong as if not stronger than their associational ones. This was as true of the more assimilated Central European Jews "uptown" as of the Eastern European immigrants in the great "ghettos." Whether one formally joined a synagogue or not, in those neighborhoods a Jew was surrounded by family, friends, businesses, and institutions operating within an essentially or substantially Jewish milieu. The move to the suburbs broke up the old neighborhoods and, with each successive move outward from them, weakened the extent to which the immediate environment was "Jewish" and lessened the proximity of Jews to one another. Under such conditions, Jews who maintained their Jewishness through *organic* relationships had to seek more formal *associational* ties simply to keep those relationships alive. The local synagogue offered the easiest and most acceptable means (in the American context) for making the transition.

Consequently, synagogue membership soared in the 1950s (parallel-ing similar developments in local Christian churches, which were affected by the metropolitan frontier in similar, though not identical, ways). Whether those membership gains represented a "return" to Judaism, as was assumed at the time (e.g., by Herberg), or simply a transition to more formal affiliation on the part of those already committed, as demanded by changed circumstances, is a question that still remains unanswered.

The resurgent synagogues capitalized on their position by reaching out to embrace functions not inherently "local," but not inherently "cosmo-politan" either. They became the primary custodians of Jewish educa-tion, establishing synagogue schools on their premises as means of attracting additional members, adapting those schools to the new conditions of suburbia and creating an ideology to justify the new trends they initiated, virtually eliminating the private and communal Hebrew schools of the previous era. They became the primary organizers of the youth, either on a congregational basis or through their national organizations, virtually replacing both the Zionist organizations and B'nai Brith. They began to undertake recreational and social service functions that had been the province of the Jewish community centers and the local Jewish welfare agencies. In order to play their expanded role, synagogues had to become large institutions, often with member-ships of over 1,000 families. Indeed, synagogues with fewer than 500 families came to be considered less than viable.

While this was occurring on the local plane, the countrywide synagogue bodies were also laying claim to a special importance in American Jewish life that transcended their earlier efforts to foster congregations of their respective "persuasions" in a rough competition for the unaffiliated, challenging all other national bodies in the process. Though their challenge was only marginally successful, it did represent a continuing area of contention within American Jewish life.

The struggle between the federations with their constituent *agencies* on the one hand and the national synagogue bodies with their constituent *congregations* on the other was a classic manifestation of the "cosmo-politan—local" dichotomy. The federations, dominated by the cosmo-politans of the Jewish community, had their eyes focused on typical *cosmopolitan* interests, ranging from those of the local community-as-a-whole to those of world Jewry-as-a-whole. The focus of the synagogues was equally and typically *localistic*, whether in reference to immediate congregations or to the interests of the separate quasi-denominational "branches" in their competition with one another and with the extra-synagogue elements in the overall community. As the leaders of the

synagogue bodies sought to coopt additional functions into the synagogues under their jurisdiction, they increasingly came into conflict with
the leaders of the federation bodies whose conception of the functions of
the community-as-a-whole was expanding at the same time.

By the 1960s, then, the American Jewish community had developed
certain organizational patterns which were more or less replicated in over
800 organized Jewish communities and countrywide as well. The
patterns were all derived from the associational basis of American
Jewish life described above.

PRESENT AND PROJECTED TRENDS

The trends of the postwar period reached their culmination in the early
1960s. The ostensible religious revival came to an end; membership in
synagogues as in local churches stabilized and then, by the late sixties,
began to decline; and new challenges emerged to threaten the established
organizations. By the end of the sixties, the trends toward sorting out the
various elements in the organizational structure of the Jewish community
and harmonizing them within a common communications network had
taken another step forward, though partly as a result of the decline of one
segment of the structure and partly as a result of the redefinition of the
other.

The synagogues represented the declining element. It was not that
their loss of membership was decisive; for indeed despite the reversal of
the trend, the actual losses were still relatively moderate by the end of the
1960s, stabilized early in the 1970s and may even have been turned
around by the mid-1970s. What had happened, however, is that a series
of events had robbed the synagogues of much of the basis of their claim to
primacy. On one hand, the changed American attitude towards organized
religion made the Jewish champion of organized religion, namely the
synagogue, far more vulnerable to outside criticism, especially from the
ranks of American youth. Second, the emergence of a disaffected
segment of the youth population, drawing disproportionately from
Jewish ranks, led to direct challenges to the synagogue as an instrument
of the "establishment." Finally, the Six-Day War, in June, 1967, made
it clear for all Jews to see that it was *not simply* a common concern with
religious affiliation which bound Jews together so much *as* it was a
sense of a common fate *as a people*, symbolized and reaffirmed by the
Israeli-Arab crisis.

After 1967, it became apparent that the synagogue's claim to be able
to harmonize Judaism with Americanism by redefining Judaism in
predominantly, if not exclusively, "Protestant" structural terms was not
all that it was cracked up to be. The redefinition of Judaism in strictly
Protestant terms, instead of attracting American Jews in ways that no

other definition of Judaism could, turned out to be less attractive than the *broader* definition set forth by Jewish tradition, which gave the land of Israel a central place as a means for attracting most Jews. The definition of Judaism as a strictly religious phenomenon proved even to be a handicap when it came to a certain segment of Jewish youth who were "turned off" by Judaism as a "churchly" phenomenon in a secular age. Those same young people were often able to find meaning in the *more ethnic* aspects of Judaism at a time when ethnic nationalism was on the upsurge in America and around the world. Significantly, it was not esoteric ritual or tradition that the young people rejected—quite to the contrary, there was something of a boom in traditionalism among certain youth—but the overly sanitary religious schools of suburban congregations, originally introduced in the name of modernity.

While synagogues were on the decline, the federations were busy redefining their role in an expansive manner.

In the 1950s, as we have seen, the leadership of the federations began to concern themselves with the problem of Jewish survival as something more than an issue of welfare or overseas relief. This tendency became a trend after 1960, with federations developing deepening concerns for Jewish education and culture and wider interest in community planning in a whole host of ways. All this tended to strengthen the hands of the federations as the all-embracing agents of Jewish communal life. At the same time, the federations became more mindful of traditional Jewish practices which have usually been called "religious." They began to embrace the public observance of Jewish religious practices in their own programs and to encourage traditional and observant Jews to involve themselves in their ranks, thereby building a bridge into that segment of the Jewish community which had previously been outside their normal purview. The decade culminated with the federations taking the most effective action towards developing a means to reach out to the disaffected Jewish youth.

At the same time, new organizational and functional patterns have begun to emerge in response to the dissatisfactions which have surfaced since the mid-1960s. Perhaps the best way to describe those patterns and the trends in Jewish organization which they may have initiated is to examine them with respect to the functions which the Jewish community is called upon to perform. These functions include: organization of religious rites and worship, defense, external relations, education, welfare, enforcement of norms, and public finance.

The organization of religious rites and worship, the central concern of the Jewish revival of the 1950s, is also the issue which has provoked the greatest dissatisfaction and generated the most portentous changes today. In general, the ferment among the young has led to an assault upon the contemporary organization of Jewish religious life, particularly upon the *large suburban congregation* with what they perceive to be the inauthentic modes of religious observance which have developed within its confines, the essential impersonality of its operations, and the privatism which animates its members' participation, all of which they see as having replaced the more intimate and communally oriented goals and patterns of the traditional synagogue. Those young Jews who are seeking an authentic religious experience are also searching for new ways to organize their religious life. The development of fellowships, the increase in the number of *small* congregations devoted primarily to worship and fellowship, and the emergence of new seminaries dedicated to both are all features of Jewish religious organization and innovation of the last few years.

In most respects, these innovations represent a return to traditional standards, although in new format. Thus, it is not surprising that the pioneers of this reaction to the forms of American Judaism were traditionally-minded Jewish academics and scientists, who in the late 1950s and early 1960s began to create their own synagogues which were both Orthodox and traditional. That is, while committed to the meticulous observance of Jewish law, they also involved a revival of the style of congregational organization common before the day of the larger synagogue, emphasizing smaller membership composed of families highly committed to one another and seeking a great deal of interpersonal interaction aside from that built around the worship experience proper.

Since the mid-1960s this pattern has been followed with considerably more fanfare by Jewish intellectuals from Conservative and to some extent Reform backgrounds, primarily through fellowships and "underground" seminaries. But their efforts are still too new to be assessed, other than to say that they have infused a certain dynamism into Jewish religious life that has carried over beyond the confines of their fellowships and seminaries.

The relationships among the branches of Judaism also are undergoing a certain change. Orthodoxy, which a generation earlier was becoming more like Conservatism, has taken on new strength and sharpness as a small but growing minority seeking to return to the tradition in the fullest sense. Conservatism and Reform, on the other hand, have come closer together in practice if not in theory, although their closeness should not be exaggerated.

Notes

1. For a discussion of these two elements and the relationship between them in the context of American religion, see Gerhard Lenski,

The Religious Factor (Garden City, N.J.: Doubleday Anchor Books, 1961).

2. Among the many sources discussing the dimension of the War's covenant, see R.A.F. Mackenzie, S. J., *Faith and History in the Old Testament* (New York: 1963), particularly Chapter 3.

3. For a record of past opportunities, see Salo W. Baron, *A Social and Religious History of the Jews* (Philadelphia: Jewish Publication Society, 1952) 14 volumes. Howard M. Sachar's, *The Course of Modern Jewish History* (New York: Dell Publishing Co., 1958) gives a good description of the contemporary situation.

4. The close connection between the theological and the political are made manifest in Jewish literature beginning with the Bible. In our time, Martin Buber has been the foremost expositor of those connections. See, in particular, his *Kingship of God*, trans. Richard Scheimann (New York: 1967). See also, Hans Kohn, *The Idea of Nationalism* (New York: 1944), ch. 2; and Harold Fisch, *Jerusalem and Albion* (New York: 1964).

5. A broad picture of this "associational" community is available in any of the better sociological studies of American Jews. See, for example, Marshall Sklare and Joseph Greenblum, *Jewish Identity on the Suburban Frontier* (New York: Basic Books, 1967).

6. Mackenzie, op. cit.

7. For the Israelite origins of the federal idea, see "Federalism", *International Encyclopedia of the Social Sciences* (New York: Crowell-Collier-Macmillan, 1970) and the citations appended thereto.

8. Salo W. Baron describes this situation and process in *Social and Religious History, op. cit.* and *The Jewish Community* (Philadelphia: Jewish Publication Society, 1942).

9. See Sachar, *op. cit.* and Ismar Elbogen, *A Century of Jewish Life* (Philadelphia: Jewish Publication Society, 1945).

10. See, for example, Jacob Katz, *Traditional Crisis* (New York: Basic Books, 1965).

11. See Daniel J. Elazar, "The Reconstitution of Jewish Communities in the Postwar Period," *Jewish Journal of Sociology* (December, 1969); and Ernest Stock, "In the Absence of Hierarchy: Notes on the Structure of the American Jewish Community," *Jewish Journal of Sociology* (June, 1970).

12. Elazer, op. cit., from which the following typology is drawn.

13. This section is based on the standard sources of American Jewish history and sociology. See, particularly, Nathan Glazer, *American Judaism* (Chicago: University of Chicago Press, 1957).

14. For Jewish population statistics, see the *American Jewish Year Book* published annually by the American Jewish Committee and the Jewish Publication Society.

15. A bibliography of the leading studies dealing with these phenomena is available from the Study of Jewish Community Organization, Center for the Study of Federalism, Temple University.

16. Will Herberg, *Protestant-Catholic-Jew*.

17. See, for example, Sklare, *op. cit.*; Albert I. Gordon, *Jews in Transition* (Minneapolis: University of Minnesota Press, 1969) and *Jews in Suburbia* (Boston: Beacon Press, 1964); Ben Halpen, *The American Jew: A Zionist Analysis* (New York: Herzl Press, 1956); Oscar I. Janowsky, ed. *The American Jew: A Reappraisal* (Philadelphia: Jewish Publication Society, 1964); Peter I. Rose, ed. *The Ghetto and Beyond* (New York: Random House, 1969); and C. Bezalel Sherman, *The Jew Within American Society* (Detroit: Wayne State University Press, 1965).

Part Two

Selected Agencies and Subgroups

Introduction to Part Two

Ross P. Scherer

Part Two presents sociological analyses of selected agencies and sub-groups of denominations. Chapters 4 by Gannon and 5 by Winter cover what in effect are task-oriented social movements—Roman Catholic religious orders and Protestant mission societies. Chapter 6 by Hartley and Schuller deals with an important service agency, the theological training school, and Chapter 7 by Perry with probably the single most important denominational subelement—the local congregation or parish. Chapter 8 by Hesser applies open systems analysis to the plight of an important functional component of denominations—the role problems of the full time, male religious professional. While Hesser primarily treats the ordained Protestant male, much of his analysis also applies to priests and female ministers.

Gannon in Chapter 4 provides a historical review of the origins of Roman Catholic orders and a summary of some recent sociological research on their changing character. While he treats male orders, at least some of his generalizations apply also to female religious. His chapter should be an eye-opener to non-Catholics, since information on background and structural nomenclature of orders is seldom summarized so succinctly. In some ways his delineation of the different styles and structures of different orders over time reminds us of the diversities found within the Protestant denominations in Chapter 1. Different times called for different styles and forms—a shifting from withdrawal from life to participation in society, from "particular" to general goals, from traditional to utilitarian outlooks. Just as an early medieval period called for the geographically stable Benedictines, the modern evoked the mobile Jesuits. In his delineation of the order as a general type form, he notes the importance of the environment in precipitation, the increase in autonomy of members as later orders defined mission as lying in the environment, together with a consequential increase in bureaucratization. We see here illustrated the important process of *cooptation*, whereby a parent organization and offspring function in a dialectical relationship of mutual support and strain. Of special interest is the requirement in orders of what Max Weber termed "virtuoso religiosity," expressed in the special disciplines of obedience, communal ownership, and celibacy.

The real genius of the orders, however, is revealed in his comparison of members of a selected number of orders with the Catholic clergy *not* in orders—the diocesan priesthood. The order clergy tend to be more self-selected and, concomitantly, to be more positive about and "satisfied" with their lot in a number of ways—they find specialized occupations more compatible with their view of mission; they are more accepting of celibacy; they experience more communal support in their lifestyle; they experience more variety and challenge, assisted by availability of wider choices in reassignment. Gannon's comparisons of four male orders remind us again that there is *no one best way*. The Jesuits, for example, appear more able to gain satisfaction from work specialization. In general, order members seem more able to adapt to environmental demands and to achieve work satisfaction *without undermining mission commitment*. Nonetheless, the orders are experiencing difficulties in recruiting the young, and their median age is rising. Among other things, perhaps this reflects the problem of working in an era when many young people have become wary of long-term commitments.

Chapter 5 is a kind of companion piece to Chapter 4. Winter here seeks to probe how and why emerging Protestantdom first lost, then partly recovered the functional equivalent of the religious orders. The groups he studies are largely from the independent "evangelical" tradition which have become so successful in the last decade. With a good sense of history, he terms the split between the central, denominational governing structures (termed "modalities") and the specialized, autonomous, voluntary mission agencies (termed "sodalities") as the "other Protestant schism." Thus, he sees groups like the Inter-Varsity Christian Fellowship, the Navigators, and Campus Crusade as functionally equivalent "Protestant orders" possessing commitment and discipline. While the Protestant agencies made marriage permissive, they made "poverty" their main evangelical counsel.

Winter delineates four types of structural relationships for these mission agencies, ranging from maximum unification and integration with denominational governments (type A) over to minimum integration and total independence (type D). He traces a long-run shift from type D to C (and even to A by 1950); but more recently he notes an increase in independent societies (type D), whereby even local organizations financially sponsor and commission missionaries. Whereas he sees most Catholic orders and European Protestant mission societies as *intermediate* and so fitting under type C, most American Protestant mission operations appear to fall at either extreme, either type A or D. He thinks the strong development of independent type D groups gives evidence of a lack of consensus in American denominations. He sees in the independents a parallel to the Catholic "military" orders and a free enterprise, entrepreneurial style. He is not uncritical of the evangelical movements, however, noting that they at times appear to bypass even the local congregation, as well as the denomination. On the one hand, he urges denominations to reassess their "abandonment" of such voluntary agencies and construct a new cooptative relationship with them; on the other, he urges the independent societies to reevaluate their condescension over against the denominations and develop ties with them, especially in the task of theological training. It is interesting that the same kind of competition occurred over 100 years ago in American church history. (A related type of competition, but on a different scale and related to the recent ecumenical movement, will be treated in Chapter 11 of this volume).

In Chapter 6, we move on to a different type of denominational sub-agency—the seminary, or "theological school" as it is more and more being called. The theological school is an important service agency of denominations, frequently serving as a kind of ecclesiastical "flagship" for the denomination as-a-whole. The seminary has often acted as an entry-point for change in theology and the denomination's "lifestyle." Hartley and Schuller in their chapter provide an impressionistic summary of trends related to theological schools, especially focusing on a view of the interorganizational field and network in which they are imbedded. American theological schools in the recent period appear to have moved to Emery and Trist's "disturbed-reactive" stage, including the development of a seminary "trade association." The authors note the major influence variables acting upon the seminary—the parent denomination and its confessional tradition (if any), the American university, the government, foundations and funding organizations, the seminary's local area. Of these, the denomination has been the most important for faculty, students, finances, field experience and placement of graduates, etc. Since World War II, however, seminaries have begun to lose their isolation, and many have begun to take the university and its scientific learning as their reference group and intellectual resource for faculty and students. The Association of Theological Schools as the trade association assists this declining isolation. Theological schools, however, may soon be confronting the dilemma of too little vs. too much isolation. How can they maintain ties to both the "world" and their denominational constituencies?

Among the strains being felt by theological schools Hartley and Schuller mention the following: a growing gap between number of graduates (including women) and pastoral positions available; the competition between university-scientific and denominational-confessional norms; choice of emphasis in curricula between a charismatic-spiritual vs. organizational focus; local-regional vs. national accountability in funding; beaming program to the theological candidate vs. the veteran-in-service as the seminary's constituency. The presence of these strains makes it very clear that the seminary's present situation is truly an "open system."

Of all denominational elements, the parish or local congregational level is the one to which most sociological and in-house denominational researches have been directed. Unfortunately, however, the models used to direct this research have seldom been made explicit. Everett Perry, in Chapter 7, seeks primarily to elucidate the models historically in use. He draws from his thirty years of observation as a national executive of a leading Protestant denomination strongly involved in research and planning for the local church. On the basis of his own experience and the vast, informal, in-house literature on parish planning, he points to the dialectic existing over the years between the missionary tasks as seen by the denominations and the particular models of parish employed in church planning strategies. He notes also the tension existing between individual and social conceptions of mission, between the concepts of "to be" over against "to do."

Perry then evaluates the strengths and weaknesses of each of the following models successively employed for congregational planning: the ecological, the goal attainment, and the voluntary association models. The ecological, while placing a premium on adaptation to the external environment, perhaps went too far overboard in making the congregation a prisoner of its environment. The goal-attainment approach allowed more room for informal definition of purpose, use of outside consultants, initiation on the part of the congregation, and linkage with sister congregations in the same geographic area as a way to expand resources. More recently, in the face of local resistances to national planning, the congregation is now seen as a voluntary association, frequently composed of a diversity of laypersons who are led best via a process of persuasion. He underlines the complexity of the process of trying to develop consensus among groups of diversified lay members;

also the difficulty of trying to combine "solidary"-expressive and task-oriented emphases in the same group. Thus, it becomes exceedingly difficult to develop a radical concept of mission and simultaneously maintain group solidarity. He also raises the question of specializing for "mission" on various levels within the denomination. Undoubtedly, it is easier for church professionals somewhat removed from local accountability to employ more radical concepts of mission (e.g., social justice); however, the parish level may be better suited as an expressive rather than goal-attaining organization. He concludes his chapter by recommending that all strategies be combined in what he terms a "systems motivational" model.

In the last chapter in this section, Chapter 8, Hesser treats a denominational "element" on another level than that of the sub-groups of religious order, mission society, seminary, and congregation—the level of the religious professional. In many ways, the clergyman (or clergyperson, as Hesser terms this individual) is a microcosm of the structures in which he (she) must operate. Perhaps people in no other occupational position have had to face as many conflicting demands as do ministers, priests, and rabbis. In his treatment of religious professionals (primarily Protestant clergymen), Hesser adopts an open systems perspective utilizing the concepts of "institutional dilemma" and "role strain." The pastor of a local church is burdened with the dilemmas not only facing churchmanship-in-general in modern society but also those of being a kind of manager or man-in-the-middle poised between the competing expectations of his lay employers, his local community, and the "higher" levels of his ecclesiastical system. Hesser notes that, in contrast to "problems" (which respond to diagnosis and solution), the pastor's "dilemmas" *defy* solution and can only be "lived with" or accommodated to. Dilemmas are strains which grow out of the complexity of having simultaneously to meet several competing demands.

To begin, the pastor is and isn't prepared for the task by background. The clergyperson's personal strain is aggravated by unrealistic expectations, mixed motivations, being compelled to undergo premature adult socialization as a child (!), idealization of future role while in seminary, lack of coordination between the training, recruiting, and hiring systems, and lack of organizational sophistication and realism in the hortatory (reference group) literature on the ministry (at least that existing prior to World War II—he maintains that a sociological naivete concerning "organization" has been present in both theological and practical literature). Furthermore, the "anti-institutional" criticism of the late '60s has been no help either in comprehending such dilemmas. (The sole exception was the recommendation by H. Richard Niebuhr and associates in the 1950s, of the concept of minister as "pastoral director.")

The congregation itself may impose multiple and often conflicting goals—mission vs. maintenance (just referred to by Perry in the preceding chapter), change vs. conservatism (like Perry's "to do" vs. "to be"); choosing between clergy peers vs. lay members as standard for role performance. The religious professional also experiences gnawing inadequacies over "authority"; isolation, social distance, and lack of feedback; and lack of know-how in building small, communal group structures. Then there is the tragic irony whereby pastors complain of "having to spend too much time on administration," yet feeling no legitimate warrant for this task.

His solutions for these problems are continuing education, changes in recruitment process, provision of more training of seminarians as group catalyzers and facilitators of decision-making. He has omitted an important strategy noted by Sister Kim in Chapter 2—the articulation of a system of specialization within ministry and possibly also within congregations by means of restructuring them into types of specialized corps.

The chapters in this section again illustrate the point that there is no one best way; and that churchmen should feel free to borrow liberally from models and stances in other sectors—as long as they also can maintain the genius and unique "mission" of the churches as divine-human organizations.

4

Catholic Religious Orders In Sociological Perspective

Thomas M. Gannon, S. J.

One of the more intriguing organizational phenomena within Roman Catholicism is the religious order. Weber and Troeltsch were the first in sociology to point to the importance for a large institutional body like the Catholic Church of affiliated monastic groups with a highly religious ethic.[1] The idea that such communities represent a "leaven within the lump" which is somehow able to revive and stimulate the larger organization is familiar to theologians, historians, and sociologists alike. It is also apparent that similar groups play a parallel role in political parties.

My purpose in this chapter will be to examine this organizational phenomenon as a major instrument for carrying out the mission of the church in maintaining and communicating religious beliefs to laymen and non-believers, as well as a vigorous embodiment of a rigorous interpretation of the normative obligations existing in the Christian tradition. This examination will include a brief historical review of the origins and development of Catholic religious orders and a summary of some recent empirical research on the changing attitudes and beliefs of those who belong to religious orders today. These historical and sociological data will provide some insight, I believe, into what contributions such specialized organizations can make to the future development of the church's mission, as well as the particular problems these organizations create for large church bureaucracies. The focus will be on religious orders within Roman Catholicism, since even though this organizational phenomenon can be found in many religious systems—in Eastern and Western Christianity, as well as in Buddhism, Hinduism, Mohammedanism, and Taoism—it is in the Roman Catholic Church that they have reached by far their fullest development.

The major themes of the present chapter, therefore, will center on the social organizational aspects of the religious order. As a result, many sociological and theological issues will be omitted. One of these, for example, is the puzzling question arising out of traditional Catholic doctrine on the "states of perfection," which appears to place those who choose membership in a religious order in a qualitatively "superior" elite status which more closely approximates the ideal of following Christ than does the lay state. Such an anachronistic survival of the feudal system seems incongruous in the context of Vatican II's emphasis on the "pilgrim church" and the collegial relationship of all sectors of the church to its collaborative mission in the world.[2]

If we leave aside the purely religious aspects of these groups and confine ourselves to their sociological significance, several key issues are pertinent to the concerns of this chapter. First, there is need to define the religious order as an organizational type. This will involve distinguishing orders from mass religion, purely charismatic movements, and sects and comparing them with other related types of organization commonly treated in sociology, e.g., voluntary organizations, total institutions, normative organizations, etc.[3] A second major concern is the influence which religious orders have on the lives of their members. The formal definition of "religious life" establishes an ideal against which individual members must balance their expectations and those of their peers, as well as clients and other "outsiders." In the process of balancing these forces, members arrive at an organizational structure and style of life which is unique to them and which represents a true social compromise between their life as defined by formal religious principles and life as it must be lived by men and women in a particular society. Perhaps "compromise" is an improper choice of terms; for in meeting the demands of their vocation, individuals do not set out to devalue religious ideas, but to give them substance in the exchanges they have with fellow "religious" and those outside the order. Members of an order, therefore, give religion a reality through their *lifestyle*.

Because religious orders are both social and historical entities and because the various organizational forms they have taken are strongly linked to the historical situations in which they arose, I will then turn to the question of a formal definition of religious orders as an organizational type, drawing upon relevant literature in sociological theory and the sociology of organizations as this applies to religious orders. The next section of the chapter will present a review of some recent empirical data on the present situation of the orders and their influence on members' beliefs, attitudes, and behavior. The chapter will conclude with an assessment of the problems facing Catholic religious orders today in a period of rapid social and religious change and some remarks about their future.

THE RELIGIOUS ORDER IN
HISTORICAL PERSPECTIVE

Origins and Development

Religious orders within Catholicism owe their origin to two major factors. First, there was the gradual differentiation within Christian consciousness between the realms of the secular and sacred. As Durkheim stated with some creative exaggeration: "Originally [religion] pervades everything; everything social is religious; the two words are synonymous. Then, little by little, political, economic, and scientific functions free themselves from the religious function, constitute themselves apart and take on a more and more acknowledged temporal character."[4] Second, there was an increasingly felt need for more radical Christian witness—both prophetic and charismatic—than what could be proclaimed within the hierarchical structure of the church.

These two factors came together as a combined influence in reaction to the great persecutions which Christianity endured in the third century.[5] To these persecutions Christians reacted in different ways: some remained steadfast in their faith and became martyrs, some lapsed from the church, others hid themselves in remote places. Thus, in the deserts of the Near East, there arose the first monastic communities which continued to exist, even to multiply, after the persecutions had ceased. One of the reasons for the interest in monastic isolation was its appeal as a peacetime martyrdom. In the lull following the Diocletian persecution, when accommodation was reached between church and empire, the more zealous Christians began to flee the "city of man" for the "desert of God." They formed themselves into celibate communities and bound themselves to the ascetic and evangelical virtues of chastity, poverty, and (later) obedience. The hard desert life became a dry martyrdom replacing the bloody witness of the persecutions. Sometimes men were encouraged to go out to the desert because they had spoken up prophetically against heresies and social and political injustice. As the early Theodosian Code proscribed: "If any persons shall be found in the profession of monks, they shall be ordered to seek out and to inhabit desert places and desolate solitudes."[6]

The traditions of early monasticism indicate that the monks were a rugged and unruly group. The need for rules was seen quickly. The most important monastic rule in the Eastern church is associated with the name of Basil (d. 397). Western monasticism, however, became and remained *Benedictine*, so named after Benedict of Nursia in Italy, who founded his first community at Monte Cassino in 528. Its vitality and flexibility can be judged from the fact that Benedictine monasticism endures in modern Catholicism in a vigorous condition. Without question, it represents the mature development of the monastic ideal.

The power of the Benedictine Rule lies in its simplicity.[7] It calls for a rhythmic balance and order among the essential components of the monastic life: personal prayer and asceticism, solemn communal prayer and public liturgy, manual labor. The life is lived in common, including common meals and common recreation. The ancient Benedictine tradition, in fact, left the monk little privacy, and the type of intellectual and pastoral work in which many modern Benedictines engage has forced some revision of this tradition. Benedictine government is loose and paternal, its spirit of community is fraternal. The head of the community (the abbot) is elected for life; like the father of a family he does not serve a term of office. His government is more the work of his personal charisma than of executive management. Such an organization allows for variations in the spirit which can be found in different monasteries, all accepting the same rule. In theory and practice, each Benedictine monastery is a fairly independent religious community, in spite of Catholicism's traditional proclivity toward centralized administration.

The strong community orientation of Western monasticism typified a manifest change in orientation from the earlier forms of "pre-monastic" hermit (or "eremitic") life. Committed by a vow of "stability" to live within the monastery they joined, original Benedictinism still retained the earlier Eastern tradition of "withdrawal" from the world. The harmony between prayer, liturgy, and work was designed to prevent the purely individualist pursuit of austere asceticism. Their daily solemn and communal public prayer exemplified a new form of communitarian religiosity. Likewise, the Benedictine motto, *ora et labora*, stressed the inherent value of work as well as prayer. The Benedictine model did not maintain complete withdrawal from the activities of society and culture, despite the limitations placed upon it by confinement to the cloister. Because of their emphasis on public liturgical prayer, as well as their increasing involvement in pastoral activities, the Benedictines jettisoned the earlier anti-clericalism so prevalent among the premonastic forms of religious life. Moreover, life self-governing and economically independent family households, the abbeys formed a natural part of the secular community and exercised significant influence on the society around them.

The overall importance and positive strength of the Benedictine model does not imply that it had no unfavorable aspects; nor does it imply that monasticism endured for all these centuries with no ups and downs and no reforms. One of the recurring themes in the various reform movements within Benedictinism was the desire both to return to a more solitary kind of life emphasized in early hermit-type monachism (the "eremitic ideal") and to place greater emphasis on the single-minded pursuit of holiness through prayer and reflection (the "contemplative ideal"). The attractiveness of these two ideals was certainly strengthened by the desire to break monasticism's ties with temporal society and prosperity —bonds that developed during the Dark Ages and led many monasteries away from certain fundamental observances of the religious life. Consequently, these reform movements sought to restore separation from the world, real poverty, and manual labor. Moreover, the low level of Christian life itself, especially among the diocesan clergy, drove men up the wild mountain sides just as the corrupt state of society in the fourth century had driven men into the desert. Behind this movement, therefore, stood the profound belief that the austere and holy life of the man of God would powerfully contribute to the Christian upbuilding of society at large.

The monastic reform movements reached their peak in the eleventh and twelfth centuries, and a number of the orders founded during that time continue to the present day. This reform represented a significant stage in the development of Catholic religious orders and promoted a qualitatively different monastic-type orientation. One of the best known of these reform orders is the Cistercian Order of the Strict Observance, more commonly known as *Trappists*, because of their origin from the French Cistertian Abbey at La Trappe. Like other eleventh and twelfth century semieremitic movements, the Trappist follow the Rule of Benedict and interpret it most strictly. The Trappist life is one of poverty, simplicity, self-support by the monk's own labor, and hermit-like solitude achieved by strict silence. The single goal of this type of order was and remains the pursuit of the contemplative life.

This swing of the pendulum between relaxation and stricter observance of an original religious rule (e.g., the Rule of Benedict) is a noteworthy feature of the historical development of religious orders and the shifts within individual groups. It is also significant that the reforms in the old-established monastic orders had two effects: they limited the autonomy of individual abbeys and, at the same time, demonstrated the need for a common bond of authority between them. To supply this need, there arose monastic congregations, i.e., associations of several independent monasteries of the same order, under the control of a single superior. Monastic autonomy was preserved, however, since this superior was not directly responsible to the Roman administration of the church.

Parallel to the reform of monasticism was the emergence of a modified monastic movement called *Canons Regular*.[8] When celibacy for the diocesan clergy was universally introduced in the early Middle Ages, many of these priests also felt the desire for community life, even though they were occupied with pastoral work in the world. In particular, the clergy attached to cathedrals and large churches formed themselves into "chapters" and developed a lifestyle which had much in common with traditional monasticism. Members of these chapters were called Canon Regulars. The Canons were mostly recruited from wealthy and aristocratic families. Except for the fact that each person retained his own personal property, the Canons regulated their lives by the general observance of monastic practices. They formed independent communities under their own superior; they were exempt from the direct authority of the bishop, but continued to fulfill their pastoral and parochial functions (e.g., the Norbertines). The kinds of work they did, however, made necessary some departures from the purely monastic way of life. Complete segregation from the world and permanent residence in one place was impossible and pastoral activities necessarily replaced manual labor. In short, the lifestyle of the Canons Regular clearly demonstrated how religious life could be combined with active service to the church in the world.

The Emergence of "Apostolic" Religious Orders

A new chapter in the history of religious orders opens at the beginning of the thirteenth century with the appearance of the so-called "mendicants"—the *Dominicans* and *Franciscans*. These orders were products of the revolutionary political and social changes of the late Middle Ages: the collapse of feudalism and growth of towns and cities, the emergence of a town and country proletariat, migratory movements of the population, the progress of physical science, and the prevalence of heresies. The uneducated diocesan clergy were ill-equipped to supply the needs of a society that had broken adrift from its spiritual moorings. The older (rural) monastic orders were even less able to supply these needs.

The Franciscans set up their chapels and "convents" among the people, in the "suburbs" outside the town walls. Under the kindly leadership of the poverty-loving Francis of Assisi, they broke away from the traditional isolation of monastic life, a life sheltered from economic want which in the older orders had too often led their members into worldliness and materialism. Dominic, a Canon Regular, was a contemporary of Francis. He joined his followers into a centralized organization to combat heresy by means of the spoken word. Dominican houses were founded in the neighborhood of universities and in the center of cities near the residences of its leading citizens.

Thus, the emergence of the mendicants gave substantial evidence of a corporate desire to pursue the ideal Christian life in a way that would avoid the corruptions experienced by so many monasteries.[9] Even though a large portion of the original patterns of monastic life was still retained in the structure of the Franciscan and Dominican orders, these groups also represented a further rationalization of religious orders in the direction of emphasizing service to the world by preaching and good works. The mendicant groups were, most simply, apostolic brotherhoods that reintroduced indefatigable journeying for the sake of the gospel. They were international and centralized bodies divided geographically into regional provinces, which elected or appointed their major administrators according to a recognized constitutional system. These administrators and general meetings of the order held full jurisdiction over every house and friar. The resulting unified command and the abandonment of monastic-type stability gave the friars a flexibility and mobility that were completely new in the history of religious orders. Founded also when the papacy had reached the zenith of its influence, the mendicants were closely tied to Rome and soon became effective agents of papal policy.

Although there is great similarity between the Franciscan and Dominican orders, one particular difference is significant. The Franciscan movement originated as a *sectarian form of lay religion* and, in its beginnings, received no formal recognition by the church. Gradually, however, the church recognized its value and incorporated it into its structures, using it precisely to win back the religiously endangered city populations. Despite this incorporation, the Franciscans still retained a strong orientation toward lay religion and a form of spirituality which was egalitarian and somewhat unsympathetic to the feudalism of the institutional church.[10] The Dominicans, in contrast, were notably more clerical in orientation and the order was directed toward scholarly research and teaching and the integration of secular thought and Catholic theology (best exemplified by one of their early members, Thomas Aquinas).

This trend toward what Etzioni calls a "dual normative-utilitarian" type organization,[11] exemplified by the mendicants, reached its full development in the sixteenth century with the founding of the Society of Jesus, more commonly known as the *Jesuits*. From the days of the Renaissance, Western society had grown continuously more complex and presented the church with an increasing variety of problems. The perennial need to supplement the ranks and effectiveness of the parish clergy, the demand for institutions to care for orphans, the sick, and the aged, the growing educational needs of Catholics, the opening of new areas of the world to European influence, and the challenges raised by the French Revolution posed new and unanticipated challenges. This was the social context within which the Jesuits originated. Like the Friars, the Jesuits chose a sphere of activity that had no geographic limits, and they constructed an organizational form that was intended to respond to the mentality of a new society as radically different from that of Francis and Dominic, as the latter had been from that of Benedict—in particular, a society which was attaching ever more importance to secular activity and a church that was struggling with widespread corruption of morals and the religious doubts raised by the challenge of Protestantism.

Probably the most significant characteristic of this new order was its institutionalized diffuseness of purpose. While most *earlier* religious groups were founded with *specific* goals in mind, the Jesuits' organizational goals can be stated only in *diffuse* terms, such as "service to the church" or the "salvation of ourselves and our neighbors." Quite simply, the purpose of the Society of Jesus was to go out into the world, to influence it, and to Christianize it by direct contact. To this end it encouraged all kinds of apostolic endeavor in any part of the globe. To insure the greatest possible success in this work, it was willing to adopt any reasonable methods that were appropriate and was ready to depart from traditional ideas if necessary. In a word, *tradition*, so powerful in the older groups, *yielded to* practical *utility*. Preaching, teaching, scientific work—all were to be organized in whatever manner might be most efficient in the prevailing circumstances. The stereotype of the "Jesuit" is a person who craftily adopts whatever dubious means are available to accomplish his intended purposes. Such an image can at least partly be attributed to the multiplicity of forms that Jesuit activity has taken, as well as to the bureaucratic rationality and instrumental character of the organization, exemplified by the rapid interchangeability of work roles. In its structure, the Jesuit order much resembles a modern business organization. Authority is centralized, the responsibilities and powers of each individual are clearly defined, the division of labor is based on practical needs and aptitudes, and working conditions and discipline are to be adapted to each member's capabilities.

The emergence of the Jesuits, therefore, represents a highly original structure and came at the end of a long process of organizational development.[12] Its central features included professionalism, rationality, geographical mobility, individual autonomy, and radical "this-worldly" asceticism. Risking over-simplification, it might be said that the abbey of early monasticism looked *inward* toward the sanctification of the religious order. The mendicant orders looked in two directions: *inward* toward community holiness, *and outward* toward salvation of the neighbor. The Jesuits looked *upward, outward, and inward*: up toward the glory of God, out toward the apostolate, in toward personal holiness. In overall thrust, however, it was the apostolate (or mission) that provided Jesuits with their organizational and individual focus.

More Recent Variations

Although the history of Catholic religious orders does not end with the Society of Jesus, all orders established since then have been strongly influenced by the Jesuit model. While most of these groups may seem like "variations on a theme," the variations bear the marks of the spiritual and social conditions of the different times they were founded. For example, in addition to the Jesuits (and other groups of similar structure which fall under the Catholic juridical classification of "Clerks Regular"), the sixteenth century saw the introduction of the *Religious Society*—a type of organization much different from the orders we have been discussing, because its members were priests living in community but *without vows*. Philip Neri originated this form of life when he founded the Oratory at Rome in 1575. Its members sought holiness by following the evangelical counsels and engaging in the priestly ministry. The Oratorians are made up of individual foundations united only by the bond of fraternal charity, common Constitutions, and general statutes; one of the most famous of the Oratorians was John Henry Newman. Other early Religious Societies included the Vincentians, founded by Vincent de Paul in 1625 for preaching missions to the rural poor, and the Paris Foreign Mission Society (1660), that chose Asia as its field of labor. Some, such as the Sulpicians (1642) and Eudists (1643), were founded to provide seminary training for diocesan clergy. More recent Societies like the Paulists (1858), the Josephites (1866), the White Fathers (1868), the Society of the Divine Word (1875), the Maryknoll Missionaries (1911) and the Glenmary Missionaries (1939)—the last two of which were established in the United States—devote themselves to the foreign missions or other largely non-Catholic home regions.

The eighteenth and early nineteenth centuries witnessed the growth of another variation in the religious order—the development of *religious congregations*. Similar to the other orders already described, these groups emerged during a time when the Catholic population faced profound crisis. Seldom before, in fact, had the position of the church been so critical. Not only was it faced by radical unbelief, the passing of an old social and political order, the dechristianization of society, but it had also lost many of its traditional educational, social welfare, and other church-related agencies. The French Revolution, the secularization of church property in Germany, and the subsequent suppression of religious communities in Latin countries greatly weakened Catholic religious life nearly everywhere in Europe and Latin America. The Church had already been deprived of the services of the Jesuits, with their suppression in 1773. Where other religious groups survived, they were weak and ineffective. The large number of new groups that rushed in to fill this vacuum did so on the presumption that it was easier to begin new communities than to revive the old ones. Such groups including the Passionists (1720), Redemptorists (1732), the Fathers of the Sacred Heart (1800), the Congregation of the Holy Cross (1837), and many others devoted to the Virgin Mary or one of the saints sought to revitalize

Christian life by appealing to fundamental Christian mysteries and devotions.

In organizational form, most of these new groups resembled the Jesuits: purpose and utility dominated their lifestyles to the subordination of "internal" goals such as community prayer and stability. They differed from the Jesuits in that most were founded for specific rather than diffuse purposes—education, foreign mission work, care of the sick. A further difference is constitutional. All religious communities pronounce three vows of poverty, chastity, and obedience. Sociologically, these vows represent the voluntary commitment of members to the group and form the basis of the group's solidarity. Theologically, vows are distinguished as "solemn" and "simple." Although this distinction is not easy to explain in practice, theoretically, *solemn* vows admit of *no dispensation*; they are considered a dedication which approaches the permanence of marriage or priestly ordination. *Simple* vows may be taken *for a specified period* of years, and such temporary vows are common practice in many of these newer religious groups.[13] Except for Religious Societies, all the groups previously described are groups in which *solemn vows* are taken; in canonical terms they are called *orders*. Groups whose members are bound together by *simple vows* are, in canon law, called *congregations*. The importance of this distinction, however, lies neither in theological nor canonical terms, but in its implications for the social organization of the particular group in question, namely, an organization which rests on a solemn, permanent, and theoretically non-dispensable voluntary commitment versus an organization which rests on a simple, temporary, renewable group commitment.

To complete this brief sketch of Catholic religious orders, some mention should be made of the fact that throughout their history many groups have become further differentiated by the addition of different organizational branches. What might be called the male branch is called the "first order." Where they exist, female branches are called the "second order" (e.g., Benedictines, Trappists, Franciscans, Dominicans). Diocesan clergy, laity, and other religious not under solemn vows, may join a "third order" (e.g., Benedictines, Trappists, Franciscans, Dominicans). Besides these "second orders," semi-autonomous orders of women have been in existence since the fourth century.[14] The largest increase in these female groups occurred during the eighteenth and nineteenth centuries, and most of them took the form of religious congregations. For present purposes, it can be said that the history of women's orders parallels that of men's orders in major developments and characteristic themes. While the principal focus of this chapter is on the male groups, most of the following analysis and comments aptly apply to female orders as well.[15]

THE RELIGIOUS ORDER AS AN ORGANIZATIONAL TYPE

The enormous variety of religious orders within Roman Catholicism has remained a significant aspect of its organizational life. It is no easy task to group these orders together within a single sociological category. As a first step, several important conclusions can be drawn from the preceding historical description.

1. Common to all religious orders is separation from the world, in greater or lesser degree. Members of these orders withdraw or detach themselves from worldly pursuits to devote themselves to higher spiritual goals which they feel cannot be achieved in the social and cultural milieu in which they would otherwise live. They are ascetics, giving up the satisfaction of life in secular society in order to devote themselves more to God and the service of their fellow men. But this separation can never be absolute or entire. It is, rather, a highly selective modification of a given social and cultural pattern. The common basis of all orders is a spiritual idea, expressed by selective emphasis on particular Scriptural injunctions and rules of conduct, which the Catholic Church does not impose upon all its members but leaves to the free choice of individuals or groups who strive for greater spiritual ideals and more formal and full-time involvement in religiously related activities.

2. The founders of religious orders came forward during times of religious crisis, and only after a period of waiting. The declining fervor of the early church ended with the beginning of hermit life in the desert. Reaction to the decay in Christian living in the Dark Ages (c. 850) produced the first monastic orders in the West and the later movements of monastic reform. These reforms looked for inspiration to the Scriptures and the example of the early church, and from this renewed interest there arose the trial and error of the itinerant preachers, the Canons Regular, and the penitential apostolic brotherhoods. Both saints and heretics came from these brotherhoods and, after a century of experiment, Dominic and Francis. The stagnation of the late Middle Ages resulted not only in Martin Luther but in Ignatius Loyola. The aftermath of the French Revolution occasioned one of the most flourishing periods in the history of Catholic religious orders.

3. The long history of Catholic "religious" has gone through two great phases. An inverse process of growth took place in each. From Anthony to Dominic, the community constantly gained at the expense of the individual religious. Moving from the complete liberty of the hermit to the first community under Pachomius, monasticism constantly progressed toward an

ever-greater control over the individual monk. Since the thirteenth century, however, the individual religious has gained greater freedom and mobility, and the influence of "community" has lessened. The Canons Regular slackened the ties of community enough to permit a limited sphere of worldly activity. Dominic and Francis threw the door wide open. The Friars carried the religious life out into the world. With Ignatius, this loosening of the bonds of community was greatly accelerated. Freedom of movement became the symbol of modern religious life and created the context for extensive involvement in a large number of works. This opening of the doors that kept the monk in his monastery began when the priestly and religious professions were united. Until the rise of the Canons Regular, monasticism was predominantly a *lay* institution, even after its choir monks became priests. But it took 200 years more before the Friars broke the shackles that bound the Canons to a single church. Since then, the priestly orders have brought to mature development the two principal elements of professional religious life—the contemplative and the apostolic.

4. Over time, religious orders have also experienced a continuous leveling process, similar to what Weber called the "routinization of charisma."[16] Regardless of an order's originality, it is inevitably influenced by the society and culture around it, as well as by the emergence of new orders and religious movements. For example, the free-wheeling, unsystematized asceticism of the medieval orders was strongly affected by modern spiritual practices: retreats, systematized methods of meditation, etc. This routinization is also related to the fact the members of religious orders are usually involved in very similar kinds of work. Almost all religious order priests preach, teach, work in the foreign missions, run parishes, etc. Moreover, in contrast to the other major organizational unit of Catholic priests, the diocesan clergy, religious order priests as a whole—regardless of their specific group identity—represented a break with past institutional clerical forms and thus offered the possibility of *new* patterns of priestly community and work style, functioning as a flexible work force within the Catholic Church. Since they were neither bound by the territorial limits of a parish or diocese nor operated entirely under the jurisdiction of a local bishop, these groups could be used and, in fact, were used by the papacy to provide important specialized services for the church in education, social work, and missionary activity.

5. Despite this leveling process and similarity in work functions, the major religious orders each contain within their own traditions a distinct character. It is difficult to explain to the outsider how religious orders each feel they have a peculiar

spirit and style which differentiates them from every other group. Not only do they feel this, but members of a group can usually describe it if they are asked. They are quite jealous of their identity; and their preservation of peculiarities in domestic customs and costume, as well as their achievements and the great men who have been among their members, have much to do with this sense of group identity. Therefore, religious orders are convinced that each of them has its "corporate personality," and one who does not see it is kindly forgiven as not being very perceptive!

6. While this distinctiveness is an aspect of the multiplication of these orders throughout the history of Catholicism and contributes to their sometimes bewildering diversity, a rather clear theoretical distinction can be made between the *monastic* (e.g., Benedictines, Trappists, etc.) and *apostolic* orders like the Jesuits. The "ideal type" monastic order conforms to a type of relatively small, personalized group, all of whose members live and work within the same physical community; work is more generalized and, in the stricter monastic groups, more focused on the needs of members and their common life; when the monastery engages in service, it brings outsiders to it in the fashion of a resource center. Both to members and outsiders, consequently, the definition of the order is based on the direct experiences of every member with every other member of the group. In contrast, the apostolic order represents a more abstract and complex form of social organization that permits more impersonal, segmental relationships among its members. Its government is more centralized and bureaucratic; its members more mobile. Work is more diverse and often more specialized, and the objectives of service center more on those outside the religious order than on the order's own members. Consequently, the apostolic order's self definition is based more on abstract notions about who belongs to the group, the work and status roles of its members, value systems and symbols common to the group.

7. One of the most striking features of Catholic religious orders is to their amazing durability. Christianity has always been sufficiently vital to throw off new rules, austerities, and forms of asceticism. But in so doing, the older forms do not die; all the major Catholic religious orders still survive. And sometimes an older type order returns to prominence, holds public interest, attracts members, and inspires a generation until its place is taken by another. For example, the near extinction of the Jesuits after 1773 has been so completely reversed that the order is stronger in numbers and influence today than it was before Pope Clement XIV suppressed it. The Dominicans, described by Newman as a "great ideal now extinct," sprang back to life under the influence of Lacordaire precisely when

that gloomy judgment was being written. The first half of the twentieth century witnessed an unexpected growth in candidates to centuries-old contemplative orders.

8. This durability is linked to what Weber called "virtuoso" religion.[17] Virtuoso religion follows what is taken to be a pure and rigorous interpretation of obligations which already exist in a religious tradition. It is extremist, and the monastic ideal of perfection or the apostolic ideal of perfection and service has always been seen in terms of extremism. While all the major orders have been founded by leaders with certain charismatic qualities, the resulting formal organizations should be distinguished from charismatic movements. In contrast with the vigorous restatement of an existing religious tradition, charisma shatters what already exists and articulates an entirely new basis of normative obligation. Charismatic movements aim not at pursuing ethical or religious ideals "to the letter," since to members of charismatic movements "the letter" has been effectively destroyed. While the typical statement of charismatic religion can be given as, "It is written, but I say to you. . .," the characteristic statement of virtuoso religion is "It is written, and I *insist*. . ." *Charismatics proclaim a message; virtuosi proclaim a method.* This distinction is important because it helps to explain how religious orders have been legitimated historically. Virtuoso religion typically refers back to a strongly-valued source of tradition which it restates and seeks to emulate. Thus, tradition is the basis on which virtuoso religion claims legitimacy. The way in which the tradition is used, however, involves a specific version of historical change. It is this traditional *legitimation* that also *distinguishes* religious *orders from sects*. The sect internalizes its own authority, while orders derive their authority ultimately from the parent church. Moreover, as offshoots of a more universalistic church, orders do not involve the same rejection of church compromise with the world or the same hostility to society as sects.[18]

9. Although Weber's concept of virtuoso religion helps to identify orders as religious phenomena, the preceding historical survey also provides direction for identifying religious orders as an organizational type. Broadly defined, a religious order is an organization recognized by the church, either centralized and hierarchically governed or locally governed but bound to uniformity of Rule and observance; its members are priests, or laymen (brothers), or priests and laymen, or laywomen (sisters) who have committed themselves to the goals of the organization and who live "in community"—the degree of which will vary between different orders—and who accept as binding on themselves more exacting moral and spiritual injunctions than those proposed for the church at large.

This definition can be given more precision by making explicit the elements it implies, thus constructing characteristics that form an "ideal type," compared with which we can study concrete examples. In sociological theory, this type most closely approximates Etzioni's concept of a normative organization.[19]

a. The religious order is an organization in that the behavior of each member is in some way coordinated with the behaviors of all other members; thus, a certain unity of action will be found among members of an order. The goals of this action are cultural and expressive rather than economic or related to maintaining or fostering social order (i.e., instrumental).

b. The religious order only exists as part of a larger church-type body, although it always maintains a certain degree of moral and organizational autonomy.

c. The members of the order consider themselves and are considered members throughout their period of membership. Hence, to some degree the order always forms a quasi-familial and permanent, participating, community-based group. In principle, all the individual's behavior is incorporated into the order. If an individual occasionally exercises a high degree of autonomy, these occasions are provided by the order and are considered as an empirical result of his commitment to the order through the vow of obedience. This obedience is considerably more than the obedience the church demands from either its lay members or its clergy.

d. The religious order demands that its members renounce in principle any possession of property, so that any property used is considered to belong to the individual only insofar as the order provides for or permits such possession. In a sense, the religious order can thus be considered as a corporation, whose assets (and liabilities) are its members.

e. The religious order requires that all members of any particular branch (or the whole order, if it has no branches like "second" or "third" orders) are of only one sex and are committed to celibate chastity.

f. The religious order demands total voluntary commitment, and membership may only be gained and maintained by proof of special merit.

g. The religious order is a collection of *religious virtuosi* with an uncompromising interpretation of the Gospel ethic which is sanctioned by the church but is not mandated for all who belong to the church. Members of the order, therefore, basically seek personal perfection (or a high degree of union with God) whose spiritual ideals are specified by the goals and tradition of each order and may be defined in terms of individual or social goals or of an active or contemplative life. This spirituality is highly dependent on the orientation of the order's founder and is contained in the specific set of rules (or Constitutions) which must be submitted to church authorities before the organization is recognized.

RELIGIOUS ORDERS IN AMERICA:
THE PRESENT SITUATION

Religious order priests played a significant role in American Catholicism since before the founding of the Republic. The French and Spanish colonies in the New World were established through the efforts not only of explorers and soldiers, but of Jesuits like Louis Hennepin and Jacques Marquette, explorers of the Middle West, and of Franciscans like Junipero Serra, who established the California missions.[20] When, in the mid-seventeenth century, the English colonies of Maryland and Virginia were left without priests in the wake of the virulent Anti-Catholicism that had resurfaced in the 1640s, it was with the Jesuit Superior in England that Lord Leonard Calvert pleaded to send priests to replace those who had gone.

The first American Catholic bishop was John Carroll, cousin of a famous signer of the Declaration of Independence and brother of a signer of the Federal Constitution. John Carroll had left home for Europe at the age of thirteen, joined the Jesuits, and after the suppression of the Society of Jesus in 1773, returned to live quietly in his mother's home in Rock Creek. There he became a leader in the development of "the Corporation of the Roman Catholic Clergymen," the first priests' association in the United States, which had been established by the ex-Jesuits of Maryland and Pennsylvania who had then become diocesan clergy.[21] With the increasing number of immigrant Catholics, this original small band of American priests was augmented by Irish missionaries, groups of Dominicans and Augustinians sent from Europe and, following the Revolution in France, by a band of French refugee priests, among whom was a group of Sulpician Fathers—a teaching order that played an important role in educating the next generation of American priests and setting a model for clerical piety which would hold on for many years. And it was from these religious priests that many of the early bishops of the American Church were chosen.

Turning to contemporary times, the annual statistics published in the *Official Catholic Directory* show that, in 1975, the total number of religious priests in the United States numbered 22,904; for the same year, the *Directory* lists the number of religious sisters at 135,225 and religious brothers at 8,625.[22] Table 2 (see Chap. 2, p. 100) puts these statistics in temporal perspective by showing total United States membership of men and women's religious orders beginning in 1920 (the first year these official statistics were published); the table also provides comparable figures for diocesan clergy over the same period. Tables 1-3 provide additional information on the present situation of religious orders in the United States in terms of the geographical distribution of membership and the work religious priests do. The data cited in the last two of these tables come from the 1970 survey of the American Catholic priesthood conducted by the National Opinion Research Center.[23] The comments that follow, therefore, are principally concerned with religious priests, but since some analysis will be given of differences between diocesan and religious clergy, comparative data on diocesan priests is included in Tables 2 and 3.

The data presented in these four tables (Table 2 in Chapter 2, Tables 1-3 in present chapter) show, first, that the number of diocesan and religious clergy in the United States steadily increased since 1920, reaching its peak in the mid-1960s. The high point for diocesan priests was 1969, for religious priests and brothers 1967, and for religious sisters 1966; after this, a small but relatively steady decline has set in. Second, over the last decade, there was a 7% drop in the total number of American clergy, but a 56% decline in seminarians. Religious priests actually decreased by 10% compared to a 5% decrease in diocesan clergy. Religious order seminarians also declined by 62%, compared to a 51% decline in diocesan groups. Third, during the same ten-year period, there was a decline of 23% (from almost 170,000 to just below 130,000) in the number of religious sisters and a decline of 28% (from almost 12,000 to about 8,500) in the number of religious brothers. Fourth, in 1978 there were 25 religious orders with 200 or more priest-members; of these, four orders account for 44% of the religious priests in the United States.[24] Fifth, over half these priests (55%) are clustered in the older established Catholic regions of the northeast and north central United States. Even more diocesan clergy (75%) are located in the same regions. In addition, 16% of the religious clergy are currently working outside the United States, in contrast with 2% of the diocesan clergy. Sixth, the majority of religious priests are involved in educational work, non-parish pastoral activities, and social ministries. The largest proportion of diocesan priests do parish work. Finally, the geographical and work distributions of religious priests underscore the fact that orders function as a flexible work force in the Catholic Church. Bound neither by the territorial limits of a diocese nor operating entirely under the jurisdiction of a local bishop, these groups are used to provide important specialized services for the Church.

Additional published information allows some elaboration of the numerical decline among religious clergy in Table 2, p. 100.[25] Over the past ten years, the number of seminarians in religious orders has dropped from over 21,000 in 1967 to fewer than 6,000 in 1978. Across religious groups, this decline is not only 10%-20% greater than for diocesan clergy, but in itself has been a decline of considerable magnitude. Novices in 1978, for example, even after an exceptional rise in one year, were still only about 30% of their 1967 strength. Thus, although figures for 1976-78 indicate that the decline in novices of religious orders may be fading, sample statistics from among religious orders of men indicate

TABLE 1
NUMBER OF AMERICAN PRIESTS IN MAJOR RELIGIOUS ORDERS*

Century Founded	Initials	Name	Membership		
			1976	1977	1978
16th	S.J.	Jesuits	5,209	5,208	5,166
16th**	O.F.M.	Franciscans	2,254	2,227	2,211
6th	O.S.B.	Benedictines	1,572	1,521	1,485
18th	C.SS.R.	Redemptorists	1,023	943	938
13th	O.P.	Dominicans	990	976	931
16th**	O.F.M. Cap.	Capuchins	820	812	712
19th	O.M.I.	Oblates of Mary Immaculate	810	810	811
17th	C.M.	Vincentians	776	764	752
13th	O.F.M. Conv.	Franciscans (Conventuals)	683	670	671
19th	C.S.C.	Congregation of Holy Cross	627	618	610
4th	O.S.A.	Augustinians	602	598	596
18th	C.P.	Passionists	557	541	532
19th	C.PP.S.	Precious Blood Fathers	418	414	405
18th	C.S.Sp.	Holy Ghost Fathers	362	364	357
19th	O.S.F.S.	Oblates of St. Francis de Sales	362	371	377
19th	M.S.	LaSalette Missionaries	328	321	319
19th	S.V.D.	Divine Word Fathers	290	292	296
19th	S.M.	Marist Fathers	276	273	261
13th	T.O.R.	Third Order Regular of St. Francis	265	247	249
19th	S.D.B.	Salesians	269	264	284
19th	S.M.	Marianists	245	242	249
19th	C.S.P.	Paulists	230	237	240
19th	C.R.	Resurrectionists	219	219	218
11th	O.S.C.O.	Trappists	212	216	220
12th	O. Praem	Canons Regular of Premontre	190	189	203

TABLE 1 CONTINUED

*Source: *The Official Catholic Directory*, 1978. Reprinted by permission of P.J. Kenedy and Sons.

**Only those orders with a membership of over 200 priests in 1978 have been listed. The Franciscans originated in the early 13th century, but the order experienced considerable internal conflict from the very beginning which makes its history both interesting and complicated. The Order of Friars Minor (O.F.M.) and the Capuchins (O.F.M. Cap.) represent reform movements which eventually achieved final autonomy in the 16th century, although their formal designation retained explicit continuity to what they conceived as the "true" Franciscan tradition.

TABLE 2

GEOGRAPHICAL DISTRIBUTION OF AMERICAN PRIESTS
(Per Cent)

Geographical Region	Diocesan Priests	Religious Priests
Northeast	39%	27%
North Central	36	28
West	10	13
South	13	16
Outside U.S.	2	16

Source: 1970 NORC Survey on the American Catholic Priesthood. The weighted Ns are Diocesan = 36,035; Religious = 29,199. These are approximately twelve times the size of the actual number of observations.

TABLE 3

WORK DISTRIBUTION OF AMERICAN PRIESTS (Per Cent)*

Primary Work**	Diocesan Priests	Religious Priests
Pastoral (parish work, counseling, retreats, religious instruction)	73%	37%
Administration (in dioceses, religious orders, Catholic educational institutions)	6	12
Education (teaching in high schools, colleges/universities, seminaries)	8	24
Intellectual/cultural (writing & research, mass media, arts, further studies)	2	10
Social Action (work in agencies, community organizing, etc.)	2	1
Chaplancies (institutional, campus, and military)	7	6
Other	2	10

* The weighted Ns are Diocesan = 36,035 and Religious = 29,199. The case base varies slightly due to nonresponse.

** Primary work is defined as the job in which the priests spends the largest amount of time each working week. The category "other" includes: home missions, monastic observances, and other jobs not listed in the NORC questionnaire.

they now may have about eight novices per 100 members. While this number may be sufficient to maintain today's number of religious priests, the steady advance in the average age of today's religious personnel points to an increasingly serious replacement problem in the institutions and projects staffed by religious clergy.

The general decline in membership of religious orders due to increased withdrawals and a decrease in new recruits is but one obvious manifestation of a profound transition which Roman Catholicism has been experiencing for at least fifteen years. The Second Vatican Council (1962-1965) was a result of the early stages of this transition and a catalyst for its later stages. And as a second look at p. 100 will confirm, the steady decline in religious orders began very soon after the end of the Council.

Certainly the Council did not intend to deplete the ranks of active priests and religious professionals in the Church. The *aggiornamento* initiated in the early sixties was based on the assumption that a sincere effort to clarify and implement the practical implications for modern society of the Church's teaching, together with some additional changes in structure designed to foster fuller participation in worship and apostolic works, would revitalize and unify the Catholic population in rendering active witness to Christ. An essential condition of this revitalization was the conviction that the Church must open itself to a world which was undergoing dramatic secularization. To accomplish this revitalization, many in the church felt that *aggiornamento* must involve much more than updating of religious practices and reapplying old principles to new sets of facts. The challenge posed by the Council called for a more radical change, a sincere *resourcement*, a searching return to the ultimate sources of faith and a critical reappraisal of current structures and teaching in terms of their practical impact on human affairs.

Despite the original intent of Vatican II, by the end of the decade it became clear that the *aggiornamento* had resulted in segmentation and polarized disunity rather than unity, in disaffection and indifference rather than renewed vitality.[26] The once-clear norms and social roles within the Church no longer seemed to serve their original purpose. Official teachings of the Church on matters of sexual morality, for example, are considered unacceptable to an increasingly large number of Catholics—both clerical and lay. More insistent questions are being raised about the functioning of such Church structures as the priesthood and the traditional role of laity, as well as such Church institutions as parishes, schools, and hospitals. The previously unquestioned role of such structures and institutions within the Church no longer seems to satisfy the needs of an increasingly large number of Catholics. Since religious clergy have long functioned as a radical witness of Christian values, their sense of Catholic norms and values is critical to the Church as a whole. The next few pages will discuss these normative problems as experienced by religious priests in the second half of the 1960s.

COMPARISON OF DIOCESAN AND ORDER CLERGY

The pressures of living and working in the post-Vatican II Church are not felt in precisely the same way among all the clergy. As the 1970 NORC data reveal, some interesting *differences* can be found *between diocesan and religious priests*, as well as among different key religious orders. One of the major indices designed for the 1970 survey was a set of questions that explored priests' religious beliefs and theological perspectives.[27] These questions fall into two categories. The first concerns beliefs that focus on the relationship between God and man, conceptions about faith, the church, and the meaning of earthly existence; these beliefs offer a distinctive model of reality which constitutes an intrinsic component of priests' total religious world view. For present purposes we will concentrate on those questions which stress traditional formulations of these beliefs: the essentialist and unchanging aspect of Catholic belief, the "otherness" of God, the value of the next life, faith as acceptance of defined doctrine, the world as a moral battleground, and the church as the conscience of the world. The second category of belief items conceptualize what it means to be a priest. The identity of clergymen is, after all, qualitatively different from laymen. The clergyman focuses primarily on the realm of non-empirical and religio-ethical absolutes, functioning as a mediator between man and God. A priest's identity is also different from other professionals. The priest lacks a clearly defined technical body of knowledge that can be applied to solving empirical problems. Hence, he does not *practice* a profession as much as he *lives* it. For the most part, his base of knowledge is normative and closed, rather than scientific and open. He interprets, while his secular professional colleagues prescribe; he tries to give meaning to the event since he cannot control it.[28] In the NORC survey, then, priestly identity was measured in terms of traditional perspectives which stress the distinctness and institutional status of the priest, the primacy of preaching and sacramental (and ritual) ministry, and the priest's life-long commitment.

What the NORC data reveal is that, in 1970, approximately half the clergy endorsed traditional perspectives on basic religious beliefs (53%) and almost two-thirds (66%) on priestly identity. Clearly, the strongest predictor of theological perspective is age (= .60); only 30 per cent of those under 45 strongly subscribed to traditional formulations. There were no significant differences between diocesan and religious clergy's responses to these belief indices until one considers the degree of priests' involvement in secular work (cf. Table 4). Here, only one-third (34%) of the priests whose principal job involves high school or university teaching or administration, writing or research and publication, or some other kind of work not directly religious employment support traditional religious beliefs (34%) and traditional priestly identity (37%). However, over half of those in non-secular (or directly religious or religiously-related) jobs like parish work, counseling, institutional chaplaincies, etc. strongly endorsed traditional beliefs perspectives (55%) and identity (54%).

Examination of some other central variables in the NORC survey (cf. Table 4) shows that commitment to continue in the priesthood, acceptance of traditional church teachings on sexual morality and the positive value of priestly celibacy are all negatively affected by priests' involvement in secular work. Secular work also somewhat increases priests' problems with loneliness and authority and the likelihood of forming close friendships outside their family, clerical colleagues, and Catholics with whom they work (i.e., forming more "universalistic" friendships). In contrast, more priests whose primary job is in secular work live in larger priest-residences and appear slightly more satisfied in their jobs. Secular work is most strongly related to educational achievement.

Without doubt, these clergy differences based on secular vs. nonsecular work are influenced by age and education. Regardless of the effect of other variables, there is strong evidence that younger priests are typically less traditional in their basic beliefs, definition of priestly identity, attitudes toward celibacy and sexual morality, more lonely, and less satisfied in their work. Younger priests comprise nearly two-thirds (62%) of those engaged in secular work as their primary job. Moreover, quite apart from age differences, the consistently higher level of education among those doing secular work demonstrates the importance of this relationship.

At the same time, the impact of secular work is experienced differently in the diocesan and religious clergy. The negative influence of secular work is consistently stronger on diocesan clergy—a pattern which is particularly noticeable in clergy's basic beliefs and theological perspectives. Lack of agreement with traditional perspectives is much more evident among diocesan than religious clergy. Similarly, almost two-thirds (65%) of diocesan priests in secular work are unsure about their decision to continue in the priesthood. More of them also reject traditional perspectives on sexual morality and priestly celibacy and are more likely to report having significant problems with loneliness and authority. Despite the fact that they live with more priests, these men do not appear to have more priest friends than diocesan priests in nonsecular work nor do they express any stronger orientation toward community life. Instead, secular work increases "universalistic" friendships for diocesan clergy; it does not have this effect for religious.

TABLE 4
DIFFERENCES BETWEEN DIOCESAN AND RELIGIOUS PRIESTS IN
SECULAR AND NON-SECULAR WORK (Per Cent)

Characteristic	Diocesan		Religious	
	Secular	Non-secular	Secular	Non-secular
Education (beyond MA)	60%	25%	81%	46%
Work Satisfaction	46	37	56	44
Little Problem with Authority	24	37	37	44
Little Problem with Loneliness	43	54	56	61
Feeling of Personal Fulfillment	68	70	79	77
See Celibacy as a Value	33	53	57	66
Many Priest Friends	22	29	39	43
Many Priests in Residence	35	19	82	64
Derive Satisfaction from Being Part of a Community of Christians Working Together	60	60	62	69
Derive Satisfaction from Living the Common Life with Like-Minded Colleagues	29	37	57	65
Tendency to Form Mainly Particularistic Friendships	22	37	37	37
High Degree of Colleague Support	45	40	49	47
Endorse Traditional Beliefs	25	55	37	54
Endorse Traditional Sexual Morality	28	48	39	52
Endorse Traditional Priestly Identity	30	53	41	55
Certainly Plan to Continue in the Priesthood	35	58	55	69
Number of Cases	4,467	31,568	9,677	19,522
Per Cent	12%	88%	33%	67%

Source: 1970 NORC Survey on the American Catholic Priesthood.

Finally, even though diocesan priests in secular work are more highly trained and somewhat more satisfied than those doing non-secular jobs, a *higher educational level and greater work satisfaction remain more characteristic of religious priests*, regardless of the type of work religious do. The same inference can be made about the religious clergy's positive orientation towards community life.

The major differences, then, between diocesan and religious priests center on type of work, level of education, work satisfaction, attitudes supporting the need and value of community life, and exposure to what might be called the "clerical subculture," i.e., the number of close priest-friends, the tendency to form most of one's close friendships with other priests and Catholics with whom one works (i.e., more "particularistic" friendships), and living in large priest-residences. In Parsonian terms, these differences pertain to the adaptation and integration imperatives of the two clergy organizations.[29] Fewer diocesan/religious differences were found in those areas related to basic religious beliefs, priestly identity, continuance in the priesthood, and attitudes toward sexual morality, celibacy, and the church's use of authority and distribution of power (i.e., to the Parsonian categories of pattern-maintenance and goal-attainment). In explaining differences between these two groups, the impact of secular work is critical; and when secular work, education, and age are considered together, their combined influence is different within each of the two clergy organizations, diocesan and religious.

Although age tends to promote more agreement with traditional beliefs about God, the church, faith, and the nature of priesthood, involvement in secular work notably lessens this effect, especially when linked with higher levels of education. By itself, education appears to have a slight "de-traditionalizing" influence—an effect particularly in evidence among diocesan priests. Since the religious clergy have a much higher proportion of men doing secular work and men with more advanced and specialized education, it is not surprising that the combined influence of these factors is different in the two units. The "de-traditionalizing" influence of education on the diocesan clergy is weakened by the influence of secular work. For religious, the effect is neither as consistent nor as strong. In fact, for religious, education seems to prepare for the impact of secular work. As a result, *while religious priests in secular work* are generally *much less traditional* in their beliefs and values than those in non-secular work, *there remains more pluralism of opinion among religious priests* as a whole than is evident in the diocesan clergy. In contrast, the number of diocesan priests in secular work is smaller and so they are much more isolated as a group in their willingness to assume less traditional religious perspectives.

Variations Among Order Clergy

In comparison with these overall diocesan/religious differences, variations among specific religious orders of priests are, as one might expect, more subtle. Still, the NORC data do provide some interesting information. From the religious priest groups in the United States included in the 1970 survey, four specific groups were chosen for analysis here: the Order of St. Benedict, or more simply Benedictines (OSB); the Order of St. Francis, or Franciscans (OSF); the Society of Jesus, or Jesuits (SJ); and the Maryknoll Missionaries (MM). These groups were selected not only because they parallel the historical development of religious orders discussed earlier in this chapter, but also because they represent most of the variations in structural characteristics that distinguish the 91 groups in the NORC sample.

Preliminary analysis of these four orders reveals somewhat different patterns of influence. The SJ has more priests involved in secular work than any of the others; its members are also most likely to have the highest level of educational achievement, more job satisfaction, and stronger patterns of particularistic friendships. The link between secular work and education is characteristic of all four orders, but weakest in the OSF. In contrast to the OSB and MM, however, the OSF and SJ are alike in the relationship between secular work and particularistic friendships. Job satisfaction is again different for the SJ. For them it is linked with education and secular work. For the other three groups it is more strongly linked with expressive satisfaction (i.e., feelings of personal fulfillment, overall happiness, and fewer problems with loneliness).

For the OSB and OSF expressive satisfactions are associated with conformity to traditional views about religious beliefs, sexual morality, celibacy, and fewer authority problems. For the SJ, expressive satisfaction seems to be more a function of attachment to the clerical subculture and conformity to traditional values and norms, and is more associated with this attachment (especially number of priest friends) than in any other group. For the SJ and MM, attachment to the subculture and particularistic friendship patterns are also related to colleague support. For the OSB, however, this is not the case. Rather, number of priest friends is what most specifies the meaning of particularistic friendships. Similarly, the meaning of attachment to the clerical subculture is different in these four orders. The OSB and OSF more conform to the general religious (vs. diocesan) pattern of making a sharp distinction between the value placed on fostering community among all Christians and the value of priests living in community with likeminded colleagues. It is especially this latter value that is stressed by religious, and among the four orders under consideration, the OSB and OSF. The SJ and MM (as well as diocesan priests) do not make this distinction: they are, in other words, much more likely to see the two meanings of community are interrelated in their own values.

Thus, the NORC data only partially confirm E.K. Francis' application of the *Gemeinschaft/Gesellschaft* model to religious orders. For the SJ (the most *gesellschaftlich* group), work plays a more important role than it does for the other groups; and work satisfaction and expressive satisfaction are certainly interrelated, although separate issues. For the OSB, the reverse pattern appears: attitudes toward community life and expressive satisfaction are more influential, particularly in terms of the positive influence they exert on traditional perspectives. The OSF stand between the OSB and SJ, and the MM are closest to the diocesan clergy. This does not mean that the SJ place lower value on community life, but that community (and personal satisfaction) incentives are separated from work incentives, even though they are interrelated. The SJ seems to take a more inclusive view of the meaning of community at the same time they score higher on involvement with the clerical subculture and in their preference for particularistic friendships.

How, then, are these variations among religious orders to be interpreted? The preceding analysis strongly suggests that an *order's involvement in secular work and the value* it places *on community life* (as the central measure of organizational integration) are *associated with different patterns* of influence. For religious and especially for diocesan priests, secular work raises new and special problems not unlike those created for other large-scale organizations when they increase work specialization.[30] The larger cultural base represented by secular employment provides colleagues who act as reference groups that stand in occasional opposition to the norms and role expectations of the priesthood. For all the religious orders, education helps to prepare for the impact of secular work. As a result, while religious priests in secular work are generally much less traditional in their beliefs and values than those in non-secular work, there remains more pluralism of opinion among religious clergy as a whole. This pluralism seems to relate directly to the size of the order's involvement in secular work.

The influence of community life depends upon how "community" is conceived: whether a distinction is made between the more "expressive" (and "local") notion of community ("the well-being that comes from living the common life with like-minded colleagues") or the more "instrumental" (and "cosmopolitan") view of community ("being part of a community of Christians who are working together to share the good news of the Gospel"). For all religious, secular work increases work satisfaction and expressive satisfaction. But in groups where the expressive meaning of community is stressed and socialization is hence more locally focused (e.g., the OSB and OSF), job satisfaction is more a function of satisfaction with community than of involvement in secular work. Personal satisfaction, in turn, is more related to conformity with traditional beliefs and values than with attachment to the clerical subculture. An emphasis on the importance of "local" community and the socializing processes at work in local communities are, as John Barrett suggests, most likely tied to modeling and persuasion; "leaders" and peers are the agents of socialization.[31] In addition to an atmosphere which positively emphasizes organizational norms, the individual is confronted with experiences which serve to undo old values so that new ones can be learned. For groups that stress the expressive ties of local community, these experiences must be related to what happens within that community. To assume a non-traditional priestly identity, therefore, would be more associated with weaker community ties than to possessing non-traditional beliefs and values.

However, when attitudes favorable to community life are more instrumental and cosmopolitan (e.g., particularly in the SJ, and to a lesser extent, in the MM), secular work heightens particularistic friendships and attachment to the subculture. Conformity with traditional beliefs and values is more linked with attachment to the subculture, but is sharply decreased if loneliness needs are not met. Similarly, nontraditional perspectives are increased by secular work, loneliness, lack of colleague support, and especially, non-traditional religious beliefs. Loneliness has a particularly strong effect in the SJ. Lack of support for traditional beliefs and values are much stronger factors in the MM and account, in large part, for the much greater proportion of men who are unsure whether they will continue as priests.

RELIGIOUS ORDERS IN TRANSITION

The purpose of this chapter has been to delineate the form and function of religious orders within the social organization of Roman Catholicism. For this reason, we began with historical material drawn from a broad range of examples, then moved to a theoretical discussion of Catholic religious orders as an ideal type of organization, and finally turned our attention to some recent empirical data on the present situation of Catholic orders of priests in the United States. The chapter amply demonstrates, I believe, that in examining the social organization of Roman Catholicism, the distinction between diocesan and religious clergy and among various orders of religious priests not only has had important consequences for the diversity and adaptiveness of the priesthood but of Roman Catholicism in general. These consequences continue to have sociological relevance. With reference to the priesthood itself, this relevance is mainly related to the clergy's adaptation and integration. The *greater adaptiveness of religious priests*, especially those *with more involvement in secular work and higher educational achievement*, not only *contributes to more work satisfaction*, but *also to a wider acceptance of new theological perspectives without*, however, *undermining commitment* to the profession's long-term beliefs and norms or the goals of Roman Catholicism. A community life-style and wider networks of clergy interaction help to prevent cleavages observable in the diocesan clergy—cleavages especially noticeable when one compares the perspectives of those engaged in secular versus non-secular work.

However, the steady decrease in membership due to increased withdrawals and decline in recruits (especially sharp in religious orders of women and non-clerical orders of men)[32] plus the data from the 1970 Priesthood Survey also suggest that Catholic religious orders in America are undergoing a profound transition which is likely to take another twenty-five years to run its full course. Shrinking membership will produce an aging religious clergy and necessitate serious cutbacks in the institutional commitments religious have made to the work of the American Catholic Church. The diversity of beliefs, values, and norms that have appeared since the end of Vatican II prevail throughout the whole Catholic priesthood, regardless of diocesan/religious affiliation or membership in a particular religious order. Large numbers of American priests have rejected traditional theological formulations about God, faith, the church, the meaning of priestly identity, the value of celibacy, and norms regarding sexual morality. These men have clearly been influenced by the criticism of the old consensus which has been implicit in recent changes within Catholicism, but there is no evidence that they have accepted a new coherent theological perspective in its place, even though the majority of priests vigorously endorse a wide variety of specific changes in the post-Vatican II church.[33]

What, then, can be said about the future of Catholic religious orders? Several clues to this question can be found in their historical development. First, despite periods of growth and decline, successes and failures, religious orders as an organizational type have shown remarkable staying power. A glance at history makes it most reasonable to conclude that religious orders will persist as long as Roman Catholicism endures. Second, the form and function of the religious order has undergone several major transitions as this organizational type evolved in the Catholic Church. Four clearly distinguishable transitions can be identified: the development of monasticism from the scattered and loosely organized hermitages in the desert (500-1200); the emergence of the mendicant orders in the high Middle Ages (1200-1500); the establishment of apostolic orders in the wake of the Protestant Reformation (1500-1800); and finally, the growth of new teaching and missionary congregations in the aftermath of the French Revolution and the subsequent movement to educate the masses (1800 to the present).

Third, these major transitions have always been associated with uprooting external and internal events; the principal external factors and events have been fundamental shifts in secular culture. The stabilizing regularity of Benedictine monasticism, for example, represented a successful adaptation of religious life to the feudal society of the Dark Ages and the early medieval period that followed the barbarian invasions and the breakup of the Roman Empire. The new image of the apostolic religious order spurred religious to confront the secularizing trends of the scientific revolution, enlightenment philosophy, and the rise of nationalism in Europe. The principal internal events affecting transition have stemmed from a prolonged period of social breakdown or disintegration within existing religious orders. In each of these transition periods, the breakdown of existing orders can be charted in terms of a dismantling of the institutional structures and belief systems that arose in the prior time of expansion (after the early period subsequent to the order's founding) and which served the order well during its stabilization. This collective decline, associated with decreasing membership and ideological cleavage, gives rise to stress and doubt about the degree to which the order's lifestyle and work are equipped to handle important new challenges. The order loses its sense of identity and purpose, service to the Church becomes haphazard and without direction. Moral norms are relaxed, particularly those regularizing chastity and poverty, and there is a loss of membership through increased withdrawals and decreased recruitment of new members.[34]

Fourth, three outcomes are possible for religious orders during periods of transition: extinction, minimal survival, or revitalization. Extinction has been the fate of 76% of all men's religious orders founded before 1500 and of 64% of those founded before 1800. From an historical perspective, it is reasonable to predict that most religious orders in the Catholic Church today will eventually die out. An order which does not disappear may go through a long period of low-level or minimal survival. The membership patterns of presently existing orders founded before the French Revolution reveal that most of them enter into a prolonged period of very low numbers. In fact, only 5% of all men's orders founded before 1500 and only 11% of those founded before 1800 have current worldwide membership larger than 2,000. Finally, a small percentage of religious orders which survive the breakdown period enter into a period of revitalization. This revitalization has involved personal and collective transformation in terms of reappropriating the founding charism, reforming the internal structures of the order to promote greater fidelity to its ascetical ideals (prayer, poverty, chastity, obedience), and an innovative insight regarding its "mission" or work. This transformation and supporting insights signal the emergence of a new theory which gives meaning to the experiences of individuals and the shared events lived within the community; it also spurs the creation of new models of living together as a community and new ways of serving the needs of the Church and the larger society. This new vision and the new models that result attract more recruits and the order finds a future.

There is considerable evidence to support the argument that both the prerequisite external and internal factors and events for transition are presently occurring. Should this line of argument prove valid, it is also probable that the main feature of the next era of religious life will not emerge in discernible form for some time. In the interval, Catholic religious orders must face the painful task of reappropriating their original charism, searching and experimenting with new variations in their life and work, selecting those experiments which most correspond to the order's charism and today's challenges, and then establishing new tasks and priorities. This is the formula for adaptive renewal advocated by Vatican II.[35] What the formula implies is that Catholic religious orders today face the kind of long and troublesome road suggested by the old Chinese curse: "May you live in a time of transition."

Notes

1. Max Weber, *The Sociology of Religion* (Boston: Beacon Press, 1963), pp. 619-678; 733-757; *Economy and Society* (New York: Bedminster Press, 1968), pp. 1166-1173; Ernst Troeltsch, *The Social Teaching of the Christian Churches* (New York: Harper and Row, 1931), p. 723.

2. *The Documents of Vatican II*, ed. Walter M. Abbott, S.J. (New York: Guild Press, 1966), pp. 9-106; 183-316.

3. The most careful examination of the distinction between the religious order and other types of organization is presented in the excellent study of Michael Hill, *The Religious Order: A Study of Virtuoso Religion and Its Legitimation in the Nineteenth-Century Church of England* (London: Heinemann, 1973), pp. 61-84. I have drawn extensively on Hill's analysis, particularly in the second part of this chapter. In addition, some of the data and analysis used in this chapter also appear in my "The Religious Order in American Catholicism," *The Annual Review of the Social Sciences of Religion*, Vol. 3 (1979).

4. Emile Durkheim, *The Division of Labor in Society* (New York: Free Press, 1964), p. 169.

5. Cf. Adolph Harnack, *Monasticism: Its Ideals and History* (London: Williams and Norgate, 1901), pp. 25-29 Herbert Workman, *The Evolution of the Monastic Ideal* (Boston: Beacon Press, 1962), pp.

10-36. Two other important sources on this period are David Knowles, *From Pachomius to Ignatius* (Oxford: Clarendon Press, 1966) and Helen Waddell, *The Desert Fathers* (London: Collins, 1962).

6. *The Theodosian Code*, tr. C. Pharr (Princeton: Princeton University Press, 1952).

7. Cf. Thomas M. Gannon, S.J. and George W. Traub, S.J., *The Desert and the City* (New York: Macmillan, 1969), pp. 51-80; Lowrie J. Daly, S.J., *Benedictine Monasticism: Its Formation and Development Through the Twelfth Century* (New York: Sheed and Ward, 1965); *The Rule of St. Benedict in Latin English*, tr. Justin McCann (London: Burns, Oates, 1952).

8. Cf. Gannon and Traub, p. 99; Workman, pp. 258-268.

9. Gannon and Traub, pp. 81-83; see also, Ronald Knox, *Enthusiasm: A Chapter in the History of Religion* (Oxford: Clarendon Press, 1950), pp. 75-77; John-Baptist Reeves, O.P., *The Dominicans* (New York: Macmillan, 1930).

10. Troeltsch, p. 355; see also, Raphael M. Huber, O.F.M. Conv., *History of the Franciscan Order, 1182-1517* (Milwaukee: Nowing Publishing Apostolate, 1944).

11. Amitai Etzioni, *A Comparative Analysis of Complex Organizations* (New York: Free Press, 1961), pp. 51-56.

12. It is also true, as Francis remarks, that each order was influenced in its own development by the extant civil organizational models available. However, Francis, as well as Lewis Coser, push this point a bit too far in their comparison between the Jesuits and the military organizations of sixteenth century Europe. The quasi-military characteristics of the Jesuits are more properly linked *to* the military experiences of *their founder*, Ignatius of Loyola, and to his fondness of military imagery—a fondness shared by many Roman Catholic leaders, theologians, and preachers during the counter-reformation. Cf. E. K. Francis, "Towards a Typology of Religious Orders," *American Journal of Sociology*, Vol. 55 (March, 1950): 437-449; Lewis A. Coser, *Greedy Organizations* (New York: Free Press, 1973), pp. 110-128.

13. Take, for example, a simple versus solemn vow of poverty. Those with a simple vow of poverty retain the nominal (but not the beneficial) ownership of their property and may acquire additional property unless the rule of the group expressly forbids it. Those with a solemn vow of poverty renounce for life both the nominal and beneficial ownership of their property. Further, religious congregations may be established by a bishop or even a parish priest to deal with particular local needs. Religious orders are national and mostly international organizations whose existence must be approved by the Pope. The last Catholic religious "order," strictly so called, that has been established is the Jesuits.

14. Regarding the history of religious orders of women, see Suzanne Cita-Malard, *Religious Orders of Women* (New York: Hawthorne Books, 1964); *The New Catholic Encyclopedia*, Vol. 12 (New York: McGraw-Hill, 1967), pp. 287-294.

15. On the current situation within religious orders of women, see Marie Augusta Neal, "The Relations between Religious Belief and Structural Change in Religious Orders: Developing an Effective Measuring Instrument," *Review of Religious Research*, Vol. 12 (Fall and Spring, 1970-1971): 1-16; 153-164; "A Theoretical Analysis of Religious Orders in the U.S.A.," *Social Compass*, Vol. 18 (Fall, 1971): 7-25; "Cultural Patterns and Behavioral Outcomes in Religious Systems: A Study of Religious Orders of Women in the U.S.A.," *Acts of the 13th International Conference on the Sociology of Religion*, Lloret de Mar, Spain, August, 1975: 61-85; Helen Rose Fuchs Ebaugh, *Out of the Cloister* (Austin: University of Texas Press, 1977).

16. *From Max Weber: Essays in Sociology*, ed. Hans Gerth and C. Wright Mills (New York: Oxford University Press, 1958), pp. 245-252.

17. *Ibid.*, pp. 287-288.

18. In addition to similarities between religious orders and both charismatic movements and sects, Goffman's concept of "total institution" has been applied to orders. Indeed, there are certain superficial features which monastic orders do share with total institutions (e.g., prisons, mental hospitals, the military) relating to the way they center daily activity on a strict timetable and insist on members performing many functions in the religious community. But orders are *voluntary* organizations whose members have consciously chosen to adopt this particular way of life, whereas members of total institutions are typically *non*-voluntary (cf. Erving Goffman, *Asylums,* Garden City, New York: Doubleday, 1964).

19. Cf. Etzioni, pp. 41-42; Hill, 19-60. These characteristics are "typical" in that no one religious order will contain all of them or any of them to the same degree; they are "ideal" in that they constitute a set of characteristics toward which the orders tend in an always imperfect approximation.

20. For a more detailed account of the early history of religious orders in America, see John Tracy Ellis, *American Catholicism* (Chicago: University of Chicago Press, 1956), or Thomas T. McAvoy, C.S.C., *A History of the Catholic Church in America* (Notre Dame, Ind.: University of Notre Dame Press, 1969).

21. James Hennesey, S.J., "Jesuits in the United States," *Yearbook of the Society of Jesus: 1976-77* (Rome: Curia Generalis Societatis Iesu, 1976), pp. 13-35.

22. *The Official Catholic Directory* (New York: P. J. Kenedy and Sons).

23. National Opinion Research Center, *The Catholic Priest in the United States: Sociological Investigations* (Washington, D.C.: United States Catholic Conference, 1972). The sample design for this survey called for a stratified two-stage cluster sampling with probabilities proportional to size of unit. Individual responses were subsequently weighted for analysis. The sample comprised 85 of the 155 American dioceses, 91 of the 253 self-governing religious priest-communities, and 7,260 of the 64,000 bishops and priests in the United States. All bishops and major religious superiors, diocesan and religious priests in the sample were sent a 46-page self-administered questionnaire; the response rate for active priests was 71 per cent (N = 5,155; diocesan = 3,045, religious = 2,110).

24. These four orders (and their 1976 memberships) are: the Jesuits (5,029), the Franciscans (2,254), Benedictines (1,572), and Redemptorist Fathers (1,023). Source: *The Official Catholic Directory, 1976*. It is interesting to note that in the entire history of the church only thirteen men's religious order ever surpassed 10,000 members at some point. Listed in the order of their date of founding, these orders include: Cluny Benedictines, Cistercians, Premonstratensians, Franciscans, Dominicans, Carmelites, Augustinians, Minims, Capuchins, Jesuits, Christian Brothers, Marist Brothers, and Salesians. Cf. Raymond Hostie, S.J., *Vie et Mort des Ordres Religieux* (Paris: Desclee, 1972), pp. 340-342.

25. The principal sources for this additional information include: *The Official Catholic Directory, 1920-1976*; William J. Mehok, "Religious Life in Transition: An Analysis of Membership Trends and a Projection to 1982," *CARA: Forum for Religious*, Vol. 1 (Fall, 1976): 3-5; Raymond L. Fitz, S.M. and Lawrence J. Cada, S.M., "The Recovery of Religious Life, *Review for Religious*, Vol. 34 (No. 5, 1975): 690-719; *The Nineteen Centuries of the Roman Catholic Church* (New York: American Institute of Management, 1956).

26. Cf. Gannon, "In the Eye of the Hurricane: Religious Implications of Contemporary Trends," *Social Compass*, Vol. 19 (Winter, 1972): 213-228 for a discussion of the various conflicting assumptions with which people approached the Second Vatican Council.

27. An explanation of the index construction used in the NORC analysis can be found in *The Catholic Priest in the United States*, pp. 333-48.

28. Cf. Gannon, "Priest/Minister: Profession or Non-Profession," *Review of Religious Research*, Vol. 12 (Winter, 1971): 67-79.

29. See Talcott Parsons, Edward Shils, et al., *Theories of Society* (New York: Free Press, 1961), pp. 38-41 for perhaps the clearest explanation of the four functional imperatives.

30. Philip Selznick, "Foundations of the Theory of Organization," *American Sociological Review*, Vol. 13 (February, 1948): 26.

31. John H. Barrett, *Individual Goals and Organizational Objectives* (Ann Arbor: Institute for Social Research, University of Michigan, 1970), p. 10.

32. Fitz and Cada, p. 713.

33. Andrew M. Greeley, *The American Catholic: A Social Portrait* (New York: Basic Books, 1977), p. 156.

34. Cf. Fitz and Cada, pp. 700-707.

35. *The Documents of Vatican II*, pp. 466-82.

5

Protestant Mission Societies and The "Other Protestant Schism"

Ralph D. Winter

As a fairly narrow *Presbyterian* seminary student, one of the first shocks the writer experienced was to encounter *Baptist* Kenneth Scott Latourette's statement that, for all intents and purposes, the early band of highly evangelistic *Methodist* circuit riders adhered to characteristically *Roman Catholic* vows of poverty, chastity, and obedience. This disturbing thought germinated and, along with other broadening influences, eventually wreaked havoc with my typically Protestant limitations.

It was the beginning of an intellectual pilgrimage in which the writer would eventually come to see the emergence of the Protestant mission society as a parallel to the Roman Catholic order despite the fact that it is viewed as a major, yet somehow "foreign," structure within the Protestant stream of history. He would come to see the Protestant mission society as unintentionally and unfortunately the basis of a veritable "schism" not often confronted and analyzed structurally, an internal strain in Protestantism between church and parachurch organizations which profoundly frustrates the contemporary tasks of renewal and unity as well as mission.

PROTESTANTISM REVISITED

The undoing of a mindset takes years. The writer has not easily or happily yielded to the eventual and inevitable conclusion that the major Protestant traditions (Reformed, Lutheran, and Anglican—if we can stretch the word "Protestant" that far) became in their state-church postures every bit as Constantinian as they had ever imagined the Roman Catholic tradition which they spurned. Many a seminary student seeking the renewal of the church tends early to side with the so-called "radical reformers" who, though they existed long before the Reformation, were still protesting Protestant Constantinianism long after the Reformation. What dismay that many of these once radical traditions today bear many of the traits of the state-church syndrome.

In other words, from the particular bias of many Americans, state-churches of any kind may appear to have been a "mistake." But in seminary studies, new disappointments greet even "believer's church" or "gathered church" enthusiasts. Gradually they realize that, once on the free soil of America, these once elite and sectarian traditions, now totally untrammelled, have apparently descended over the decades to a nominalism—an in-name-only membership not strikingly different from that of the state church, whether Protestant or Catholic. Eliteness and vitality, it is discovered, are not very durable in any tradition. It seems almost a rule that *every Christian tradition, whether Protestant, Mennonite, or Roman, insofar as it depends heavily upon a family inheritance—or, shall we say, a biological mechanism—for its perpetuation over a period of time, will gradually lose the spiritual vitality with which it may have begun.* Such a loss of vitality occurs simply because biological and spiritual types of reproduction are fundamentally dissimilar. No exception, Protestantism as a movement has to a considerable extent survived both *in spite of and* curiously *because of* the constant *emergence* and reemergence *of new groups*—the fissiparous tendency which Latourette highlights. Thus, each new religious body represents and maintains a somewhat elite selection out of the general population only in its first or second generation. To the Roman Catholic, but also to the Protestant ecumenist, this type of constant rebirth, when it keeps on creating separate new churches, may seem to be an apparently fragmenting and therefore horrifying tendency, such that whatever recovery of zeal it may embody is commonly and with some justification disparaged.

Is there "a more excellent way"? The writer is convinced that the *Roman Catholic* tradition embodies in its much longer experience with the phenomenon of the "order" a *superior structural approach to both renewal and mission.* Gannon in the previous chapter has already described it. The writer believes that Protestants must begin to see their "parachurch" structures in a similar light. That is, they can better understand how best to fulfill their own profound obligation to unity, renewal, and mission if they see their own forms in comparative reference to those of the Roman Catholic tradition.

THE ENVIABLE ROMAN CATHOLIC SYNTHESIS

Personal reactions to the inadequacies of the Protestant tradition no doubt give the writer a particular slant on the history of the Roman Catholic church. For example, I tend to interpret the very survival of the Roman Church into the high medieval period as being to a considerable extent the result of the sheer durability and spiritual and Biblical vitality of the earlier monastic tradition. (Thus it seems perfectly proper that the monastic and religious orders should be called "regular," while the diocesan tradition is labeled "secular." As a Protestant deeply concerned about the inherent limitations of Protestantism's typical pair of alternatives—state-church nominal religion vs. sectarian disunity—the writer is quite likely to be *over*reacting in favor of that fascinating middle way constituted by the relationship between the diocesan tradition and the religious communities of the Roman tradition. I try not to be blind to several periods of long, drawn out competition between orders of friars, or the recurrent seesaw of power between bishop and abbot. I have not totally forgotten the typical Protestant stereotype of the ascetic anchorite fleeing the world instead of endeavoring to save it. But Protestants in their own ways have also achieved most of these excesses, and on balance I am convinced that the inherent *decentralization, mobility, and eliteness* of the Roman religious communities *must* urgently *be recovered by the Protestants*. To a considerable extent, in fact, Protestants do now possess in various parachurch structures functional analogues, if they could somehow see them in a new light and develop a new relationship to them that will be both supportive but also accountable. (This theme is developed later in the chapter.)

THE WARP AND THE WOOF

In order better to deal evenhandedly with parallel structural forms in Catholic, Protestant, and secular traditions alike, the writer has found it helpful to employ a pair of neutral terms: "modality" and "sodality." It would appear that every human society, whether secular or religious, needs *both* modalities (i.e., overall, given *governing structures*) and also sodalities (i.e., other structured, decentralized, especially *voluntary initiatives*). Even primitive tribes, for example, possess in addition to a tribal governmental system other structures long called *sodalities* by anthropologists (borrowing and modifying the Catholic term). These are substructures within the community that have an autonomy within and under the tribal government. Although not all are voluntary, they do not include whole families and are therefore not biologically perpetuated. American life itself is to a staggering degree the result of the work of thousands of organized, voluntary initiatives—business, social, and cultural—which are watched and regulated but not administered by the government. It is fair to say that most Americans are friendly to this type of "private enterprise" and fear creeping "big government." On the other hand, many Protestants at the same time deplore the fact that within the Christian movement there are hundreds of Christian organizations that are for the most part not directly administered by the denominations. Their misgivings are mostly rooted in the absence within Protestantism of a responsible relationship between denominations and paradenominational organizations.

Just as the word "church" is used sometimes to refer to the entire Christian movement, sometimes to denominations, and sometimes only to a local organization within that movement, I have coined the word *modality* to refer to the overall governmental structure of a human community (or communal-like group) that is biologically complete and biologically sustained, whether city, state, church, denomination, synagogue, etc. The term *sodality* then refers to those structures that are more likely to be voluntary, contractual, purposive, and not deriving in the main from biological momentum, where membership is not as likely to be automatic nor presumed nor pressured, thus where for example whole families as such are not generally admitted. Examples of sodalities include everything from commercial enterprises to what Catholics call *orders* and *religious societies* and Protestant historians have called *voluntary societies*.[1]

Why am I so concerned to recognize the legitimacy of both structures? Because I believe the Reformation tragically abandoned the second of these two structures and unwittingly produced another, less noticed internal "schism" that has created monumental problems for Protestants to this day. I recognize and value both the synagogue (modality) and the Pharisaic missionary band (sodality) in the Jewish community before Christ. Both the New Testament "church" (modality) and the Pauline missionary band (sodality) are reasonable and helpful borrowings of those two earlier structures. The diocese (modality) and the monastery (sodality) are later functional equivalents. We can apply this distinction, as already mentioned, to the contrast between bishop and abbot, secular and regular priests, and fairly recently in Protestantism to the uneasy distinction between "denomination" or "congregation" (modality) and "Christian movement," "society," or "parachurch" structure (sodality).

The use of the phrase "parachurch" organization for the second structure, the sodality, may even be questioned if neither structure is any more normative, any more "church," than the other. (Why not call churches "paramissions"?) Thus, just as it is impossible to make cloth without threads going both crosswise and also up and down, it is crucially important to regard these *two* structures working together *as the warp and the woof* of the fabric, the fabric being the Christian movement—the people of God, the *ecclesia* of the New Testament, the church of Jesus Christ. To make one of the two structures central and the other secondary, as the term *parachurch* seems to do, is probably unwise. The two are indeed interdependent. The evidences of history do not allow us to understand either of them as complete without the other. Their relationship is at least potentially, as in the Roman tradition, a beneficial symbiosis. The problem is that within Protestantism today the tension between the two is as great as or greater than ever before.

Thus, for well over half the brief history of Protestantism, the Reformation tradition has to a great extent been engrossed in the attempt to establish a *middle* ground between what the Reformers viewed as the nominalism of the Catholic masses and the heroic asceticism of the Catholic monastery. Again and again sects have started out from within Protestantism, often with a vital fellowship during the first or second generation, but have soon and inevitably swung from vitality to a nominal religiosity once they have become dependent upon family perpetuation for survival. The vitality of the sects has always been made possible by their newness and the opportunity this gave them to be selective in their early membership. All attempts to impose stricter standards on a *given*—rather than a *called out*—group have backfired: thus, Oliver Cromwell's ill-fated attempt to clamp all of England in a Puritan vise, and Calvin's attempt to turn Geneva into a Protestant-style monastery. Yet Protestantism in general has made no serious attempt to recover the voluntary tradition of the Catholic orders. As a result, while the Protestant tradition at many points attempted very desperately to be healthier, by cutting off the orders the Protestant body gave up arms and legs and virtually put unity, renewal, and mission out of reach.

The uniquely American experience with post-Revolution disestablishment produced briefly what was hailed as the "voluntary church." In the early days of the new republic, when church membership was less than 10 per cent of the population, there was more reason than now to place great hope upon a much more elite and selective approach to membership than that of the state-church tradition. But the phrase *voluntary church* has turned out to be virtually a contradiction in terms. Within neither connectional nor congregational denominational experience have social pressures on the younger generation in the long run allowed for voluntary mechanisms easily distinguishable from the state church. Both rely mainly on familial perpetuation. Thus, Kelley's *Why Conservative Churches Are Growing*[2] (really "why non-selective churches are not attracting select people") chronicles the "inevitable" trend to nominalism, whereby it remains clear that the voluntary principle lies mainly in the sodality (not modality) structures.

This does not at all mean that the modality or communal body is inferior to the sodality or contractual group. It means that the continuing life and work of the Christian movement ideally requires both a mainly non-voluntary, inherited structure and a whole array of optional, voluntary structures for deeper community and effective service. The two types of structures, the one with a benefit-of-the-doubt membership and the other with ideally a strict and voluntary one, are together the warp and the woof of the fabric. Thus, when the voluntary structure is not valued and employed effectively, as is the case within Protestantism, the very fabric of the Christian movement is accordingly weakened.

WILLIAM CAREY'S DISCOVERY

Thus, it was very important when an unlikely village school-master-preacher-cobbler fought his way out of this impasse and bequeathed to succeeding Protestant Christendom what was, in effect, the reinvention of the Catholic-originated "wheel." I refer to the brilliant and awesomely determined, young man named William Carey. It may some day be acknowledged that his tightly reasoned essay, *An Enquiry into the Obligation of Christians to Use Means for the Conversion of the Heathens*, has been the most influential single piece of literature in Protestant history since the Reformers.[3] His essay is at minimum the *literary* basis for the reemergence in Protestantism of a whole rash of what he called "means"—religious societies, voluntary societies. Thus, at the crucial point of modern history when the French Revolution cut the European roots of the global network of Catholic missions, Protestants suddenly discovered how to sprout the organizational arms and legs that were not only to carry them around the *world* in the extension of their faith, but also potentially to rebuild and renew their home traditions from *within*.

Beginnings were slow and humble, but twelve significant mechanisms for missionary extension were forged along these lines in the next twenty-five years. These mission societies in great measure were influenced by William Carey's genius, example, and insistent spirit as mediated foundationally by his *Enquiry*. This remarkable document (1) systematically reviewed past efforts to extend the faith, (2) summarized statistically the actual religious status quo of every continent and country, and (3) pleaded forthrightly that Christians without embarrassment employ the kind of *organizational means* that were so well known in the Protestant commercial world and had by then reached out in such commercial "callings" to the farthest corners of the world. His knowledge and appreciation of the existence of Catholic missions, however, was embarrassingly scant and negative. It would be a few years yet before those who followed in his steps would have sufficient contact with Catholic missionaries for there to be any possible revision of their stereotypes of the latter. But reinvent the wheel they did.

The impact for unity and mission of this sudden acquisition of arms and legs by the body of the Protestant tradition is not often fully appreciated, but it is widely recognized that Protestant efforts for unity have gained impulse from the field contacts between different missionaries; and mission executives back home have simultaneously grown in awareness of their oneness via pursuing a single international task. Both the World Council of Churches and the National Council of Churches in the United States came into being by this route. That is, the WCC owes a great deal to the 1910 World Missionary Convention in Edinburgh, to the International Missionary Council, and indeed to four other sodalities— the worldwide Young Men's Christian Association, the World's [sic] Christian Student Federation, the Student Volunteer Movement, and the national and international activities of the amazing Christian Endeavor movement. Who knows whether, without these transdenominational sodalities, the present degree of fellowship between Protestant church traditions would have been possible? In the case of the National Council of Churches in the United States, the principal forerunner was the Foreign Missions Conference of North America, which actually brought a wider variety of Christians together than the present NCC, including as it did Southern Baptists, denominational societies, and interdenominational societies.

The Protestant reinvention of the mission sodality in particular and the parachurch organization in general did not merely affect mission and unity. One of the most fascinating phenomena in the history of Christianity in the United States was the almost unbounded creativity of new Christian sodalities in the Carey era—the first third of the nineteenth century. Literally hundreds of reforming, renewing, campaigning, evangelizing, reviving, and missionizing societies burst into existence. Not merely did the famous visitor from France, Alexis de Toqueville, remark on this bursting forth of voluntary activity from the civil body politic. The proliferation of activist voluntary societies was so great that William Carey himself, had he been present, might easily have been horrified, even though all these societies, whether or not foreign mission societies, were indeed organized "means" of the very kind he had proposed. However, there was no "pope" in Protestantism to moderate their growth. Denominational leaders inevitably reacted as they saw so many of their key laymen and so much of their members' money flowing into these novel channels. No wonder, then, that Episcopal Bishop Hobart[4] inveighed against the societies, but we do wonder about his assumption that the denomination was a divinely instituted structure, while the societies were merely human creations. A growing literature[5] has described the development of the American denomination as a religious form that is neither church nor sect (See Introduction). In this literature there is also the persistent issue of what to do with the amazing growth and novel structure of the voluntary societies. A temporary and inadequate answer came gradually as it became prevalent in America for the various *denominations to establish their own boards for overseas mission operation*—a new pattern we can call the *American pattern*,[6] which did not characterize either the approach of Roman Catholics or European Protestants. For the latter, the emergence of missionary societies was far too limited a phenomenon to demand total capture by the churchly structures.

Following the Civil War, however, a whole new plethora of voluntary, interdenominational mission societies sprang up, a breed now termed "faith missions." These were to a considerable extent inspired by the example of a second "William Carey," Hudson Taylor, who also plotted statistics of unreached people and urgently proposed a *means*. By 1910, the immense stake of American Protestants in organizations of this type working all over the world was so significant that in the United States even *Roman Catholic* foreign mission initiatives were for once (in a unique switch) *spurred on by Protestants*. Another vast new boost in American Protestant involvement in missions resulted from the Second World War which among its other functions dramatically familiarized American citizens with the rest of the world as no other event in American history, setting the stage for another 150 voluntary foreign mission societies to burst forth.

Looking back, however, it is only fair to say that William Carey, working as he did within the Protestant tradition, could not have exactly reproduced the Catholic orders even if he had consciously tried. Unlike Catholics, Protestants have always tended to *overlook the usefulness of unmarried* people. Yet Carey did not deem it necessary for his wife to accompany him to India when he first ventured forth, and Hudson Taylor's followers often lived as though they were single men, leaving their wives back in coastal cities as they probed China's interior for a year at a time. Having to provide schooling and care for the missionaries' children inevitably focused on another significant contrast between Protestant and Catholic mission societies, involving both advantages and disadvantages.

Nevertheless, the comparison between the two traditions is still feasible and useful. What about poverty, chastity, obedience? The acceptance of "poverty" as a lifestyle has characterized virtually every Protestant mission society. "Functional chastity" of a sort we have just mentioned. But chastity is as much an attitude as anything else. Obedience? Until recent times, becoming a Protestant missionary was as permanent a call as any solemn vow in the Roman tradition. The biggest difference between Protestant and Catholic, in regard to this matter of disciplined, additional-commitment communities, is not so much the difference between the *internal* functions of Protestant and Catholic missions as the difference in the *external* relationships of these sodalities to their respective parent denominational traditions. Yes, in this respect, Protestants are indeed very different from Catholics. Note, for example, that Vatican II assumed the existence, the value and permanence of the orders, while the Bangkok meeting of the World Council of Churches' Commission on World Mission and Evangelism in 1973-1974 virtually assumed the *passing* of the Protestant mission societies. This leads us to look more closely at what we may call the "other Protestant schism".

THE "OTHER PROTESTANT SCHISM"

Generally, Protestants are committed to the principle of cultural self-determination and are therefore not offended by the idea of a world-wide fellowship of separate autonomous, national (cultural, ethnic) or nation-oriented churches. This holds as long as every possible continuing effort is made for these legally independent churches to develop a sharing relationship between themselves. But while the Reformers conceived of the legitimacy of such autonomy for their *own cultural spheres*, they did not successfully understand and apply this insight as a *general principle*. In fact, it was not until their own missions belatedly arose that the Protestant mind encountered full-blown cultural traditions in the non-Western world where for them the shoe was now on the other foot and the issue of those "non-Western degraded cultures" being self-determining really arose to test the Protestants' untried general principle. Today, of course, the need for "indigenization" (or "contextualization") is commonly discussed and widely accepted among both Protestants and Catholics (although seriously unresolved dimensions remain).

Thus, the well-known schism between the Mediterranean-Romanized and the Northern-European, non-Romanized populations was both inevitable and in some sense beneficial. Scholars have sometimes termed the Reformation the "Protestant Revolt," but in one sense this "revolt" may have misfired since the sons of the Reformation have not generally understood the point that was made: that the schism was a cultural decentralization. In any case, Protestants unwittingly created another and even more significant *internal* "schism" deriving from and resulting in a truncated view of the church: this other organizational hiatus resulted as *the Reformers conceived of an overall church structure getting along nicely without any voluntary sub-communities worthy of being part of the church.* In one respect, the resulting situation constitutes to this day Protestantism's own still unresolved "investiture controversy." But alas without a pope, the Catholic solution (of orders becoming free from local control) is not directly applicable. It is as though the Protestants are still living prior to Cluny and cannot proceed because they have no higher power (other than the secular state) to which an elite community in a given locality can be subordinated instead of to a denominational church government.

As a result, although Protestant foreign mission societies finally surfaced—and there are by now more than 600 in North America, raising more than $700 million annually–nevertheless, Protestant church structures in America have somehow not yet fully resolved their relationship to such structures. As a result, they either *ignore* their existence, *or try to make them into an ecclesiastical type of "government agency"* that suffers other handicaps:

1. About half of all North American Protestant missionaries are sent out by organizations owing no allegiance to any denomination by name. These suffer from imperfect accountability.
2. The other half are sent out by organizations that function basically at the initiative of denominational governments. These are often frustrated in the outworking of their highly specific, especially "prophetic," goals by being ultimately required to seek majority approval from the denominational constituency.[7]

Figure 1 shows two extreme (A and D) and two intermediate (B and C) models of relationship. Back in William Carey's era, the new initiatives

FIGURE 1
RELATIONSHIPS BETWEEN DENOMINATIONS AND PARADENOMINATIONAL ORGANIZATIONS

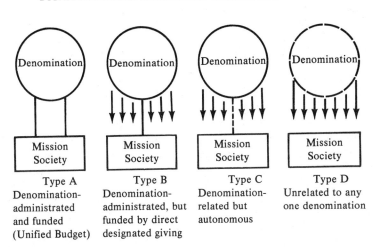

Type A	Type B	Type C	Type D
Denomination-administrated and funded (Unified Budget)	Denomination-administrated, but funded by direct designated giving	Denomination-related but autonomous	Unrelated to any one denomination

were mainly *outside the church governments* (i.e., Type D), although Carey himself finally secured the limp backing of a local Baptist conference of churches, so that his society was really Type C. In America this pattern of mere church recognition and/or tacit approval of virtually autonomous mission structures went much further. Thus, in reaction, we see the development of a pattern almost unique to America (already referred to as the "American Pattern") whereby the U.S. denominations, which were pretty elite in the voluntary sense, in the early 1800s one by one began gradually to coopt or create their *own internal* voluntary societies for mission, such that by 1865 most of the Type C or D societies had become B or C. Even though the "faith mission" movement, following 1865, resulted in a whole new crop of unrelated Type D societies, and still another new set of Type D societies emerged following World War II, nevertheless by 1950 most of the older societies or boards with C and B relationships had finally moved to Type A (unified budget) relationships. Meanwhile also, newer or younger denominations generally followed this latter pattern from the time it became well known.

Figure 2 impressionistically portrays this longstanding trend *away from* the nearly universal use of *voluntary* societies as a means of active service, *toward* the use of *denominational* boards and then the *reversal* of that trend.

The three most reliable points—1969, 1972, and 1975—are a substantial indication of the present trend.[8] This is partly the result of a general trend within the denominations *toward* greater *internal diversity* and thus *away from* expectations of a majority *consensus* in regard to social and missionary interests, especially in mainline U.S. denominations. That is, in a democratic polity very little initiative can be taken without a numerical majority.

From the perspective of this chapter, the trend to the A and D extremes of relationship between mission structures and churches—call it the Bear-Hug or Abandonment Syndrome—is further evidence of the continuing internal schism or uneasy tension between the denominations and the voluntary societies. We need to ponder today why all Catholic orders and nearly all European Protestant societies fall into Type C while American Protestant missions nearly all fall into the A or D extremes. In the terminology of church historians, this phenomenon is also described as a tension between (1) the model of a church government being directly *responsible* for only its *internal* life and discipline and depending upon external voluntary societies as its arms and legs in social and missionary activism; and (2) the model, advanced in opposition to the interdenominational voluntary societies, that each *denomination*, being itself a voluntary society of sorts, *should* also *function as its own "missionary organization."* A recent essay by a church historian, Fred

FIGURE 2
PROPORTION OF AMERICAN MISSIONARIES UNDER
VOLUNTARY SOCIETIES AND UNDER DENOMINATIONAL
BOARDS SINCE 1800

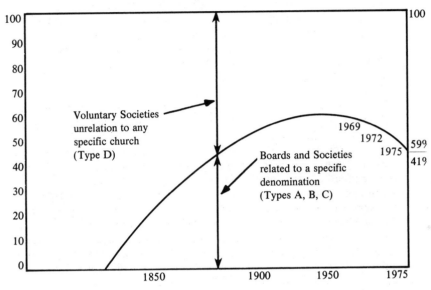

J. Hood, describes these two concepts nicely (although extended treatments are only available in unpublished dissertation form).[9] Today, the bulk of all U.S. Protestant denominational leaders would readily affirm the *second* model, in keeping with the activist mood of our time and the by now well developed "theology of the church in mission." Nevertheless, as seen in Figure 2, the tide seems to be flowing in the opposite direction in the last few years, if we judge by the number of North American Protestant missionaries sent out by denominationally related structures as compared to the number sent out by Type D structures.

This curious transition back is due in part to the rapid increase of new independent, Type D voluntary societies. It is also due to the phasing out by older boards of mission work in places overseas where domestic churches are by now well established. The fact, however, is that *new work* has always been begun mostly by *independent voluntary societies*. One example will suffice: The Reformed Church in America as a "church in mission" directly sponsors mission work in 24 countries. *In not a single case* were these locations *pioneered by denominational board initiatives*. In every case, *informal* initiative spearheaded the initial activity and then the denominational board later shouldered ongoing responsibility. This is not to be considered ominous but does underscore the crucial importance of allowing breathing space for initiatives too small to gain a 51% approval in a democratic church body. Figures 3 and 4 show more of the details of the expansion of independent voluntary societies and the simultaneous contraction by denominational boards of the number of overseas workers.

Figure 4, on the same scale as Figure 3, concentrates the shaded and white areas to show the actual percentages plotted as the three final points in Figure 2. It is not our purpose to make predictions, much less to take sides in this struggle, but we may contrast this tension in America with the Roman Catholic (and European-Protestant) patterns, almost entirely Type C, which seems to gain a great deal by being *neither* totally *independent* of nor totally *dominated* by the churches. The most significant example in America today of the Type C pattern is the Conservative Baptist Foreign Mission Society, which sustains a close fellowship with the Conservative Baptist Association of some 1300 local churches. The CBFMS not only antedated the Conservative Baptist Association, to which it still loyally and faithfully relates itself, but is still legally autonomous and is not actually governed by any of the overt ecclesiastical processes of the CBA. Furthermore, it receives support from 700 *other* churches that are not part of the Conservative Baptist Association; many belong to other Baptist groups, but some are Presbyterian, Episcopal, etc. The Type B relationship may also be preferable to either A or D (most Type A "unified budget" boards were once Type B in their relationship to their respective denominations). Thus, although the Type A relationship (not Type B) is the dominant pattern today among denominational boards, the impersonal processes of the unified budget system are now no longer defended as unqualifiedly as they once were by denominational leaders.[10] As a concession to human weakness, as some put it, most denominations are now beginning to make greater allowance for the "designated giving" pattern of the earlier Type B relationship.

It may be observed that the tension between church governments controlled by a majority and the pressures of a minority for activism on foreign or home mission frontiers is clearly a general phenomenon and not merely a problem arising from mission work. John R. Fry in his recent book, *The Trivialization of the United Presbyterian Church*, gives the poignant and eloquent outcry of an activist deeply concerned about a whole array of social concerns. He takes great satisfaction in the fact that, for a relatively brief period in the 1960s, top leadership in the

FIGURE 3
GROWTH OF DIFFERENT TYPES AND CATEGORIES OF MISSION SOCIETIES

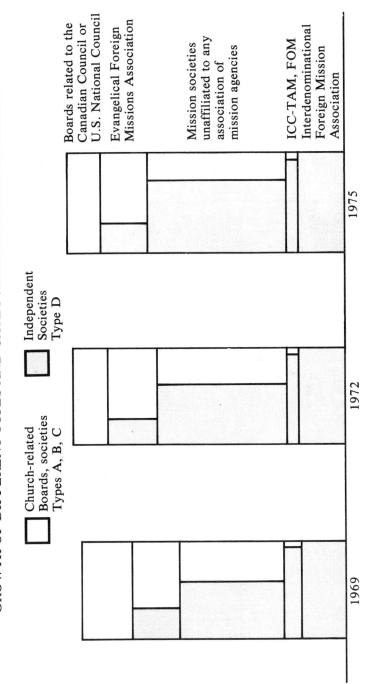

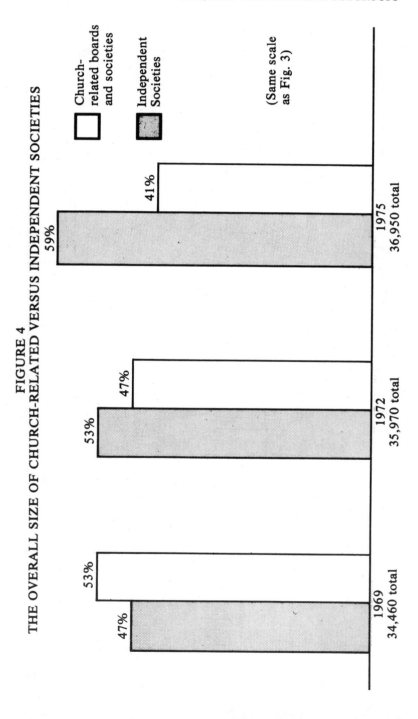

FIGURE 4
THE OVERALL SIZE OF CHURCH-RELATED VERSUS INDEPENDENT SOCIETIES

Church-
related boards
and societies

Independent
Societies

(Same scale
as Fig. 3)

41%

59%

1975
36,950 total

47%

53%

1972
35,970 total

53%

47%

1969
34,460 total

United Presbyterian church was able to gain widespread consensus (or so it seemed) for official church involvement in political, social, and economic issues of all kinds. In that period, nearly every regional presbytery developed a "church and society" committee, and even many local congregations followed suit. This did not last, however, and he terms his denomination's reverting to internal concerns a "trivialization."

The problem with trying to move whole denominations to take a specific policy stance on programs (e.g., the table grape boycott) was anticipated clear back in the early 1800s when the proposal that the churches should officially promote "missions" was at that time generally considered improper. There was also less than complete agreement that voluntary societies were the proper way to go. This difference of opinion contributed significantly to one of the more spectacular church splits in U.S. history when, in 1837, 2,400 Presbyterian ministers were divided almost exactly into two equal parts by the "New School/Old School" schism. As always, there were a variety of issues; but by 1847, the leaders of the Old School branch decisively settled for themselves the matter of structure by declaring *their half* of the denomination to be itself a "missionary organization." The schism in attitude toward the external voluntary societies remained for a time as the New School continued to express its activism through voluntary societies not under the direct control of the church.

But the tide was toward doctrinal purity, and thus denomination-controlled boards. The New School was anxious to provide proof to the "triumphant" Old School that it was equally Presbyterian (and not Congregational). Other groups participating in the American Board of Commissioners for Foreign Missions gradually withdrew for similar reasons. Thus, at the time of the reunion of the Old and New Schools a generation later, the various overseas fields of the ABCFM, the oldest ecumenical foreign mission organization in America, were simply divided between the Congregational and Presbyterian traditions; and when the New School Presbyterians withdrew, the office of the ABCFM became the office of the denominational board of the Congregationalists. The same thing happened to the British older sister of the ABCFM—the London Missionary Society.

Thus, the various churchly traditions pulled up their skirts from contacts that would muddy or compromise their distinctives. The New School was subjected to unblinking doctrinal rigidities in the reunion, and in such a climate it was naturally unthinkable to mix doctrine and polity either in home mission or foreign mission endeavors. It was such exclusiveness that put the cooperative voluntary societies in a bad light back in 1837. By *exclusiveness* we mean the setting aside of the earlier idea of a denomination being only one of a set of jointly embattled and equally legitimate church enterprises working together to try to redeem an overwhelmingly non-Christian world. The very success in church growth of the cooperative period ironically ushered in an era of greater confidence about the future of Christianity and a resulting sense of competition between denominations. This further heightened tendencies to separation and a sense of superiority. Thus there arose a new concept of *denominations* which conceived of the development of internal action groups as the essential characteristic.[11]

It is highly crucial to note, however, that by deciding against cooperation between denominations, nothing at all was stated or settled regarding the relative merits of the various structural options of *internal* voluntary societies (e.g., Types A, B, C). In the New School/Old School reunion there were in effect five Type B societies that carried forward the outreach of the church but recruited personnel and funds on a semiautonomous basis. It would take another hundred years for the work of all these internal boards to be merged completely into a single Type A structure whereby it would be very difficult for people to give specifically to any one of the various causes (home, foreign, women's work, etc.).

The irony of this story is seen in the fact that at a time—say 1865— when a virtual consensus among the denominations had come to pass, that each one should sponsor its *own* denominational outreach, a whole new uncontrollable host of other forces were already actively at work— the YMCA, the Student Volunteer Movement, and Christian Endeavor— that powerfully *united* people all *across* the denominational *boundaries*. One example was the flourishing of the new breed of "faith missions" that were not exclusively related to any specific denomination or congregation.

Similarly, by 1950, when the "unified budget" approach had gained widespread consensus among the denominations as a further step toward centralization, another vast new crop of powerful voluntary societies was being born, the money from individual church members somehow constantly gravitating to the specific. These new societies account for much of the growth trends noted in Figures 3 and 4. Thus the peculiar proclivity of American Protestants to support causes and channels of action other than just denominations and denomination-administrated good works is strikingly illustrated by the mounting number and power of independent voluntary societies. At the same time, the continuation and increase of the Type D category is continuing evidence of the Protestant schism between the modality and sodality, that is, church and parachurch organizations. But before we go on to ask how there can ever be a healing of the breach constituted by this other, Protestant, internal, structural "schism," we need to take a good look at the facts, noting both differences and similarities between Protestant mission structures today.

PROTESTANT MISSION STRUCTURES TODAY:
THEIR DIFFERENCES

There are five useful general questions that can be asked of any particular structure, and each question brings additional dimensions of distinctiveness. The possible answers mentioned here are merely illustrative.

A. How Closely is an Agency Related to the Organized Church?

(We have already covered four types of relationships—Types A, B, C, D, as in Figure 1.) The various relationships give rise to three common distinctions:

1. Church-related/independent (ABC vs. D)
2. Denominational/interdenominational (ABC vs. D)
3. Intradenominational/interdenominational (C vs. D)

B. How is the Agency Related to Churches That Exist in the Field of its Mission Efforts? Two more distinctions:

4. Church planting agencies/service agencies

While there is no reason a so-called service agency could not be dedicated to planting churches as a service to various denominations, most such agencies offer other specialized services, such as in medicine (Medical Assistance Programs), aviation (Missionary Aviation Fellowship), mass communications (Far East Broadcasting Company), literature (World Literature Crusade), etc., and operate alongside the churches in their areas of ministry.

5. International church/national church

Here is an interesting distinction rarely used. By "international churches" we mean those U.S. churches whose overseas work has not produced autonomous national churches. They are fairly numerous, examples being the Church of Jesus Christ of the Latter Day Saints, the Seventh-Day Adventist Church, the Roman Catholic Church, and in some ways even the Church of the Nazarene and the Christian and Missionary Alliance. This alters the church-to-church relationship somewhat and may soften or at least postpone mission/church tensions since members everywhere are a part of a *single* church. It may tend to limit the full autonomy of the newer subdivisions, however.

C. How is the Agency Related to Other Agencies?

The Foreign Missions Conference of North America was founded in 1893 and eventually embraced most U.S. mission societies. However, by the time this structure was subsumed into the National Council of Churches in 1952 (as what is now called the Division of Overseas Ministries or the DOM), the interdenominational agencies had long withdrawn, some of which now belong *instead* (rather than *in addition*) to the Interdenominational Foreign Mission Association (IFMA). The

Evangelical Foreign Mission Association (EFMA) came later and has both church-related and independent agencies as members. Many agencies, however, have no affiliations with others.

    6. Affiliated/unaffiliated

D. How is the Agency Structured Internally?

    7. Board-governed/member-governed/donor-governed
    8. Centralized/decentralized administration
    9. Polynational/mononational
    10. "Home office" in one country/"home offices" in many countries
    11. Formal/non-formal

A jungle of complexity faces us if we try to give the details of the internal structure of the various agencies. Most are board-governed. Some (e.g., Wycliffe) are member-governed. Some, e.g., the Evangelical Alliance Mission (TEAM), are essentially donor-governed. Whatever the ultimate source of governing power, however, the actual day-to-day administration may be in the hands of a fairly influential nearly permanent staff. Differences in fund raising may affect the degree of centralization of power. The Overseas Missionary Fellowship (OMF), for example, theoretically raises money for the *society*, not for individuals, while the Sudan Interior Mission (SIM) requires each *missionary* to raise his *own* support. The result is that, in some ways, the OMF has greater centralized control than the SIM.

Some organiztions draw their members from many countries (e.g., Wycliffe Bible Translators, Andes Evangelical Mission). Most express the missionary concern of a single nation (distinction #9, above). Some agencies have "home offices" for support, and even governing purposes in more than one country. Such agencies are sometimes called international but could also be called multinational.

One large, virile tradition stemming from the Disciples or Restorationist tradition does not approve of agencies as such, and yet without the help of any formal mission agency (distinctive #11), several thousand missionaries are sent out by individual local congregations belonging to either of two "brotherhoods." This is an explicit rejection of William Carey's proposal to use "means." Nevertheless, the non-formal coordination of teams of such missionaries to specific fields does in fact provide the functional equivalent of a mission agency. The very absence of formal cohesion sometimes elicits greater teamwork than in cases where a formal relationship is prescribed or inherited. The record thus far, however, is unclear.

E. For What Function is the Agency Designed?

    12. Home missions/foreign missions
    13. Sending/non-sending

14. Church planting/service (same as #4)
15. Evangelistic/Christian presence
16. Institutional/non-institutional
17. Cross-cultural/mono-cultural
18. E-1/E-2/E-3

These distinctions are mainly self-evident. Number 13 refers to the sending of people to live and work in a different place. Literature missions may send mainly literature, not people. The same is true of agencies mainly sending funds to support overseas (national) workers, projects helping orphans, or for relief in cases of disaster. Number 16 refers to the fact that some agencies do not found any schools, hospitals, industries, but perhaps focus only on the establishment of new congregations. Numbers 17 and 18 are very significant. They refer not to *geographical* or *political* distance, as in #12, but to cultural distance. E-1 means evangelism where the only barrier is the "stained glass barrier"—the special culture of the church. E-2 means there is an additional, serious culture barrier, but at least some significant common denominator. E-3 means the work is being done in a totally different culture. For example, reaching Navajo tribal peoples in the U.S. may be for Anglo-Americans far more difficult than working among Spanish-speaking people in the U.S. (or Argentina) since Spanish is a sister language and Navajo is not. Thus, to an Anglo-American, the Navajos (and Zulus and Chinese) are at an E-3 distance, that is, totally different, while Spanish are only E-2, and a non-church-going Anglo next-door neighbor (or Anglos among the G.I.s in Spain or Tokyo) are merely an E-1 distance away.

Furthermore, agencies working cross-culturally (e.g., E-2 or E-3) must organize their internal training programs properly to take into account the linguistic and cultural barriers. E-2 agencies, for example, typically "fumble" an E-3 opportunity that happens to be in the same area of their work. This is why most U.S. missions working predominantly among the Spanish-speaking people of Latin America (an E-2 task) fail miserably to reach the American Indians (who are at an E-3 distance). It usually takes a specialized E-3 mission, like Wycliffe, to traverse that extra cultural distance.

Table 1 gives the list of mission agencies, each with an annual income of $5 million or more in 1975. These 29 entities took in more than half of the total of $656 million given in 1975 by North American Protestants to overseas ministries. These are not all sending agencies, and in some cases work in the U.S. may be included. The purpose here is to display the relative strength of the larger organizations, and to show the varying relationships they sustain to church organizations, as per Figure 1. Two of them (Restoration Churches and Brethren Assemblies) operate with the non-formal structure commented on earlier (distinction #11). Note that about one-third of the organizations, drawing about one-third the

TABLE 1
OVERSEAS MINISTRIES ANNUAL INCOME
(1975, IN MILLIONS)

Denomination	Structural Type			
	Type A	Type B	Type C	Type D
Southern Baptist Convention		48.30		
Campus Crusade for Christ				27.33
World Vision International				27.00
Seventh Day Adventist	25.00			
Church World Service		23.50		
Assemblies of God		21.79		
United Methodist Church	19.06			
Wycliffe Bible Translators				16.90
American Bible Society				13.24
Church of the Nazarene	12.40			
Restoration Churches		12.00		
Christian & Miss. Alliance	11.39			
Sudan Interior Mission				9.95
Lutheran Ch.-Missouri Synod	9.59			
Evangelical Alliance Mission				9.07
United Church of Christ	7.61			
Baptist Bible Fellowship				7.04
Mennonite Central Comm.		6.96		
Episcopal Church (USA)	6.56			
Navigators				6.25
Cons. Baptist For. Miss. Soc.			5.98	
OMS International				5.92
Lutheran Church in America	5.84			
Presbyterian Church in U.S.	5.75			
American Baptist Ch. in USA	5.69			
Baptist Mid-Missions				5.63
Bretheran Assemblies		5.50		
American Lutheran Church	5.49			
United Presby. Ch. in USA	5.08			
Totals	119.46	118.05	5.98	128.33

funds, are of Type D—totally unaligned to any specific denomination.
Note that there is only one Type-C agency.

PROTESTANT MISSION STRUCTURES TODAY: THEIR SIMILARITIES

If the American experience has proven anything, it has demonstrated that disestablishment was no disaster to the Christian movement. But if establishment could sometimes ignore the grassroots, and pastors were paid whether or not people attended, disestablishment altered things irretrievably. Clearly, despite the wide diversity of types of organizations, virtually all U.S. Protestant denominations today are coalitions or federations of local congregations of mainly married people who own (or act as though they own) the local church plant. They sense the fact that they are needed to support its leadership and exercise a great deal of/or total control over the very choice of that leadership. Even the Anglican tradition in America underwent this kind of democratization as the post-revolution, restructured Episcopal Church emerged. The reason for this leveling is a conscious or unconscious parallel between church government and the accepted pattern of democratically controlled civil government—and vice versa.

In a similar sense, despite wide diversity in organizational details, there are certain sweeping *common denominators* which hold true *for* virtually *all mission structures*. In the latter case, unlike the structure of the denominations, however, these owe nothing to democracy. Why? Because the conscious and unconscious *parallel* is not to *civil government* but to the *Catholic orders,* the *military, and* the structure of *private enterprise*, in that order. In a way, similarities are more difficult to describe than differences. But our task is easier due to the valuable check list Gannon (Chapter 4) gives for Catholic orders. The parallels are striking (giving titles in our own words to the enumeration of characteristics he describes):

1. Voluntary, deeper commitment
2. Response to a challenge
3. Stress on both devotion and active involvement
4. Task forces ready for any good work
5. An organizational esprit de corps
6. Both come-structures and go-structures
7. Amazing durability (of purpose and existence)
8. Stress on Christian basics
9. A normative pattern of discipline, for example:
   a. community of members
   b. related to a church but yet semi-autonomous (e.g., Type C, see Table 1)
   c. a structure of authority—"quasi-familial"
   d. common property
   e. celibate chastity, mono-sexual membership in any one order
   f. & g. elite commitment beyond that of ordinary church members

As we have already noted, there is a congenital reticence among Protestants to acknowledge the wealth of their inheritance from the Roman tradition. This reticence alone may account for the fact that the obvious parallels between practically every item in Gannon's trait list and the Protestant mission movement have not been more often acknowledged. American Protestants generally recoil from any whiff of one group being "holier than thou," and in particular from the concept of celibacy. But virtually every other trait holds substantially true for the Protestant mission societies and even for some of the Protestant renewing societies. The practice of holding all property in common is not widespread. Yet for a Salvation Army officer, for example, house, automobile, and even uniforms are owned in common, and it is impossible for such officers to earn anything independently or even inherit money that does not become the property of the group. On the other hand, by now many Protestant structures may take the concept of poverty as seriously as (or perhaps even more seriously than) many Catholic orders. Neither poverty nor simplicity of lifestyle is mentioned in Gannon's list of traits, even though these traits do not appear to be automatic correlates of the renunciation of personal property, which he does mention.

However, *Protestant missions do plan for poverty*, so to speak. It is almost universal among Protestant missions for all field personnel under any given agency, whether medical doctors, teachers, or whoever, to *receive modest and identical allotments*, once the cost-of-living and national exchange-rate adjustments have been made. The actual amount may vary significantly from one agency to another. For example, United Presbyterian overseas personnel have more recently been paid on a standard related to the average U.S. United Presbyterian pastor's salary, while workers under the Wycliffe Bible Translators receive more nearly half that amount. On the other hand among Protestants, little thought is given to "poverty" as a specific spiritual virtue. The actual parity and comparative austerity of allotment is more likely the result of pragmatic, situational considerations—"making the money go further." Recently, however, the idea of simplicity of lifestyle has gained considerable interest even in secular circles, partially due to the ecological crisis, and there is at least one Christian organization pledged to promoting "simple lifestyle" as an ideal.[12] The plan is to extend to the families of *donors* the same pattern of comparative austerity and simplicity of lifestyle the field missionary follows and in turn to ask missionary personnel to accept lifestyle simplicity not as a nuisance (to be endured only as long as field service continues) but as a permanent way of life. In any case, it may be that *poverty* rather than the former hardships involved in living overseas may *perform for Protestants* much the *same function as celibacy does for Roman Catholics*—that is, serve as a barrier to the faint-hearted or the uncommitted.

As an extended illustration let us consider three independent, Protestant mission enterprises which in some respects may be viewed as *Protestant counterparts of religious orders*. Table 2 shows the rapid growth of these three associations. Even though all three work in the United States as well as overseas, they involve varying degrees of controlled income per worker just as the standard mission societies do. All three are heavily involved overseas as well, although the overseas affiliations of Inter-Varsity are not included in these figures. Various factors operate in the flourishing of these three groups. All three are heavily involved in ministries on college campuses, where they function almost as "surrogate denominations," but despite good intentions, do not really try very hard to sustain or nourish the denominational relations or backgrounds or foregrounds of the students they touch. None of them, for example, produces or routinely employs any literature that would explain the different denominational traditions to students or acquaint them with present-day denominational problems, successes, or personalities, even though all three are active publishers (Inter-Varsity Press being a major religious publisher today). On the other hand, all three make a rather unusual contribution to the development of Christian leadership among college youth and are justly proud of the literally thousands of traditional ministerial vocations that have resulted from their work. Campus Crusade is especially careful to require its staff to be loyal and supportive to local churches.

Similarities between these organizations can be highlighted by certain fascinating differences. Inter-Varsity, expressive originally of the Plymouth Brethren tradition much more than now, came to the U.S. from England via Canada and retains a British flavor—a certain reserve and cautiousness—a slight de-emphasis upon the role of married women but a healthy

TABLE 2
GROWTH OF THREE PROTESTANT "ORDERS"
INCOME IN $ MILLIONS

Year	Inter-Varsity Christian Fellowship	The Navigators	Campus Crusade
1970	1.1	2.5	8.6
1971	1.2	2.8	12.6
1972	1.4	3.1	17.3
1973	1.8	3.5	22.5
1974	2.5	4.0	23.6
1975	3.2	6.3	27.3
1976	4.0	11.0	34.8
1977	4.9	15.3	43.2
Increase 1970-77	445%	612%	502%

recognition of the vocation of the unmarried. Inter-Varsity's style of ministry is characterized (in sharp contrast to the other two) by exceedingly loose and informal relationships with campus groups, many of which often don't know or sense whether they are or are not "an Inter-Varsity group." The Navigators and Campus Crusade take their style of ministry from the U.S. Navy and the business world, respectively, the former being primarily a fellowship within the Navy in its early years, the latter being founded by a businessman and its current top administrator being a Harvard Business School graduate.

All three, in regard to their internal staff, are highly disciplined organizations and follow a system of an equivalent or parity of consumption-level, each member (as with the "faith missions") raising his or her own support. By now each has a meticulously developed manual of discipline or procedures comparable in function to the *regula* of a Roman Catholic order.

Curiously all three, while heavily involved in *campus* ministries, spurn *worldly* knowledge in favor of constant, daily study of the Bible; and none of them very extensively encourages its staff to work toward higher degrees. In this, they resemble the Franciscans more than the Jesuits. Nevertheless, Inter-Varsity, in particular, which has a far greater intellectual emphasis than the other two, counts hundreds of faculty in American universities who have come through its local student fellowships. The emphasis of all three on disciplined Christian life tends to prepare their people for challenge and/or disappointment once they graduate and depend more heavily upon church traditions for their nurture and continued ministry. But the very fact that graduation provides a major transition from college, usually to a new place as well as a new set of relationships, means probably that these three agencies are not likely to lose their parachurch status and become denominations. The same cannot be said for some organizations that perform ministries that are not localized to a specific age-span; and because celibacy is not inherent in their scheme, any of the three at any time could quite successfully decide to move from order status to church status. Here an important similarity encompasses many Protestant parachurch groups.

The Christian and Missionary Alliance is an example of a parachurch organization that became a denomination against its own will. To some extent derived from what is now the United Presbyterian Church, it is less than 1/30th as large in membership, but sends out twice as many missionaries as the United Presbyterian Church. Now in its third and fourth generation, it is uneasy about its nearly exclusive emphasis upon overseas missions, and it is already tending to broaden its range of involvement in Christian ministry. However, it began as an alliance of congregations seeking to focus attention upon home and foreign missions and, for its first 60 or 70 years, simply made missions its primary concern, in effect expecting those families or members of families not so disposed to go to other churches. In this sense, it has always until recently presumed the existence of "ordinary" local churches concerned with the ordinary spectrum of Christian ministries.

A similar case is that of the Salvation Army, to which we have already made reference. Family members not drawn to the rigorous, inner-city ministry characterizing this group have simply fled and attached themselves to other churches. If it were not for such a reverse selection process, it is doubtful that the durable focus of this group could have been maintained for 100 years. Interestingly enough, at present, profound changes are already taking place in both the Christian and Missionary Alliance and the Salvation Army, both of which are about 100 years old and have about 100,000 communicant members. The latter in 1976 dramatically outstripped almost all denominations in the United States in its percentage increase in membership. This was primarily the result of its recent decision to reverse a long-standing policy of not welcoming new people into its fellowship unless and until such people were ready to become involved in the rigorous, active ministry of the Salvation Army. (In India, where they could not expect converts simply to go to "other" churches, and the organization has long been a church rather than an order, there are four times as many Salvation Army churches as there are in the U.S.)

The durability of the specific goals of these two organizations is thus brought into question by the recent tendency of each of them to accede to the general pattern of American church life and to foster growth in membership whether or not this sustains the rigorous task-oriented emphasis of the past. Both began as auxiliaries to existing church patterns, the Christian and Missionary Alliance largely to the Presbyterian, and the Salvation Army largely to the Anglican. In both cases, the church tradition balked at allowing this type of specialization in its membership, although in neither case was there any significant antagonism on the part of the internal sodality. Just as a Roman Catholic Pope balked at Peter Waldo's lack of upper-class credentials (and another Pope reluctantly made up for that omission by allowing Francis of Assisi to go forward with a similar lack in credentials), so the Anglican authorities in England decided that William Booth's Salvation Army could not properly belong within that Church, but then the (Anglican) "Church Army" was begun in its place.

All this leads us to the very threshold of a concluding discussion about the healing of the "breach" in Protestantism between church and order, denomination and voluntary society, democratic rule and minority initiative—between modality and sodality.

THE HEALING OF THE BREACH

One of the hardest things for Protestants to deal with has been the matter of a mechanism for perpetuation—the inevitable divergence in the products of biological or familial reproduction and spiritual reproduction. Elite, ascetic perfection was not in fact rejected by the Reformers. They merely rejected the *celibate mechanism* that transcended normal biological perpetuation. In what remains perhaps the most brilliant essay on the medieval period, Lynn White, Jr.[13] observes:

> In both intent and practice Protestants were ascetic. . . When the Venetian ambassador called Cromwell's Ironsides "an army of monks," he was close to the truth. For if the Puritans rejected the distinction between a religious and a secular life, it was to monasticize the laity; if they destroyed abbeys, it was to make an abbey of the whole world. Only so one can understand Calvin's Geneva, Knox's Scotland, or colonial New England.

But whether we look closely at Calvin's Geneva or today's Salvation Army, we see that all Protestant attempts to combine elite commitment with a nearly automatic mechanism of perpetuation have resulted in repeated cycles of failure.

Yet the Protestant mentality is not likely soon to embrace celibacy as the only solution. Neither do modern sensitivities about family life encourage the thought that family-based church traditions like the Christian and Missionary Alliance and the Salvation Army can long practice the effective exclusion of their own children who do not wish to sustain their ministry emphasis or the shunning of "mediocre" outsiders in order to maintain pristine goals of specialized service. Protestant mission societies have not found it impossible to allow the children of missionaries to choose some *other* form of Christian service than overseas missions, but the remaining problem of how to allow the children to grow up in two worlds—and thus be able to choose *not* to be missionaries—is becoming more and more serious as sensitivities about quality in family life heighten. Clearly, the Protestant missionary family has brought a valuable new touch to the history of missions; yet there is no doubt that in many circumstances the missionary family is a clumsy and inefficient instrument of ministry.

But if Protestants will not give up children, neither can we expect their denominational leadership soon to be reconciled to the existence of external voluntary societies that are *accountable only to donors uninformed about technicalities and IRS agents unconcerned about goals*.

This leaves us with a Protestantism plagued by denominations that by themselves won't stay elite and associations that, if rejected by the denominations, are no longer accountable to them. For Protestants, certain important principles seem to emerge.

1. There must be a renewed commitment to a denominationalism that acknowledges both the incompleteness and yet the authenticity of each denomination as part of the *una sancta*.

2. At the same time, there must be recognition of the very real dependence of the modalities—the family-based, mainly genetically perpetuated structures called congregations or denominations—upon the sodalities—the more selective, second-choice, purposive, voluntary structures of fellowship and service that tend to be ignored or fought, especially *where* they are *not accountable*. This means American denominational leaders must reevaluate the assumptions which have led to the abandonment of the Young Men's Christian Association, the absorption of the Student Volunteer Movement, the destruction of the Society of Christian Endeavor, and the resistance to the Christian and Missionary Alliance in its early stage as an auxiliary to the churches.

3. Equally, there must be a reciprocal renewal of respect and responsibility toward the denominational traditions on the part of the interdenominational voluntary societies. This means that the Protestant order-like enterprises, especially those of the Type D variety which are not related to any denomination as such (e.g., Youth for Christ, Young Life, Youth with a Mission, Operation Mobilization, Inter-Varsity, Navigators, and Campus Crusade, which are in greater and greater measure custodians of the young), must follow the lead of the David C. Cook Publishing Company (which recently produced popular books on specific denominational traditions) and be willing—intentionally and not just accidentally—to reinforce the non-elite, benefit-of-the-doubt structures (e.g., the congregations and denominations) which all too often they now only abide with subconscious condescension. This also means that staff membership in a Protestant "order," such as Navigators or Wycliffe Bible Translators, should not obscure that person's relationship to his/her own denominational affiliation. Indeed, there is nothing preventing those staff members of the Navigators—who are simultaneously members of the United Presbyterian denomination—from drawing a dotted line around themselves and their work and sending a formal annual report of what could be called "the Presbyterian Navigators Fellowship" to the United Presbyterian General Assembly.

4. Finally, Protestants must accept the example of the Roman Catholic achievement of equivalent training programs ("priestly formation") for the leadership of the two functional arms of the Catholic tradition—diocese and order. This means that the voluntary societies must come to terms with what has become the near universal standard of a graduate theological seminary education as basic for a good proportion of their leaders. This pattern of education not only has considerable intrinsic value but, as it is adopted more extensively by the parachurch agencies will expand the foundation upon which respect and communication between church and order can be built. At the same time, the

seminaries must modify both their course structure and their very perspective of the history of the Christian movement in order that the role of the "Protestant orders" may emerge and gain proper visibility in academic currency.

Notes

1. I realize the dictionary gives several little used and unrelated meanings to the word *modality*, and I realize that both the Catholic and anthropological uses of the word *sodality* are slightly narrower than mine. I am not myself particularly attached to these terms, but I am certainly very concerned to suggest that the two kinds of structures to which I refer are the very warp and the woof of the fabric of all healthy societies and as such are both to be considered legitimate elements in any human community—religious or secular. As a result, much of my own writing has dealt with the dangers resulting where either modality or sodality are missing, or either is not fostered and respected (Winter 1969, 1970, 1971, 1972, 1973, 1974).

2. Kelley, Dean M., *Why Conservative Churches Are Growing* (New York: Harper & Row, 1972).

3. It is not as though Carey's ideas were a new creation. There were a number of mission societies already in the U.S., and of course the Moravians had been active for many decades. Neither is it that no one had ever proposed in writing that a mission society be formed in the Protestant tradition. Justinian Welz, had he been dealing merely with a rural Baptist association, might have succeeded more than a hundred years earlier, but the Lutheran hierarchy was too much for him. If Carey's *Enquiry* was immensely influential, then it is to his honor, not so much to his credit. It was well done, but so was what Welz did. Carey's material simply played an infinitely greater role. *The Protestant missionary movement is in some ways as important as Protestantism itself.* See James A. Scherer, *Justinian Welz, Essays by an Early Prophet of Mission* (Grand Rapids, Mich.: William B. Eerdmans, 1969).

4. See the quote from Bishop Hobart in the second volume of *American Christianity, 1820-1969* by H. Shelton Smith, Robert T. Handy, and Lefferts A. Loetscher (New York: Scribners, 1963), p. 77.

5. See, for example, Robert Baird's *Religion in America*, Henry Bowden, ed. (New York: Harper & Row, 1970); Philip Schaff's *America*, Perry Miller (ed.) (Cambridge: Harvard University Press, Belknap Press, 1961); D. B. Robertson (ed.), *Voluntary Associations* (Richmond: John Knox Press, 1966), especially the chapter entitled

"Voluntary Associations as a Key to History" by James D. Hunt, pp.
359-373; James Gustafson, *Treasure in Earthen Vessels* (New York:
Harper and Brothers, 1961); Milton B. Powell (ed.), *The Voluntary
Church*, (New York: The Macmillan Co., 1967); and J. Roland Pennock
and John W. Chapman (eds.), *Voluntary Associations* (New York:
Atherton Press, 1969). Very new are Howard A. Snyder's *The Problem
of Wineskins: Church Structure in a Technological Age* (Downer's
Grove, Ill.: Inter-Varsity Press, 1976) and Russell E. Richey (ed.),
Denominationalism (Nashville: Abingdon Press, 1977).

    6. My own first use of this phrase was in "The New Missions and
the Mission of the Church," *International Review of Mission*, LX (No.
237): 89-100.

    7. For a fuller discussion of this problem, see "The New Missions
and the Mission of the Church," *International Review of Mission*, LX
(No. 237): 89-100, or *The Warp and The Woof of the Christian
Movement: Organizing for Mission* by Ralph D. Winter and R. Pierce
Beaver (South Pasadena: William Carey Library, 1970).

    8. The data underlying these calculations and those in Figures 2, 3
and 4 are as follows:

	Year	Conciliar		Non-conciliar				
	1925	11,020		2,588				
	1952	10,416		8,160				
		CCC + NCCCUSA	EFMA	Unaffiliated	TAM + FOM	IFMA	TOTALS	
	Type A,B,C	8986	4564	4784	37	0	18,371	= 53%
	Type D	312	1992	6088	1612	6085	16,089	=47%
1969	Totals	9298	6556	10,872	1649	6085	34,460	
	%	27%	19%	31%	5%	18%	100%	
	Type A,B,C	6921	4848	5106	43	0	16,918	=47%
	Type D	0	1839	9755	1008	6450	19,052	=53%
1972	Totals	6921	6687	14,861	1051	6450	35,970	
	%	19%	19%	41%	3%	18%	100%	
	Type A,B,C	5339	4892	5003	49	0	15,283	=41%
	Type D	0	2120	11,673	1468	6406	21,667	=59%
1975	Totals	5339	7012	16,676	1517	6406	36,950	
	%	14%	19%	46%	4%	17%	100%	

Code: CCC = Canadian Council of Churches
           NCCCUSA = National Council of Churches of Christ in the U.S.A.
           EFMA = Evangelical Foreign Missions Association
           TAM + FOM = The Associated Missions & The Fellowship of Missions
           IFMA = Interdenominational Foreign Mission Association

    9. Three examples are Earl MacCormac's "The Transition from
Voluntary Missionary Society to the Church as a Missionary Organi-
zation Among American Congregationalists, Presbyterians and Metho-
dists" (Yale University, Ph.D. dissertation, 1960); Fred J. Hood's
"Presbyterianism and the New American Nation: A Case Study"
(Princeton University, Ph.D. dissertation, 1968); and Marybeth Rupert's

"The Emergence of the Independent Missionary Organization as an American Institution" (Yale University, Ph.D. dissertation, 1974).

10. See "Pluralism and Consensus: Why Mainline Church Mission Budgets Are in Trouble" by Richard G. Hutcheson, Jr. in *The Christian Century*, XCIV (July 6-13, 1977): 618-624.

11. Refer to Hood, Op. Cit.

12. The United Presbyterian Order for World Evangelization, 1605 Elizabeth Street, Pasadena, CA, 91104.

13. See the chapter entitled "The Significance of Medieval Christianity" in *The Vitality of the Christian Tradition*, edited by George F. Thomas (New York: Harper & Brothers, 1945), pp. 87-115.

6

Theological Schools

Loyde H. Hartley and David S. Schuller

Theological schools in North America exhibit a wide variety of organizational patterns. Some are affiliates of major universities, while others are free-standing institutions without formal relations to any other higher education establishment. They vary in size, having as few as 9 and as many as 3,202 students in 1976. They differ in the requirements they demand of students, in the nomenclature and duration of degree programs, and in the nature of internal governance structures.

Those institutions of higher education which provide *training for* persons interested in entering denominational service as *professional religious leaders* constitute the limits of this brief review. Several theological schools emphasize in their promotional materials the importance of theological education for persons entering professions *other than ministry* and for general liberal arts enrichment. The preparation of persons for ministry as an occupation, however, is the thread that holds together this fairly diverse set of organizations.

The Association of Theological Schools in the United States and Canada (ATS) is the "trade association" and accrediting agency for a majority of Protestant, Catholic, and Jewish theological schools in the United States and Canada. It has developed a set of criteria for accrediting those institutions which provide theological education at the post-graduate level.[1] A substantial number of schools, however, do not

225

qualify for accredited membership in this federation because their constituencies do not require or perhaps even wish to have a college-educated clergy. Furthermore, some schools which train persons for ministry deliberately do not seek the relationship to other seminaries implied by professional accreditation, although the religious bodies supporting these schools do recognize the importance of *some* education for the practice of ministry in their midst. A few theological schools have sought accreditation with regional academic accrediting agencies rather than professional accreditation with ATS. Over the years, moreover, there have emerged a large number of "Bible Colleges" which offer regular college courses and a large number of "religious studies" courses developed and taught with sensitivity toward particular religious persuasions. Often such Bible colleges train people who enter directly into the ministry without additional theological education beyond the undergraduate level. (Bible Colleges are accredited by the American Association of Bible Colleges.)

In order to understand the complexity of these organizational patterns, it is necessary to look at the various forces in the external environment which can and do impact upon the organizational patterns of theological schools. The two most critical external environments are the *denomination* and *academia* (as noted by Niebuhr[2]), to be treated shortly in detail.

More specifically, the primary documents and/or confessional doctrines and traditions of denominations constitute an important external factor for theological schools. Furthermore, a sometimes obscure and often hypothetical group which seminary administrators refer to as the "constituency" may also be an important factor, being sometimes subdenominational and at other times ecumenical in composition. Many other organizations also have effects upon theological schools: other theological schools, state and federal governments, philanthropic foundations, private benefactors, business and industry, and demographic and ecological characteristics of the community in which the seminary is physically located.

The first part of this chapter, then, identifies the basic resources needed by theological schools as well as the external organizations controlling these; the second part reviews the ways in which seminaries are organized to secure and use these resources; the final section discusses some of the tensions which have emerged.

THEOLOGICAL SCHOOLS AND THEIR INTERORGANIZATIONAL CONTEXT

Role of the Denomination

For most theological schools, the single most important external organizational structure is the denomination. Access of theological schools to a church tradition and its essential resources most frequently is through direct affiliation with a particular denomination. But this may also occur by means of working arrangements with specific congregations, clergy who are alumni or friends of the school, and/or a variety of ecumenical structures.

Theological schools depend, in differing extents, on the denomination for the following resources: foundational legitimacy, basic theological outlook and informing traditions, basic financial support and monthly cash flow, recruitment of faculty members and approval of faculty appointments, recruitment of students, field education settings for interns or students needing short term experience, placement of students after graduation, and evaluation of educational programs.

While theological schools clearly could not survive without confessional documents or doctrines of the faith, they are in little danger of being deprived of them. These documents not only provide identity and a link to the past but in some instances establish doctrinal standards for students and faculty. In some instances students and faculty are asked to pledge their allegiance to the Heidelberg Catechism, the Westminster Confession, or some other article of faith. Some theological schools expect their faculty to sign yearly statements indicating their agreement with doctrines. In other instances, theological schools have sensed the educational and financial values of sharing faculty, courses, and libraries. Where ecumenical composition is strong, some are struggling to define the points at which they seek to educate leaders in a specific theological, ecclesiastical tradition—that a person be graduated as a Methodist minister or a Roman Catholic priest—within a broader religious setting. Many seminaries which hold to a strict doctrinal standard are able to discuss broader educational issues with schools of radically differing theological viewpoints through the forum of agencies such as the ATS.

The relationship of origins to organizational control is illustrated in the statement of purpose in the charter of Reformed Theological Seminary, Jackson, Mississippi:

> To establish, control and develop an institute of theological studies established upon the authority of the Word of God standing written in the sixty-six books of the Holy Bible, all therein being verbally inspired by Almighty God and therefore without error, and committed to the Reformed Faith as set forth in the Westminster Confession of Faith and the Larger and Shorter Catechisms as originally adopted by the Presbyterian Church in the United States.

Few theological schools are fully endowed; federal funds are not available to theological schools as theological schools; seminary alumni are not wealthy. Many theological schools, therefore, require massive denominational money to support current programs.

Most students in theological seminaries were recruited for the ministry by pastors,[3] and many such students have some denominational sanction before entering theological schools. For example, in the United Methodist Church, students interested in the ministry are listed as ministerial students in regional judicatory records; in the United Church of Christ, judicatories approve persons as "students-in-care." The suggestions which pastors and judicatories make regarding theological education are highly influential with students as they make their choices. Moreover, many theological schools require formal recommendations by pastors for applicants.

Professional placement of graduates has in the last decade become a concern of critical importance. Theological schools which have identifiable constituencies often report greater success in placing graduates in denominational positions. Several denominations have increasingly *fewer positions* available for clergy, while the number of *graduates* continues to swell, including major increases in the number of women graduates. The relationships among size of denomination, number of congregations, and number of ordained clergy on its roster may be in serious imbalance in any given period. Notice in Table 1 that only four of the twelve denominations listed experienced an increase in the members-per-clergy ratio from 1950 to 1975 (Church of God, Church of the Nazarene, Presbyterian Church in the U.S., Reformed Church). This means that the other eight experienced a *decrease* in this ratio—their numbers of clergy have grown more rapidly (or declined less rapidly) than their overall memberships, creating a potential "surplus" of pastors. Thus, it is evident that theological schools which have access to the placement systems of denominations have, therefore, a distinct advantage over those which do not.

Theological schools may use denominational channels for recruiting faculty members, especially for faculty whose expertise is related to the parish. Moreover, in some instances, faculty appointments require the approval of a church body. Denominations that adopt strong confessional positions such as the Roman Catholic, Lutheran, and Presbyterian bodies are concerned that major teaching posts be filled by members of their particular group to assure that ministerial candidates be knowledgeable and confessional church leaders. Roman Catholic teachers, for example, normally make a yearly profession of faith.[4]

To the extent that theological schools require (or make elective) courses in parish practice, the seminaries are dependent on congregations to provide the context for such education. Most schools provide at least minimal instruction in this area. As theological schools have begun to take more seriously the need to educate men and women for ministry, many have experimented with teaching significant parts of the curriculum in parish settings. Several major seminaries in the greater

TABLE 1
NUMBER OF MEMBERS, CONGREGATIONS, AND CLERGY
OF SELECTED AMERICAN PROTESTANT DENOMINATIONS
IN 1950 AND 1975

Denomination	Year	Members	Congre-gations	Ordained Clergy	Members per Clergy ratio
American Baptist	1950	1,561,073	6,768	6,200	252
Church	1975	1,603,033	5,999	8,416	190
Christian Churches-	1950	1,767,964	7,769	8,208	215
Disciples	1975	1,297,464	4,514	6,554	198
Church of God	1950	107,094	1,964	2,455	44
(Anderson, Ind.)	1975	166,259	2,239	2,905	57
Episcopal Church	1950	2,417,464	7,116	6,473	373
	1975	2,857,513	7,197	12,186	234
Lutheran Church	1950	2,395,356	5,159	4,571	524
in America	1975	2,986,078	5,760	7,647	390
Church of the	1950	226,684	3,480	4,552	50
Nazarene	1975	441,093	4,733	7,223	61
Southern Baptist	1950	7,079,889	27,788	22,293	318
Convention	1975	12,733,124	34,880	55,000	232
Presbyterian Church	1950	668,206	3,647	2,795	239
in the U.S.	1975	878,126	4,028	2,818	312
Reformed Church	1950	183,178	763	887	206
of America	1975	355,052	902	904	393
United Church of	1950	1,977,418	8,366	8,269	239
Christ	1975	1,818,762	6,552	9,536	191
United Methodist	1950	9,659,540	44,677	27,722	348
Church	1975	9,957,710	39,027	35,106	284
United Presbyterian	1950	2,391,967	8,535	9,179	260
Church in the U.S.A.	1975	2,657,699	8,630	13,771	193

Source: "Clergy Supply and Demand," research in progress, by Jackson W.
Carroll and Robert L. Wilson

New York area have experimented with teaching a full year of seminary
education in the field—in urban parishes. While field education has been
growing in popularity, what distinguishes this new design is the attempt
to do rigorous scholarly work simultaneously using the parishes as the
principal locale for study rather than the classroom. The Lancaster (Pa.)
Theological Seminary offers the entire second year of professional
studies in parish settings. Inter/Met, an experimental theological school

in Washington, D.C., offered, until its closing in 1977, the entire program of studies in parishes.

Theological schools isolated from the organization(s) which will ultimately employ its graduates run the risk of becoming superfluous. As the result, most schools provide for receiving some kind of regular *feedback from the denomination* on the nature and effectiveness of their training program. Boards of trustees generally include large represent-ations of parish clergy and denominational leaders. In some instances, the denomination may employ sanctions to induce greater conformity to the doctrines of the denomination. Southern Baptist Theological Seminary, Louisville, found itself pressured by its denomination several times in the last century (1879, 1896) to demand the resignation of a prominent professor and president.[5] During the latter half of the nineteenth century a number of church-related seminaries came under pressure to force the resignation of men whose orthodoxy was questioned. The Presbyterian Church in the U.S.A., the Congregational Church, and others were involved. Chicago Theological Seminary, Andover-Newton, Princeton, Union Seminary-Richmond were all involved in serious controversies. Most recently, Concordia Seminary, St. Louis, has been involved in a conflict that eventuated in the exodus of most of the faculty and student body in 1974. The administration and the majority of the faculty of this school lost their posts because of refusing to subscribe to the dictates for orthodoxy of the Lutheran Missouri Synod leadership.[6] (See chapter 9 for the case of the Missouri Synod and Concordia Seminary.)

Even when all other dependencies on the denomination are reduced to a minimum, an historical tie with a specific denomination (occasionally more than one denomination) is usually maintained by a theological school. For example, the dean of Harvard Divinity School recently identified "communities of faith" as the primary constituency of divinity schools.[7] The deans of Yale Divinity School and Union Theological Seminary-New York are faithful in attending inter-seminary meetings conducted by the denominations with which their schools have been historically affiliated, although their dependence on the denominations in question for fiscal survival is not great.

Theological Schools and Academia

A second major external variable influencing theological schools is universities. While theological schools which are integral parts of universities are obviously very dependent in this regard, even free-standing denominational schools remain somewhat dependent on colleges and universities.

Among the resources provided by academia are the following: training of professors, publications of journals, sponsorship and dissemination of research, sources for training and recruitment of pre-theological students, experimentation with models of education, secular scientific study of religious phenomena, and general opportunities for informal fraternizing with graduate students and faculty. Theological schools closely affiliated with universities have additional kinds of dependencies, including general governance, provision of buildings and housing, participation in larger endowments, and library services.

For theological schools *not* located on university campuses, perhaps the most significant dependency on the university is for the training of professors. Free-standing theological schools frequently lack the capacity to train their own professors and so look to the universities for providing the doctorate as well as post-doctoral training opportunities. This is especially true in an era of theology/arts and sciences cross-fertilization (e.g., theology and the arts, literature, philosophy, psychology, sociology, education, communications arts, etc). Publication of journals and sponsorship of basic research are not limited to universities, yet the universities are clearly in a leadership position in this area because of their greater resources in funds and specialists.

Those theological schools accredited by the Association of Theological Schools require a baccalaureate degree of almost all their applicants. As a result, theological schools are having to rely more on colleges and universities to provide pre-professional academic background. The training of pre-theological students has been traditionally in the liberal arts area, but more recently persons with backgrounds in business, science and technology, and other fields have been entering theological schools. In some Roman Catholic seminaries, the undergraduate education is provided in the seminary itself. At one time, seminaries in the ATS agreed on a basic pattern of courses considered necessary prior to entrance to seminary. But no one pattern is prescribed as normative for all pre-seminary education today. The current statement of the ATS regarding pre-theological studies defines the need for understandings in three areas: (1) general: understanding of human selfhood, social institutions, culture, science, the modes and processes of understanding; (2) theological: Bible, history of the religious tradition, constructive theological methodology and interpretation; (3) linguistic skills: Greek or Hebrew, Latin, German, French, or Spanish.[8]

While theological schools themselves frequently generate a considerable amount of innovation internally, innovative strategies to general education are more often generated within the universities. For instance, the notion of education by extension, the giving of academic credit for life experience, and the emergence of non-conventional doctoral programs all can be traced to experimentation within universities. Theological education relates most specifically to other areas of professional education in the universities. Many of the problems faced in the education of ministers have their counterparts in the education of doctors, architects, lawyers, or teachers. Professional education faces a perennial problem in maintaining a balance between necessary theory and the actual work carried out by practitioners in the field at any given period. Theological schools have taken this challenge seriously within the last decade, resulting in many innovations involving contextual education and the utilization of the resources of other academic, religious, and community institutions.

Persons committed to confessional study of religion have over the past years become increasingly aware of the value of disinterested scientific study of religion to the extent that most theological schools now offer or require courses in the psychology of religious experience and the sociology of religion. Yet, theological schools depend largely on universities for the *advancement* of these disciplines.

Theological Schools and the State

Because of the strength of the idea of separation of church and state, under a system of denominational pluralism in the United States it might be expected that seminaries need not be concerned about the influence of state and federal levels of government as important external factors. In some American states, the separation of church and state has led to a total "hands off" policy with regard to religiously affiliated institutions of learning which has resulted in the "diploma mills" benefitting from the protective legitimacy of established denominationalism. However, in other states (e.g., Pennsylvania), the state department of higher education may actually participate in the accrediting process of the institution and grant the charter by which degrees may be granted. In an attempt to protect the consumer of education, many states have passed legislation that establishes what amounts to another form of accreditation. Laws designed to discourage diploma mills have frequently been phrased so broadly that they have caused problems in additional reporting, yearly visitations, and increased costs for reputable, established, theological schools. For many years the federal government has depended upon voluntary accreditation as the basis for the giving of a variety of individual and institutional grants. Now the Federal Office of Education is pursuing a more rigorous policy of monitoring the field of voluntary accreditation because of its quasi-governmental functions.[9]

Theological schools, moreover, rely heavily on the state and federal governments for *tax exemption*, a privilege which is being questioned by an ever-enlarging number of state and federal legislators. Theological schools receive funds for aid to student veterans through the Federal GI Bill as well as benefit from other federal provisions for aiding students. Students may also apply for government-insured long term loans from the United Student Aid Fund.

Moreover, since university-based schools of theology often benefit from federal funds which come to the whole university, as a result they are subject to some federal regulations not applying to free-standing schools, e.g., equal opportunity and affirmative action legislation.[10]

Philanthropic Foundations and Private Benefactors

A fairly sizable number of theological seminaries benefit regularly from awards granted by private foundations. In some cases, these grants are competitive in nature. The impact of foundations is particularly notable when foundation money is used for innovation in theological seminaries. In the past, foundations participated frequently in the construction of libraries and buildings and have provided major assistance in the continuing education of faculty members. In recent years, foundations have increasingly assumed more pro-active roles in determining the specific areas in theological education for which they would provide grants programs. They consequently have become a force in determining the precise shape of theological education. Funds for theological research and scholarship, the advancement of theological consortia, the strengthening of education in predominantly black seminaries, the exploring of new directions among theological libraries, encouraging the involvement of lay people in the education of professional clergy, and furthering the planning and fiscal skills of administrators—all have been recent priority concerns of foundations.

The impact of private benefactors on theological education can be very great, even to the extent that the theological persuasion of the benefactor determines the stance of the institution itself, although most benefactors do not exert this level of influence. Head executives of theological seminaries do, however, maintain private lists of donors whom they can ask periodically for major contributions. The collective influence of benefactors is rarely exerted because their relationship to the seminary is largely through personal ties to the head executive.

Theological Schools and Business-Industry

Apart from theological schools' participation in general commerce as a consumer, theological schools have comparatively little dependency on or interaction with the business and industry sector. In some instances, seminaries may approach businesses for favorable part-time positions for students while they are enrolled in studies. Moreover, some industries make matching contributions to the gifts of their employees to philanthropic concerns, although this has not produced a major source of income for theological schools. Too, some staff members (e.g., secretaries) may receive experience in business before being employed by theological schools. The pay scales for these persons tends to be competitive with business and industry. Some seminaries are affected by unionization via hiring of unionized employees.

Other Theological Schools and the Local Community

As stated previously, other theological schools and accrediting agencies have emerged as important external factors for theological schools, especially since the organization of the Association of Theological Schools in 1936. Schools are accredited by ATS on the basis of peer-determined standards and peer evaluations. Through the accrediting process, theological schools have been able to mitigate somewhat the power of other external organizations to control necessary resources, vis-a-vis the denomination and the university. For example, accrediting commissions' downgrading of schools for insufficient faculty, poor library resources, or fiscal unsoundness provides leverage for the theological school to seek funds or other support. Some schools have changed locations and/or affiliated with other theological schools to maintain their accredited status.

The racial and ethnic composition of the neighborhood in which theological schools are located generally has less impact upon theological schools than upon other institutions in the community. The comparative lack of the significance of demographic factors is related to the fact that the theological schools have constituencies which are usually regional, often denominational, and in some cases national in scope. In some instances, however, students who would not ordinarily attend a particular seminary choose it because of its location near their home or their place of work, more true perhaps of the students of long-Americanized denominations. Over the years, this factor has contributed to the ecumenical composition of the student population in many theological schools. Methodist students, for example, often attend the theological schools of other denominations because they can be appointed to Methodist congregations in the immediate environs of the seminary.

Moreover, the particular organization of the curriculum by a theological school reflects a general orientation to standards and doctrines traditionally considered important by the school. Traditional patterns of curricula begin with Biblical studies, move to historical studies, then to theological studies, and finally to praxis. Implied in this list is a kind of ontological order which suggests that the faith derives primarily from the fundamental "symbols" and moves through history and theological reflection to the practice of ministry. As understandings of the establishing documents change, structures in the seminary change.

A number of seminaries have attempted recently to build new curricular patterns about the competencies demanded in contemporary ministry. In 1973, the Association of Theological Schools embarked on a massive project, the "Readiness for Ministry Program," initially funded for a half million dollars by the Lilly Endowment. Conducting continent-wide empirical studies, this project was able to define a core set of sixty-four characteristics or dimensions that clergy and laity across denominations use in *assessing ministry*. The project subsequently developed a package of assessment instruments that evaluate a significant number of these criteria. A large number of seminaries and church bodies are using the data and the instruments to evaluate the adequacy of their programs of theological education.[11]

PATTERNS OF SEMINARY ORGANIZATION

Theological schools have needed to fulfill both adaptive and cohesive functions vis-a-vis denominations, academia, and other sectors of society. The variety of organizational patterns found in theological schools can in large part be understood by analyzing the ways in which schools have intentionally restructured their environments so as to shape them or to be shaped by them. Below are listed seven organizational patterns extant in contemporary theological education. The first two— the *freestanding* denominational school and the *university-related* school—constitute the major patterns, with the other five being interesting variants.

Table 2 presents the distribution of theological schools, full-time faculty, and students in the United States according to organizational relationship. The reader may note that denominational schools comprise 89% of the total vs. 11% for the inter- or nondenominational. Furthermore, 91% of the schools are "freestanding" and so *not* university units, with the other 9% being units of universities either of their own denomination or no denomination affiliation. The same ratios obtain with regard to general proportions of faculty and students, with freestanding denominational schools having the lion's share of both. The interdenominational schools, however, while in the minority, have a disproportionately greater number of faculty and students than do the denominational schools. About half (77 of 153) of the denominational schools now have some affiliation with a "cluster" of kindred schools; and about the same proportion of the interdenominational or nondenominational schools (7 of 19) have cluster affiliations. The vast majority of such cluster schools (92%) have denominational ties, although they tend to have a smaller proportion of the students as compared with the nondenominational cluster schools. In other words, almost half of ATS schools in the United States now operate within types of local coalitions of kindred but denominationally varied make-up.

Denominational Schools—Freestanding and University-related

As stated, 89% of the American schools affiliated with the Association of Theological Schools in the United States and Canada (ATS) are

TABLE 2

DISTRIBUTION OF U.S. THEOLOGICAL SCHOOLS, FULL-TIME FACULTY, AND STUDENTS BY TYPE OF ORGANIZATIONAL RELATIONSHIP

Type of School and Organizational Relationships	Number	%	Number of Full-time Faculty	%	Number of Students	%
Denominational schools						
Freestanding	142	83	2,159	79	31,276	76
Integral with University	11	6	235	9	3,141	7
Inter/nondenominational						
Freestanding	14	8	235	9	5,016	12
Integral with University	5	3	116	4	1,645	4
Total	172	100	2,745	100	41,078	100
Denominational schools with cluster affiliation	77	92	1,023	87	14,186	86
Inter/nondenominational with cluster affiliation	7	8	156	13	2,223	14
Total	84	100	1,179	100	16,409	100

Source: *Bulletin*, Part 4, 1977 (Directory), The Association of Theological Schools .
Table includes only ATS member schools within United States.

denominationally affiliated, either (1) "freestanding" or (2) integrally related to a university of the same denominational affiliation. The identity of these schools is linked very closely with the denomination, and the schools very frequently carry the *name* of the denomination as a part of their corporation name (e.g., Lancaster Theological Seminary of the United Church of Christ). The reliance of these schools on the denomination's essential resources is obviously great. They may be characterized as having faculties which are largely made up of members of the school's parent denomination, and the students are likewise predominantly members of that denomination. The school exists to *train* religious leaders *for the denomination* in the style and manner required by it, and the graduates generally accept positions in the denomination. It is not uncommon, moreover, for students of another denomination who happen to attend the denomination's schools to be coopted into the sponsoring denomination, notwithstanding the fact that such schools rarely aim at deliberate proselytization.

In some instances, appointment to the faculty and/or administration of these schools is reward for loyal denominational service—a way in which denominations can encourage cohesiveness and compliance of the schools to the denominational norms.

Instruction in denomination-affiliated schools is more likely to be confessional in nature, articulating and providing apology for the denominational stance of the sponsoring church. A conservative Methodist seminary, for example, will consciously utilize the Wesleyan tradition in emphasizing patterns of holiness which it will seek to inculcate into its students through formal and informal means. More generally, courses in the life and theology of its spiritual forefathers—Luther, Calvin, Aquinas, Wesley, et al., the history and polity of the denomination, and a survey of the particular mission fields served by that given denomination will form a required part of the curriculum.

The freestanding denominational schools are administratively structured to maximize the availability of the denomination's resources and, indeed, often consider themselves an integral part of the denomination's structure—whether it be the equivalent of a judicatory, a congregation, or a denominational program agency.

Of course, theological schools may organize themselves in such a way as to *introduce innovation* into the denomination. For example, several "liberal" Protestant seminaries have promoted the critical, scientific study of the Scriptures as a major exegetical device. As the result, this stance has come to be supported by the denominational leaders, as well as pastors and to a lesser extent laity, in these denominations.

Non-Denominational University-Related Schools

Theological education in university-based theological schools (e.g., Harvard Divinity School, Yale Divinity School, University of Chicago

Divinity School, etc.), especially in those instances where the university is *not* integrally affiliated with a particular denomination (only 5 of 172), may more often be characterized as being like a "Department of Near Eastern Studies" than exclusively as a training ground for clergy. In general, the survival of a university-based school is *more* dependent on *finding its place within the university structure than* within a *denomination.* The quality of instruction and research here reflects the disinterested, "scientific-academic" stance vis-a-vis the phenomenon of religion rather than a stance of "confession."

Students are more likely to be recruited from a wide background of ethnic and religious heritages, and orthodoxy is determined on the basis of the canons of *academic* research rather than standards of *spirituality.* The faculty will typically include persons representing a range of theological positions within the broad Christian tradition as well as Jews, Moslems, and Hindus. Frequently, in addition to degree programs leading to ministry, several other programs will prepare graduates to assume teaching posts in "religious studies" at seminaries and colleges. A center for the study of world religions often bridges the seminary and the graduate department of the university. Lodged within the Divinity School of Harvard University, for example, is the "Center for the Study of World Religions." The School's register describes it:

> The Center was established in 1958 to encourage the pursuit of a coordinated study and understanding of different religious and historical traditions. It is particularly concerned with the relationships between various religious committees in both practice and theory, past and present, and with the religiousness of man in its varieties.[12]

An intermediate type between the university-affiliated school of theology and the freestanding denominational school is the school of theology situated in a university setting but with strong connectional ties to a denomination. These schools reflect some of the characteristics of *both* types. Perkins School of Theology of Southern Methodist University and Princeton Seminary would illustrate schools that still educate *primarily* for the *parish* ministry *but* have maintained structural or functional *ties with their universities.*

Clusters of Theological Schools

In the 1960s, several theological schools which were located near one another decided it would be advantageous to affiliate and to promote cooperative efforts among their respective institutions. Their cooperative efforts included tuition-free cross registrations, inter-institutional team taught courses, ecumenical seminars, and sponsorship of special lectureships. Some institutions were motivated to participate in this cooperative effort because they anticipated it would reduce the cost of operations, thereby reducing their dependence on the denominations or universities which sponsor them for financial resources. Over half of all American schools have such "cluster" affiliation. (See Table 2.)

Charles L. Taylor identified fifteen such clusters in the United States and Canada, eleven of which he studied for his report.[13] These vary considerably in the size, strength, and degree of cooperation. The Toronto School of Theology functions as a school incorporating the resources of seven schools of theology. The Graduate Theological Union in Berkeley is composed of nine seminaries plus a center for Judaic studies and a center for urban-black studies. The Boston Theological Institute coordinates significant programs for the nine theological schools of the greater Boston area. These three clusters are "federations" with full time staffs and complex programs. In other cases, two or three schools in a given area cooperate informally, with the strength of cooperation rising and falling with the interest and initiative of administrators and faculty at any given time period.

Ecumenical or Nondenominational Schools

Some schools have intentionally constructed faculties and recruited student bodies which are *ecumenical* or nondenominational in their compositions. These schools are distinguished by the fact that they identify as their constituencies persons from a *wide variety of denominations.*[14] Fuller Theological Seminary in Pasadena, for example, is a large evangelical school that stands on a clearly defined statement of faith. The school is ecumenical, drawing its faculty and student body from the conservative groups within a variety of Protestant denominations.

Parish-Oriented Schools

Concerned that traditional seminary education often draws students away from the active life of parishes, sequestering them in classrooms and libraries, some attempts have been made to educate primarily in the parish setting. The most significant experiment has been Inter/Met in Washington, D.C. Founded in 1972, its goal was to educate for ministry "on the job." It designed a curriculum that used the resources of personnel and settings of the Washington metropolitan area, seeking a new wedding of the academic and the practical. Instruction and supervision were provided for the candidates by parish clergy, professors from other institutions, staff advisors, and lay teachers from a variety of settings. The new institution was begun with substantial foundation support. However, because of its inability to find necessary funding, Inter-Met ceased operations at its 1977 commencement.

Bible Colleges

While Bible colleges are not theological schools per se in the sense that they do not offer post-baccalaureate professional education, a sizable number of their students intend to enter the ministry without additional theological training. There were 61 accredited and 14 non-accredited such schools in 1976-1977. Often these Bible schools are affiliated with conservative denominations or sect-type groups. These religious bodies do not require as high an educational standard for clergy as do other religious bodies which sponsor post-bachelor degree theological education. The organizational pattern of these schools is quite different, because the perceived needs of their sponsoring bodies are different. It is interesting to observe the steady development of graduate departments in many Bible colleges that bear a striking resemblance to those of mainline Protestant seminaries. Graduates of the college divisions often sense a need for additional education after several years in a parish ministry. The graduate departments have been developed to provide a more thorough gounding in theology and practice either before or after entry into the ministry.

Theological Education by Extension

Theological education by extension originated in Central and South America, although there are now some sizable extension programs in the United States and Canada. At least nineteen ATS schools are now offering such courses for credit. Fuller Seminary has a notable extension program serving persons as far away as Seattle and Denver from its home campus in the Los Angeles area. Theological education by extension has also found particular appeal in the Episcopal Church, which ordains a sizable number of persons who have had no training in theological seminaries. The primary advantage of theological education by extension, cited by those who support it, is the ability to serve students without disrupting them from their life setting. Hence, it represents another approach of theological schools to meet the needs of the church and church leaders.[15]

SOME SOURCES OF CONFLICT AND TENSION

When a theological school depends on more than one external organization for essential resources, conflicts and tensions emerge as the school tries to accommodate to the conflicting interests of these multiple influences. In this regard, theological schools are similar to other organizations which span more than one major social institution (e.g., religious bookstores which are oriented to both denominations and business, Amtrak which is related to both government and the railroad business, etc.). The conflicts and strains may contribute to the strength of these organizations as well as to their weaknesses.

For example, the universities which train professors for most theological schools characteristically emphasize adaptation to a *disin-*

terested stance in the study of religion, while the denominations which sponsor theological schools expect cohesiveness via *confessional* stances in the study of religion, if not as a denominational policy at least as the normative expectation of many practicing clergy and laity. Moreover, students from a confessional background often spend enormous amounts of energy combatting the disinterested study of religion, with little effect.

Another kind of strain is that between the model of spirituality and religious goals inculcated by documents and doctrines as taught in the theological school, on the one hand, and the more pragmatic outlooks demanded of graduates once in the ministry for maintaining and "promoting" the structures of the church, on the other. (See Chapter 8) for elaboration of this dilemma.) Academic rigor may in some instances be construed as competing with competence in professional skills for the loyalty of students and faculty alike. Programs of theological education for the vocationally committed often seem too narrow for the "seekers" or persons who want to study religion for its liberal arts value. Students and faculty interested in rigorous study of the more academic areas of theological curriculum (e.g., church history, Biblical archaeology, etc.) often consider students and faculty interested in praxis to be shallow and lacking in substance; and the latter, in turn, are known to accuse the former of irrelevance.

At best, however, this tension contributes to the production of knowledge about religion undergirded by academic integrity, while not undercutting the institution of religion which is the object of study. Confessions or beliefs which are clearly far removed from that which can be validated are revised or allowed to become obsolete, as the result of this tension.

For the last decade, a "crisis of values" has been observed at the heart of American society. But traditional religious institutions are accused basically of not having become suspect as have other institutions in that society. On the other hand, each of the various organizational patterns of theological schools (noted earlier) appears to have a potentially constructive contribution to make toward defining the role that religion might play in the creation of a set of values for our contemporary age. Thus, universities with their various graduate departments, including religion, might continue to serve as centers for the critical analysis of religion as a humanistic and scientific phenomenon. Denominational, confessional schools will continue to educate the men and women who will teach and guide the various communities of faith, large and small. University-related schools have the resources to pursue creative scholarship and prepare a highly educated corps of persons as potential teachers in church-related institutions. Extension programs can serve people who otherwise might have no access to theological education. Strains and conflicts tend to arise as advocates of a particular pattern seek to duplicate the tasks better performed by one of the other structures, or when they get into competition over scarce resources such as students or funds.

Another kind of tension is produced by the shifting locale of power in denominations. As centralized denominational structures weaken, some theological schools have necessarily moved *from central to decentralized* sources of denominational funding (e.g., to regional judicatories, local congregations, individual benefactors related to the denomination). For example, in 1975, the United Church of Christ (UCC) ended all *national* denominational fiscal support for theological education, and what denominational support the UCC theological schools now receive is through regional offices (conferences) or local churches. The change in source of funding provided the occasion for theological schools to develop new configurations of relationships to different persons within the denominational structure, with new patterns of influence emerging.

The nature of educational programs in theological schools has changed in order to adapt to the market of persons *already possessing* theological training. That is, in recent years, many theological schools have introduced major programs in *continuing education* of the clergy rather than trying to increase the enrollment of persons entering the profession for the first time. This change may be understood, in part, as the schools' response to an oversupply of clergy in many liberal Protestant denominations. The growth of the Doctor of Ministry (D.Min.) programs offering a second professional degree for clergy illustrates this change in program for theological schools. The enrollment in D.Min. programs was 201 in 1969, but it reached *4,252* students *in 1976*; while during this same period, Master of Divinity and kindred programs increased only from 20,620 students to 24,683.[16] (It may be noted that a small minority of theological schools offer the D.Min. as a first theological degree.) Likewise, enrollment in graduate programs for persons not entering the professional ministry (M.A., M.A.R., M.R.E.) has also increased during this same period. In 1969, 79% of persons enrolled in theological school on the whole were in first professional *degree* programs; while in 1976, only 63% were so enrolled. The change may in a large part be attributed to theological schools adapting to the changing market of persons already possessing the first professional degree in theological education.

Finally, there occasionally is disagreement over the proper model and orientation of the theological school in relation to the larger society. Should it mainly be a place of reflection and integration and so located in a cloister shut off from the mainstream of social activity? Or, should it be a catalyst and observer of the intersection of the human and the divine and so be located in the marketplace where theology can impact everyday life? (Cf. Hesser's discussion in Chapter 8.)

To summarize, these conflicts can be analyzed by noting the multiplicity of expectations which external organizations and reference groups have for theological schools. Denominations and local churches expect clergy trained in their tradition to be suitably fitted for the practice of ministry. Academia expects academic integrity and rigorous scholarship. The community in which a seminary is located expects a fair share of community service. Conversely, theological schools also have reciprocal expectations toward these agencies, as has been previously outlined. Imbalance between forces for adaptation and forces for cohesion involves strain and at times conflict. Change from centralized to decentralized decision making has required changes in the organization of theological schools. Changes in the market for persons with theological educations have led schools to introduce new programs for laity and existing clergy.

Notes

1. The Association of Theological Schools, "Procedures, Standards, and Criteria for Membership," *A.T.S. Bulletin* 32, part 3 (1976).

2. H. Richard Niebuhr, Daniel Day Williams, and James M. Gustafson, *The Purpose of the Church and Its Ministry* (New York: Harper, 1956).

3. See, for example, Loyde H. Hartley, *Placement and Deployment of Professionals in the United Church of Christ* (Lancaster, Pa.: Research Center in Religion and Society, 1973), pp. A 80-83.

4. Frederick W. Danker, *No Room in the Brotherhood* (St. Louis: Clayton Publishing House, 1977).

5. George H. Shriver, *American Religious Heretics: Formal and Informal Trials* (New York: Abingdon Press, 1965). For additional discussion of disputes in theological schools, see Arthur C. McGiffert, Jr., *No Ivory Tower* (Chicago: University of Chicago Press, 1965).

6. James E. Adams, *Preus of Missouri and the Great Lutheran Civil War* (New York: Harper & Row, 1977).

7. Krister Stendahl, "Rooted in the Communities of Faith: A Reaffirmation of a Learned Ministry." *Theological Education* XIII (1977): 61.

8. Association of Theological Schools, "Policy Statements," *A.T.S. Bulletin* 32, part 5 (1976).

9. Jesse Ziegler, Comments made at ATS Meeting, Boston, 1976.

10. Stendahl, *op. cit.*

11. David S. Schuller, Milo L. Brekke, and Merton P. Strommen, *Readiness for Ministry.* Vols. I and II. Vandalia, Ohio: Association of

Theological Schools, 1975 & 1976. See also *Ministry in America* (New York: Harper and Row, forthcoming in 1980).

12. *The Divinity School 1976-1977, Official Register of Harvard University*, LXXIII, no. 1, p. 24.

13. Charles L. Taylor, "Cooperation in Theological Education in the United States and Canada," *Theological Education* X (1973): 3ff.

14. "Ecumenical" and "non-denominational" seminaries may be understood to include Harvard and Yale as well as some very small conservative schools supported by several denominations too small to support their own theological schools.

15. Wayne C. Weld, "The Current Status of Theological Education by Extension," *Theological Education* X (1973): 225.

16. Marvin J. Taylor, ed., *Fact Book on Theological Education, 1976-77* (Vandalia, Ohio: Association of Theological Schools, 1977), Table 4.

7

Congregational Models for Mission—Factors in Adaptation and Goal Attainment

Everett L. Perry

In this chapter we are providing a brief overview of the three major models or perspectives—the ecological, goal, and voluntary—by which congregations have been viewed by scholars, practitioners, and church administrators. These models, in historical and ideological perspective, provide a frame of reference for considering the variety of factors which bear upon the functioning of present-day congregations. Making them consciously explicit should benefit people having a concern for the congregation as an effectively functioning unit of community and denominational life.

This approach should be helpful, in the context of the diversity of present-day life, not only for advancing sociological thinking about the "lowest rung" in ecclesiastical organization, but also theological thinking as to what really constitutes the mission of the church.

The special importance of this chapter is found in the recognition that the congregation—or the local church-parish-synagogue, or local entity by whatever name it is called—is fundamental to the organization, functioning, and support of each religious group in the United States.

We draw our material from a variety of studies and reports—published and unpublished—viewed through the lens of more than a third of a century of experience by the writer in congregational studies for the United Presbyterian Church in the U.S.A. and for national and local ecclesiastical bodies.

DIFFERING VIEWS OF MISSION

To raise the question of adaptation or goal attainment in the 1970s immediately involves us in a prior question: *what is the mission* of the church? We do not propose to give a simple answer. Rather, a semi-historical sketch of the main ways in which mission has been defined in the U.S. will highlight the fundamental complexity of the answer to the question.

In the early days of the republic, "mission" meant to take the church westward to the people building community life on the frontier and to reach "the heathen" on the frontier and beyond. Soon mission was to "the heathen" overseas and also to immigrants to our major cities through health, educational, and welfare activities all of which were so fundamental to the neighborhood house, the institutional church, and the work of denominational mission societies. Mission was conceived of as involving both spiritual sustenance and tangible service to people with special needs.

In the post-World War II period, the developing frontier was replaced by the rapidly growing suburbs where organizing the white middle-class suburbanite into new congregations became an important mission. Later, as a concomitant of the civil rights movements of the 1960s, a new mission emphasis emerged directed toward organizing and empowering the minorities and the poor to secure their rights, as part of the Gospel imperative to feed the hungry and to free the prisoner. Exerting influence to change the institutional structures of society and thereby provide more justice to the poor became an aspect of "mission" for some.

As a reaction to this more radical trend came a demand to serve more directly the spiritual and psychological needs of the middle-class white constituency of the churches. Along with this came a parallel realization on the part of some church leaders that the age-old mandate to change the hearts of *individuals* is fundamental and prerequisite to implementing *social* changes and institutional applications of the Gospel of Christ.

The role of the *local* church in mission has been tending to shift from support of mission *elsewhere* to concern for its *own* community.

These varying views of mission are all still with us, sometimes as strands or dimensions of the task and sometimes as contrasting approaches. Thus, to raise the question of "mission goals" and "adaptation" moves us into a substantive diversity out of which can come no easy answer.

Metz[1] attempted to categorize mission goals into those labeled "survival" versus "formal," using a modified Parsonian model. But survival goals may be, in some instances, clearly *indispensable* and instrumental *to* the pursuit of *formal* goals, even though they may seem to be geared to institutional maintenance per se (e.g., membership growth, building, financial support, etc.). We refuse to attempt to draw a line between the legitimacy and illegitimacy of mission directions, on the basis that *to be* in witness in some situations (e.g., where the very existence of the church is threatened) may be as significant as *to do* good deeds in other situations.

DIFFERING VIEWS OF FACTORS IN ADAPTATION AND GOAL ATTAINMENT

To raise questions about *the factors* which contribute to adaptation and goal attainment of a congregation involves us in a similar complexity. Without an overall frame of reference, one can discern an almost endless variety of factors which seem to be of importance, depending upon the situation and who is analyzing it.

In a Midwestern city several years ago pastors, church officers, and members who were not church officers were asked, "What is this congregation's understanding of its mission?," followed by another question, "What led to this understanding?"[2] Altogether 62 pastors and other staff and 327 members, over half of whom were also members of the governing boards of these congregations, were interviewed. About 80% of the congregations of one old-line denomination located in this metropolitan area were included. Following are some illustrations of the responses.

Presidential Heights Church, organized in the early 1900s, found itself by 1970 in a racially changing neighborhood. Rather than moving to a suburb or attempting to serve its traditional middle-class white constituency, wherever they lived, this congregation adapted by setting up and working toward goals of mission to its neighborhood which it considered to be in "obedience to the commission of our Lord, worldwide and local, of reconciliation between people and God and ourselves and others." People of the congregation identified five factors which brought the congregation to this kind of adaptation:

1. A conservative but open theological stance, which both allowed and encouraged services to the community.
2. Ability of the church leadership to interpret the ethical implications of panic selling of homes when blacks began to move in.
3. Members who were concerned residents of the community and sensitive to its needs, rather than outsiders who commuted to church services on Sunday.
4. Willingness of the governing board to support the idea of integration of the congregation and of its community, with sponsor-

ship of a bi-racial committee to deal with community concerns.
5.   Pastoral leadership open to, rather than being threatened by,
     change, and willing to take seriously the positive action of the
     board, exploiting for change what might otherwise have been
     only a formal commitment.

Northwoods Church is in a white community which has had an influx
of Appalachian people and the aging. It has faced a wide range of
community problems characteristic of the older residential areas of a
large city and developed a broad range of constructive programs, quite in
contrast to what might have been expected from its less than 400
membership.

Interviewees attributed the unusually broad program to the ideas
coming out of a diversity of points of view which were brought into
creative tension in the congregation in an annual planning retreat; a
pastor who himself fed in ideas and encouraged program development;
conduct of a community study which broadened the understanding of
local needs; significant communication with other congregations, both of
its own denomination and of others; a serious response to Confessional
directives from the denomination in support of community action.

Central Church, on the other hand, is essentially a mission in a black
area which has been maintained by a combination of two factors:
motivation from people of the community who have felt the hurts of
society, and substantial financial aid from the denomination's regional
organization.

In sharp contrast to all the above is the *Jesus Church of Milltown*, an
unsuccessful new church development of several years ago. It had not
paid on its building debt for nearly ten years, spending all its funds on
pastor's salary and other pressing operational expenses. While its people
focused their comments on building and financial problems, the church is
limited by the lack of growth of Milltown, compared with the earlier
favorable projections. It is also limited by a theological stance which had
not proved relevant to the times, or to the people of Milltown.

It is clear that the people of these various congregations not only were
in different situations, but also looked at themselves through different
lenses.

It is our purpose, through the following models, both to trace the ways
in which congregational life has been viewed in recent decades, and to
provide a set of paradigms or frames of reference which will help to
organize and make sense of the variety of concrete and important
analyses illustrated by the above cases.

THE ECOLOGICAL MODEL

The *ecological* model has been fundamental to a large proportion of
congregational studies in the twentieth century. Ecology sees the church

as a territorially-based organization which has roots in the social life of a community and may be *in competition with*, or in symbiotic relationship to, other forms of organization in that same territory. *Adaptation*, a key notion (following concepts of Darwin), may result in both survival and shifts in the nature of relationship to the social environment. *Specialization* in program occurs as a consequence of the *interaction of the organization* (congregation) *with its environment* (community).

H. Paul Douglass, a student of both urban and rural churches during the first half of this century, supported the generalization that types of urban churches are definable primarily in relation to the degree of developmental adaptation from rural stock to urban.[3] The measure of this adaptive trend was viewed by Douglass as statistical—the number and diversity of programs supported by the church. He allowed for exceptions to this "normal" adaptive rule by citing factors such as a church's strength and resources, its distinctive religious convictions and specialization, self-complacency, tradition, and philanthropy. He did not attempt to describe the way in which such factors bore upon the congregation, nor the degree to which they affected the church in relation to the ecological factors.

William P. Shriver provided a similar perspective when he noted that urban Protestant churches, in their ten types, "tend largely to reflect the economic neighborhood to which they minister."[4]

S. C. Kincheloe, a younger contemporary of Douglass and Shriver, studied congregations in the framework of the Burgess concentric zone hypothesis of urban structure and growth. Rather than stressing the statistical description so apparent in Douglass, Kincheloe looked at congregations as organic entities and made case studies in depth, often over periods of time. This could easily be done in the Chicago scene, since his research laboratory was based there and was supported not only by the Congregational Church and other denominations but also by the Church Federation of Greater Chicago.[5]

Particularly in that unique monograph on "The Behavior Sequence of a Dying Church,"[6] Kincheloe moved beyond the rather mechanistic approach of Douglass and gave attention to some of the inner dynamics and relationships of the congregation. At the same time, however, he saw the dying congregation's fate dominated by the social, economic, and racial forces which moved so inexorably across the face of the metropolis, distributing population groups as well as shaping the congregations.

Hawley, at a much later period, echoed the same phenomenon when he concluded, "A stratification of churches has matched the stratification of population."[7]

The ecological approach represented a monumental step forward in the study of congregations. It moved the study of churches away from both ecclesiastical moralizing and ad hoc description toward scientific principles. Such principles focused upon the congregation in relationship to its local environment, in an attempt to "explain" the behavior of the church as an urban voluntary organization. It was basically a very pessimistic approach, however, and seemed to say to the congregation in rapidly changing urban areas: "adapt, serve as best you can during a transitional period, but then probably die." From such a perspective, the capacity of a congregation to determine its future became severely limited. The church was seen as the ecclesiastical counterpart of other urban phenomena, such as the hobo, mental illness, the family, and vice, the forms and distribution of which were perceived largely *as determined* (by the ecology of the city) *and not determining*.

APPROACHES TO GOAL-ATTAINMENT MODELS

Efforts at goal attainment, implicit but largely undeveloped in ecological approaches, were a natural outgrowth of an increasing consciousness that congregations should be *determining their own futures*, rather than playing simply a responsive role to the trends in the society around them. Support for this approach was also found outside the churches, where city, regional, state, and national planning were in vogue.

Dependence upon Rational Response to Data

Initially the survey and self-study processes so popular in the churches in the 1950s and early 1960s were a bridge from the adaptation model of ecology. The demographic-type data of population characteristics and distribution, community characteristics and changes, all with a territorial base, were used. But the leading assumption was simple—that *people are rational* in their decision making and would adjust their behavior to conform to the implications of the demographic and ecological "facts" which were presented to them, or which the people themselves were instructed to gather.

The survey, and the self-study guide,[8] of that era generally produced considerable data, charts, maps of membership distribution, population pyramids of community and constituency, etc. These were based on U.S. Census data, other locally collected community data, and analysis of membership and constituency of the congregation itself. However, it became clear that two assumptions were false: (1) such "facts" themselves did not imply one, specific "right" course of action; and (2) even in cases where there seemed to be a clear link between data and implied action, *facts by themselves did not necessarily lead to rational decision making*. Stratification and power considerations tended to be ignored.

Broadening the Base of the Model

A second step was taken in the late '60s by the United Presbyterians in the development of a guide, not for self-study but for exploration of mission,[9] which attempted to take into account the deficiencies of the earlier approach. Again, it implied and was based on principles that reflected judgments about what factors were of importance in goal attainment that went beyond simple survival, adaptation-to-environment factors.

While the *Guide to the Exploration of Mission in the Local Congregation* included data-gathering suggestions borrowed from older approaches, it put a major emphasis on several other factors: selection, for membership on the exploration committee, of innovators rather than representatives of various organizations and segments of the congregation; an initial Biblical and theological study by the exploration committee to highlight the mandate for mission; personal involvement of exploration committee members in interview of community leaders; guidance in a process of goal definition, designed to be used on a piecemeal ad hoc basis; use of an outside consultant to facilitate and guide the process.

Extensive studies by Bartholomew[10] of the actual operation of the exploration process, based on interviews with people who had been involved, concluded that two factors were particularly important to an effective exploration: the preliminary Biblical study and the use of consultants from outside the congregation.

Dependence on Processes

A further development occurred in some places, which moved the pendulum further away from concern with external and over toward internal considerations.

One of these was an emphasis on the planning process, as a way of determining goals and making decisions about them. The assumption behind this direction was that, *if* it were possible to define and follow the *right process, then proper goals* would be selected and they would be achieved. Thus emerged comprehensive planning as an alternative to ad hoc planning. Most recently, it has emerged in the form of program budgeting (PPBS), the initial model of which was developed for the military, and was used particularly by NASA.

As applied in the church, for example in the United Presbyterian Planning/Budgeting/Evaluating (PBE) system,[11] it begins with review and analysis of what the organization has been doing and moves to consideration of priorities among these and other programs which the planning committee can think up. Comprehensiveness is emphasized.

While consideration of external factors of ecological import are still part of the process, their importance is downplayed in contrast to what the church decision makers perceive they *can* make some decisions about. The result is a tendency to assume that these factors are unimportant. PPBS and the church version, PBE, are found to work better in an atmosphere of *growth* rather than *retrenchment*.

The other process upon which dependence has been placed is that of organizational development.[12] Again, this has paralleled secular trends in organizational development to utilize the findings of various behavioral sciences in an effort to achieve a smooth-running and efficient organization, without pressing the issue of goals very hard, in contrast to the planning process. The emphasis becomes that of achieving "organizational health," with the exception that a well-operating and healthy institution will adapt itself successfully to its environment and make relevant and proper choices among goals. As in the Exploration of Mission approach, intervention by an external consultant is considered to be an important part of the process.

Findings of Studies on Factors in Change

Several studies provide concrete data which help to identify factors which are either roadblocks to or facilitators of change. Metz in *New Congregations* found that, when formal (i.e., mission) goals were *vaguely defined*, it was easy for the congregation to be *subverted to* an emphasis on *survival* goals. He also found that an orientaiton toward concrete goals as related to survival (e.g., building a new structure, holding a financial campaign, or carrying out a drive to secure new members) is sometimes used to reduce internal conflicts but that this actually subverts the internal mission of the church. He also found that, if the professional staff had a sense of job security, they tended not to feel compelled to concentrate attention upon survival goals as a means to prove their "success" to themselves, to their congregations, or to their peers and superiors who evaluated them

Goodman,[13] in a series of case studies of congregations which have undergone renewal, found that change comes through the influence of an *innovator* in the congregation—whether it be pastor, officer, or member, or a group within the organization. The innovative party is often strengthened by an influx of new people resulting from the mobility of population in many communities. In partial confirmation of the Bartholomew findings on *Exploration of Mission*, Goodman also found that people in congregations were inspired to support change when they were convinced that the direction of change had a sound theological basis, and also when it was apparent to the church that it was not meeting its mission responsibilities if it failed to make the change. She finally pointed out that a variety of change mechanisms were utilized geared to a variety of circumstances. It took innovative thinking, however, to select the *right* mechanism for the *right* set of circumstances.

A study of growing congregations, initiated by the UPCUSA Department of Evangelism,[14] was based on discussion of and reflection upon recent membership trends among people from a small group of congregations selected by computer analysis. It found that growing congregations were more likely than others to have *met and* successfully *solved* a crisis in their history, rather than merely *never having* had *to face* such a crisis.

Hessel,[15] in a study of congregations involved in study and action on social issues, found larger congregations more likely to be involved (perhaps because of the diversity of people in their membership). Gibbs and Ewer also found large congregations in large communities more likely to be socially involved than smaller congregations but attributed this to greater availability of personnel and leadership resources.[16] Both Hessel and Hoge discovered that black congregations also tended to be more socially involved than white, probably because of their having more directly experienced hurt from discrimination in our society.

"Project Test Pattern," sponsored by the Episcopal Church and aimed at renewal of congregations, involved working in an organizational development style. The director of that project, Loren B. Mead,[17] looked upon these congregations ideally as "centers for learning, experiencing, and sharing the truths of the faith." From its material, Cynthia Wedel pointed out certain recurring patterns, however, which hindered development of mission: problematic relationships between pastor and people, including the tendency of some pastors to make decisions and to carry out tasks without involving the laity; lack of clear goals; poor communication within the congregation and between the congregation and its environment; the direct influence of community patterns and norms.[18]

Mead identified five learnings directly related to the process of change in a parish: "that third-party consultation assists change; that contracts or covenants can help change to happen; that the clergyman is a key to change; that support systems are important; and that failure itself can produce significant learnings."[19]

External Linkages and Change

We have already seen that recently much emphasis has been placed on the expectation that the intervention of a consultant will produce change. Change is generally defined as a change in goal perspectives or generation of new insights rather than in the survival characteristics of the congregation as an organization. The study of Bartholomew and experience of Mead and his associates have tended to confirm that there has been such an impact. Other evidence tends to support Bartholomew and Mead and help clarify what can and what cannot be done by such outside intervention.

In the late 1940s Henry Pressler completed a comprehensive study of the Presbyterian Churches of Chicago, 1871-1942, to determine what effect subsidy had on them and on the presbytery itself. (Presumably intervention of a consultant was also involved, as well as subsidy, but Pressler did not take into account that aspect of the relationship.) From statistics and also case studies, Pressler found substantial support for the notion that *subsidy is ineffective* in bringing a congregation to self-support, *depending upon* the presence of *certain conditions,* as land-use and cultural factors:

> Presbyterian Churches were helped by subsidy to reach self-support in neighborhoods where the land use was residential, largely free from commercial and industrial properties, which neighborhoods were not fragmented by transportation thoroughfares (main automobile highways and street car lines, railroads, canals, and rivers), and which neighborhoods were not threatened by encroaching non-residential properties or transport lines; provided such neighborhoods contained dominant British-American populations having Calvinistic religious heritages.[20]

In short, Pressler found that what a presbytery can do to support, strengthen, and modify its congregations is strictly *limited by* the *ecology* of the city. The social forces of land use and cultural background limit and even dominate conscious plans.

The "larger parish" in rural areas, and more recently the inter-parish "clusters,"[21] which are frequently an urban phenomenon, coincide in recognition that in some instances the local congregation can benefit by *outside linkages* as it seeks to develop and attain mission goals.

While the older larger parish concept was built on the idea of *concentration* of resources, the more recent *cluster* concept[22] extends the *cooperation* to a combination of innovators *across* congregational and, sometimes, denominational *lines*. The cluster is based on cooperation in particular tasks rather than simply on an organizational relationship, or on cooperation in joint staffing. It is an *application of the coalition idea* to congregations. Cooperation may be directed specifically at Christian education, music, dealing with community concerns, or social action. Clustering opens up the possibility of cooperation between congregational members interested, for instance, in housing with like-minded people from other congregations, permitting a sharing of human resources and interest which could not be found in one congregation by itself.

Despite the potential value, however, there are negatives, one of which is the threat posed to the establishment—the pastor, the session, etc.—in introducing a different dimension of relationships into the established structure of a congregation. Competition and ambiguity of responsibility between the local church and the cluster, with suspicion that the cluster would take over and usurp a local congregation's prerogatives, were mentioned by participants. Greater diversity of people and ideas sometimes produced conflict and polarization.

Clustering in one sense seems to have been a fad of the late 1960s, but it used basic principles and procedures which are not time-bound to a particular era of popularity. The cluster phenomenon was built on the very realistic principle that many, if not all, congregations can benefit from the additional resources and new ideas that can come through the establishment of relationships with lateral units on the same ecclesiastical level. It is a form of ecclesiastical "community organization." "Clusters" which were set up by external initiation, e.g., as an aid to synod or presbytery planning and programming, appear generally to have been less successful than those which grew from local intiative.

THE LOCAL CHURCH AS A
VOLUNTARY ORGANIZATION

Whether the congregation is viewed as the primary and basic organizational unit of a religious group, as among the Baptists, or whether it is considered to be a mere convenience because of the unmanageable size of the whole church, as at least theoretically among the Presbyterians, to complete our review of models we must consider the congregation as a *voluntary organization* based on and composed of individuals.

Simply, whether a church adapts or defines and attains its goals depends in large part on its membership base, which is composed of individuals. The voluntary organization is based on decisions to participate or not participate which, according to current theory, revolve around the satisfactions that individuals derive from such participation. The needs and goals of individuals and of the organization must to some degree coincide. From this perspective, the church is seen to be in competition with other voluntary organizations for loyalty and commitment of its people. Consideration of member attitudes and opinions becomes essential.

The dichotomy raised by Glock in *To Comfort and to Challenge*[23] is very relevant. Will the person support the congregation only for what "comfort" he himself can get out of it? If so, the possibilities for goal attainment are severely limited. Again, are the people in the neighborhood congenial to what the church is and is doing or not? If not, from an ecological-ethnic perspective, the future of the local church may be severely limited. Are people of the congregation willing and even anxious to be challenged to external mission tasks? If so, the possibilities of formulating and reaching mission goals will be enhanced.

Hoge, who has explored mission priorities extensively, finds a current dichotomy between evangelism and social action,[24] i.e., an apparent "conflict" in the church. However, *another* reading of the data might be that there are minorities of people at each of these extremes, while the large block of membership is in between, eager to be deeply involved *neither* in evangelism *nor* in social action, but, if anything, wanting to be "comforted," in Glock's terminology.

Unfortunately, relatively little of this kind of exploration of member attitudes toward priorities for mission has been related to specific congregations but has usually been based on samples of members drawn across congregational lines. Nonetheless, to the extent that in-depth survey has been applied within congregations, it is usual to find *wide variations* in mission priorities of people *within any one congregation*. This was certainly true of Westminster Presbyterian Church of Detroit, Chestnut Hill Presbyterian Church of Philadelphia, several Methodist and Presbyterian congregations studied by Carroll and Hoge, and a sample of Presbyterian congregations in New Jersey.

Within this diversity, there is sometimes a dominance of one priority direction which can set the atmosphere of the congregation and result in selective recruitment of new members, providing for continuity of congregational mission direction over time. However, sometimes a radical change at some point, for instance in the type of minister combined with membership changes from mobility of population, may result in a radical change in the congregation's mission direction. In Chicago, for example, this process was documented in the transition of several Congregational churches to Bible Church status.[25] This became possible, in part, as a result of lack of financial or property ties to the Congregational organization.

The effect of diversity emerges in another way. Some students point to a conscious effort on the part of some congregations to minimize differences in points of view in order to avoid conflict. A planning process, ostensibly designed to sharpen mission goals, may actually select *only* those goals on which there can be *agreement*, reducing the possibility of conflict but also watering down the goal statements. Special structures may be needed to avoid inaction and mere surface consensus and to serve as a logistical "hedge." The organization of task forces or groups with special interests and goals of a more radical nature than could secure approval by the whole congregation has long been advocated. By means of such *informal structures*, some members can proceed to take action without securing the participation and/or assent of all, or even of a majority of the total congregation.

In tracing these diversities back to more basic factors, Hoge has a key finding. Behind these individual differences in mission priority, there may be a theological factor which is rooted in the social and educational contexts in which people live. The conflict of priorities, as he sees it, is based on a conflict between two world views—the academically-oriented scientific world view, which is unitary in nature, and the dualism of the church's traditional world view.

In this situation, it is frequently beyond the ability of a congregation to provide broad satisfaction, over goal attainments, to a spectrum of individuals *except at the level of vagueness and mediocrity*. Further-more, Demerath and Hammond point out the ease with which vague goals can be displaced by more concrete goals which had originally been only means to an end (e.g., recruiting members becomes a goal replacing salvation of souls).[26] Thus, the fact that a congregation is a voluntary organization needing a high degree of consensus *limits* its ability to develop positive *mission* goals.

This raises a key question which emerged in the Midwestern study.[27] It is the very threatening idea that an important part of the mission of the church today is to *change individual lives* and lifestyles. People tend to back away from this central theme of the Gospel when they meet it in the context of local church life, either spiritualizing it or believing that it really refers to someone else, not themselves.

One student of congregations[28] defines "satisfaction" as "meaning," designating the church as the institution which can provide meaning to life. He hypothesizes that, to the extent people perceive of a church as being *a carrier of meaning* for their own lives, it will have their support. We might hypothesize a step beyond: to the extent that they *find meaning*, they will produce a dynamic for aggressive action by the congregation, within the limitations of the context in which that mission is being carried out.

LOOKING TOWARD THE FUTURE

We have reviewed three models, or views, of the local church which have been directed toward adaptation and change: (1) the *ecological* model, which views the congregation in large part as determined by social forces external to itself, with its internal processes directed largely at adaptation to those forces; (2) various approaches to a *goal-attainment* model, which through a planning process, organizational development, and/or with interventions from the outside attempts to take the future in its own hands, downplaying but not completely disregarding ecology; and (3) the church as a *voluntary association*, which focuses on the members who are behind the processes which relate congregations to their ecological base, either for growth or death, and which also injects a grass-roots dimension into the goal-attainment model, either supporting or serving to water down the goal-definition process and dulling any sharp edge to goal attainment.

The Systems Motivational Model

As we look toward the future of the local congregation and efforts of local, regional, and national church leaders to stimulate and direct successful adaptation and the selection and attainment of mission goals, we find that no one of these three models, however popular by itself, is adequate. At the same time, each has elements that are critical and cannot be disregarded.

Our proposal, therefore, is that we must currently view the congregation in a perspective which will include all three, but in a frame of reference which adds up to more than the sum of its parts. Thus, it is necessary to view the *congregation as a system* comprised of closely interrelated sub-systems, some of which are internal, some external, and some internal/external. Such a congregation-system must be seen not only as operating *within the community* as context, but also *as part of the community* and the community as part of it. This both affirms the Pauline conception of the church as an organism and extends it beyond that of a self-contained entity working in an external and often foreign environment. Not only through programs but also through the attitudes, opinions, and priorities of individual members is this internal/external linkage maintained.

That the local church is fundamentally an *expressive* organization limits its ability to be a full-fledged, goals-oriented organization, similar to a manufacturing or sales organization. *To be* (i.e., to witness to) and to discern God's work in the world and to cooperate with it is different from selecting a secular goal and figuring out ways of attaining it, even if it is or seems to be in the direction of justice and liberation. (Conversely, national denominational offices, two or more steps removed from the grass roots, can strategically operate with a more thorough goals orientation.)

The motivational element must be included, since a primary dynamic for any action, expressive or goal-oriented, comes from the relation of individual goals and satisfactions to organizational goals. Argyris[29] points out that in organizational theory the relation to the individual has often been neglected. By virtue of the nature of the church as a voluntary association, this aspect can be disregarded only at great peril. "Exchange" or "need" theory deals with this micro-level of social analysis.

The writer maintains that one should not create a dichotomy and so demand a choice *between* the systems approach and the goal-attainment model, as Etzioni seems to do. Use of rationality in defining goals and figuring out how to attain them is important and possible within a sound theological context, within the political context involved in the internal dynamics of ecclesiastical behavior, and within the limitation of the social environment.

This view brings us beyond the scope of any of the previous models. While the systems motivational model is more complex and provides no easy solutions, it does not leave the church merely at the mercy of external forces, or subject only to the whims of uninformed members, or only in a "healthy" but goalless state of being.

Some Reflections on Implications for Policy

Policy, defined as statement of intention and commitment to certain lines of action or procedure, must arise out of the experience of the body which affirms the policy. Our suggestions relate to understandings important to consider in the formulating of a policy, not recommendations for policies to be adopted:

1. Need for a strong affirmation that congregational health, vitality, and setting of realistic goals is one of the highest priority concerns for the whole church and its future.
2. Provision of consultants and material helps making available a broad range of skills—including theological and Biblical perspectives, community analysis, organizational development, planning, and attitude probes and analysis, rather than depending upon any one limited approach as the answer.
3. Recognition that congregations vary greatly and that their needs for external help are equally varied.
4. Recognition that helps which can come from the outside, both as to finances and consultant skills, while important, are relatively limited in potential effectiveness compared with the development of inner strength and vitality and sense of direction in the congregation itself.
5. Further development of an understanding of the systems motivational approach, utilizing a growing body of experience which is being collected, and upon which there is reflection and design of further approaches.

Notes

1. Donald L. Metz, *New Congregations, Security and Mission in Conflict* (Philadelphia: Westminster Press, 1967).

2. *Congregations in Mission*, Asking 58 Congregations About Their Mission Concepts, Programs, Budgets, and Relationships (New York: Program Agency, United Presbyterian Church in the U.S.A., 1972).

3. H. Paul Douglass, *1000 City Churches* (New York: George H. Doran Co., c. 1926), p. 90.

4. *Ibid.*, p. 249, quoting from the Interchurch World Survey, American Volume, p. 31.

5. S. C. Kincheloe, *The American City and Its Churches* (New York: Friendship Press, 1938).

6. Samuel C. Kincheloe, "The Behavior Sequence of a Dying Church," *Religious Education* XXIV (April, 1929): 329ff.

7. Amos H. Hawley, *Urban Society, An Ecological Approach* (New York: Ronald Press Co., 1971), p. 256.

8. *Self-Study Guide for the City Church* (New York: Board of National Missions, United Presbyterian Church in the U.S.A., 1955).

9. *Guide to the Exploration of Mission in the Local Congregation* (New York: Board of National Missions, United Presbyterian Church in the U.S.A., 1965).

10. John Bartholomew, *A Study of Planning Techniques for Local Congregations* (New York: Institute of Strategic Studies, Board of National Missions, United Presbyterian Church in the U.S.A., 1967). *Congregations Explore Their Mission*, Experience in Use of the Guide to the Exploration of Mission with Special Emphasis on the Role of the Consultant (New York: Institute of Strategic Studies, Board of National Missions, United Presbyterian Church in the U.S.A., 1970).

11. *Planning/Budget/Evaluating in the Local Congregation* (New York: General Assembly Mission Council, United Presbyterian Church in the U.S.A., 1976).

12. Warren G. Bennis, Kenneth D. Benne, and Robert Chin, eds., *The Planning of Change* (New York: Holt, Rinehart & Winston, second edition, 1969). See particularly pp. 299-305 for comparison of system and developmental models.

13. Grace Ann Goodman, *Rocking the Ark* (New York: Division of Evangelism, Board of National Missions, United Presbyterian Church in the U.S.A., 1968).

14. *A Study of Some Growing Churches in the United Presbyterian Church, U.S.A.* (New York: Division of Evangelism, Board of National Missions, United Presbyterian Church in the U.S.A., 1971). See particularly the comment: "In all but two of the churches studied, historical events were of such significance that they became the bases for new emphases or beginnings of new life for the congregation. Termination of a long pastorate, a decision to relocate the church, a traumatic experience with a dominant personality, a confrontation with the presbytery were some of the historic occasions which resulted in a new self-awareness and a spur to new prospects," p. 9.

15. Dieter Hessel and Leslie Galbraith, *Occasional Paper #6 on the Church and Conflict* (Philadelphia: Board of Christian Education, United Presbyterian Church in the U.S.A., 1971).

16. James O. Gibbs and Phyllis A. Ewer, "The External Adaptation of Religious Organizations: Church Response to Social Issues," *Sociological Analysis* 30 (Winter, 1969): 223-234.

17. Loren Mead, *New Hope for Congregations* (New York: Seabury Press, 1972), Preface, p. 10.

18. Elisa L. DesPortes, *Congregations in Change* (New York: The Seabury Press, 1973), Foreword, p. vii.

19. Mead, op. cit., p. 201.

20. Henry Hughes Pressler, "The Effects of Subsidy on Presbyterian Churches in Metropolitan Chicago, 1871-1942" (unpublished Ph.D. dissertation, the Divinity School, the University of Chicago, 1948), p. 3.

21. Consultation on Church Union, Task Force on Local Church Clusters, *Report to Plenary*, September 27, 1971.

22. Edward M. Huenemann, Robert S. Macfarlane, and Everett Perry, *The Cluster Phenomenon*, Occasional Paper VIII (New York: Division of Evangelism, Board of National Missions, United Presbyterian Church in the U.S.A., 1971).

23. Charles Y. Glock, Benjamin B. Ringer, and Earl R. Babbie, *To Comfort and to Challenge* (Berkeley: University of California Press, 1967).

24. Dean R. Hoge, *Division in the Protestant House* (Philadelphia: Westminster Press, 1976).

25. Everett L. Perry, "Socio-economic Factors in the Rise and Development of American Fundamentalism" (Unpublished Ph.D. dissertation, the Divinity School, the University of Chicago, 1959).

26. N. J. Demerath III and Phillip E. Hammond, *Religion in Social Context*, Tradition and Transition (New York: Random House, Inc., 1969), pp. 173ff.

27. *Congregations in Mission*, op. cit.

28. Theodore H. Erickson, "Leadership and Church Growth," remarks at Church Growth Symposium, Society for the Scientific Study of Religion/Religious Research Association, New York, April, 1976.

29. Chris Argyris, *The Applicability of Organizational Theory* (London: Cambridge University Press, 1972), pp. 118-119.

8

Organizational Dilemmas of Religious Professionals (Or, "I Never Promised You A Rose Garden")

Garry W. Hesser

Sample test

What is the function of a "religious professional"? (Circle one answer below.)

a. Pastoral director
b. Counselor
c. Leader
d. Facilitator
e. Priest
f. Prophet
g. Resident Theologian
h. Administrator
i. Name your combination

Professional[1] activity, by definition, does not take place in a vacuum. The role is performed in an organizational setting which alternately facilitates and constrains those activities by influencing the rights and obligations "belonging" to those who opt for that position. To the professional collage are added personality factors and wider societal developments, such as secularization, which influence the daily and long-range vocational behavior of a pastor.[2] And these organizational realities comprise inescapable warp and woof with which the religious professional must cope.

THE CRISIS AS DILEMMA

From the outset, let us substitute the term "dilemma" for the overly dramatic "crisis."[3] It is often helpful to differentiate between "problems" and "dilemmas", which though interrelated are two quite *different* phenomena. For example, low salaries and inadequate training in denominations may be seen as unpleasant conditions or "problems" confronting religious organizations. Often they can be "solved" if the various decisional parties (clergy, laity, official leaders) of the institution are willing to *define* them as "problems" and redirect resources to remedy them. Dilemmas, however, are more enduring strains or paradoxes basically *inherent in the institutionalization process itself* and, as such, probably *unsolvable*.

Thomas O'Dea has lucidly underscored the "dilemmas in the institutionalization of religion" by nothing that:

> The unusual and creative performance of the hero, sage or saint, though of great exemplary and genetic importance, is too unpredictable to become the basis of everyday life. . . . Yet the achievement of the necessary stability involves a price. . . . It would remain a fleeting and impermanent element in human life without its embodiment in institutional structures to render it continuously present and available. Yet in bringing together two radically heterogeneous elements, ultimacy and concrete social institutions, the sacred and the profane, this necessary institutionalization involves a fundamental tension.
>
> In other words, religion both needs most and suffers most from institutionalization. The subtle, the unusual, the charismatic, the supra-empirical must be given expression in tangible, ordinary and empirical social forms.
>
> The nature of the religious experience tends to be in conflict with the requisites and characteristics of the institutionalization process and the resultant social institutions.[4]

Thus, some of the popular "crises" of the ministry can be consequences of simply the unwillingness to mobilize and/or redirect resources to solve "problems". But other dimensions of the "crisis" are rooted in *fundamental and enduring tensions* between the Scylla and Charybdis *of two seemingly equally necessary alternatives* and stem from *both theological and institutional* realities. Thus the notion of "dilemma" takes on the imagery of keeping the teeter-totter balanced, or "living on the boundary" as Paul Tillich so aptly phrased the tension of living creatively with social contradictions.[5] Consequently, there may be *no resolution*, only a more or less effective style of abandoning false dichotomies and holding in tension both the theological and institutional realities confronting religious organizations. The religious institution is not unique in this regard. A major emphasis among the observers of organizations is upon the "stress and strain" which manifest themselves at both the personal and organizational levels.[6] Just as an individual pastor is affected by the internal and external demands and resources at his/her command, the congregation itself has internal realities, inconsistencies, and conflicts which influence how it responds to the demands of the community or society of which it is a part.

Central to the thesis presented here are the concepts derived from viewing the religious institution as an "open-system" possessing an inevitable tension between the values/ideals and the organizational-instrumental means necessary to accomplish any goals deriving from those values. The religious professional's congregation, socialization, training, and family are viewed as overlapping social or institutional systems[7] operating within the environments of denominations, as well as wider societal and community systems (see Figure 1). Such a professional context requires training and continuing education which utilizes a dynamic planning and evaluation approach for coping creatively with the blossoms and thorns of the parish rose garden.

ANTECEDENTS TO THE DILEMMA

Characteristics of Recruits into the Profession

Accumulating factors lead to a career decision and the continued "stabilization" in a vocation. In their total combination, these factors seem to account for decisions and/or social behavior which are antecedents to a career. In addition to particular sociocultural and biographical factors, the profession is colored by two thousand years of church history and is marked by career training that shapes a "new" person. For example, during the years of training, the pastor may even subconsciously *absorb* the "right intention" by learning what his motives *ought to be*. Although research on motivations, commitments, and self concepts is very problematic, there are a number of salient factors that emerge from that literature. These tendencies suggest that *unrealistic expectations* and *mixed motivations*, whether material or idealistic, are a part of the religious professional's organizational dilemma.

Upward mobility. One tendency is indeed ironic. Studies reveal that for the average seminarian and clergyperson, the profession represents a channel of upward social and economic mobility. Pastors tend to come from families of moderate economic circumstances, are usually sensitive to considerations of prestige, and have indicated that they desire to use their educational advantage to rise in the social and economic structure.[8] Complementary findings reveal that Protestant pastors tend to have grown up in small communities and relatively small churches and go from them to small denominational colleges.[9] Similarly, Catholic priests tend to come from families of lower to moderate incomes.[10]

The importance of the motivation implied in economic and social mobility is underscored by evidence from a national study of Protestant pastors conducted in 1969. The respondents were asked to compare their own salaries with those of others. Analysis by the author revealed that occupational stress increased significantly as the actual gap or the subjectively perceived financial deprivation increased.[11] Thus, knowing a clergyperson's attitude toward his/her salary is very helpful in understanding how he/she copes with the dilemmas of the profession.

A cursory view, then, leads one to conclude that the "parochial" and lower socioeconomic tendency in the background of clergypersons is a potential for stress, especially when unacknowledged. This motivational dimension needs to be recognized and dealt with openly, lest the organizational dilemma be intensified by the drive for status and mobility. The profession does appear to offer social and material status rewards higher than previously experienced, leading to outcomes ranging from (1) satisfaction with the rewards if they represent real vertical mobility, to (2) considerable dissatisfaction if the rewards fail to approximate expectations.

Non-material motivations. Numerous studies document the developmental importance which religious professionals attribute to parents,[12] the actual vocational decision,[13] their pastor's influence,[14] and altruism within an ecclesiastical context.[15] These tendencies are congruous with James Dittes' thesis that many pastors grew up as "little adults" who internalized the expectations and values of the adult world. Dittes hypothesizes that this tendency to be a spokesperson and agent of the transcendent adult world among their childhood and teenage peers transfers very naturally into the clergy role of articulating and urging transcendent values among their peers.[16] These tendencies, coupled with commitments to world needs, reform, serving God, and other such transcendent motivations lay the early groundwork for later tensions with the organizational realities. The critical point to be made here is the importance of stressing *organizational realities* in the recruitment and training process. Idealism and high expectations will definitely contribute dynamic leadership to the institution; but if those so motivated do *not* take into account the basic organizational nature of the religious institution, a likely consequence will be unnecessary disillusionment and the compounding of the dilemma.

Professional Training

The professional training process itself makes a major input to the understanding and behavior associated with the role performance. Yet very little empirical research has focused upon the effect of the seminary experience *per se*. Only a few seminary administrators or denominations have initiated comparative, longitudinal educational research to evaluate the relative effectiveness of various types of seminary education.[17] Professional education ranges from three to seven years for Protestants, with the not-too-surprising generality that the end results represent neither uniform nor systematic, professional socialization.

For example, some seminaries are structured to include students with considerable theological background as well as those with very little. Others channel such differently prepared students into more homogeneous student bodies. Some seminaries were deliberately located in large cities near universities and others in the countryside away from "liberal" higher education and the distractions of the city.[18] One especially salient conclusion emerges from the few empirical attempts to assess the effectiveness of seminary training vis-a-vis the practice of the profession. Namely, seminaries have, in the past, consistently operated with a *different conception of the ministry from* the one which actually exists in *ecclesiastical* life.[19]

Perhaps the best systematic study of the clergy which addressed itself to the conflicts emerging from the multiple agents and dimensions of clergy professionalization concluded that:

> Under the present setup the recruiting system is separated from the training system, which, in turn, is separated from the hiring system. And even in many instances the hiring system is separated from the real constituency to be served. Young people choose the ministry with one set of ideals and occupational images, they are introduced to a radically different set in the seminaries, and when they emerge as neophyte ministers into local parishes they discover additional roles and obligations for which they were never trained. It is a well-nigh universal complaint among younger clergy that they had to learn to be ministers after they left the seminary. The young pastor discovers that the training system and the hiring system of the church are really out of touch. He is simply not trained to handle all the elements of his work when he actually gets on the job. And when we look carefully at the scene we see, too, that the training system simply does not exercise sufficient judgment about who should and should not enter the parish ministry to enter that field is both a sin against that person and a sin against the church.[20]

But to what extent can or should a professional education introduce a "pre-professional" to parish realities? Can theological and scriptural tenets have authenticity when the training is grounded in those realities? Conversely, is theological education really connected if it is not plugged into the people of God in a very concrete way? In what ways can or should the seminary equip a pastor to understand and work effectively within an organizational context, to understand conflict management, consensus formation, the coordination of volunteers, administration and staff interaction, power, or change strategies? In other words, what training *can* seminarians receive which would equip them to creatively cope with organizational realities instead of being overwhelmed or seduced by them?

Four organizational ideologies embedded in traditional seminary education. The past reveals very little evidence of an overt or conscious attention to such a synthesis. Colin Williams highlights an underlying *opposite* tendency. He stressed that, as a consequence of its being taken-for-granted that the function and organization of the church were obvious, little direct or self-conscious attention was even given to ecclesiology (i.e., the theology of organization) until the early stages of the ecumenical movement.[21] The hortatory literature on the ministry and the church written prior to World War II is largely apologetic, usually with a "recruitment" or socialization orientation.[22] Books on the ministry stressed "the strong man," "the social gospel,""moral leadership and the ministry," "clerical types," the "duties of the ministry," and "the Christian pastor in a new age." Some attention was given to organizational emphases such as "practical papers on parish problems," "the building of the church," "an efficient ministry," or "the minister and the community."

This was the literature which nourished and shaped the training and socialization of most present-day pastors. A review of this material reveals at least four distinct emphases, none of which have sharply focused upon the inherent organizational dilemmas nor equipped religious professionals to deal effectively with the realities of the organizational nature of the church. Clearly there were several crucial exceptions, but these counter-trends did not sufficiently challenge the ruling paradigms.[23]

The first emphasis, with many nuances, focused upon the *"call"* or the view that the ministry rests fundamentally upon a personal experience or relationship that can only be described and not analyzed. Included here would be the almost "mystical" conviction that the church and the performance of ministry are "gifts of the Spirit" and, thus, humanly uncontrollable "events."[24]

At the other extreme was a second emphasis seen in the *"how to"* manuals which were adopted, often with little alteration, from the dominant business management orientations. Techniques were passed on, ranging from how to organize a financial drive to building a youth group, from "functionally" organized churches to more effective filing systems and uses of duplicating machines. As Lyle Schaller has noted, there was a tendency to view the church as a "strictly 'business-like' venture to which good business administrative principles can be readily applied in the same way they are applied to the administration of most institutions in society."[25] As one clergyman noted:

> The seminary prepared me for preaching and taught me the difference between preaching and public speaking; it helped me to become a pastoral counselor and not simply a counselor; it

prepared me for the work of Christian education; but it gave me no preparation to administer a church as Church; what I learned about church administration was a nontheological smattering of successful business practices.[26]

The third emphasis, largely a post-World War II phenomenon, was almost exclusively *theological*. Names like Barth, Nelson, Welch, and Newbigin are but a sampling of the plethora of those who challenged the supremacy of the first two trends. One underlying assumption appeared to be that theological clarity and/or Biblical rootedness would "automatically" give birth to "organizational integrity," an implicit conclusion derived from the virtual absence of attention to "organizational realities" per se. In addition, this "queen-of-the-disciplines" superiority complex naively took for granted that things would fall into place if the theology was authentic and the Word and sacraments rightly administered.[27]

Even at their best, a certain organizational naiveté appears to be inherent in all of these positions. Whereas the first seemed to rely upon the Spirit to create and orient one to the "right" forms or instruments, the second bought wholesale the methods of the business schools with too little attention to the inherently different goals and purposes of businesses and churches, Reacting to both these, the theologians, at times, focused too exclusively on the theological foundations without dealing explicitly with organizational realities of the "body."

The fourth and final reigning pattern was the *anti-institutional* literature of the 1960s. Castigating the success of the 1950s as the "noise of solemn assemblies," "suburban captivity of the churches," and "civil religion," this approach usually stopped with a critique of "what is" without suggesting positive viable alternatives except for "religionless Christianity" or the "underground church." Clear exceptions were those critics who found hope in the rediscovery of small groups, e.g., Koinonia, Bible study, Christian Family Movement, or Yokefellows. But even here, the "small group" was often viewed as "over against" the organizational realities and tended either to merge with the Spirit-led trend or be another uncritically adopted import from the business-research world of T-groups and group dynamics. On the whole, like its predecessors, the renewal advocates and experimenters reflected a certain naiveté as regards organizational reality, especially in their failure to stress the critical aspects of authority and charisma in leadership.

MINISTRY IN EARTHEN VESSELS: A VISIONARY SYNTHESIS GROUNDED IN REALITY

Ironically, the middle 1950s gave birth to an approach to the church marked by *both theological* (as well as *Biblical*) depth *and sociological-*

organizational sophistication. This balance emphasis advanced a reasonable, faithful and alternative synthesis. H. Richard Niebuhr and his colleagues, Daniel Day Williams and James Gustafson, provided the themes in their study of "theological education in the U.S. and Canada." Niebuhr's concept of "pastoral director" seemed to forthrightly face the tensions inherent in the "institutional dilemmas." These insights were further brought to focus in works like *Treasure in Earthen Vessels*[28] and "The Organizational Dilemma in American Protestantism."[29]

Yet this emphasis, which seemed a plausible synthesis, faded into the background. One hypothesized "cause" as to why it faded grounds in the rise of social activism and the civil rights movement which often branded such "realism" as "compromising" and "unprophetic." Many turned myopically to replicate the experimental Church of the Savior or "New Life in the Church" but failed to fully appreciate the qualities of charisma and the uniqueness of context that were critical to most such "experiments." Perhaps others seemed masochistically turned on by the devastating critiques of surburban "captivity" and took delight in branding quantitative success as the "noise of solemn assemblies." On the other hand, others simply rode the continued spillover from these earlier waves of success.

Whatever the cause, and it was likely a consequence of *many* factors coalescing in the "spirit of the times," the Niebuhr-Williams-Gustafson-Lee synthesis of a theological understanding of ministry with the insights of the social sciences played second fiddle until a recent upsurge of interest.[30] One consequence of that lapse has been a continual stream of religious professionals whose patchwork training in *"practical* theology" did little or nothing to adequately sensitize them to or provide them with a perspective or set of strategies and tools to cope creatively with the inevitable organizational realities.

The 1970s. A systematic review of current curricula in Jewish, Catholic, and Protestant seminaries[31] shows greater sensitivity to organizational realities but mostly tendencies similar to the past. In general, current seminary curricula do *not* seem to be addressing themselves systematically or thoroughly to the issues being raised here. Specifically, the norm seems to be one course which attempts to cover everything from office management and the sacraments to group dynamics, motivation, and denominational policy. Another tendency is to allow students to choose their own course focus either individually or as a group, i.e., according to the "interests of the students." Further, there is a tendency to utilize somewhat dated material with three fourths of the Protestant seminaries surveyed using an organizationally sensitive but somewhat outdated text published in 1965. Except for some Doctor of Ministry programs and a few innovative seminars which almost require classification as "unique," there is no trend nor apparent pressure to embrace the administrative-organizational dimension as anything more than a stepchild to the queen(s) of theological education.[32] Thus, George Webber's "obvious" observations of 1964 appear equally salient and in need of operationalization today:

> By the same token, it is possible to evolve a brilliant and relevant theology of mission, but to find it serves no useful purpose unless and until it is given concrete institutional expression that takes into account the reality of the human situation in all its particularity.[33]

THE DILEMMA IN ORGANIZATIONAL CONTEXT

Such an approach views every clergyperson as functioning in two specific and overlapping social environments: namely, (1) the religious institution, and (2) the non-religious social fabric or society in which the religious organization(s) operate and of which they are a part.[34] Figure 1 suggests that for any given behavior, attitude, or interaction, there are potentially salient "audiences" or influences originating from (A) the religious organization, (B) the "non-religious" social environment, and (C) the total set of statuses, roles, beliefs and values of the particular clergyperson. Certain decisions and behavior may be salient only to the pastor and the congregation (#2), e.g., a salary raise, the choice of curriculum. Other matters may involve the pastor in the wider social environment (#3), e.g., personal political activity, a housing purchase, or the pastor's participation in the local PTA. And frequently behavior and attitudes are variously affected by all three systems (#1), e.g., stands on school busing, tax deductible salary arrangements, or recruitment of new members from other congregations.

FIGURE 1
OVERLAPPING SOCIAL ENVIRONMENTS OF
RELIGIOUS PROFESSIONALS

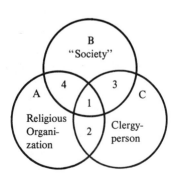

This orientation emphasizes the social, cultural, and/or institutional context in which organizationally salient decisions are perceived and acted upon. Religious professionals and the religious organizations in which they are inextricably enmeshed operate within an environment which affects and is affected by their activities. The environment includes competitors, resources (both human and material), colleagues (both individual and collective), regulatory agencies (both secular and religious), technologies which enhance or undercut their goals, and the socio cultural (political and economic) milieu(s) of the communities and nations in which they operate.

Organizational Climates

The relevance of this perspective is illustrated by a recent study which examined the cycles of work success as influenced by (1) organizational conditions and (2) the personal characteristics of Catholic priests. Hall and Schneider[35] emphasize *both* the critical importance of the *initial* work experiences *and* the more recent or *current* experiences in the religious organization. They posit that the climate in which career work is accomplished is critical to a clergyman's self-image and career commitment.

> The increased commitment and self-esteem resulting from the success will feed back to increase the person's probability of setting further challenging career goals. . . . *Challenge* is important to permit the setting of difficult goals. *Autonomy* is important to permit the individual to set his own goals and the means of achieving them . . . goals central to his self-image.[36]

The tension between competing goals and values. Often the tension between the professional ideals and organizational realities (i.e., the attractive challenges of service, creativity, and collaboration vs. the day-to-day maintenance activities and expectations) constitute an ongoing dilemma both requiring and undermining responsible and competent professional activity. Consequently, the dilemma seems also to derive from the reality that increasingly skilled and theologically sophisticated full-time clergypersons often "serve mainly to guarantee the manpower necessary to continue the 'bureaucratic maze' of ecclesiastical structures."[37]

These same religious organizations came into being to coordinate activities aimed at achieving the lofty goals set forth by the founders. Usually that goal is narrowly conceived at the beginning, with a tendency to expand and multiply over time. These goals provide a focus, a legitimizing rationale for the persistence of the group; ideally they direct the group's activities and its allocation of time and resources. But as an organization emerges, the initial goals are often supplanted by "acquired" or secondary goals, namely, the *maintenance* of the organizational structure.

Metz, for example, details the dilemmas associated with "formal" goals (largely derived from formal doctrine) and "survival" goals (keeping the congregation "alive" as a viable organization).[38] The overwhelming evidence suggests that *survival or maintenance* goals tend to *become dominant* in most organizations, with churches being no exception. Again, the religious professional appears caught between the organizational Scylla and Charybdis. Paradoxically, he/she often criticizes the loss of mission and shifting of goals, yet professional prestige, salaries, and social and material rewards and satisfactions are tied to the maintenance and survival of the organization, reflecting what Lyle Schaller terms the ability to "pay the rent."

Furthermore, there are significant tensions within the realm of the formal goals as suggested in Figure 2. To some, the church is primarily a source of *comfort* in an unstable world (otherworldly), while to others its major purpose is one of *social responsibility* (this-worldly). In addition, there is disagreement as to whether the focus of the church should be on working among those *outside* the group (missional) or concentrating on the relationships *within* it (communal).

FIGURE 2
TYPOLOGICAL SCHEME FOR CLASSIFYING THE
GOALS OF RELIGIOUS ORGANIZATIONS

	This-worldly	Other worldly
Communal		
Missional		

Faced with these divergent goals, many attempt to give "equal" emphasis to the this-worldly and otherworldly, as well as the communal and the missional. Thus, they view both tendencies as complementary rather than as contradictory. Others find themselves and subgroups within their congregations clearly located in different quadrants.

Professional clergypersons themselves often engage in goal displacement by overconforming to the rules and regulations, the expectations and perceptions of congregational and hierarchical influentials. Whether for purposes of "orderliness," efficiency, or career enhancement, the effect can be to displace the primacy of formal goals with those aimed at maintenance and stability.

Subsequently, the "goal" dilemma frequently takes three forms: (1) disagreement with the membership, (2) balancing maintenance goals vs. formal goals, and (3) balancing and integrating multiple goals. Most organizations tend to be *multiple* in focus, resulting in an almost *constant need for balancing and phasing* both within the congregation and in coordination with other levels of the religious organization. This is why management is an *art* calling for much skill.

Minimally, most religious organizational goals focus upon (1) individuals and (2) their social and cultural environment(s). Resources are allocated to celebrate, worship, educate, "save," give hope to, feed, nurture, and care for individuals. At the same time, attention often focuses upon altering or preserving social structures, including the further advancement of other "formal" goals such as justice, peace, human rights, education, care for elderly and children.

To facilitate these goals, most congregations coordinate their own activities with other levels or subsystems whose functions are the coordination of activities and moneys of the system, the institution of new programs, the training or orientation and supervision of personnel, the setting of standards of performance, the allocation of rewards to the successful, the application of punishment to the deviants, and the setting of goals of the system. Each subsystem of the total organization has a formal organizational table with job description and job differentiation. Each subsystem has explicit formal goals and implicit organizational self-maintenance goals of its own.

The local clergyman, in turn, is sandwiched between the values and expectations of the members of the local parish *and* those articulated by these wider subsystems.[39] And *both* possess resources and "control" in the form of promotions, salaries, and recommendations, as well as valid needs and programs deserving the pastor's support and attention.

In short, clergypersons continue to find themselves faced with an ubiquitous struggle *to balance sets* of goals which may seem *opposed but are all* probably *necessary* (or perceived so by some elements in the system) for the overall success of the enterprise. The degree to which time and talent are expended on activities which are defined as "valuable," "challenging," and "worthwhile" will largely influence how religious professionals *perceive and evaluate* their profession, the religious organization and its managerial claims, as well as themselves.

A clue seems to lie in the extent to which "organizational-administrative" work is planned and perceived as *legitimate means* toward the more ultimately conceived *ends*. And this leads to the organizational locus of authority: namely, the degree to which the pastor *plans* his own activities or *has them planned* for him, or some combination of the two.

AUTONOMY, AUTHORITY, AND LEGITIMATION

The Venn diagram (Figure 1) suggests that the autonomy of the religious professional ranges along a full panoply of constraints. These "outside" influences or controls stem from such sources as a sense of accountability to one's call or understanding of God, other colleagues on multiple staffs, hierarchical influentials whose control varies with respect to the particular situation and organization, as well as the "client-members" whose voluntary participation exercises considerable influence over the ministerial autonomy. Thus, the evidence points to *significant limitations* to professional autonomy which are inherent *in the organizational climate*.

Although religious organizations can be located along a continuum ranging from hierarchical to charismatic, the religious professional is confronted with one clear reality: his/her professional status has neither "legitimacy nor existence" apart from the religious organization.[40] The issue of autonomy, then, is really best seen as a dialectic which takes seriously the bases by which legitimacy and authority are bestowed upon the clergyperson. Sources of authority range from that inherent in the role itself (e.g., bishop, rabbi) to that deriving from a sense of being "called," as well as from expertise, competence, and tenure. In addition, the personal magnetism and capacity to gain and hold a "following" can impact the authoritative base of the clergyperson.

One irony in the gaining and retention of authority is the tendency of members to take a day-to-day passive stance, which allows or necessitates that someone "steer the ship." As a result, power often consolidates over time in the hands of the ones who keep the ship moving. Thus, *tradition and growing expertise accumulate to form considerable authority* which is able to withstand efforts at reform and change when and if the passengers wake up and want to help steer too.

However, overriding the entire issue of autonomy and authority is the *voluntary, localized nature of American religious institutions* and their denominational variations. The followers or clients possess a power and autonomy of their own as joiners, contributors, and employers in this ongoing dialectic of mutual influence, legitimacy, and autonomy. Consequently, a critical organizational reality affecting the professional's autonomy and sense of challenge becomes manifest in the goal-establishing process, especially as it juxtaposes the goals of the institution with the career or personal goals of the pastor.

CHANGING AND CONFLICTING PERCEPTIONS OF THE CLERGY ROLE

In the ensuing twenty plus years since Samuel Blizzard's catalytic work, observers and participants have documented, analyzed, and witnessed to the numerous and often contradictory expectations associated with the clergy role. Sidney Skirvin has poignantly summarized the discussion of multiple roles (and multiple audiences) and points specifically to the dilemmas of the religious professional

> ...He or she is involved intricately in the complex network of relationships which comprise the church. Though not necessarily desirable, the pastor, more than anyone else associated with the church, functions as the center of these networks. In the words of James Dittes, the pastor is "on the spot." As the parish professional, this person stands at the point of intersection between expressive purposes [i.e., the increase of the love of God and neighbor] and instrumental means [i.e., the organizational realities necessary to achieve such purposes].... And to add to the confusion, this role diversity [i.e., preacher, pastor, priest, teacher, organizer, administrator...] is set within the context of a very human, very diverse voluntary association which is a part of a society undergoing the agony of normlessness.... This person is, in other words, a generalist, both willing and able to be sustained by the purposive vision of the church and to express it. At the same time, he or she is committed to being an unabashed ecclesiastical politician for the sake of the instrumental means of the [religious organization].... This dynamic tension continues to be the determinant of pastoral roles and functions.... It is the power of this dynamic tension which causes some professionals to be perplexed, some to be enlivened, and some to move their ministry into other contexts.[41]

Graphically, Skirvin suggests the imagery of multi-dimensional vectors converging upon the "minister on the spot." Both laser-like and latent, these conflicts derive from (1) a "unique set of client/employer/employee relationships ... (where) the clients and employers are the same" with a tendency for congregations to evaluate performance in terms of "invested money" and "pastoral return" rather than mutual ministry; (2) denominational, hierarchical, and ecumenical demands for loyalty; (3) the dynamic and complex realities of the community and social context of ministry; plus (4) a theologically and ideologically informed perspective represented by such titles as "servant," "priest," "teacher," "professional," "prophet," "preacher," "scholar," and "organizer."

Intensifying the impact of conflicting expectations and tugs-of-war between differing definitions of goals and authority is the general absence of a comprehensive support or evaluation/feedback system. No doubt this is a consequence of the highly autonomous behavior of clergypersons, due both to their own self-perceptions and to the expectations of others. One could add (as does Skirvin) the impinging realities of scarce monetary resources and rewards, the "sluggishness" of institutions to adapt, especially when such actual and potential dissonance is manifest or always lurking below the surface of tranquility whether actual or simply feared.

The frequent consequence of these multiple pushing and pulling realities is either immobilization of both pastor and congregation, or a caution that inhibits growth and candor. Thus, a first step might be to embrace the parish dynamic, and "for both pastor and parish to acknowledge" the realities and relate to each other as a body mutually "called out for ministry."[42]

PROLIFERATION OF ROLES AND CONTRADICTORY EXPECTATIONS

Perhaps the most dynamic example of this is seen in the redefinition of the Roman Catholic priest's role as a consequence of Vatican II. One Catholic writer posits that the liturgical reform shifted the priestly function from "saving souls by administering the sacraments [as an] intermediary between God and the faithful" to the essential function of "presiding over religious communities."[43] Such a redefinition of responsibilities suggests that competence in *directing and unifying the "community"* becomes crucial. Ironically, however, professional training has rarely included such emphasis or content, even though repeatedly observers have noted the importance of a theologically informed pastoral-director role for rabbis and pastors, as well as priests. Nor has such an orientation or training been allowed to mature from its stepsister role to that of a legitimated, full-fledged family member alongside the biblical-theological-historical-homiletical-educational hegemony.

Between ten and twenty role categories have characterized this "master role" which encompasses both the general function of presiding over a religious community and numerous specialist functions such as counseling, preaching, and teaching. If the proliferation of roles gave birth to compatible or complementary expectations, dilemmas would primarily concern the matter of competence and time. However, the dilemma is underscored by the often conflicting expectations attached to each sub-role and accentuated by the fact that some are quite traditional (e.g., evangelist, shepherd, and scholar) and others more contemporary (e.g., community problem-solver, counselor, and planner).

Research has noted that ministers and laity are not too far apart in their preferences for how a clergyperson should spend his/her time, namely with priorities upon preaching and pastoral-visitation. But an organizational paradox is that, in spite of the rhetoric about and commitment to these priorities, pastors generally lament that they actually spend most of their time organizing and administering programs, but with little sense that there is a legitimacy, much less a theological perspective, for the organizing, planning, and evaluative tasks necessary for effective goal attainment by the religious community.

Social identities. Alvin Gouldner[44] extends the often cited role conflict approach by unravelling and examining the strands at the end of the rope utilized in the "tug of war" between the roles. Utilizing the perspective that views a social role as a set of expectations pertinent to the occupant of a position within a social group or system, he stresses the multiplicity of "social identities" which specify all or some of the "correct" activities for pastors. These "social identities" may be "manifest" or "latent." This suggests the importance of giving careful attention to how and why some social identity is regarded as valid for a given social or professional situation while another role behavior might be labelled as being irrelevant, inappropriate, or illegitimate by some or all of the various social audiences or climates that have an influence on the pastor[44] (see Figure 1).

Such an approach suggests that some *latent* social identities, although defined as *irrelevant* or illegitimate say by the parishioners, may represent strong influences upon the pastor's performance of his role(s). For example, a female or minority group pastor may identify a great deal with a group or ideology associated with such statuses, whereas official boards or sessions might define such influence as irrelevant or inappropriate. Less dramatic latent identities might stem from clergy support groups, family commitments, as well as professional aspirations and fantasies. On the other hand, the personnel decisions made by a denomination or congregation may be significantly affected by sexism or a traditional definition of the pastor's role neither of which might be defined as relevant by the particular pastor, even though the outcome might lead to unemployment or a promotion.

Consequently, latent social identities may potentially be very influential for clergy role behavior and be especially critical in the role conflict tug of war. These *latent* social identities and roles are important because they exert pressure upon obvious or *manifest* roles, often impairing conformity to the taken-for-granted role behavior accepted as "agreed" upon by the congregation or denomination.

With reference to the clergyman's role, the congregation as a social system may by consensus disregard the norms of an outstanding theologian or the valuations of denominational leaders as unimportant or irrelevant to a *job description* for *their* pastor. But in fact, such latent social identifications may be quite influential to the behavior or attitudes of a particular pastor, however irrelevant or illegitimate they may be to the congregation or subgroup of parishioners.

Identity Incongruities

Like countervailing magnetic force fields, the social identities of most clergy are grounded in organizationally related reference groups or social systems. These may be stable in their intensity of influence or, more likely, receive new weightings depending upon the task and the intensity of importance assigned it by the respective audience. Minimally, most clergypersons have as reference points their congregations (and its numerous subgroups), the denomination and its infrastructure, a theological and/or ideological position(s), and other professionals (clergy as well as non-clergy who perform functionally similar tasks in such domains as counseling or social change). In addition, there are the potentially powerful influences of racial and sexual identity, prospective members, and colleagues in multiple staffs, to mention but a few.

Analoguous to the vectors referred to above, these significant social networks and individuals interact with and often compete for influence over the pastor, often displacing or usurping the centrality of the "officially recognized" role definitions. Viewed in another way, these social identities represent four levels of influence: ranging from *self-definitional* to *associational* (the congregation), to *inter-associational* (denominational), to *societal* (external to the religious system *per se*). Peter Berger succinctly describes the relationship between the first three and some implications for the clergy:

> The clergy occupies an interesting position in this situation. On the one hand, the clergyman appears as the local representative of the organization (as though he were its principal "retail man"). On the other hand, he is very much dependent on the good will of his lay members and, in most Protestant and all Jewish cases, he is actually *employed* by the lay members insofar as the economic base of his existence is concerned. It is easy to understand how this in-between position is bound to lead to conflicts of all kinds. The conflicts tend to be centered on the definitions of the actual role of the clergyman. The theological definition of this role (which, at least in the beginning of his career, tends to be identical with the clergyman's self-definition) may not agree with either the organizational or the associational expectations concerning the role. The clergyman thus finds himself being pulled at by at least three different sets of expectations, sometimes in diametrically opposite directions. There is good evidence, certainly in the Protestant case and very likely in the Jewish one, that the expectations of the lay members (who constitute the clergyman's most continuous social "reference group," in addition to being his source of finances) have the strongest pull in the long run.[45]

Strong evidence has accumulated which supports the thesis that *no other occupational group has as many potential* (and actual) *conflicting social identities* which are salient to professional activity. Any response to the organizational dilemmas of the clergyman must also face squarely what Richard Niebuhr observed over two decades ago:

> The contemporary church is confused about the nature of the ministry. Neither ministers nor the schools that nurture them are guided today by a clear-cut, generally accepted conception of the ministry, though such an idea may be emerging.[46]

And, the evidence noted above suggests that a consensus seems, if anything, to be equally remote at the present time.

THE RESIDENT THEOLOGIAN AS A "PLANNER-PASTOR-PRIEST"

"Without a vision, the people perish" (parish?); but it is equally valid to note that, without effective collaboration and coordination, the *vision perishes* for want of an instrument to translate the ideals into mission and service. Recently such phrases as "management by objectives," "organizational development," and "the self-guiding society" have been used by those who posit that there are dynamic, flexible administrative approaches which can be utilized to tap the rich resources of the individuals constituting an organization. And at the same time such administrative investment provides articulate concreteness for the visions or goals which transcend and give purpose and perspective to the day-to-day endeavors.

The first step, then, toward equipping the congregation and its resident professional(s) is to reaffirm both the Biblical witness and the informing insights of the social and administrative sciences. Attention must minimally focus upon a self-consciousness which leads to co-creativity, the transcending goals to which the theologically informed community is called, and the power and strength inherent in groups.

It is ironic to find social scientists and students of administration using such language as

> . . . .[increasingly] greater vision in more persons, and—most gradually—a decline in the emphasis on material wealth in favor of increased symbolization. . . . The members themselves are transformed . . . consensus, one whose growing value-realization hinges on a continued interplay between members and structures. . . . To be active is to be aware, committed, and potent."[47]

Certainly the synagogue and parish are organizational forms that can gain from developing more effective and active social covenants, utilizing the approaches and insights of "social planning" and "management by objectives," while all the while utilizing and adapting these tools with theological integrity.

Underlying the central thesis of the preceding analysis has been the assumption that the clergyperson's task is "not a bundle of miseries or a vocational hair shirt."[48] Rather, it is a dynamic, tension-filled career with distinct stresses. To function creatively in an organizational "earthen vessel," consisting of human beings enmeshed in "institutional dilemmas," seems to require both a special orientation and training. In fact, it seems even to require *special kinds of persons* who neither become immobilized by nor who "sell out" to such organizational realities as seem inescapable when organizations endure over time and *make demands of their own.*

Assuming, therefore, that it is unlikely that we can "eliminate human frailties," what can be done to enable clergypersons and congregations, as well as all levels of the religious organization, to probe into the internal dynamics of a shared task of ministry and emerge both wiser and better equipped to live with organizational dilemmas? Following are some questions and some possible alternatives posited for consideration.

RECRUITMENT AND TRAINING
FOR THE "THEOLOGIAN-PLANNER"

Recruitment

Can that deeply personal and sacred sense of "call" be left unexamined and explored? What can be done that simultaneously honors both the individual's sense of commitment *and* the realities and "requirements" of that dynamic, tension-filled profession with all its organizational demands? Cannot some process of value clarification and reality testing screen, filter, or redirect persons? As pointed out above, the motivations and personalities of clergymen seem to be as susceptible to human foibles as those of all people. Psychological tests may be very revealing, as may career development counseling which begins early and continues to be available throughout the career.

Yet while pursuing such objectives, care must be taken to avoid the pitfalls of a mangement development program that produces carbon copies. Here much insight can be gained from the organizational development approach which strives to incorporate a wide variety of individual styles and input by means of coordination and confrontation.[49] To suggest such a process cannot ignore the likelihood that Moses, Luther, St. Francis, or other notables might have been screened *out* by any such process. But that must not prevent efforts by the religious organization to address itself to the career requirements and to counsel and train accordingly, especially since there are quite legitimate and needed alternatives to serving a congregation.

Training

The training process should minimally confront the seminarian with the sense that effectiveness is to no small degree dependent upon his/her expressive awareness of people and an instrumental skillfulness in getting jobs done.[50] There is strong evidence to suggest that the training of theologically sensitive "pastoral directors" might include leadership skills so that they can effectively and sensitively act as catalyzers within parish situations. In addition to much more intensive on-the-job training and feedback, such skills could easily include experience with the following administrative orientation:

1. Taking seriously the idea of planned change which assumes that human beings are willing and able actively to create and recreate organizations, i.e., play an active role in controlling rather than being controlled by the social forces influencing the organization.[51]
2. Carefully attending to the skills relative to "participative management," which recognizes that training in congregational administration is a co-equal element in the seminary curriculum.
3. Dealing forthrightly with the political realities of conflicting goals and values to be found in the internal and external relationships characterizing congregations.

In short, seminary training must introduce and equip her/him to (1) be a self-conscious and knowing participant within an organization; (2) be a facilitator enabling the congregation to focus upon its goal(s), as well as the resources and commitments required to achieve them; and (3) take seriously the importance of power and influence at the heart of planning, change, and organizational reality, i.e., the political realities of parish life. Some approaches, such as case studies, point in this direction, but extensive on-the-job reality testing and feedback are also essential.

Decision-making as a Core Ingredient

Decision making links the warp and woof, the ends and means, of any organization. Decisions range from those related to the expenditure of limited funds (e.g., redecorating classrooms), to hiring or nominating, as well as ethical responses to core beliefs. And yet, in spite of its everyday nature, decision-making skills do not receive the central attention they require, and rarely is such "training" grounded in the dynamic realities of actual congregational decisions. What is being posited here is that one of the most critical roles of a professional clergyperson is that of a facilitator of corporate and individual decisions which are theologically, morally, and organizationally sound. Such a role rests upon the following assumption: that, for a pastor, a monopoly on authority is neither practically possible nor grounded in voluntary organizational theory *or* in theology.

Increasing membership sophistication requires what has perhaps always been theologically implicit, namely, the involvement of members in the questioning, comparing, and making of decisions related to the complex internal situation and external environment of congregations. In order to facilitate its mission in an effective manner, the religious enterprise demands planning skills and expertise, for both pastors and members. These include:

1. An *empirically* and *theologically* based evaluation procedure which incorporates sufficient amounts of systematically and objectively gathered information.[52]

2. A process of planning in which problems/issues are clearly posed and articulated. That is, goals must be specified in relationship to where one is at any moment; and alternative solutions to the obstacles must be presented, analyzed as to probable consequences, then selected and evaluated in terms of whether the chosen solution did in fact enhance the desired goal.

PLANNING WITH THE ORGANIZATIONAL DILEMMA PERSPECTIVE

The following model is suggested as an alternative to the polar tendencies to berate or underplay the organizational potential or the "idolatry" exhibited by those who take the organization itself *too* seriously. The planning process represents a dynamic alternative for a parish actively and creatively: (1) to cope with the societal and ecclesiastical environment of a congregation; (2) to clarify, establish, and be more effective in attaining the goals for which the organization exists, i.e., its *raison d'etre*; (3) to integrate the membership into a working entity actively involved in goal formation, strategy assessment, and evaluation processes; and (4) to establish its "*own* way of doing things," a normative and localized order which simultaneously avoids the too rigid parochialism of "this is how we always do things here."

Process Planning: A Useful Tool

The very dynamic nature of parish organizational life require continuous decision making and evaluation of those decisions in light of the dilemmas posed. In order to maintain the balance between external and internal pressures upon the allocation of the limited resources of the congregation and as professional(s), it is essential that there be *systematic* and continuous planning and feedback which might be addressed in the following manner:[53]

1. Identifying the possible goals, distinguishing between (a) a goal system, i.e., an integrated, unified, comprehensive set of objectives which have relative stability and universality; and (b) more precise, concrete, operating goals which actually "determine" or specify action.[54]
2. Clarifying the problems or obstacles obfuscating the accomplishment of those goals.
3. Developing consensus on possible and feasible *targets* for solving or neutralizing the problems.
4. Ascertaining the alternative options for action, including *all* the alternatives and *who* would have responsibility for expediting each strategy or tactic.
5. Systematically analyzing the implications of each option as to its obvious and not-so-obvious consequences (i.e., manifest and latent) to the internal and external realities of the

congregation, with particular attention to the *finite* fiscal, human, and community resources available for the solution of any organizational problem.[55]

6. Utilizing a variety of skills to reach *compromises* and consensus on the most viable strategies which honor the integrity of theology and organizations.

7. Forging cooperative and mutually beneficial relationships with other congregations, levels of the religious organization (i.e., district, regional, and national systems), community groups, as well as subgroups and individuals within the congregation.

8. Effecting a division of labor which makes consignments which are just, agreed upon, and sufficient to carry out the option(s) including sufficient attention to the coordination function.

9. Establishing key criteria and priority to a quantative monitoring and evaluating of the progress toward the goal and the peripheral consequences of the means utilized; e.g., unanticipated detriments to other important programs or goals of the congregation, denominations, or wider social milieux.[56]

Decision-making processes and planning which address these intrinsic dimensions are adaptable to the highly interrelated dilemmas facing every clergyperson, namely how to focus energies most effectively and efficiently in the collective mission of the particular congregation. Such an approach or style further leads to a more open acknowledgement of and creative response to the political realities of the local congregation, especially the disagreements over goals and values. And instead of adopting a static or ad hoc resolution of problems, the congregation is enabled to deal with diversity and changing needs or priorities on a more "system"-oriented basis.

CONCLUSION

Such a professional "planner-pastor-priest" orientation offers a challenging and effective instrumentality for working creatively with the dynamics instead of succumbing to the dilemma. Not only are the responsibilities for decision making expanded in a more democratic manner, but the utilization of more, salient, and systematically secured information has the potential of leading to more effective decision making, more efficient use of resources, and better evaluation of the consequences. In short, the pastor and his/her congregation can make significant strides *toward regaining control* over their organization, because they actively and systematically seek to be more "aware, committed, and potent" relative to the goals and purposes of the religious organization.

Such a style requires human sensitivity, humility, self- and corporate-restraint, as well as learning to live and grow by the inevitable tensions;

otherwise the corporate life together will more likely be characterized by the taking of short-cuts, with ill-informed strategies, or operating by the "seat of one's pants" in and out of the dilemma of congregational life.

In short, on-the-job experience with the planning-feedback model is essential as an integral and coequal dimension of seminary and continuing education. Then, as theology and organizational realities articulate with one another, there is an increased possibility for a creative coping with the dynamics of congregational life. A dialogue that begins in seminary thus continues throughout the professional career.

Ultimately, the key issues confronting the professional are integrity, competency, and accountability for the consequences of individual and corporate decisions made in the name of religious goals. But even a rose garden is blessed with prickly thorns. Despite the thorny "pastoral dilemmas," deliberate and thoughtful cultivating can reestablish the garden of ministry as an exciting non-utopia, a dynamic and rewarding context in which to expend a career and a life.

Notes

*I am indebted to several colleagues and research assistants who made significant contributions by way of editorial and bibliographic suggestions: Nancy Homans, Marilynn Duker Bergman, Karen Fritz, and Linda Buda and to the Faculty Development Fund of the College of Wooster which provided financial assistance for the preparation of the manuscript.

1. Debate rages about the applicability of a professional model for clergypersons. An assumption made here follows Douglas T. Hall and Benjamin Schneider, *Organizational Climates and Careers: The Work Lives of Priests* (New York: Seminar Press, 1973), namely that, although "no occupation is totally professionalized, and no individual in a profession acts totally professionally," there is considerable usefulness in using the model or concept to refer to occupational groups that tend to have: (1) specific skills or techniques, (2) authority deriving from knowledge, (3) control or influence over training of new members, (4) a code of ethics, (5) a cultural tradition, (6) service orientation, (7) collegial identification, (8) work with a standardized product, etc. Although the religious professional operates more or less within a bureaucratic structure and a social context in which some see the "deprofessionalization of everyone," the chapter is essentially a discussion of the qualifications and influences exerted on the role, especially those derived from the organizational nature of the religious group. Cf. Thomas M. Gannon, "Priest/Minister: Profession or Non-Profession,"

Review of Religious Research 12 (Winter, 1971): 66-79; Marie R. Haug, "The Deprofessionalization of Everyone?", *Sociological Focus* 8 (August, 1975): 197-213.

2. In an attempt to avoid the denominational, specifically religious, or sexist connotations implicit in the terms "priest," "rabbi," "clergyman," etc., the more neutral terms "clergypersons," religious professionals," and "pastors" will be utilized.

3. Edward C. Banfield, *The Unheavenly City Revisited* (Boston: Little, Brown and Company, 1974), pp. 3ff. In discussing the urban crisis, Banfield points out that the word *crisis* is often used indiscriminately to discuss situations ranging from those that are merely uncomfortable or inconvenient to situations that cannot be changed or are "too costly" to merit changing. Like Banfield, the author prefers to reserve the term *crisis* for those issues involving the "essential welfare" of the individual or the "good health" of society.

4. Thomas O'Dea, *The Sociology of Religion* (Englewood Cliffs, N.J.: Prentice-Hall, 1966). Cf. James Dittes, *Minister on the Spot* (Philadelphia: Pilgrim Press, 1970), who argues that the very human dilemma of being on the spot is the place of ministry.

5. Paul Tillich, *On the Boundary: An Autobiographical Sketch* (New York: Scribner, 1966). Note the editor's emphasis on "phasing" and "balancing."

6. J. Eugene Haas and Thomas Drabek, *Complex Organizations: A Sociological Perspective* (New York: The Macmillan Company, 1973), emphasize that the persistence and change in organizational performance output varies with the patterns of stress and strain, i.e., inconsistencies, among and within three key structures or elements basic to every organization: (1) the norms (and sanctions) which constitute the rules of organizational life; (2) the person-to-person understandings and orientations; and (3) the physical resources available to the personnel, including persons, buildings, equipment, and information.

7. Cf. David A. Moberg, *The Church as a Social Institution* (Englewood Cliffs, N.J.: Prentice-Hall, 1962); Ross P. Scherer, "The Church as a Formal Voluntary Organization," in David Smith, et al., eds., *Voluntary Action Research* (Lexington, Mass: D. C. Heath, 1972).

8. Observers have long noted the tendency for religious professionals to perceive of their mobility in status terms such as a "better parish," even though they rationalize such aspirations in other terms such as "called to a new challenge," "God's will," or "an opportunity to utilize special talents." Cf., Kenneth R. Mitchell, *Psychological and Theological Relationships in the Multiple Staff Ministry* (Philadelphia: Westminster Press, 1966); Eli Ginzberg, *et al., Occupational Choice: An Approach to General Theory* (New York: Columbia

University Press, 1951); and Keith P. Bridstron and Dwight W. Culver, *Pre-Seminary Education* (Minneapolis: Augsburg, 1965).

9. Cf. Bridston and Culver, *Pre-Seminary Education.*

10. For example, in an extensive study of midwestern seminaries, Francis A. Lonsway, *Seminarians in Theology: A Study of Backgrounds and Personalities* (Washington, D.C.: Center for Applied Research in the Apostolate, 1968), concluded that over 40 per cent of these Catholic seminarians' fathers and 60 per cent of their mothers had not graduated from high school, with only 12 per cent of their parents receiving a college degree. Typically, the father was in a clerical, agricultural, or skilled occupation, although frequently managerial and unskilled service occupations were also noted. A nationwide study done in 1968 by Raymond H. Potvin and Antonas Suziedelis, *Seminarians of the Sixties: A National Survey* (Washington, D.C.: Center for Applied Research in the Apostolate, 1969), further revealed that the majority of Catholic seminarians came from families with incomes ranging from $5,000-$15,000.

11. Edgar Mills and Garry Hesser, "A Contemporary Portrait of Clergymen," in G. Bucher and P. Hill (eds.), *Confusion and Hope* (Philadelphia: Fortress Press, 1974), pp. 20ff.

12. Cf. Bridston and Culver, *Pre-Seminary Education*; Lonsway, *Seminarians in Theology*; Gerald Jud, et al., *Ex-Pastors: Why Men Leave the Parish Ministry* (Philadelphia: Pilgrim Press, 1970).

13. Cf. Bridstron and Culver, *Pre-Seminary Education.*

14. Ibid. and also Joseph Fichter, *America's Forgotten Priests* (New York: Harper, 1968).

15. Cf., Jacob Jay Lindenthal, *The Delayed Decision to Enter the Ministry: A Study in Occupational Change* (New Haven: Yale University, 1968); Bridston and Culver, *Pre-Seminary Education*, 1968; and Lonsway, *Seminarians in Theology.*

16. James Dittes, *Minister on the Spot*, pp. 130ff.

17. Donald W. Shriver, "An Educational Research Program. Why?", *The Union News*, October, 1976, pp. 1-2, who cites G. Ellis Nelson, *Using Evaluation in Theological Education.*

18. Franklin Littel, "Protestant Seminary Education," in James H. Lee and Louis Putz, eds., *Seminary Education in a Time of Change* (Notre Dame: Fides Press, 1965), pp. 533-556. Walter O. Wagoner, *The Seminary: Protestant and Catholic* (New York: Sheed and Ward, 1966).

19. James M. Gustafson, *Treasure in Earthen Vessels* (New York: Harper and Row, 1961); cf. Jud, et al., *Ex-Pastors*; and James Glasse, *Profession: Minister* (Nashville: Abingdon, 1968).

20. Jud, et al., *Ex-Pastors*, p. 129. Reprinted by permission of Gerald J. Jud and Pilgrim Press.

21. Colin Williams, *The Church* (Philadelphia: Westminster Press, 1968). Compounding this rather belated "self-conscious ecclesiology" were some tendencies which seem to have greatly detracted from systematic attention to the organizational realities of congregations. For example, at the First Assembly of the World Council of Churches (1948), the Anglo-Catholic Bishop Gregg of Ireland defined the church in terms of its "givenness" as the body of Christ in history, stressing the visible continuities of its life in ministry, creeds, sacraments, and fellowship. Then, Karl Barth insisted upon the humanly uncontrollable character of the church as "event", insisting that it occurs as a gift of the Spirit where the Word evokes faith (cf. Williams, 1968: 13). Note also the theme of being at a "cross-roads" following Vatican II and the various roles and functions of the priest in such documents as the *Decree on Priestly Training* or the *Pastoral Constitution* on *The Church in the Modern World* (Rahner, 1969).

22. For example, the contributors to the work edited by C. R. Brown, ed., *Education for Christian Service* (New Haven: Yale University Press, 1922), focused almost exclusively upon an historical and spiritual understanding, relying primarily upon the scriptures and theology.

23. The author searched out the literature in a seminary library in an endeavor to ascertain the emphasis placed upon the ministry and the church as an organization. These observations rely on both a systematic and impressionistic content analysis. For example, ten works published between 1800 and 1900 were examined; sixteen between 1900 and 1925; only three between 1926 and 1948; and thirty-three published since 1948. Further research using systematic content analysis would appear to be fruitful.

24. Cf. Colin Williams, *The Church* (1968).

25. Lyle Schaller, *Planning for Protestantism in Urban America* (New York: Abingdon Press, 1965), p. 89.

26. H. Richard Niebuhr, et. al., *The Purpose of the Church and its Ministry: Reflections on the Aims of Theological Education* (New York: Harper, 1956).

27. Cf. Claude Welch, *The Reality of the Church* (New York: Scribners, 1958); Karl Barth, *Dogmatics in Outline* (N.Y.: Philosophical Library, 1949); and Emil Brunner, *The Christian Doctrine of the Church, Faith, and Consummation* (Philadelphia: Westminster, 1960).

28. Gustafson, *Treasure in Earthen Vessels* (1961).

29. Robert Lee, "The Organizational Dilemma in American Protestantism" (*Union Seminary Quarterly Review*, Nov. 1960).

30. Hall and Schneider, *Organizational Climates and Careers* (1973); Jud, et al. (1970); Glasse, *Profession: Minister* (1968); Dittes, *Minister on the Spot* (1970); Fichter, *The Forgotten Priests* (1968).

31. In order to assess the current seminary emphasis, the author randomly selected a cross-section of seminaries, fifty-nine of which were

randomly selected from Constance Jacquet, ed., *Yearbook of American and Canadian Churches* (Nashville: Abingdon, 1976): pp. 183-188, and requested syllabi and bibliographies currently in use. These observations are based upon the twenty-three responses.

32. There are some notable exceptions which include extensive use of case studies, simulations, conflict management, planning processes, and the understanding of organizational structures and climate. The frequently used text is Alvin J. Lindgren, *Foundations for Purposeful Church Administration* (Nashville: Abingdon Press, 1965), with its attention to administrative principles, church as persons in community, flexible principles for adaptation to unique situations, and emphasis upon "purposeful" activity and planning.

33. George W. Webber, *The Congregation in Mission* (New York: Abingdon Press, 1964).

34. This conceptual distinction between "spheres" is arbitrary as is best illustrated by how to "classify" other religions, other denominations, or even "competing" congregations of one's own denomination, e.g., other orthodox synagogues or Roman Catholic parishes within the same city.

35. Douglas T. Hall and Benjamin Schneider, *Organizational Climates and Careers* (1973).

36. *Ibid.*, p. 3; cf. Edgar W. Mills and John Koval, *Stress in the Ministry* (Washington, D.C.: Ministry Studies Board, 1971); Yoshio Fukuyama, *The Ministry in Transition* (University Park: Penn. State University Press, 1972).

37. Thomas M. Gannon, S.J., "Priest/Minister: Profession or Non-Profession," *Review of Religious Research*, 12 (Winter, 1971): 71.

38. Donald Metz, *New Congregations* (Philadelphia: Westminster Press, 1967); cf. Dean R. Hoge, et al., "Sources of Conflict Over Protestant Church Goals and Priorities," paper presented at Annual Meeting of American Sociological Association Meeting (August, 1975); T. C. Campbell and Y. Fukuyama, *The Fragmented Layman* (Philadelphia: Pilgrim Press, 1970).

39. Cf. Sidney Skirvin, "Christian Ministry in Earthen Vessels," in Glenn Bucher and Patricia Hill, eds., *Confusion and Hope* (Philadelphia: Fortress Press, 1974), pp. 37-39; Jud, et al., *The Ex-Pastors*; Hall and Schneider, *Organizational Climates*, 1973; and J. Kenneth Benson and James Dorsett, "Toward a Theory of Religious Organizations," *Journal for the Scientific Study of Religion* (Summer, 1972): 138-151.

40. Gannon, "Priest/Minister": 74.

41. Skirvin, "Christian Ministry . . .", 1974, pp. 36-39. Reprinted by permission of Fortress Press.

42. Ibid., p. 42.

43. Emile Pin, S.J., "The Priestly Function in Crisis," in Karl Rahner, S.J., *The Identity of the Priest* (New York: Paulist Press), pp. 45-58.

44. Alvin Gouldner, *Patterns of Industrial Bureaucracy* (Glencoe, Ill.: Free Press, 1954), pp. 282-284; cf. Jackson Carroll, "Structural Effects of Professional Schools on Professional Socialization," *Social Forces* 50 (Sept. 1971): 61-74, regarding seminary impacts on self image.

45. Peter Berger, "Religious Institutions" in Neil Smelser (ed.), *Sociology* (New York: Wiley, 1967), p. 368. Reprinted by permission of John Wiley and Sons.

46. Niebuhr, et al., *The Purpose of the Church and Its Ministry* (1956), p. 50.

47. Warren Breed, *The Self-Guiding Society* (New York: The Free Press, 1971), pp. 9-10.

48. Jud, et al., *The Ex-Pastors*, pp. 53.

49. Warren G. Bennis, et al., *The Planning of Change*, 2nd edition (New York: Holt, Rinehart, and Winston, 1969).

50. Cf. Skirvin, "Christian Ministry . . ." and Glasse, *Putting It All Together in the Parish* (1972), and *Profession: Minister* (1968).

51. Cf. Amitai Etzioni, *The Active Society* (New York: The Free Press, 1969); Warren Bennis, *Organizational Development* (Reading, Mass.: Addison-Wesley, 1969).

52. Richard Gorsuch, "Research and Evaluation: Their Role in Decision Making in the Religious Setting," *Review of Religious Research* 17 (Winter, 1976): 93-101.

53. The planning process model, though widely utilized in all types of organizations, is adapted from a report by the Washington Council of Governments, *Toward the Year 2000*.

54. Cf. Kevin Lynch and Lloyd Rodwin, "A Theory of Urban Form" in Robert Gutman and David Popenoe, eds., *Neighborhood, City and Metropolis* (New York: Random House, 1970); pp. 756-776. For example, the local church's goal system may be "preaching the Good News," serving mankind, or being a community; but its specific goals may *more* likely be establishing and raising a budget, determining an optimal location, providing a religious educational system, and so forth.

55. There is a certain parallel here to cost-benefit analysis which examines the value of costs of a strategy or program relative to its benefits. Its strengths lie in that it "forces" the congregation and its leadership to obtain considerably more information than the traditional "intuitive" or "charismatic" appeal to the past (i.e., what has worked) or some vague, utopian future. There are decided benefits in examining the

costs to other programs or goals, i.e., trade-offs, and the effects of the various actions upon the personnel, community, congregation, and finite budgets of time and money. The difficulty of calculating qualitative and unknown costs and benefits qualifies the "cost-benefit" approach considerably, but the struggle to assess the wider implications of organizational decisions and programs offers a significant strength to planning.

56. For example, the time and energy required by the pastor may undercut his/her effectiveness in other areas or the monetary cost to other programs within the congregation. The writer's own experiences with a building program illustrate how the benefits, such as cohesiveness and purposeful activities, have to be weighed and reassessed in terms of the cost to other effective programs, e.g., the disillusionment experienced by many as they observed a subtle shift in the overarching goal system or "mission" of the church.

Part Three

Strain and Change in Denominations

Introduction to Part Three

Ross P. Scherer

Many of the preceding chapters have dealt with change. Burkart has focused on organizational development in his treatment of Protestant denominations; Kim has traced the effects of Vatican II on Catholicism; Gannon and Winter have dealt with structural shifts in religious orders and missions societies; Perry has treated the successive models used in parish planning; and Hesser has traced the growing lack of fit between the outer society and ministerial preparation. All these chapters, then, have dealt with "strain"—the continuous presence of imbalances between resources, goals and expectations, and performances—as an unavoidable accompaniment of organizational life. The chapters in Part Three go further than this in treating "stress" in denominations—an exaggerated form of strain or of the imbalances just referred to, frequently eventuating in outright conflict. Stress and even conflict, however, are not viewed as bad per se from the open systems perspective, since they may assist in clarifying direction, establishing boundaries, and building in new "variety" into the organization. It is true, however, that stress can be very threatening to religious organizations, since their members tend to pride themselves on their internal "harmony."

In this section, Takayama in Chapter 9 develops a comprehensive, theoretical review of the forces affecting denominational consensus and conflict. Johnson and Garrett in Chapters 10 and 11 deal with more specific problems—grass roots-leader disagreement; the problem of the wider environment and intrusion of the denominational "trade association," the National Council of Churches, upon the turf of member denominations.

Takayama's discussion of "strains, conflicts, and schisms" in Protestant denominations in Chapter 9 is really a continuation of the open systems perspective found in the introduction. Much of what he says applies to all voluntary organizations and movements which undergo politicization. He asks how inconsistency is inherent in the structural make-up of denominations, how environment in turn affects this, and what combination of conditions is necessary for conflict to emerge. He sees both disagreement on the concept of organizational authority and the high "permeability" of a denomination to environmental influence as crucial to the development of schism. Yet, environmental influence can to some degree be mediated by leading denominational actors, so that denominations probably respond selectively to outside influences. Sometimes, the leading contenders agree on both goals and means, sometimes on one only, or even on none. In denominations, because ideology is the basis of cohesion, disagreements on goals or on both goals and means probably occur most often, resulting in resort to "compromise" or "inspirational" strategies, he says. This is all complicated by the diffuseness of ends and requirements of grass roots' consent in denominations. Thus, denominational decision making becomes more political than economic. As in civil politics, great finesse and skilled churchmanship are frequently required to maintain sufficient consensus and avoid outright schism. Takayama maintains that the particular ideological and constitutional-political traditions of the denomination determine the modes of stress resolution actually adopted.

Takayama notes that religious organizations are especially vulnerable. Because of their special emphases upon ideals and commitment, they tend to suffer more than other organizations from ideal-actual discrepancies. Furthermore, they tend to emphasize communal and expressive functions (more than instrumental ones) and so probably put a premium upon harmony as an operative goal. Thus, "solidary" incentives when combined with "purposive" goals tend to produce stress, especially on the congregational level. (This point was also made by Perry in Chapter 7.)

As denominations have taken on more functions and have had to face problems of enlarged scale, Takayama says they have tended to think they can dispense with clear authority patterns and so underestimate the need or justification for a central coordinating structure. Their makeshift efforts at coordination thus lack legitimacy and accountability, making the leaders vulnerable to power blocs. The local grass roots may consider as "overcentralization" what the more cosmopolitan leaders may view as "efficiency" in central management. Takayama sees the particular brand of church polity as affecting the internal politics of denominations—leaders in episcopal- and presbyterian-type denominations probably having more sanctions at their disposal for controlling resisters.

Cataclysmic change occurs when internally and externally induced changes combine. The external acts as a catalyst to the internal. Today, denominations are operating in a turbulent environmental field, being affected by the changing social texture, information explosion, changing mores, and the other pathologies of modern society. Takayama believes that denominations will need to rely more on structure than ideology to retain their cohesion. Amid such turbulence, external societal conflict may not breed internal solidarity but rather will exaggerate already existing strains of internal disunity.

In the last section of his chapter, Takayama treats two recent cases of schism—those of the Southern Presbyterians and the Missouri Lutherans. Both have involved conflict between conservatives and moderates; both foundered on the shibboleths of "inerrancy" and ecumenism. Both involved controversy over a seminary, prominence of factional publications, caucuses, and protests from within, charges of "abandoning historic norms." On the other hand, the differences between the two cases are striking. The Southern Presbyterian split involved conservative exclusivists who seceded, whereas in the Missouri Synod it was the moderate inclusivists who were practically forced out in order to survive. The Southern Presbyterian secession was a largely lay movement; the Missouri, a clergy one. The Missouri situation was a much more atypical development in that it involved a purge by conservatives. The Missouri situation has produced a plethora of book-length reports which need to be reanalyzed and assessed in the years to come. Takayama's perspective should form an important part of the theoretical basis of such assessment. The incipient schism of strict constructionists over women's ordination in the Episcopal Church in September, 1977, seems more like the Presbyterian than the Missouri Lutheran case.

Johnson in Chapter 10 deals with the continuous problem of politicization in the context of diminishing resources and a period of fiscal retrenchment. During the mid-1960s a number of Protestant denominations got caught up in the turbulence of the civil rights (and partly the anti-Vietnam War) movements. Simultaneously, however, the United States ran into national economic difficulties, precipitating cutbacks in voluntary giving and a slowing of the "trickling up" process by which voluntary giving reaches the denominational and National Council of Churches levels. Johnson focuses upon the dissensus between denominational grass roots and leadership regarding program and the consequences for staffing and executing denominational programs, especially unpopular ones. Thus, he is dealing with the way in which communication and feedback malfunction in denominations as systems.

He points to what Robert Michels termed the phenomenon of "oligarchy" in organizations which are nominally private but which are constituted on a popular-democratic basis. He notes that several Protestant denominations suffered drops in per capita giving during this period; that staff specialists (including editors and media specialists) took wholesale cuts, resulting in a vast loss of innovative and adaptive power, since information resources are critical to denominational effectiveness. The problem was complicated, he thinks, both by insensitivity in timing of program emphases by national leadership and the coming on the scene, in some cases, of new leaders in a time of turbulence. Church structures generally are ill-equipped to resolve conflict. Hence, he views the role of denominational leaders as a difficult one. On the one hand, theological conviction constrains them to try to be prophetic; but simultaneously, on the other hand, the grass roots constrain them to offer program formulae which will satisfy them so that they will continue to contribute. During periods of national economic turndown, leaders must be especially adroit at finding a successful balance. In effect, as Takayama implies, they must be successful at acting as "politicians for God."

In Chapter 11, the final chapter in this section, Garrett demonstrates the historically conditioned nature of structural arrangements. He deals with the interorganizational relations of a number of Protestant denominations to each other and to their ecumenical organization, the National Council of Churches. Whereas joint, ecumenical cooperation was successful in the 19th century on the local and regional levels amid relatively simple problems of scale, the more recent attempt to coordinate national denominational efforts in the 20th century via the National Council of Churches has met with severe difficulty. He thinks the flaw lies in trying to repristinate a 19th century organizational pattern in the 20th! Ecumenical fervor still burns today, but a workable structural formula has not yet been produced.

What happened was this. In the 19th century, denominational organization was simpler and was geared to assisting sacramental functions and local church staffing; special program tasks were handled by interdenominational mission societies. The simple denominations and the task-oriented associations worked in a complementary balance, resulting in a decentralized, grass-root variety of ecumenism. As time went on, however, the early task-oriented ecumenical efforts were *coopted by the aggrandizing denominations*, which then grew at the expense of the ecumenical. The independent mission societies could deal with individuals and congregations but not with increasingly bureaucratizing denominations. (Winter in Chapter 5, however, notes a reversal of this in the present period).

The first major interdenominational effort was the Federal Council of Churches, founded in the first decade of this century by a number of more Americanized Protestant denominations. The denominations did not view the FCC as a threat, however, since it was involved in something they did not give much attention to, social service. And since denominations did not support the FCC very much, the latter turned to outside funding, becoming a movement alongside but not integral to the former. The successor to the FCC, the National Council of Churches, began originally as a *council of interdenominational agencies* in the early 1950s but began to be transformed into a *council of denominations* in the early 1960s. But the denominations, when faced with the problems of fiscal retrenchment coupled with program disagreements, began to have second thoughts. The member denominations of the NCC, while willing to "conference" together on common problems, feared the Council was becoming "another denomination" and one with which they would have to share a shrinking resource "pie." A concomitant problem was that ecumenical structure could not generally articulate very well with existing denominational reward systems for executive career advancement. Thus, Garrett maintains, while in the impoverished 19th century, decentralized ecumenical societies thrived in a pluralistic market, in the affluent 20th, a more centralized ecumenical structure has nearly collapsed.

His solution to the impasse—a passion for ecumenism together with a lack of a workable blueprint—is not really new but is only partly being tried. He proposes that the member denominations formalize what has operatively and informally been present—that NCC be converted into a *research and development* arm of the denominations; that NCC do for the denominations what they cannot effectively do for themselves. He urges that the development of economic and informational resources be separated from the political process of their implementation and administration; that the competition between the members and the Council be reduced and complementarity be increased. Thus, he thinks, structural interdependence and accountability would be guaranteed. His suggestion seems worth investigating, since there are existing, working exemplars of this in industry, government, education, etc. Whether fiscal and political realities will allow such a possibility is another question.

9

Strains, Conflicts, and Schisms in Protestant Denominations

K. Peter Takayama

Among the most conspicuous aspects of Protestant denominations today are the intra-organizational disputes and conflicts between various opposing leaders and groups. Denominational periodicals as well as daily papers offer dramatic accounts of these disputes and conflicts. For example, the Lutheran Church—Missouri Synod recently underwent severe internal conflicts between conservative and moderate leaders, leading to withdrawal of moderates and the formation of the new Association of Evangelical Lutheran Churches. The Presbyterian Church in the U.S. (Southern) suffered similar internal conflicts, resulting in 1973 in the withdrawal of some 275 conservative local churches which formed the Presbyterian Church in America. There are also indications that other denominations (e.g., the Episcopal Church, the United Methodist Church, the United Presbyterian Church in the U.S.A.) are troubled by internal divisions which can threaten to disrupt their organizational unity.[1]

To be sure, division has characterized the Protestant movement since its inception. In America many denominations have experienced intra-organizational conflicts since the Civil War. Internal disputes (e.g., theological issues regarding liberalism and evolutional theory) and environmental changes (e.g., industrialization, racism, differentiation of social groups and status groups) have no doubt influenced these divisions. Yet, today's disputes and conflicts seem to have greater magnitude in terms of visibility, scale, and organizational complexity.

Ecumenical movements, interdenominational coalitions and even denominational mergers strongly characterized many American churches in the 1950s and 1960s.[2] Only two decades and a half ago, Morrison, for example, was critical about the multiplicity of Protestant denominations, saying it was "scandalously wasteful of the resources of Protestantism" because it not only increased competition among themselves but also "provincialized Protestant mentality by erecting barriers against the flow of Christian thought."[3] But these cooperative ventures have apparently now come to a halt. What has happened?

We can ask several questions: (1) Are the intra-organizational strains (i.e., inconsistencies among structural elements) and conflicts inherent *in* the *basic* structural *make-up* of Protestant denominations? (2) To what extent and how do types and rates of social *change in* the external *environment* influence characteristics and magnitudes of intra-denominational conflicts? (3) What are the major *conditions for* the development of severe *conflicts* that may lead to denominational splits today?

To answer all these questions in detail is impossible. It is the intent of this writer merely to underscore the *normality of intra-denominational strain*, and even conflict, as well as to explore the major contemporary characteristics or conditions which magnify the ever present strains and conflicts.

Our approach is limited in two respects. First, the theoretical framework we use is that of formal organizations, plus that of social movements. This is limited in the sense that it is directed to the analysis of *organizational* dimensions alone. But such a perspective enables us to focus sharply on strategic problems of the denomination as a functioning organizational entity. Burkart (Chapter 1) has suggested potential sites of organizational strains and conflicts in his typological discussion of developmental patterns of Protestant denominations. Building partly on his suggestions, we extend and elaborate various sources and sites of strain and conflict, and then discuss possible outcomes as well as routes of "conflict resolution." The major focus of discussion is on the dynamic *interplay between* denominations' *normative structures*, such as ideologies, constitutions, and authorities, on the one hand, *and* their changing *environments*, on the other. Since it is through the mobilization of power and resources that all organizations confront changes, it is appropriate to stress the role of *internal* denominational *political* processes as well as environmental changes.[4]

The second limitation is that we shall primarily focus on *structural sources* of strain and conflict and their consequences in mainline Protestant denominations, since they occupy the dominant positions in the American religious scene and seem to be the most troubled by internal divisions today.[5]

The main thesis of this chapter is that (1) environmental permeability and (2) ideological basis of authority are two major conditions for splits and the development of divisions in denominations. It was H. Richard Niebuhr who identified causes of divisions in terms of heterogeneity of social base and doctrinal purity. His discussion of the role of social class, ethnic, and regional factors in denominationalism remains the classic statement of the *need for internal homogeneity* in a denomination.[6] Niebuhr, however, largely ignored organizational or "structural" aspects of the denominational life, which also are crucial factors for the development of division. Niebuhr's class, ethnic, and regional factors can be conceptually incorporated into aspects of the denomination's "internal" elements. Thus, modifying and extending his thesis we advance our argument that *the major conditions for divisions are a high degree of environmental permeability and ideological concern regarding the legitimacy of organizational authority and the behavior of the leadership, rather than doctrinal purity per se.*

The main thesis stated in this general fashion, our task is to specify these conditions in detail so that we can offer research propositions for the advancement of empirical investigation in this area. Our discussion begins first with the outline of a conceptual model for the study of intra-denominational conflicts and changes. This will be further elaborated in the second and third sections with the support of empirical evidence available in the literature. Finally, preliminary attempts to test the plausibility of the model will be made by applying it to two cases of denominational split, the Presbyterian Church in the U.S. and the Lutheran Church-Missouri Synod. (For the readers who are interested in research, the major ideas and propositions discussed in the first three sections are summarized into hypothesis statements, to be found in an Appendix at the end of this chapter.)

THEORETICAL MODEL: MAJOR ASSUMPTIONS

Organizational changes are outgrowths of conditions both within and without organizations. They are dialectical processes in the sense that the internal and external conditions mutually influence each other (see Chapter 1). Changes in conditions external to organizations and those internal to organizations are so closely intertwined that, however caused, changes become part of the cycle of dynamic interactions. It is often difficult to trace them to a supposed "original" cause or causes.

This appears especially true for what Etzioni calls "normative" organizations.[7] Because they serve culture-oriented goals, they are highly sensitive as well as vulnerable to moral climates and social issues of the society (and the world). Religious denominations and other ideological associations (e.g., political parties) are such organizations.

Changes in the external environmental conditions no doubt constitute powerful constraints and challenges with which organizations must cope. Differentiation and proliferation of social groups, major population shifts, technological-scientific innovations, changes in values and normative standards, and the like may precipitate major changes within the organization. These changes are so basic and universal that some social theorists (e.g., Marxian scholars) consider them to be beyond the power and control of many organizations.

This deterministic view of social change, while having a considerable measure of truth at a macro-general level, however, does not help us understand how social changes occur in organizations unless we analyze them *from the standpoint of those* who are leading and *participating* in specific organizational movements and activities. It was Max Weber who espoused this view forcefully. Recent organizational literature informs us that types of environmental changes affect the organization differentially, just as the various types of organizations are influenced differentially by the same environmental change.[8]

We conceive of organizations as *open systems* (see Introduction). Among others, Thompson expounds this theoretical perspective.[9] He considers the central problems for organizations to be having to cope simultaneously with both uncertainties imposed by external environmental changes and structural inconsistencies or strains generated from *within*. Haas and Drabek underscore this problem as follows:

> The critical point is that organizations are not to be viewed as identical black boxes. Environmental change is interpreted and assessed by incumbents who find themselves confronting structures with differing patterns and intensities of strain and differing capacities to monitor the environment.[10]

They consider that, in addition to organizational incumbents' definitions of environmental changes, the degree of interdependence between the organization, the sector of the environment that changed, and the organization's internal strain pattern will constrain the range of response options.

Environmental changes are filtered: i.e., organizations respond *selectively* by acting on their environment so as to try and expand their autonomy, prestige, and security. Any specific environmental change does *not* automatically result in a *single* response. Environmental changes create a set of new strains in organizations. Leaders in one organization may see their options as highly limited, whereas leaders in similar organizations, confronting similar strains, may envision a multitude of *different* yet appropriate responses.

Denominations respond to their environmental changes and internal strains in similar fashion, although the range of response options may be narrowly restricted. Their responses are likely to vary according to such factors as the nature of a particular religious tradition, the tendencies and needs of the leadership, the types and amounts of internal strains, the social characteristics of the membership, the strength and nature of the secular values and interests, and the type of population base to whom a particular denomination is attempting to appeal.

Thompson believes that the organization's "dominant coalition," i.e., those who are in a position to impose their will on the organization at a given time, plays the most crucial role in determining possible outcomes. "Strategic choice" will be made by the dominant coalition among the whole range of constraints and opportunities the organizational structure allows. He suggests that the type of strategic choice depends on two factors: (1) whether there is *agreement on objectives*; and (2) whether cause/effect relations are known, that is, whether there is *agreement on how to bring about* given objectives. The combination of these two factors produce four types of decision strategies. First, if there is *agreement on both* objectives and how to attain them, "computational" strategies are possible; that is, decisions can be based on rational calculation. Second, if there is *agreement on objectives* but cause/effect relations are not fully known so that insight is needed to decide on the best course of action, a "judgmental" strategy will be used. Third, if there is *agreement on how* to achieve various objectives but dispute on which objectives have first priority, a "compromise" strategy is required to make decisions. Finally, when there is *disagreement on both* the objectives and how to achieve them, "inspirational" strategies are likely to be resorted to.[11]

We would expect that *in denominations* the *compromise and/or inspirational* decision *strategies* are most often required. It is true that even utilitarian organizations (e.g., business and industrial organizations) are often forced to resort to the judgmental and/or compromise decision strategies when they confront severe strains. Knowledge insufficient to specify the cause/effect relations pertinent to a decision due, for example, to rapid changes in the environments of organizations, is the most obvious constraint. But there are several reasons why denominations are expected to use the compromise and/or inspirational decision strategies even in "normal" situations. To begin with, the major basis for cohesion is *ideology*; that is, ideological consensus is the basic instrument for both organizational unity and control. The second reason is the saliency of individual members' interior commitments to the organizational ends, which are often highly diffuse. That is, denominational ends often cannot be translated into concrete organizational proposals without serious risk of alienating some significant part of the membership. The third is the importance, in denominations, of maintaining democratic processes for arriving at consensus regarding the major policy decisions—deliberate decisions cannot be made at the top leadership level alone.

These conditions make decision making in a denomination a highly *political* rather than *economic* affair. Beckford is correct when he makes the point that, in religious and other ideological organizations (e.g., political parties), strategic choices are likely to be made more on political considerations than on utilitarian ones. Persuasion is the most consonant means available to these organizations. In Beckford's words: "This makes it all the more necessary for sociologists to examine the purely political aspects of decision-making in such organizations."[12]

Indeed, the leadership of a denomination, in its attempt to resolve strains, must seriously consider the political consequences which its strategic decisions bring about. For example, if a severe strain (i.e., conflict) emerges regarding a program priority and a segment of the leadership seeks to maintain or broaden its influence, it must through persuasive negotiation win the support of, or at least neutralize, other segments of the leadership and individuals actively in disagreement. Yinger describes several tactical options of this type as follows:

> Shall it oppose them fully and directly, compromise with them, or try to co-opt them into its own program? Each strategy has its costs. Direct opposition may bring defeat; compromise may require yielding on significant values; co-optation raises the question of who will take advantage of whom.[13]

If the conflict persists without solution, it may lead to the development of charismatic movements, and this development in turn may result in a split of the organization.

In their theoretical elaboration of organizational responses to strains, Haas and Drabek identify nine possible tactical options:[14]

1. Toleration—if the conflicts generated are minimal, "doing nothing requires nothing."
2. Delaying—if proposed actions to resolve strains are regarded by some to lead to further intensification of the conflicts, delay.
3. Smoke screens—if there are important areas of dissensus, groups try to keep them diffuse, ambiguous, and low in visibility so that they appear less threatening. This tactic, however, tends to generate other strains.
4. Dismissal—if the strain is largely the product of a few members, the consensus may be restored by simple explusion. However, it may seriously reduce the effectiveness of the organization to resolve future conflicts.

5. Condemnation—seek to discredit the threatening ideas rather than the individuals who propose them.
6. Cooptation—this is "the process of absorbing new elements into the leadership or policy-determining structure of an organization as one means of averting threats to its stability of existence."[15] Cooptation may temporarily resolve the strain without precipitating any type of structural change. In fact, organizations often respond to strain with cooptation approaches, but they frequently find that this tactic produces *new* areas of *strain* which become more difficult to reconcile.
7. Organizational birth—unresolved strains may result in a split; some members withdraw from the organization and form a new one. Where bringing a new organization into existence does not require huge resources, as for a religious or even a political organization, new organizations are formed from parts of old ones with considerable frequency.
8. Organizational death—as strains become intensified, members are less and less able to use "expectation sets" to guide their behavior. Interaction among units may decrease, and ambiguities in expectations increase. Eventually task performance declines. "No one seems to know what the problems are or what to do about them."
9. Self-renewal—the strains are uncovered, separated, and examined. Conflict and change are encouraged, but there are procedures to facilitate the resolution of conflict and the stimulation of change. Integrations of old and new are encouraged through major structural organization.

Many of these nine response options may be used simultaneously as leaders of denominations attempt to cope with strains. The question of which response options denominations will resort to is very much influenced by the type of strain and its degree of intensity, as well as the location and general pattern of strain within their institutional structure. Of course, this question must ultimately be answered through empirical investigation. But if we know *the dominant mode of institutional structure*, at least theoretically we may be able to predict probable response patterns. We have argued that the *ideological and political* structures play the pivotal role in the decision-making process of denominations. We suggest that those institutional structures provide definite limitations within which response options are selectively used.

Zald's "political economy" approach to organizational change provides useful conceptual tools for our purpose.[16] Zald argues that the analysis of organizational polity must include not only goals, power, and environments but also *institutionalized and authoritative patterns of decision control*. The latter refers to traditionally sanctified and normatively shaped aspects of organization such as *ideologies* and *constitutions*. These aspects are especially important for understanding the strain-reducing activities in *purposive* organizations (i.e., religious and other ideological organizations). Ideologies define "theories" of proper authority. Relative compatibility of symbol systems regarding the belief of proper authority becomes a major source of potential strain when organizations confront change. Consider, for example, the principle of local church autonomy in congregationally organized denominations and its implications for the development of new administrative structures for denomination-wide coordination and control. According to Zald, analysis of constitutional norms is critical to the understanding of organizational control and change for two reasons. First, differences in constitutional norms underlie variations in the political economy of organizations. Second, "Constitutional norms provide the context within which organizational elites confront change."[17] We suggest that *denominational constitutional norms limit* as well as specify *the range of discretion* and decision responsibilities of officers, local units, clergymen, and individual members. Consequently, when denominations confront changes, questions of functional responsibility, autonomy, and degree of centralization-decentralization become basic constitutional parameters having great import for strategic decisions of denominational leaders.

INTERNAL SOURCES OF STRAIN

Up to this point we have been primarily concerned with general questions concerning three analytically distinct processes: (1) how environmental changes are filtered into the denominational structure, (2) how strains are generated and intensified, and (3) how denominational leaders respond to strains in terms of their attempt to cope with them. In this section, we want to discuss *internal* sources or sites of strain in some detail; then, we will detail the significant role of the environmental change in precipitating structural change of denominations.

Strain sources originating from within the denominational structure are many, but the following are ubiquitous: discrepancies between the "ideal" and the "actual," shifts in the authority structure, changes in the values and perceptions of the executive, the differentiation of tasks and responsibilities, membership turnovers, the rise of charismatic leaders, leadership succession in goals, and the development of conflicts of interests among the organization's groups and their leaders. These are pervasive and systematic in the sense that they are *not simply accidental accompaniment to products from external* sources. None of these strain sources is likely to be the major one in producing the actual strain. It is well to remember that, however begun, these factors become interdependent with one another. For the present context of discussion, however, we believe that the first two factors (the ideal-actual discrepancy and shifts in the authority structure) are particularly critical sources of strain.

Moore argues that the disjunction or lack of a close correspondence between the "ideal" and the "actual" is almost a universal source of strain, and therefore becomes an important cause of change in most social systems. Social order is a moral order; human societies (and all social groups) are committed to values (including cultural symbols and beliefs), and human behavior is goal-directed. This is the reason for the persistence of "ideals." Yet, all social structures are organized around conventional rules, norms, and procedures (actuals) that make orderly interaction feasible. It is likely that these ideals and actuals never coincide. Ideals not achieved, however, are neither ineffective nor unimportant; they "endure as a perennial challenge to imperfection" and influence the shape of actual patterns and practice.[18]

Religious organizations and institutions more than any other social systems remain the repository of "ideals," that is, of truth, symbolic value commitments, and aspirations. Yet, they are equally subject to conventional norms and procedures if they affect people and stay viable. A religious system almost inevitably requires many actions that its adherents would not perform without religious ideals and motivations to achieve them. These actions, as Yinger correctly argues, would have no meaning in the context of purely egocentric, economic, or hedonistic criteria. "Certain ascetic restraints, taboos, self-torture, sacrifice, and so forth, can be understood only in relation to religiously motivated desires."[19]

O'Dea presented the thesis of "Five Dilemmas in the Institutionalization of Religion."[20] He argued that because religious organizations are preeminently symbolic and idealistic in their core structures, they *suffer most from* the dilemma of the *ideal-actual discrepancies.* He was thinking of large-scale, institutional religions as are embodied in denominations. For example, denominational leaders have always been confronted with questions such as these: shall we translate the religious message into concrete rules and norms, running the risk of making them inflexible?; or, shall we state it as a guiding spirit, running the risk that it will not be understood or will be interpreted according to contradictory individual perceptions? Because denominations emerge in different historical eras, face varying contingencies, and develop different traditions and characters, they have attempted to solve these problems differently. But the solutions always leave a large number of uncertainties or strain-producing areas.

The "incentive theory" of organizations of Clark and Wilson points to different sites of internal strains, strains that are also generated essentially from the ideal-actual discrepancies. Previously we identified religious organizations as "purposive" organizations. They are purposive organizations because their major incentives derive from stated purposes. The dominant "inducements" to participate are suprapersonal ends and the intrinsic worth of the ends themselves. Churches are oriented toward the fulfillment of supra-empirical and universalistic values. Yet, local congregations of denominations as *concrete functioning structures* can be viewed as predominantly "solidary" or communal organizations. (Solidary organizations are ones in which the dominant inducements to participate are such incentives as socializing, congeniality, the sense of group identification, and the maintenance of social distinction.) We are suggesting that church congregations are *covertly*, not overtly, solidary or *communal* organizations. They are oriented toward *harmony*, not toward "issues." They seek to avoid internal conflict.

The use of the two incentives, solidary and purposive, within the denominational structure is a potential source of strain and instability. For example, it is often observed that denominational executives and program professionals who head the administrative structure, as well as denominational seminary professors also, are actively committed to the solution of critical social problems. These tend to show a willingness to change as well as the power to act according to their judgments. This is the case because they work in "rational-bureaucratic" and academic-professional settings and because they are relatively *free from local community constraints*. But this attitude and exercise of discretion often make them appear to a significant grass-roots minority as excessively "independent" and "authoritarian." After all, the functional responsibility of the executives must be approved by denominational assemblies, and exercise of academic freedom by denominational seminary professors is expected to be within the bounds of denominational doctrinal "purity."

In contrast, local churches' moral standards are often shared with the surrounding community through the congregational members. Because local churches are *voluntary* local groups functioning in specific community contexts, they are highly *vulnerable to* the sentiments and interests of *the local* population. Despite its universalistic orientation, the very fact of the individual congregation's identification with the "community" it represents tends to fasten upon it the limitations and constraints of that community. Glock and Ringer saw local church membership as a restraining force. The church was seen as wanting to act, but was able to do so only in situations where actions would not alienate its parishioners.[23] In their study of minister's role conflicts in Little Rock's racial crisis, Campbell and Pettigrew documented a similar pattern.[24] According to Hadden, a significant proportion of young men who chose the ministry in the 1960s were doing so out of a strong commitment to the solution of critical social problems. But many soon discovered in the manner of "a cruel awakening" the realities of parish life and "the disparity between their expectations of the ministry and those of their congregation." For some the disparity was so great that they left the ministry.[25]

Shifts in the authority structure occur in a double sense. First, as Michels and Selznick[26] have shown, the organization's administrative structure is recalicitrant and tends to generate its own needs for greater control and security. Second, as an organization expands and its administrative structures differentiate, new centers of power and tasks emerge for a more efficient coordination of the entire organization. These shifts pose serious problems especially for normative (or purposive) types of organizations because they are likely to bring about the fundamental question of proper *authority*.

The difficulty of coming to terms with the shift in the authority structure is likely to be greatest in Protestant denominations. Ideologically, Protestants in general deplore the legality, hierarchy, and tradition which are found in the organizational structure of the Roman Catholic Church. They believe that their organizations can operate effectively without recourse to a well-defined line of authority. In fact, most American Protestants view the looseness or even the absence of authority in their ecclesiastical organizations as a singular blessing.[27] For them, supralocal church bodies are useful and important as long as they serve congregations and Protestant individuals. Logically, this implies that any organization should be readily altered or cast aside if it is no longer meeting a need as viewed by the local churches.[28]

This ideological stance of course stems from the fact that American Protestantism is made up of "voluntary churches." Voluntary churches, however, "have always had grave difficulties with the problem of authority" because *ideological* (theological) *definitions* regarding church polity, such as the principle of local church autonomy, and *the realities of organizational power structures* have *not* been *harmonious*.[29] Harrison supplies a fine illustration of this in his study of the American Baptist Convention.[30] Officially, the Baptist principle of church government does not recognize the power of supralocal church organizations. This norm has therefore been placed under an increasingly heavy strain as result of growth of new administrative structures as well as their translation into informal, de facto power. The need for efficient coordination allowed the development of powerful administrative structure. Administrative executives, for example, having no formally legitimated power over local churches are obliged to enlist the congregations' support by other means, i.e., persuasion. The more persuasive among them are able to build a large following among the laity by the sheer force of their personalities. On the other hand, the agency without this kind of leadership is an easy target for hostile power blocs within the denomination.

In addition to the ideological strain, there are other strains toward decentralized administrative organization. As in most voluntary associations, denominations are *not* based on a functional division of labor. For example, functions of local churches *duplicate* each other. Furthermore, local churches depend on congregational members for financial support, and they are for the most part self-sufficient. Functional *duplication* and economic *self-sufficiency* have far-reaching implications for the control and coordination of the denomination. Unlike functionally interdependent units within, say, a business organization, local churches expect and generally receive only minimum coordinative direction from supralocal church structures (e.g., denominational headquarters).

Denominational structures, originally formed to coordinate maintenance and extension of local churches, have over time slowly expanded their functions. Recent literature suggests that particularly since the end of World War II they have considerably expanded. Expansion of denominational size, increased problems of intradenominational and interdenominational communications, and commitments to influence highly a mobile population demanded that denominations broaden their coordinative functions.[31] Local churches in actuality have increasingly come to depend on national agency bureaucracies for many services. According to Harrison, for example, a situation has arisen in which the local church, instead of *being served* by the bureaucracy, now *serves* the bureaucracy.[32]

This clearly suggests that shifts in the authority and power structures have occurred. In general, the *more efficient* an administrative structure becomes, the *more* it is likely it will be *viewed* by local leaders as *"overcentralized."*[33] We suggest that one major reason why many local churches today sever relations with their national denominations is their resistance to this alleged over-centralization. We shall elaborate on this later.

As Burkart (See Chapter 1) and Westhues suggest, the contemporary denominational structure can be viewed as a coalition of a variety of semi-autonomous groups.[34] The coalition includes the membership at large, the local church, the judicatory (e.g., a diocese, synod, or regional conference), the clergy, the lay leadership, the clerical executive (e.g., an episcopacy), the chief executive officer (president or stated clerk), councils (e.g., executive council or general board), staff agencies (like publication office, religious education directorate), and special organizations (e.g., missionary groups). Each of these can be expected to hold particular goals, preferences, and interests congruent with its structural position. On the other hand, a *de*centralized denominational structure dilutes the *need for* functional *interdependence* and tends to foster *different* sets of ideologies and priorities among the elements.

The behavior of groups in the coalition interdependency, however, is expected to vary according to the constitutional norms of denominations we described previously. There is good evidence that the social structures of contemporary denominations have made formal polity distinctions less meaningful.[35] But recent research suggests that differences in formal church polities have significant effects upon the *political behavior* of groups. For example, with data from twenty-eight major denominations, Wood found that the ability of policy-makers to establish civil rights policy *varies directly with the degree to which the formal polity legitimates their power.* Denominations with hierarchical polities (episcopal and presbyterian denominations) have a high degree of leader authority, using certain formal (or constitutional) sanctions against resisters; those with congregational polities have a lower degree, having no authority to sanction the resisters.[36] Examining the results of administrative differentiation and expansion in twenty-nine Protestant denominations, Takayama showed the increased *discrepancy between the traditional definitions of polity and the realities of administrative power.* In particular, he noted that the *discrepancy was the greatest among large congregationally structured denominations*; they appeared to have *more difficulties* than other denominations in terms of *coping* with the problem of maintaining internal democracy. But he observed that, because commitments to the formal-traditional polity structures (that embody politico-religious ideologies regarding church government) are stronger and more enduring than commitments to organizational efficiency and stability, the discrepancy and its accompanying strains would continue.[37]

McNamara attributed the success of New Mexico Catholic priests involved in anti-poverty programs to the church's polity structure, "which traditionally is not open to response from the laity" and which "enabled the priest directors to proceed regardless of opposition from conservative lay Catholics."[38] Takayama and Sachs have shown that Memphis local churches' responses to court-ordered busing for the public school integration *differed considerably according to their degree of political independence.* Local churches affiliated with congregational denominations sponsored many more new private academies than churches affiliated with hierarchical denominations, even controlling for degree of theological conservatism, social class of church membership, and size of the congregation.[39]

The internal sources of strain just described in terms of the two major headings, the ideal-actual discrepancy and shifts in authority structure, illustrate the fact that internal structural *inconsistencies* and their accompanying uncertainties always *exist* and develop *beneath the apparent stability* and continuity of the denominational structure. Blau and Scott consider that new *"dilemmas"* are internally *generated* in organizations *in* the very process of *solving existing ones.* This is because organizational certainty or effectiveness depend on many factors, and some factors are incompatible with others. They give a familiar example: an expansion of organizational size and increase in task complexity call for administrative differentiation such as departmental specialization, and effective coordination of the differentiated structures usually requires their vertical arrangement by increasing the number of administrative levels. These processes, however, tend to impede the flow of information which is vital to effective decision-making. Such a dilemma occurs in all organizations.[40]

This is a dialectic view of organizational change. New dilemmas continuously occur, and the ways in which dilemma resolutions are met become "cumulated" in organizations so that the patterns of resolution do not repeat in exactly the same manner; rather, they are directional. This theoretical view coincides with the "tension-management" theory of social change expounded by Moore. Moore conceptualized that "tension-reducing" measures often produce *new* tensions, resulting in directional i.e., evolutional change.[41]

CATALYTIC ROLE OF ENVIRONMENTAL CHANGE

Can internal strains or dilemmas account for changes both *in* and *of* denominations? Our immediate answer is: yes, they could. But we are reminded by Nisbet of two types of change:

> The crucial point is that of envisaging social change in a way that allows us to distinguish clearly between mere adaptation or minor modification on one hand and, on the other, those profound mutations of structure which always involve crisis.[42]

This suggests that, when and if a structural change of a denomination such as a split occurs, the unresolved strain must have a "crisis" character, a heightened or urgent feeling (at least on the part of some segments of the leadership) that the present mode of operating should no longer continue.

In our view, a structural change of denomination will result from the dynamic interplay of *both* internal and external uncertainties, not just internal uncertainties alone. In other words, *internal strains themselves are not likely to cause splits of denominations*. Rather, *external environmental changes act as catalysts to internally generated and unresolved strains*, producing crises.

Goffman once described organizations as being surrounded by "semi-permeable membranes," stating that the degree to which environmental changes are permeable varies with the type of organization.[43] Discussions on internal characteristics of the denomination presented in the preceding part suggest that denominational structure has a *highly permeable membrane*. It opens to a heterogeneous environment on a variety of fronts. Depending on their structural positions and interests, denominational units or groups experience different kinds and degrees of environmental pressures.

For most organizations, environmental change is a major source of uncertainty. In our view, the environmental contexts in which denominations have been operating in recent years have increasingly been exhibiting what Emery and Trist called *turbulent* features (see Introduction). In the turbulent "field," "the environmental contexts in which organizations exist are themselves changing, at an increasing rate, and towards increasing complexity" so that "individual organizations, however large, cannot expect to adapt successfully simply through their own actions."[44]

Denominations as normative organizations are especially sensitive, as well as vulnerable, to cultural and moral sectors of the environmental changes. Among many, such changes as the erosion of community cohesion, the uprooting of "traditional" human bonds (e.g., the decline of family authority structure, increased divorce rate), the shifting of cultural symbols and value standards (e.g., the "death of God" theology, increased importance of secular "good things in life"), and the revolution of rising expectations (e.g., civil rights and women's liberation movements) have profoundly influenced institutional religion.

These changes are largely products of unprecedented macro-level structural revolutions. They include large-scale population shifts and mobility, technological-communicational changes, differentiation of interests and proliferation of groups and associations, bureaucratization and centralization of virtually all large-scale organizations (including governmental organizations), and increased interdependency among all social systems including nations.

Churches and denominations have adapted themselves to the changed and changing environments rather reluctantly, only because they by and large have had no alternatives. Glock and Stark, for example, concluded that the church in the 1960s was *informed by, more than it was informing, the values of the larger culture.*[45] Any single church or denomination has had little power of control or capacity for regenerating value symbols required for a significant impact on any of the social trends we mentioned.

This is not to suggest that churches in earlier periods did possess capacities to withstand their environmental changes. A brief historical review of American Protestant divisions by Hoge, for example, has led him to conclude that "tensions in Protestantism are more or less a direct outgrowth of the broader tensions in the culture."[45] The critical national issues and problems that divided the nation also divided Protestant denominations. The Civil War, the industrial revolution, racism, liberalism (or scientific humanism), and regionalism profoundly influenced the divisions of denominations.

This means, as suggested earlier, that denominations have highly environmentally permeable boundaries. Nevertheless, the *environments* of contemporary denominations appear to be *quite different* from those of their past periods. The lack of general cultural consensus and the overflow of information and knowledge in the society have filtered into denominations and have generated high degrees of internal uncertainties and strains.

The denominations' environments in the 1950s and early 1960s were predominantly characterized as what Emery and Trist called the "disturbed-reactive" type (See Introduction). In their efforts to influence a secularized and mobile population, as well as to maintain church membership, most denominations were constrained to resort to organizational means. Demerath and Hammond argue that, when the distinctively religious *ideology* no longer serves as a binding force in controlling the behavior of individuals, organizational *structure* correspondingly becomes urgent.[47] While there is ample empirical evidence to support this proposition, the following quotation from a theologian, Gilkey, suffices to indicate that churches in the 1950s and 1960s were forced to resort more to organizational *structures* in order to attract people.

> As of now, the variety of American church life has little theological, liturgical, pietistic, or even Biblical content, but it is nonetheless burgeoning with air-conditioned sanctuaries, ladies' and men's societies, large Sunday School plants, 'holy name' baseball teams, and innumerable suppers and dances. It is a religious institution of immense power, wealth, and prestige, but one characterized largely by secular values such as recreation, sociability, and sporadic good works in the community.[48]

In order to cope with the environmental onslaught, denominations expanded their administrative structures unprecedentedly. Winter and Takayama, in their separate studies, documented the results of this bureaucratic "rationalization" of many denominations from comparative perspectives of organizational theory. The findings suggested that the bureaucratization processes were for the most part haphazard, for denominations were not *theologically* equipped for such administrative expansion and control. The discrepancy between the needs for greater administrative coordination and deficiencies in ecclesiological definitions of polity brought about serious internal strains.[49]

The 1950s and 1960s were also a period of unprecedented Protestant ecumenism. The ecumenism was also marked by the significance of organizational instrumentalities. Denominational mergers and interdenominational cooperative efforts of many kinds dominated the institutional religious scene. For example, the United Church of Christ, the United Methodist Church, the Lutheran Church in America, and the American Lutheran Church were formed via organizational mergers of separate denominations. The National Council of Churches was founded in 1950, and its ecumenical programs were expanded enormously in the 1960s. The most comprehensive church union plan was the Consultation on Church Union, a plan of merging the main National Council-affiliated denominations. But in 1972 the Consultation met a severe blow in the withdrawal of the United Presbyterian Church.

Since the end of the 1960s, the environments have increasingly been exhibiting "turbulent" features. A variety of national crises such as the intensification of the Viet Nam War, protest movements, the rise of violence, increased senses of alienation and "relative deprivation," and the end of economic abundance have begun to divide the nation. Zald's conceptualizations help us to describe this change for denominations. Denominational environmental contexts of the 1950s and 1960s were characterized by the "politics of abundance," in that adequate economic resources allowed denominations' dominant leaders to pursue organizationally initiated programs without much visible conflict. Since the end of the 1960s, however, the "politics of scarcity" has been set in motion, reflecting largely the conditions of the larger social structure. "Organizations changing in a system of scarcity are likely to experience greater conflict and discontent than those in an 'economy of abundance'."[50] Denominational actions and programs "invisible" in the past have now become "visible," and formerly uninterested and apathetic groups and individuals have now become concerned. In other words, the politics of abundance allowed the dominant leaders considerable latitude in initiating a variety of liberal programs, but the politics of scarcity has constricted their freedom of action and has encouraged greater responsiveness. More importantly, power balances have shifted as different groups within the denomination assume greater or lesser salience as a point of reference for leaders' decision-making.[51]

The classical sociological proposition states that "conflict with *out*-groups increases *internal* cohesion." However, empirical evidence supportive of this proposition has derived largely from research on small groups and nation-states. The effects of environmental conflict upon large-scale formal organizations have been largely ignored. Brager is probably correct when he states that "in-group cohesion is not so frequent a response to external threat as the literature has suggested."[52] Certainly, the proposition seems to require an important qualification when it is applied to the relationship between the structure of the denomination and its environmental threats. Thus, we suggest that *environmental conflict leads to internal conflict* or dissensus and that the *structure* of denominations predisposes this outcome.

We have argued that the patterns of intradenominational cohesiveness and strain would make differences in denominational responses to environmental threats. In this regard, what Coser offers is very instructive. He writes:

The relation between outer conflict and inner cohesion does not hold true when internal cohesion before the outbreak of the attack is so low that group members have ceased to regard as worthwhile or actually see the outside threat to concern 'them' rather than 'us.'[53]

Once environmental conflicts are filtered into the structure of denominations in which strains have been persisting or internal patterns of cohesion have been low, conflicts are likely to become intensified, and various tactics and strategies described previously will be used for the resolution of the conflicts. In the meantime, "we" and "they" relations are likely to be intensified, producing "crises" in the ideological consensus. One outcome of these processes will be an organizational split.

TWO CASES OF DENOMINATIONAL SPLIT

Organizational splits very recently occurred in both the Presbyterian Church in the U.S. and the Lutheran Church—Missouri Synod. These seem to provide strategic cases by which the theoretical model and propositions can profitably be examined. But the dearth of gathered information and limited space remaining in this chapter do not allow extensive pursuit of this at this time. What we offer here are tentative accounts of probable causes of the splits. Hopefully, systematic analysis of the cases will come in the near future.

The Southern Presbyterian Schism

On May 18-19, 1973, a "convention of sessions," claiming that the positions of the Presbyterian Church in the US (PCUS) were out of step with its constitutional and doctrinal requirements, voted overwhelmingly (349-16) to begin a new Presbyterian church. The first general assembly of the new conservative denomination, which adopted the name, National Presbyterian Church, was held in Birmingham, Álabama, in December, 1973. The group included about 75,000 members from 275 churches in the Southern and border states. Ruling Elder W. Jack Williamson, a Greenville, Alabama, attorney who had presided at two preparatory meetings, was elected the first moderator.[54]

The Presbyterian Journal, a conservative magazine and strong supporter of the separation movement, featured a resolution (first adopted by two local churches and later approved by many in the new denomination) with the headline, "Perhaps this should be nailed to the PCUS' front door!" The resolution declared:

We feel that the time has come when we can no longer tolerate the marked departure from historic Presbyterian doctrine and the repeated violation of its constitution which have been taking place in our denomination.[55]

Historically, the political structure of Presbyterian and Reformed bodies has been "ecumenical" in its implications. Presbyterians in the South have long lived with some strain between the demands of this heritage and the cultural legacy of the South which latter had encouraged a pervasive congregationalism, localism, and theological conservatism.

During the late 1940s and 1950s, one heard rumbles in the PCUS about alleged "liberalism." In the late 1950s and early 1960s, when the civil rights movement gathered strength in the nation, the denomination began to experience severe internal strains. As the General Assembly broadened its social concern and began to make pronouncements on "critical" social issues, voices of conservative leaders rose to condemn them. The conservative leaders not only opposed ministers and laymen pushing for greater racial integration in the church but also the positions of the General Assembly that favored and supported ecumenism.

Until the early 1960s, conservative leaders found it possible to achieve their objectives through ecclesiastical structures themselves. They made appeals to persons worried about current trends in society. But when they became apprehensive about losing their influence, they began to form an independent seminary and para-ecclesiastical bodies through which to extend their efforts.

The independent seminary was opened in Jackson, Mississippi, in 1966, implicitly repudiating the four existing denominational seminaries. It was committed to the "verbally inspired, infallible Word of God"and to the Westminster Confession of faith.

A group called Concerned Presbyterians (CP) was formed in 1964 for the purpose of "returning the Presbyterian Church in the US to its primary mission—winning the unsaved for Christ and nuturing all believers in the faith." Apparently this group was formally organized to counteract a group of socially committed young ministers who formed the Fellowship of Concern for the advancement of racial integration in the churches. The Concerned Presbyterians stressed the "strictly spiritual" mission of the church with "no meddling in secular affairs." They strenuously objected to pronouncements made by the General Assembly on such matters as the United Nations, the war in Vietnam, the public school system, welfare reform, poverty, family planning and a host of other secular subjects. They opposed the PCUS' continued membership in and financial support of the National Council of Churches, as well as the plan to unite with the United Presbyterian Church in the USA and the Reformed Church in America.

A spokesman for the PCUS wrote about the CP in the *Presbyterian Outlook*, a moderate magazine and backer of the PCUS' positions:

> For a good many years CP leaders have reserved a bloc of hotel rooms for their colleagues during meetings of the General Assembly and have made their plans with care each year only to be

rejected time and again, thus reinforcing their conviction that the church's leadership is unsound and untrustworthy.[56]

Presbyterian Churchmen United (PCU) was formed in 1969. Recognized as the ministerial arm of Concerned Presbyterians, the PCU expressed the same dissents. This group of ministers set up an organization and staff and began working to advance the objectives of the Conservative Coalition, publishing an occasional paper, *Contact*, and sending its agents across the church.

Another organization called Presbyterian Evangelistic Fellowship (PEF) came into being gradually over the years in connection with the evangelist efforts of William E. Hill, Jr. This group attracted a base of support and regular contributors to help provide for evangelistic meetings in many parts of the denomination. Hill became the first person in the denomination to issue a public call for a separation, using the Presbyterian Journal as his forum. By the time the schedule of separation was announced by the Conservative Coalition in 1971, the PEF leadership had become an active and vocal part of it, with full membership on the steering committee.

No doubt theological differences played a significant role in the division of the PCUS. But their major significance lies in the fact that they provided ideological weapons to the conservative coalition to attack alleged violation of constitutional norms and departure from historic Presbyterian doctrine of the PCUS. The critical factors in the split were social changes and shifts of cultural-moral aspects of the society to which the PCUS' General Assembly and leadership attempted to address themselves. The political and social nature of the cause of the split can be seen in part in the constitution of the new denomination. "Congregationalism" and localism are its major emphasis.

The Moderate Seccession from the Missouri Synod

A new body was formed at the close of 1976 by moderates in the Lutheran Church—Missouri Synod (LCMS) who disagreed with the theological conservatism and "authoritarian" policies espoused by Jacob A. O. Preus, President of the Synod. The new body, which adopted the name, Association of Evangelical Lutheran Churches (AELC), was launched in December, 1976, incorporating about 150 congregations with more than 70,000 members.[57]

In the late 1960s a long-simmering controversy over alleged liberalism and doctrinal indifferentism erupted in the LCMS, centering in Concordia Seminary in St. Louis, then the largest Lutheran theological school in the world. Shortly after his upset election in 1969, Preus, as he promised he would, named a "fact-finding committee" to investigate charges of heretical teaching at the seminary. When the committee's long-delayed report was released, Preus said it made "abundantly clear that some professors at the seminary hold views contrary to the established doctrinal positions of the Synod." He demanded that Concordia's Board of Control "deal with those Professors" and "deal personally and first of all" with John Tietjen, the seminary president. In a sharp rebuttal, sent to all pastors of the Synod, Tietjen denounced the investigation as "unfair, untrue, less than Scriptual, and Un-Lutheran."

At the Synod's 50th convention in New Orleans, LA., in July, 1973, conservatives of the 2.8 million member denomination scored a major victory when a series of "scriptural and confessional principles" formulated by Preus was elevated to the status of a doctrinal statement. Earlier, these principles, which insist on a quasi-literal interpretation of biblical events, had been repudiated by the Concordia faculty.

Then, in an action believed to be unprecedented in U.S. Protestantism, the Synod's General Convention condemned Tietjen and 45 of the 49 active faculty members for "false doctrine running counter to the Holy Scriptures, the Lutheran Confessions, and synodical stance." Charges against Tietjen were referred to the seminary's Board of Control.

On January 20, 1974, the newly aligned Board of Control of Concordia Seminary, achieving a conservative majority through the 1973 Convention elections, suspended president Tietjen. The suspension led to an immediate strike by a majority of the seminary's students, faculty, and executive staff. A month later, the Board of Control ordered the striking faculty to return to the classroom and resume their teaching responsibilties. When they refused the Board's ultimatum, they were fired.

The next day, February 20, 1974, 385 students marched off campus in support of the terminated faculty and staff. Faculty and students together declared their intention to continue their theological education "in exile" and named their new school "Seminex," Concordia Seminary-In Exile (renamed Christ Seminary in 1977). In their statement, the faculty and students explained the reason for their action:

> Seminex represents not a departure from Synod but a commitment to a Synod that is rapidly departing from the best in its tradition. It is the only way we can see to complete theological education and simultaneously call the Synod back to its own evangelical fountainhead.[58]

In the meantime, the same issues which resulted in the formation of Seminex (after being debated for a period with no success among religious professional), filtered down to the parish level where they frequently brought about schisms between competing factions in local churches.

The Synod's moderates earlier had organized a protest movement called "Evangelical Lutherans in Mission" (ELIM). They said they did not intend to form "another church body" but would work for reform *within* the Synod. The Synod's Board of Directors, however, censured ELIM as "substantially a church within a church" because it solicited funds for a seminary and established an independent mission society, publications, and an organizational structure.

At the Synod's 51st General Convention in July, 1975, Preus, LCMS president, laid the central issue before delegates when he noted that "for the past two decades at least we have had two opposing theologies," and, he stressed, "no church body can long support two theologies which are in conflict." By a vote of nearly 3-2, conservatives declared ELIM to be "schismatic" and told those active in its functions "to cease such roles . . . or terminate their membership in the Synod." Eight and possibly more of the Synod's 35 district presidents were warned of possible removal from office for ordaining graduates of Seminex.

In August, 1975, dissidents met in Chicago for the third assembly of ELIM and endorsed a series of actions predicated on withdrawal from the Synod. At the same time, ELIM said it would "support, encourage and assist" those who continue within the strife-torn denomination.

In April, 1976, Preus actually suspended four such district presidents (bishops) from office, using new powers which the 1975 Convention conferred on him; an additional four presidents resigned thereafter as a result of organizational pressures.

As noted, the Association of Evangelical Lutheran Churches was officially formed in December, 1976, with the deposed presidents as prominent leaders. A spokesman for AELC said that it would give "high priority" to putting itself out of business, but that a separate association was necessary because "we need each other at least for now and possibly for some brief time to come." Meanwhile, ELIM would try to continue as a "confessional voice of protest" within the LCMS to support those members who felt they could not as yet leave the 129-year-old Synod.

It is difficult to objectively assess the sources of conflict that led to the organizational split. No doubt, the overt issue was doctrinal purity, especially the interpretation of the Bible, and indeed for many "conservative" Missouri Lutherans this is the actual issue. But there are several *non-theological* sources of conflict. The first was the end of Missouri Lutherans' long enduring cultural homogeneity. The religious-ethnic homogeneity of the population and its geographical clustering helped them to sustain their traditional symbols and lifestyle in the rapidly changing cultural environments. During the last two or three decades, however, Missouri Lutherans experienced "Americanization" in terms of cultural assimilation. The traditional homogeneity was broken down. This "normal" process provided them many occasions to reconsider their traditional values and ways of thinking. Many Missouri Lutherans became more willing to experiment with contemporary American forms in such areas as parish education, missions, and fellowship with other

Lutheran (and even non-Lutheran) bodies. These ventures and experiments were reflected in changes in theological views, in conference and convention essays, and in the preaching of pastors. These changes, however, apparently were viewed by conservative leaders as "dangerously liberal" trends in the church, particulary in undermining the domination's traditional theological integrity, that is, departure from what they believe the best of the Synod.

While the first non-theological source of the conflict has been primarily *environmental change*, the second source has been *intra-organizational.* The authoritarianism displayed by the Synod's president and other conservative leaders is believed to be the direct source of the conflict. The manner in which they rose to the top official positions of the Synod and made theologically and legally binding decisions created severe internal conflicts. Marty writes of the dynamic interplay between the environmental threat and internal conflicts as follows:

> The conservatives have been successful in obscuring their changes, in pointing to the patency of Moderates' changes, in taking advantage of the security-seeking ecclesiastical Zeitgeist of the American sixties and seventies, and in openly employing denominational political instruments to achieve their ends. What they advocate in broad outline, therefore, has appealed to at least a majority of the clientele and has been appropriated by biennial convention majorities on terms that are not likely to be altered in any foreseeable future. The Moderates, therefore, have been threatened with repression or expulsion and have organized some para-synodical structures for the purpose of survival.[59]

The Missouri Lutherans have been proud of democratic, decentralized "congregational" polity. But the Preus administration, moderates insisted, radically altered their cherished tradition for his own ends.

Closely related to the second, the third factor is the *vulnerability* of the theological seminary as a subsidiary organization within a host organization. In his organizational analysis proposal on the confict surrounding Seminex, Nickel considers that the lack of the seminary's autonomy was a major factor in the conflict. He believes that Concordia Seminary-St. Louis, as a school owned and operated by the Synod, lacked control of the vital input resources required to maintain a significant level of autonomy. When leadership in the parent organization (the Synod) became hostile to the seminary itself, the faculty majority became vulnerable.[60] This hypothesis, focused on the question of authority and control, is worth careful documentation.

There are a number of ways in which this Missouri Synod case study may be unique and instructive in the historical dynamics of religious organizations. The following assertions should be regarded as hypotheses in need of verification:[61]

1. This has been a case of inclusivists (moderates) seceding or being expelled, not exclusivists (conservatives). More frequently, conservatives are those who withdraw. Also unusual has been the moderate tack of retaining "dual membership" in the old while forming the new.

2. Unusual also was the moderate strategy to disavow the political-procedural process normally used by organizations. The moderates adopted a turn-the-other-cheek stance and a policy of "abandoning the field" rather than appealing their plight in the civil courts (where they might have had a 50-50 chance of winning). On the other hand, outside strategists may consider these moderates to have been "naive" in their approach to power.

3. The Missouri Synod has been unusual among American denominations for the proportion of home-grown, professional church sons among its pastors (in 1959, 35%).[62] There is evidence that the bulk of the moderate leadership were such professional church sons, who ironically did not stand in awe of President Preus, son of a late governor of Minnesota and a professional "convert" from the sister American Lutheran Church. Concordia Seminary-St. Louis itself long was the domain of such a professional church son leadership elite. (Undoubtedly, a consequence of Preus' political sweep is, for a long time to come, to depress the desire of pastor's young sons to continue in their fathers' tradition.)

4. Preus exercised veto power over the election of heads of regional districts. This attempt to centralize the powers of districts undoubtedly could have the opposite effect—to debureaucratize and actually *de*centralize power in the Synod. The overreaction toward decentralization in the newly formed AELC is a firstfruit in this direction. Just as the Missouri Synod itself was founded in 1847 in a reaction to an attempt to centralize power on the part of Martin Stephan, leader of the original Saxon migration from Germany in 1839, so ironically President Preus may have hastened the movement in this direction too. A concomitant of this "debureaucratization" process may also be a "deprofessionalization" process for colleagueship in the ministry.

5. Over against American fundamentalists, Preus has combined conservative zeal with a formal use of organizational machinery and sanctions that is not paralleled among fundamentalistic bodies. Most bodies which pursue conservative, fundamentalist theological principles combine them with a decentralized structure of local autonomy and a technique of "persuasion."

Preus has proclaimed that the "Battle of Missouri" is over, and he is probably correct. By early 1979, he seemed in full control. The dissident district presidents have all retired, been ousted, or have died. The vocal moderates have withdrawn into the AELC. ELIM, the internal protest movement of the moderates has settled into becoming simply an alternate news medium or "voice" by means of its biweekly newspaper, *Missouri in Perspective*. The AELC, which seems to have peaked at some 100,000 members in over 200 congregations, views itself as a transitional body which will either (1) first become a district of the ALC or the LCA and then be absorbed; or (2) be the catalyst for a three-way merger of itself with the ALC and LCA within the next decade. The AELC already is in complete "altar and pulpit fellowship" with the ALC and LCA (but not yet with the LCMS) and is a full member of the Lutheran Council in the U.S.A. and the Lutheran World Federation.[63]

And so the "Battle seems over." But various moderate LCMS district presidents continue to make noises to their ALC and LCA opposite numbers about wanting to make their church "a more tolerant . . . a more understanding churchbody" and to again widen their ties to their sister church bodies.[64] Time will tell.

Notes

1. Dean R. Hoge, *Division in the Protestant House: The Basic Reasons behind Intra-Church Conflicts* (Philadelphia: Westminster, 1976).

2. Robert Lee, *The Social Sources of Church Unity* (Nashville: Abingdon Press, 1960), Samuel M. Cavert, *The American Churches in the Ecumenical Movement: 1900-1968* (New York: Association Press, 1968).

3. Charles C. Morrison, *The Unfinished Reformation* (New York: Harper & Bros. 1953), pp. 28-29.

4. See, for example, Neil J. Smelser, *Theory of Collective Behavior* (New York: The Free Press, 1962); John Wilson, *Introduction to Social Movements* (New York: Basic Books); Mayer N. Zald and Roberta Ash, "Social Movement Organizations: Growth, Decay and Change," *Social Forces* 44 (1966):327-341.

5. Mainline Protestant denominations refers to those large Protestant denominations with a relatively large body of highly educated and professionalized clergymen.

6. H. Richard Niebuhr. *The Social Sources of Denominationalism* (New York: Henry Holt and Company, 1929). For a radical critique of Niebuhr's theory, see, for example, Allan W. Eister, "H. Richard Niebuhr and the Paradox of Religious Organization: A Radical Critique," Charles Y. Glock and Phillip E. Hammond (eds.), *Beyond the Classics?* (New York: Harper & Rowe, 1973).

7. Amitai Etzioni, *A Comparative Analysis of Complex Organizations: Revised and Enlarged Edition* (New York: The Free Press,

1975). Normative organizations are characterized by the use of identive power (i.e., the power to make people identify with the organization) as its major source of control and by high commitment on the part of participants. See also Ross P. Scherer, "The Church as a Formal Voluntary Organization," in David H. Smith, ed., *Voluntary Action Research* (Lexington, MA: Heath, 1972), pp. 81-108.

8. See, for example, Merlin B. Brinkerhoff, and Phillip R. Kunz (eds.), *Complex Organization and Their Environments* (Dubuque: Wm. C. Brown Company Publishers, 1972). Wolf V. Heydebrand, ed., *Comparative Organizations: The Results of Empirical Research* (Englewood Cliffs: Prentice Hall, Inc., 1973).

9. James D. Thompson, *Organizations in Action* (New York: McGraw-Hill, 1967). Other "open systems" expositions are, to mention a few prominent ones, Daniel Katz and Robert L. Kahn, *The Social Psychology of Organizations* (New York: John Wiley and Sons, 1966) and Michel Crozier, *The Bureaucratic Phenomenon* (Chicago: University of Chicago Press, 1964).

10. Eugene J. Haas, and Thomas E. Drabek, *Complex Organizations: A Sociological Perspective* (New York: The Macmillan Company, 1973), p. 284.

11. James D. Thompson, *Organizations in Action, op. cit.* Chapter 10.

12. James A. Beckford, *Religious Organization: A Trend Report and Bibliography* (Hague: Mouton, 1975), p. 35.

13. J. Milton Yinger, *The Scientific Study of Religion* (New York: The Macmillan Company, 1970), p. 236.

14. Eugene J. Haas, and Thomas E. Drabek, *Complex Organizations, op. cit.*, pp. 286-291.

15. This definition is from Selznick, who places great emphasis on "cooptation" for the analysis of organizational adaptation to environments. See Philip Selznick, *TVA and the Grass Roots* (Berkeley and Los Angeles: University of California Press, 1949), p. 13.

16. Mayer N. Zald, "Political Economy: A Frameowrk for Comparative Analysis," in Mayer Zald (ed.), *Power in Organizations* (Nashville: Vanderbilt University Press, 1970); Mayer N. Zald, *Organizational Change: The Political Economy of the YMCA* (Chicago: University of Chicago Press, 1970).

17. Mayer N. Zald, *Organizational Change,* ibid., p. 234.

18. Wilbert E. Moore, *Social Change* (Englewood Cliffs: Prentice-Hall, 1963), p. 11. Some remarks for the use of the "ideal" and the "actual" are in order. We use "ideal" to refer to what a set of individuals regards as right, proper, important, etc. We use "actual" as that which a scientific observer would observe, whether the people observed are aware of it or not. Actual structure refers to any structure in terms of

which behavior takes place. This conceptual distinction should not be identified with that of a "goal model" used in the organizational literature. From the viewpoint of the sociology of knowledge, organizational goals constitute a subset of still larger ideal structures. No doubt, there is substantial overlap between organizational goals and the ideal held by individuals in an organization. But the former is embedded in the associational structure (the organization) itself and the latter not only in the associational but also in the communal (*Gemeinschaft*) structures. Since discrepancy between the ideal and the actual is universal, it is a basic mistake to compare actual structures with ideal structures at only one point of time. Comparisons should be made between *actual* and *actual* structures and between *ideal* and *ideal* structures at different points in the organization's history.

19. J. Milton Yinger, *The Scientific Study of Religion*, op. cit., p. 234.

20. Thomas F. O'Dea, "Five Dilemmas in the Institutionalization of Religion," *Journal for the Scientific Study of Religion* 1 (1961):30-39.

21. Peter B. Clark and James Q. Wison, "Incentive Systems: A Theory of Organizations," *Administrative Science Quarterly* 6 (1961): 129-166. Clark and Wilson distinguish between utilitarian, solidary, and purposive incentives based, respectively, on material-monetary, status and sociability-related, and normative-ideological rewards. These distinctions lead to a corresponding typology of utilitarian, solidary, and purposive organizations. Although any organization may be able to offer all these incentives, different types of organizations have more to offer of *one* than the other. Etzioni's categories (coercive, utilitarian, and normative) overlap Clark and Wilson's and have much the same focus. However, clear distinction between solidary and purposive incentives has a distinctive advantage for our present purpose.

22. For detailed discussion of this, see K. Peter Takayama, "Administrative Structures and Political Processes in Protestant Denomination," *Publius: The Journal of Federalism* 4(1974):5-37.

23. Charles Y. Glock, and Benjamin B. Ringer, "Church Policy and Attitudes of Ministers and Parishioners on Social Issues," *American Sociological Review*, 21(1956):148-156.

24. Ernest Q. Campbell, and Thomas F. Pettigrew, "Racial and Moral Crises: The Role of the Little Rock Ministers," *American Journal of Sociology* 64(1959):509-516.

25. Jeffrey K. Hadden, *The Gathering Storm in the Churches* (Garden City, New York: Doubleday, 1969), p. 219.

26. Robert Michels, *Political Parties*. Translated by Eden Paul and Cedar Paul (Glencoe, Illinois: Free Press, 1949).

27. Paul M. Harrison, "Sociological Analysis of the Participating Communions," *Mid-Stream* 2(1963):37-49.

28. This "instrumental" conception of organizations seems to be fundamental for the understanding of the pragmatic character of denominational structures as well as their secular mode of operation. The instrumental conceptions of organizations are no doubt related to the Protestant emphasis on individualism. Individualism denotes a broad social tendency as well as a social philosophy that regards the individual as sacred and intrinsically valuable. Correspondingly, collectivities or organizations are approached as nominalistic rather than as realistic. For an excellent discussion of Protestants' approach to their denominational structures, see David A. Martin, "The Denomination," *British Journal of Sociology* 13(1962):1-14.

29. James M. Gustafson, "The Voluntary Church: A Moral Appraisal," D. B. Robertson, ed., *Voluntary Associations: A Study of Groups in Free Societies* (Richmond: John Knox, 1966).

30. Paul M. Harrison, *Authority and Power in the Free Church Tradition* (Princeton: Princeton University Press, 1959).

31. Gibson Winter. "Religious Organizations," W. Lloyd Warner, et al., eds., *The Emergent American Society: Large-Scale Organizations*, Vol. I (New Haven: Yale 1967); K. Peter Takayama, "Administrative Structures and Political Processes in Protestant Denominations," op. cit.

32. Harrison found that "the iron law of oligarchy" was an apt description of the American Baptist Convention. In his words, the power of the agencies' officials was "oftentimes considerably greater than the official ecclesiastical authority of the Episcopalian or Methodist bishop or the Presbyterian moderator." Paul M. Harrison, *Authority and Power in the Free Church Tradition*, op. cit., p. 92.

33. The criticism that an organization is "overcentralized" or "overbureaucratized" must be understood in terms of the main goals of organizations. For business organizations, the major issue is "overbureaucratization" because it implies an elaboration of rules and procedures that impairs operating efficiency. For normative organizations the major issue is "overcentralization" rather than "overbureaucratization" because the latter actually implies centralization of power in the hand of officials which impairs *internal democracy*. For the theoretical discussion of this, see Peter M. Blau and W. Richard Scott, *Formal Organizations* (San Francisco: Chandler, 1962), p. 45.

34. Kenneth Westhues, "The Church in Opposition," *Sociological Analysis,* 37(1976):200-314.

35. See, for example, Robert E. Mitchell, "Polity, Church Attractiveness, and Ministers' Careers: An Eight-Denomination Study of Inter-Church Mobility," *Journal for the Scientific Study of Religion* 11(Spring, 1966) pp. 241-258. Bryan R. Wilson, "Religion and Churches in Contemporary America," William G. McLoughlin and

Robert N. Bellah (eds.), *Religion in America* (Boston: Beacon Press, 1968).

36. James R. Wood, "Authority and Controversial Policy: The Churches and Civil Rights," *American Sociological Review* 35(1969): 1057-69.

27. K. Peter Takayama, "Formal Polity and Change of Structure: Denominational Assemblies," *Sociological Analysis*, 36(1975):17-28.

38. Patrick H. McNamara, "Priests, Protests, and Poverty Intervention," *Social Science Quarterly* 50(1969):695-702.

39. K. Peter Takayama, and Diane Sachs, "Polity and Decision Premises: The Church and the Private School," *Journal for the Scientific Study of Religion* 15(September, 1976):269-278.

40. Peter M. Blau, and W. Richard Scott, *Formal Organizations*, op. cit. pp. 250-253.

41. Wilbert E. Moore, *Social Change,* op. cit.

42. Robert A. Nisbet, *The Social Bond* (New York: Alfred A. Knopf, 1970), p. 321.

43. Erving Goffman, "Characteristics of Total Institutions," *Symposium on Preventive and Social Psychiatry* (Washington, D.C.: U.S. Government Printing Office, 1957), pp. 82-83.

44. F. E. Emery, and E. L. Trist, "The Causal Texture of Organizational Environments," in Merlin B. Brinkerhoff and Phillip R. Kunz (eds.), *Complex Organizations and their Environments,* op. cit., pp. 268-81.

45. Charles Y. Glock and Rodney Stark, *Religion and Society in Tension* (Chicago: Rand McNally, 1965), Chapter 9.

46. Dean Hoge, *Division in the Protestant House,* op. cit., p. 44.

47. N. J. Demerath, and Phillip E. Hammond, *Religion in Social Context: Tradition and Transition* (New York: Random House, 1969), p. 196.

48. Langdon Gilkey, "Social Intellectual Sources of Contempoary Protestant Theology," William G. McLoughlin and Robert N. Bellah (eds.), *Religion in America* (Boston: Beacon Press, 1968), p. 147.

49. Gibson Winter, "Religious Organizations," op. cit.; K. Peter Takayama, "Administrative Structures and Political Processes in Protestant Denominations," op. cit.

50. Mayer N. Zald, *Organizational Change: The Political Economy of the YMCA*, op. cit., p. 227.

51. Shifting of power balances has been taking place since the early 1970s in the name of decentralization or regionalization. For example, budgets allocated for social programs and the number of programs have been drastically cut. Also the number of professional staff members and employees in denominational agencies has been considerably reduced. The theological climate has shifted toward a more conservative,

individualistic emphasis and correspondingly conservative voices have strengthened. The trend in general has been to emphasize the perennial ideal of American Protestantism, the independence of regional as well as local structures.

Similarly strong general resistance to ecumenism commenced around 1970. For example, the National Council of Churches came under strong attack, and funds to it were cut by various denominations. By 1973 it was forced to cut back its program drastically and to cease publishing statements on social issues. For these changes, see, for example, Dean Hoge, *Division in the Protestant House*, op. cit.; Arleon Kelley, *Foundations for Ecumenical Mission: The Ecumenical Response to Regionalization in the Church* (New York: National Council of Churches, 1974); Dean Kelley, *Why Conservative Churches are Growing* (New York: Harper and Row, 1972); Douglas W. Johnson and George W. Cornell. *Punctured Preconceptions* (New York: Friendship Press, 1972); *U.S. News & World Report*, April 11, 1977.

52. George Brager, "Commitment and Conflict in a Normative Organization," *American Sociological Review* 34(1969):482-491.

53. Lewis Coser, *The Functions of Social Conflict* (New York: The Free Press, 1961), p. 93.

54. Sources consulted about the Presbyterian Church in the U.S. split are: 1974 *Britannica Book of the Year* (Chicago: Encyclopedia Britannica); "Who are the Dissidents?" *The Presbyterian Outlook*, 1973 (reprint circulated); Morton Smith, *How is the Gold Become Dim* (Jackson, Mississippi: Premier Printing Company, 1973); Kenneth S. Keyes, "Why the Continuing Church is a Must for Faithful Presbyterians," Concerned Presbyterians, Inc., April, 1973; "Twenty-Four Reasons" (Resolution Statement), *The Presbyterian Journal*, August 8, 1973.

55. "Twenty four Reasons," ibid. p. 7.

56. "Who are the Dissidents," op. cit. p. 7.

57. Sources consulted about the Lutheran Church-Missouri Synod split are: Martin E. Marty, "Showdown in the Missouri Synod," *The Christian Century*, September 27, 1972; Martin E. Marty, "A Clash of World Views and Styles," in John H. Baumgaertner (ed.), *A Tree Grows in Missouri* (Milwaukee, Wis.: Agape Publishers, 1975); *Report of the Advisory Committee on Doctrine and Conciliation*. St. Louis, Mo.: Concordia Publishing House, 1976; *1973, 1974, 1975, 1976* and *1977 Britannica Book of the Year* (Chicago: Encyclopedia Britannica); John H. Tietjen, "In the Language of the Children"; Ronald Nickel, "Three Possible Sources of the Faculty Majority's Vulnerability in the Conflict at Concordia Seminary St. Louis: A Review of the Literature," unpublished paper, Summer, 1976.

58. This quotation is found in Nickel's paper, ibid. p. 2.

59. Martin E. Marty, "A Clash of World Views and Styles," op. cit., p. 80.

60. Ronald Nickel, op. cit.

61. I am indebted to Ross Scherer for the suggestion and formulation of these hypotheses regarding this Missouri case study.

62. Ross P. Scherer, "The Lutheran Ministry: Origins, Careers, Self-Appraisal," *The Cresset* 26(Jan., 1963):9-17, ref. p. 10 (reprinted in *Information Service*, National Council of Churches, April 27, 1963: 1-8).

63. See Willmar Thorkelson, *Lutherans in the U.S.A.* (Minneapolis, Minn.: Augsburg, 1979).

64. *Missouri in Perspective*, " 'Surprise' Visits Signal LCMS Presidents' Wish for Better Relationships," March 26, 1979, p. 8.

APPENDIX

The following hypotheses represent a summary of what has been discussed in the first three sections of this chapter. The readers are reminded that hypotheses primarily refer to structural sources of strain and conflict and their consequences in mainline Protestant denominations.

General Hypotheses

These will be stated as *general propositional statements* for research guidelines, rather than as pure hypotheses which can be tested in a precise manner.

1. If there is a relatively high degree of value consensus in the denomination but a relatively low degree of value consensus in the environment, goal succession or a shift in target population is likely, and administrative "rationalization" (i.e., differentiation of departments and specialization of tasks) is likely.

2. If administrative rationalization occurs in order to control an uncertain environment, the denomination tends to develop normative inconsistencies (i.e., strains), especially in its authority pattern.

3. If environmental value consensus becomes increasingly low (i.e., conflict in the environment increases at a rapid rate), the denominational value consensus will also tend to become low, thus introducing internal divisions.

4. If both environmental value consensus and denominational value consensus are low, the denomination is likely to experience structural changes.

5. If denominational value consensus is low and is followed by encounter with environmental threats, the conflict with environmental values is likely to act as a catalyst for internal strains, thus producing further conflicts.

6. If cooptation approaches do not resolve strains, they tend to produce new areas of strain which become more difficult to reconcile.

Hypotheses

The following hypotheses represent sequential steps in the denominational response to strain and conflict.

1. Potential for conflict within the dominant leadership group increases as the resolution of strains requires compromises on outcome preference.
2. The more strain regarding the allocation of the denomination's scarce values and resources, the more bases there are for power and the larger the number of ideological positions on outcome preference.
3. The larger the number of power bases and of ideological positions on outcome preference, the more likely the dominant leaders will resort to compromise and/or inspirational decision strategies.
4. The fewer the resources available for the goal-setting of the denominational priorities, the more likely are official (incumbent) leaders to experience uncertain decisions makings, and the more likely are non-official (out) leaders to disagree with official leaders' decisions.
5. The less the constraints and pressures applied by official leaders to non-official (opposing) leaders, the more likely the latter are to experience relative deprivation. (Relative deprivation is the sense and feeling of deprivation in comparison with the perceived situation of another group within the organization.)
6. The more out (opposing) leaders are deprived, the more they will question the legitimacy of official leaders' authority and decision-making.
7. The greater the feeling of relative deprivation, the greater the probability that the deprived leaders will develop ideological rationalization and means to defend what they regard as perennial values of the denomination.
8. The more conflicts over the constitutionality of official leaders' authority and discretion are objectified, the more intense will be the conflict.
9. The more conflicts are intensified, the greater will be the tendency for opposing minority group and their leaders to coalesce against official leaders.
10. When both official and deprived minority leaders perceive that there is no avenue open for the reconciliation of conflict, "we" and "they" relations will be intensified and interactions between them will decline.

10

Program Dissensus Between Denominational Grass Roots and Leadership and Its Consequences

Douglas W. Johnson

A denomination is a voluntary association which operates *locally* through programs that are useful to its members. This simplified version of church programming suggests a direct correlation between satisfaction with what is happening in the local church and the amount of dollar support that people provide.

The North American Interchurch Study, however, indicated that this correlation was only partially true.[1] Persons who belong to a church expect it to develop and implement programs with which they do not necessarily agree; in fact, they will support programs with which they disagree! There is, however, a range of tolerance beyond which they will not go. The question becomes, how wide is the tolerance limit?

In order to begin to answer this question with any assurance of veracity, it is necessary to look more closely at the operative levels of program, the connecting points between the program levels, and the effects on program of diminishing funds. When these have been discussed, some implications regarding the future may be drawn.

OPERATIVE LEVELS OF PROGRAM

Within denominations there are three generally administrative defined levels at each of which guidelines and legislation are established. They are programmatic in that certain types of programs are initiated, funded, and staffed at each. A brief description of each level with its major thrust provides a background for the discussion of dissensus and funding. It is a basic assumption of open systems theory that feedback from lower levels of a system is a vital datum for program planners to insure "error correction." Continuous feedback from the grass roots would seem to be especially crucial in "popular" organizations where the general membership forms the major fount of basic resources.

1. National or Denominational Level

"Are you a Lutheran?" is the type of question which speaks in general about a denominational family. Within the Lutheran family,[2] for example, are specific denominations including the Lutheran Church in America, The American Lutheran Church, and the Lutheran Church—Missouri Synod. There are others in the Lutheran family but these illustrate the point. The denominational level is concerned not with a single congregation in a particular community so much as it focuses attention on a large number of local churches held together by tradition, polity, and denominational ethos.

It is on this level that general rules of governance for all congregations within the denomination are established. Especially important are matters of faith, ordination, and organization or polity. From a church member's perspective, the national level may be distant and somewhat amorphous, although it establishes an identity for the member.

Programs at the denominational level are general program thrusts. The philosophy and theology undergirding denominational programs are established here. These are then sent (frequently via middle-level judicatories) to local congregations which receive statements from national boards and agencies with some frequency. In addition to philosophy and theology, the national level is charged with developing and providing program resource materials, especially curricula, which may be used in all congregations. The denominational level also directs programs in mission work at home and overseas. This level receives money from congregations and uses it to carry out specific purposes, i.e., to design, support, and implement particular types of programs.

The denomination insures that clergy, staff, and laity of its congregations have opportunities for training, provides informational convocations, and maintains internal communication. It oversees seminaries, sustains publishing ventures, and supports experimental mission projects. This level sets the tone for the congregations throughout the land.[3]

Funding for national programs comes mostly from congregations; only about 9% of national level denominational monies are secured from sources other than congregations.[4] An implication is that, if congregations become disturbed over national programs, they may lessen the flow of money in that direction. Such a strategy has been documented in at least one major denomination.[5] It is also the basis for believing that cutbacks in national, denominational budgets may be related to a distaste for certain programs. Yet, the percentage of persons in the 1971 survey who reported holding back money because of programs with which they disagreed was quite small.

2. Regional or Judicatory Level

The regional level is an intermediary between national denominational office and local congregations. Its geographic area is limited, usually including only one or two states at the maximum; and the number of congregations within its bounds is limited. The number of staff supported at this level is usually no more than a dozen and often less than half that. Regional budgets may range up to three or four million dollars, which is less than the budget of one division in a national denominational board in some cases.

The ideal function of the regional judicatory is to serve as a conduit from national to local and local to national in terms of program concerns and needs. If it performs this service, it becomes a key interpretive arena for existing and potential denominational programs. It serves this capacity by calling together clergy and laity from congregations to discuss denominational thrusts or priorities and ask for their support, not only by adopting the programs but helping to raise money for their support.

It is at the regional level that auxiliary service agencies are administratively located. These include colleges, seminaries, homes for the aged, and other institutions of various sorts. This level is charged with ministerial recruitment and certification, as well as raising the money for the pension plans (in certain denominations) under which clergy may retire. These latter funds are an increasing amount for the regionals.

Another function of this level is providing direct assistance to local congregations. This takes the form of dollar subsidy, deployment of clergy, and staff assistance during times of need. In each instance, the regional level organizes itself around program areas and operates within general goals established for those areas.

Money to support staff and program at this level also comes from the congregations within its geographic bounds. About 91% of the income for this level comes from this source.[7] An implication is that when regional bodies are not perceived as helpful to congregations, income for regional staff and program may be cut. This most often is reflected in the number of persons or regional staffs and the types of programs sustained.

3. Congregational or Local Level

The program focus of congregations is upon the sacraments, education of the laity in the history and precepts of the faith, and active involvement in and support of missions. "Missions" include activities in the local communities as well as regional, national, and international enterprises. These may or may not be related solely to the denomination to which a congregation belongs.

The key figure in a congregation is the member. It is this person who gives the money that eventually reaches around the world in the name of the church. The support of national and regional programs is directly correlated with the understanding and willingness of this person to contribute to such programs. It is little wonder that hundreds of thousands of dollars are spent by national and regional denominational levels to inform and persuade members to give to such and such a program or mission.

To suggest that a local church member must be "informed and persuaded" to give to church-sponsored activities may seem inconsistent with the concept of membership. In most organizations, members are *expected* to support activities of the organization they join. The church congregation, however, is a *voluntary* association. This means there is no system for "taxing" an individual. There is, however, an apportionment system which allocates national and regional denominational budget quotas to the local congregations; such quotas are usually based on a congregation's individual membership and budget. It is as close to a "tax system" as is possible in a voluntary organization.[8]

It is possible for a congregation to ignore these requests and not pay its "fair share" to the denomination or to send only partial payments. For this reason the national level of the United Methodist Church, e.g., regularly computes a budget based on receipt of only about 91% of the prorated "shares" from congregations. It is also the reason that funds supporting an agency like the National Council of Churches (really the "fourth level up") may not be fully paid during any given year. All congregations do not send in their pledged amounts to the denomination.

The three operational levels of a denomination each have distinctive programmatic functions. The *denominational system*, however, *remains voluntary throughout*. The *key level*, in terms of money, *is the local*. Without wholehearted support at this level, the other two become fiscally vulnerable.

When congregations perceive a failure in the denomination to provide services, they may refuse to pay their share of denominational budgets. The same is true for the regional unit. The denomination as a system is closely interrelated, but it is by no means hierarchical. It is based on the *authority of persuasion* that comes as a result of meeting program needs.

CONNECTING POINTS

An operating church system depends on vital connections between the levels. This is accomplished through two means. The first occurs through people, especially staff professionals and persons serving on regional and national committees. The second means of linkage is through church-sponsored media.

1. Persons

There are three types of persons within the church system who play various roles according to leader or non-leader positions within the three levels at any given time. The first are *pastors*, the ordained leaders of congregations.

Pastors, male and female, are responsible for the program of one or more congregations. Whatever programmatic thrust exists beyond the sacraments will be a result, directly or indirectly, of the efforts of this individual. The amount of income or money available to the congregation will be a reflection of his/her activity level.

It is not necessary for the pastor to skirt controversial issues in developing programs. Congregational members have direct access to him/her and can put on pressures that will let him/her know where they stand. It is then up to the clergyperson to determine whether to press onward or to find new ways to initiate social or ecclesiastical change. He/she is aware that financial support will be a key indicator of effectiveness.

This does not mean that a clergyperson is expected to cease being "prophetic." As indicated earlier, members of congregations expect leadership in this area. It seems that the key question has to do with the *approach used*, i.e., whether or not there is a continuing communication between clergy and laity during times of tensions created by the felt call of the clergy to be prophetic.[9]

A second type of person is the *staff executive* at the regional and national levels. Such officials may or may not be ordained persons who have had experience in congregations. They are hired for expertise in a particular field, although there have been some questions raised about the use of the quota system to insure ethnic and sex mixtures on denominational staffs.[10]

Staff persons are responsible for program development, interpretation, and assistance in relation to local congregations. They have experience in their field of expertise and are expected to be efficient and effective within the church. It is not always the case that they have money with which to work—they may have money only for their *salaries*. Thus, they must be innovative in what they do. Sometimes they must spend much effort within the denominational bureaucracy to insure an adequate income for staff operations, which means a limited budget for program materials and meetings.

The third type of person is the *lay person*. Lay persons are rooted in congregations and are associated with the church not for their livelihood but as believing members. They hold expectations about what the church ought to be doing and how it should go about its tasks.[11] When their trust is betrayed, they react by withdrawing from participation, "designating" or cutting down their gifts. If they begin to withdraw from active church participation, they may stop giving altogether. Personal and monetary types of participation are correlated.

These three groups of persons interact in several ways and as such are the connecting points for the system.

In the first place, they are thrown together in national and regional board meetings dealing with programs of a national or regional relevance. Laity, clergy, and staff are all represented on such boards which establish and promote programs. At this point staff persons discover views contrary to theirs with regard to particular types of programs.

The second type of interaction occurs in a formal manner. Legislation governing all programs and funds are established, and delegates are elected to serve on conferences, assemblies, and synods. During these denominational meetings, programs are adopted and funding established. Dissent within the system is usually evident during discussions about funding. After the meetings, staff members, even in face of dissent, must promote the established programs and procure the funding for program implementation.

2. Media

Another important means for interaction between leadership and members occurs through denominationally supported media. The media are a major connecting point in the church system, serving as a means by which denominational staff can speak about programs and seek support from congregations. Church-sponsored publications are designed for this purpose.

Publications sponsored by particular boards or agencies serve special audiences within the denomination. These may deal with a specific program emphasis such as peace or hunger, or they may cover a larger interest such as overseas missions. In their coverage, such publications try to keep subscribers informed as to what the denomination is doing, what their money is being used for, and what additional needs exist. In so doing, explanations of philosophy about programs are given. The revenues from these publications are generally supplemented from program funds but the media often are conceived to be programs in themselves.

The aim of internal church media is to secure commitments from a broad range of congregational members to choose to participate in and support particular programs. The need for such promotion is obvious, given the voluntary nature of each segment of the church system.

Another function of media is to act as a sounding board on controversial issues and, as part of the process, to commission some house research. For example, prior to the United Methodist General Conference in 1976, one of the denominational publications developed an opinion poll seeking the reactions of church persons to issues that would be on the agenda of the meeting. Printing results of the questionnaire just prior to the Conference had an important effect on the outcome of that Conference's deliberations.

The two connecting points in the church system, people and media, are constantly being used to persuade. Participation and information are key concepts in a voluntary society such as the church. When there is participation and understanding, support for programs will be forthcoming. The intent in using such connecting points is to increase both participation and understanding so that funding will continue for programs.

MONEY AND PROGRAMS

The church dollar is affected by many things, as has been indicated. In addition to misunderstanding, it is affected by displeasure. A review of per capita receipts (from yearbooks of American and Canadian churches) for the years 1965, 1967, and 1969 for three denominations indicate that receipts fall when serious disequilibrium occurs within the denomination. The Reformed Church in America had per capita receipts of $131.57. $86.68, and $97.04 for these three years. This denomination experienced serious readjustment at the regional level between 1965 and 1969. In this sense, programs were affected because of organizational difficulties.

The Episcopal Church had changes in per capita income during this period as well. In 1965 it was $106.80; in 1967, it fell to $69.94; and in 1969, to $59.67. Dissent over the extent to which social action programs were being funded was a major factor. By 1970 this denomination had cut its national staff in half and restructured almost all its denominational services. The denomination was not meeting the kinds of program needs that congregations felt were appropriate.

The Lutheran Church in America experienced a decrease from 1965 to 1967 and a slight rise by 1969. The figures were $79.30, $60.92, and $66.91. This denomination was going through a time when new leadership was being installed as well as experiencing reaction to programs related to "race" within the denomination. Displeasure of members and some lost confidence in leadership appear to have been important ingredients in fluctuations of the dollar figures.

In each of these denominations there is a direct connection between income flow and program development. Data from other denominations for these same years do not show the same pattern. Indeed, the per capita giving from other major denominations increased during this period.

When members of denominations feel they have reached a point of no confidence, support for programs recedes. The question raised at the beginning is once more pertinent. How wide is the tolerance limit before members begin to cut back funding to the denominations?

1. Signals

Signals are given prior to cutbacks. Grass roots unrest is evident to the denominational leaders who "listen" to congregations. John Fry documents some "signals" for the United Presbyterian Church.[12] In this and other denominations a "signal" is the emergence of internal protest groups which raise questions about particular program thrusts and operations. This has been true in the United Methodist Church regarding missionary activity, the United Presbyterian Church in its support of particular social action activities, in the Episcopal Church as related to theological changes and social action activities, and the Presbyterian Church in the U.S. relative to theology and practice of the denomination. When the protest groups become a major force in the denomination, it is evident that denominational leaders have become insensitive to a particular segment of the membership or feel that the bulk of members are not represented by the dissenters. As one official pointed out, "This group, at the most, is 10% of the members." At such a point, leaders must make a decision to change direction, or to "stay on course" and let dissenters go their way.

This is exactly the situation with two major denominations in recent years. Protest groups were involved in denominational fractures, in one case by moving out (the conservatives in the Presbyterian Church in the U.S.) and in the other of no longer being tolerated within (the moderates in the Lutheran Church—Missouri Synod—see preceding chapter).

For those who listen, the key signals are that denominational "costs are too high" for services rendered, denominational leaders are "not listening" or at least not willing to dialogue with dissenters, and that the programs provided are the "wrong ones." Dean Kelley[13] and Virgil Sexton[14] pointed to these messages in the early 1970s. The membership was telling program developers and leaders they were on the wrong track.

It is important to realize that leaders are *expected to be ahead* of members, especially in regard to the church's responsibility to society. The question, however, appears to be whether the leaders are truly willing to *hear and respond* to what members are saying. In large denominations, this is time-consuming and expensive. Yet, the importance of tempering prophecy with some effort at listening and at explanation cannot be underestimated.[15]

The "crunch" came in the early 1970s. Money was in short supply. This crisis was really precipitated by two forces. One was internal to the church. It was not a decline in money so much as it was a designation and drain-off of money to certain program areas within denominations. For example, disaster and relief programs prospered, while missions in the urban areas went into doldrums. People giving the money were more willing to support certain types of programs than others. The problem lay in shifting sensitivities and goal expectations of church members as much as misplacing of emphasis and mismanagement by denominational officials.[16]

The second pressure was inflation. The simple fact was that each year it cost more to function administratively at the regional and denominational levels. This became especially true for those offices since major denominational headquarters have progressively been gravitating to large metropolitan areas where costs have been high in the first place. The dollar flow has actually been increasing but at a rate significantly below the inflation rate. This has resulted in a loss of dollars available for program.[17]

2. Programs Suffer

What got hurt when the money "crunch" hit? The most costly item in any budget is staff. Efforts were made to keep people, but by the early 1970s it became necessary to start the cutting process at the national and regional levels. The question was where to point the knife. A look at three or four national denominations reveals the effects on programs of the pruning that took place.

Editors and writers were let go. Trainers for special fields, especially in education and stewardship, were cut back. Specialty programs in non-urban settings were dropped. Overseas missionaries were called home. Retreat and study centers were sold or taken over by other agencies. In short, *specialists* responsible for undergirding the educational backbone of denominations *were eliminated* due to costs.

This can be illustrated by a comparison of staffs in the National Council of Churches in 1970 and 1976. (See Table 1.) This has been a period of continuing reductions for this agency because of cutbacks from denominational contributions.

The argument in these changes was that services of specialists were not as essential as those of generalists. Thus, the backbone of the services available to denominations was cut out as budgets were reduced. The same phenomenon was occurring in denominations.[18]

The generalists remained and new persons were added whose expertise related to new national priorities within the constituent denominations. These priorities had to do generally with ethnic development (programs aimed for blacks, American Indians, Spanish-speaking Americans, and

TABLE 1
COMPARISON OF SELECTED NATIONAL COUNCIL OF
CHURCHES STAFF POSITIONS IN 1970 AND 1976

N.C.C. Administrative Unit	1970	1976
Office of the General Secretary	1	1
General Secretary	1	1
Associate General Secretary	1	0
Assistant Gen. Sec., executive oper.	1	1
Executive Assistant to the Gen. Sec.	1	0
Special Project	1	1
Assistant Gen. Sec for Washington Office	1	0
Associate Director—Washington Office		
Staff Assoc., Research & Information	1	0
Services, Washington Office		
Director, Special Projects and Program	1	0
Development, Washington Office		
Exec. Dir., Office on Christian-Jewish	0	1
relations		
Sub-total	9	5
Division of Church and Society		
Associate General Secretary	1	1
Special Assistant to Assoc. Gen Sec.	1	0
Associate for Administration	1	0
Associate for Religious and Civil Liberty	1	1
Other Staff	33*	8
Sub-total	37*	10
Office of Research Evaluation and Planning		
Assistant General Secretary	1	1
Long Range Planning, Executive Director	1	0
Executive Director, Research	1	0
Research Services	1	0
Information Services	1	1
Sub-total	5	2

* These include special programs such as evangelism, new forms of ministry, church building and architecture, leisure-recreation, programs at Church Center for United Nations.

Asian Americans), human rights, and economic justice. (A review of position titles of the National Council of Churches in the 1976 *Yearbook* indicates some of these changes.) While these appear to be quite specific, the persons placed in charge of these program areas had staff roles in addition to assignment to these tasks. The consequence was that relatively *little return* in terms of significant program was felt *on* the *level of the local* congregations. Inadequate interpretation and communication, resulting because the specialists in these fields were gone, produced a declining support base.

The regional level also went the way of "restructure," again by ridding itself of specialists. In the new structures, staff members often were labeled "consultants" and were to handle several tasks. The result was that their time became scattered among several fields of interest, none of which received adequate attention. The training of staff was sometimes overlooked as another "need" was added to the job description. The obvious result was a diminution of services to congregations and some confusion regarding the direction in which the denomination leaders wanted to go.

In local congregations, one consequence of inflation was reduction of staff and curtailment of innovative programs. This latter seems contradictory because it would seem that in a time of scarcity, *innovation* would be more prevalent. It seems that the mood created by the fiscal crisis and the general form of cutbacks in the denominations was oppressive. It appeared like a great gray cloud of indecision, and apathy was unleashed in the church. Innovation occurred but this was the exception rather than the rule.

The analysis seems dire indeed. To the church member it did seem dark. At the national and regional levels of mainline denominations, church extension was dropped, youth ministry took a ten year leave-of-absence, national convocations were eliminated, the average church-goer was overlooked as denominational attention was directed to minorities, a relatively small but visible segment of the white denomination's membership, and *issues* were enjoined instead of programs.

3. The Decision Makers

In the time of crisis, persons who make the decision *think* they hold the aces; but in denominations these are people probably *least* in touch with local clergy and laity. The decision makers are executives in denominational and regional offices who hold the highest positions. As in most organizations, top leaders tend to be isolated from the remainder of the organization.[19]

Decisions made during the fiscal "crunch" in the church were rationalized by those who made them. The manner of such rationalization is discussed by Fry as well as by Wilson and Mickey.[20] In each case, the executives were confident of their ability to make judgments for the "good of the organization." There was little attention given to the *programs* which were needed or which should be instituted by the organization. The effort was toward *preservation of the organization*. The consequences for national level program were similar to those outlined by Metz for a local church looking toward mere survival.[21]

Lay members made "decisions" quite separate from the denominational and regional executives and committees. These decisions had to do with dollars, as is seen in denominations like the United Presbyterian Church. This is the reason that there continues to be a problem in funding programs. Laity can and do make decisions at odds with leaders. Leaders in a voluntary organization sometimes understand their positions as power bases rather than as privileges. They choose not to respond to those responsible for bestowing the privilege, in this case the laity.

4. Basis for Decisions

One of the intriguing developments in the churches is the use of techniques for establishing program priorities. Such processes are rooted in a limit-to-growth mentality. They are intriguing because they attempt to emphasize rationality in decision making.

The development of priorities seems to be a very biased process. It assumes two things: first, that all the potential resources are known and can be counted; second, that the group doing the priority setting is truly representative of and responsible for all other members and potential members of the organization. In actual fact, neither assumption is accurate in denominations.[22] The most glaring weakness is the lack of representation in the group establishing the priorities. Regardless of the group doing the prioritizing, there is a much larger audience outside the room which by their support or non-support can redirect those priorities.

As an example, at the 1976 General Conference of the United Methodist Church, a representational group from the Church decided that a priority should be "the Ethnic-Minority Local Church." The figure for the Advance Special (special collections above the apportioned amounts of a local congregation) was $3.5 million per year. By April 30, 1977, the amount contributed in the first four months of the first fiscal year was only $15,000, nearly half of which had come in April. The priorities of the delegates and those of the givers are evidently different up to this point.

The priority process has been used extensively in denominational and regional offices. It is fairly easy for a good executive to read the sentiments of a group and to use that knowledge to direct the group to priorities that are dear to his/her heart. This form of manipulation is subtle, hard to observe, and cannot be documented easily. It is no less workable, yet detrimental to program development. Thus, in spite of the intentional efforts of various denominational assemblies to set priorities, they are still subject to redirection by professional staffs.

Professional staff influence is not inappropriate but the priority process alleged to be in use is not truthful. This dishonesty has been a major complaint of the laity and clergy, according to both John Fry and Mickey and Wilson. There needs to be a rational process for developing major priorities of a denomination, and the staffs must be involved. However, this rational process must involve a broader net of participants than is the case when only board members are construed to be the representatives.[23]

Most denominations have the facilities to garner data about program needs from across their constituency. This can be accomplished by using direct contact with samples of members or by using regional processes for collecting information. The facilities for securing such participation are available. It seems to be the attitude of the leaders that such information would not allow them the freedom necessary to function as they feel they ought.[24]

A second consideration in decision making has been the internal denominational politics at the regional and national levels. Mickey and Wilson[25] discuss this phenomenon in terms of reorganization. The same general pattern seen at the national level has also been evident at the regional level. There were no clear-cut directions for the churches during the late 1960s and early 1970s. It was a turbulent time. The turmoil of the late sixties provided the backdrop for the scene in which the problems of dollars and jobs were being renegotiated. Society also was drifting, and for the cries of "racism" and "sexism" there seemed to be a vacuum of leadership.

A third influence on decision making was the new champions of the disenfranchised. Self-styled leaders who spoke for "all females" or for universal ethnic/racial interests without hesitancy assumed their places in the forefront of negotiations. They became unequal partners in the struggle to right a ship and find a course.

Throughout this period, which stretches roughly from 1965 through the present, little attention has been paid to programs of substance. It is true that a great deal has been said on social issues and a great deal done in social action, but most of the effects have been *symbolic*. The "crisis of the city," a costly program carried out through the National Council of Churches in the late 1960s, died without nurturing long-term effects on urban ministry. "Corporate responsibility" has been an intriguing fad for several denominations during the past few years and has drained money and staff from other programs that could affect local church members much more.

Publications, which are important connecting points in the church system, also became casualties of the fiscal crisis. Monies which had sustained them in periods when "priorities" were not so rigidly developed were diverted to other areas. Non-metropolitan and urban ministries had to be specifically directed to the concerns of the "poor" or to "race," or they were dropped. It was a time of shaping church programs in the image of new politics, new priorities, and new heroes in ways generally unfamiliar to the membership. The cost has been and continues as an erosion of confidence and support of the denomination by its membership.

IMPLICATIONS FOR THE FUTURE

If we could but see tomorrow, it might frighten us enough to be serious about today. Lacking that capacity, it is possible to note some trends that will shape program in denominations at least in the near term.

It is likely that some priorities developed at the national denominational level will not be taken seriously by church members. This is seen in the non-success of placing a high priority upon the Ethnic Minority Local Church program by the United Methodist Church. The only time when "priorities" really become important is when a large number of members have a stake in determining what those priorities shall be. To date, no denomination has designed a process which assures this will happen.

The fiscal problem will continue so long as denominational and regional leaders insist in not listening to church members. This in no way means that church leaders must be bound to do what is "requested." That is not the point. The point is that people who are paying for a program are not going to remain silent when that program is non-productive. For example, it is unlikely that contributions can be expected for funds to support "economic justice" when there are no evident results from such a program.

One of the most funded programs in denominations currently deals with "hunger." Again to use United Methodist Church data, Hunger was established as an Advance Special at the same time as was the Ethnic Minority Local Church fund. By April 30, 1977, four months into the first year, the Hunger fund had received $214,000 compared to $15,000 for EMLC. (This money is in addition to other monies for Hunger programs within the denomination.) Evidently, members of the denomination feel this is an important program. It is one of their priorities.

Both now and in the future, church executives need to court the cost of establishing priorities. This does not mean that they need to abandon responsibility and accountability. The psychology generated by the exercise is frequently negative. It does not include enough persons; and so long as it is a tool of the professional staff persons, it promotes maintenance rather than dreaming, inspiration, and innovation. Of course, setting priorities has the possibility of doing this, but the evidence is that the long trend is downward rather than positive after a series of these events.

The age-old problem of finding adequate means for "feedback" into the system still faces the church. Insulation and snobbery growing out of an attitude that staff know more about reality than others are still major problems. The money flow will continue to be a dribble until staff begin to broaden their vision.

With the level of sophistication rising each year, it is unlikely that church members will find the satisfaction they desire in programming. This can only mean more "designated" giving; but as more than one denomination is discovering, such designated funds are by no means an unhappy prospect for the future.

Notes

1. Douglas W. Johnson and George W. Cornell, *Punctured Preconceptions* (New York: Friendship Press, 1971).

2. *The Yearbook of American and Canadian Churches*, Constant H. Jacquet, Jr. (ed.) (Nashville: Abingdon Press). Annually has a listing of denominational families. It also contains information about the founding date and antecedents of denominations.

3. Paul A. Mickey and Robert L. Wilson, *What New Creation?* (Nashville: Abingdon Press, 1977).

4. Commission of Private Philanthropy and Public Need, "Interfaith Research Study" (Washington, D.C.: 1975), Protestant Section, p. 24.

5. John R. Fry, *The Trivialization of the United Presbyterian Church* (New York: Harper & Row, 1975).

6. Johnson and Cornell, ibid.

7. "Interfaith Research Study," ibid.

8. Paul M. Harrison, *Authority and Power in the Free Church Tradition* (Princeton: Princeton U. Press, 1959), esp. pp. 98-104—a description of the rational-pragmatic authority that allows an apportionment system to function in a voluntary association.

9. Report by Douglas Walrath, consultant, on two churches facing tension as result of the minister's engaging in social action, 1975.

10. Mickey and Wilson, ibid.

11. Johnson and Cornell, ibid.

12. John Fry, ibid.

13. Dean Kelley, *Why Conservative Churches Are Growing* (New York: Harper & Row, 1972).

14. Virgil Sexton, *Listening to the Church* (Nashville: Abingdon Press, 1971).

15. John Fry, ibid.; Mickey and Wilson, ibid.

16. Mickey and Wilson, ibid.

17. Constant H. Jacquet, Jr. (ed.), *Yearbook of American and Canadian Churches 1976* (Nashville, Abingdon Press, 1976), p. 250.

18. For an illustration in one program area, see Douglas W. Johnson, *A Study of High School Youth Programming in Six Denominations and Three Youth Organizations* (Ridgewood, N.J.: Institute for Church Development, Inc., 1977).

19. Peter F. Drucker, *The Practice of Management* (New York: Harper & Row, 1954), pp. 168-69.

20. Mickey and Wilson, ibid.; Fry, ibid.

21. Donald L. Metz, *New Congregations* (Philadelphia: The Westminster Press, 1967).

22. Harrison, ibid., pp. 162 ff.

23. Douglas W. Johnson, *Managing Change in the Church* (New York: Friendship Press, 1974)—discusses the need for broad participation in decision making. Harrison had described the fallacy of taking representational bodies in the church at face value.

24. Harrison, ibid., esp. pp. 115-116.

25. Mickey and Wilson, ibid.

11

Interplay and Rivalry Between Denominational and Ecumenical Organization

William R. Garrett

The advances recorded by the international ecumenical movement in the twentieth century stand in marked contrast to the recent frustrations experienced by American ecumenical organizations in attaining their manifest aims. For example, the celebrated Consultation on Church Union has now tabled its plan for organic unification in favor of a more limited "grass roots" approach aimed at fostering local and "middle range judicatory" cooperation.[1] Meanwhile, state, regional, and local councils of churches have encountered a slackening of participatory support from retrenching denominational organizations which are still reeling under the backlash generated by the tumultuous 'sixties.[2] And all across the ecumenical spectrum, cooperative church planning is languishing on the drawing boards for lack of interest in this sort of enterprise by denominational programmers. Such a somber portrayal of the ecumenical situation is surely familiar to all who have pursued the literature generated by ecumenical analysts of late. Indeed, one informed group of researchers recently concluded that we are still living in "a pre-ecumenical age."[3] Undoubtedly, many would agree that the achievement of an authentic ecumenism is far from historical realization.

Despite the dismal forecasts relative to ecumenism's probable future, however, it is still possible to discern—after carefully taking stock—some anomalous signs of life yet invigorating the several members of the American ecumenical body. One notable symptom of lifeblood pulsating through the movement finds expression in the honorific rhetoric by which churchmen continue to enshrine the *idea*—as opposed to the *practice*—of ecumenism. Like the romantic attachment to the notion of motherhood, the idea of ecumenism numbers no despisers among the stalwart leaders of the mainline denominations. Furthermore, it is precisely this striking disjunction—reflected in the ardent support for the ideal of ecumenism along with a flaccid commitment to its exercise—which thrusts into sharp relief the current strain in organizational relations between denominational and ecumenical bodies, a strain that is the central focus of this interpretation. In the interest of clarity, then, we can state forthrightly the leitmotif resounding through these reflections and linking the various segments of our analysis; to wit: *the goals and social structure of the contemporary ecumenical movement reflect* the socio-logical and ecclesiastical conditions obtaining in *the nineteenth century*. That is to say, where once a rational symmetry linked organizational goals with the structural mechanisms for attaining these ends in relation to a particular historical context, now a fundamental reordering of the social environment—occasioned primarily by the growth of denomina-tional bureaucracies—has irrevocably altered the social climate within which ecumenism must necessarily pursue its activities. Consequently, a profound organizational strain has recently emerged predicated on the fact that ecumenical goals are no longer attainable through the organiza-tional means currently employed by the movement. This basic conclusion suggests that, if ecumenism is to endure as a vibrant force amid the mounting complexities of modern, secular life and the fully bureau-cratized forms of denominational life, it must articulate renewed aims and/or strategies commensurate with the organizational environment prevailing in the remaining decades of the *twentieth* century.

A SOCIOLOGICAL INTERPRETATION OF NINETEENTH CENTURY ECUMENISM

One principle firmly established in the conventional wisdom of sociology asserts that social groups swiftly *expire when* they are consistently *unsuccessful* in attaining their specified goals. Organiza-tions which somehow retain a tenacious lease on life while simultaneously failing to reach their published aims, therefore, tend to incite sociological attention. Frequently, when groups plainly defy this iron law of sociological dynamics, researchers take refuge in the interpretation that such perservering organizations must be accomplishing some "latent function" which lies beyond the explicit purview of the organization's active participants.[4] If we proceed on this assumption with regard to the current ecumenical quandry, some intriguing possibilities for reevaluating the ecumenical enterprise emerge for our reflection.

Consider, for example, this striking fact. When measured against the backdrop of American religious experience, the stated aims of contemporary ecumenism were *more* fully *realized during* the decades surrounding the *1820s than* the *1970s*. For after the second great awakening had fanned the flames of religious enthusiasm, cleric and laic representatives from across the broad spectrum of Protestantism collaborated in developing a remarkable variety of interfaith ministries. To cite but a few examples: in 1810 the American Board of Commissioners for Foreign Missions was incorporated, followed in rapid succession by the American Bible Society in 1816, the American Tract Society in 1823, the American Sunday School Union in 1824, the American Society for the Promotion of Temperance and a Sabbath-protection society in 1826. The same years witnessed the birth of all sorts of reform organizations dedicated to the humanitarian relief of the poor, the sick, the mentally ill, orphans, women, criminals, prostitutes, and, of course, abolition societies devoted to the eradication of the peculiar institution of slavery.[5]

The distinguishing feature of interchurch societies all through this period centered in their special character as voluntary associations uniting individuals and local churches for a common expression of their ministerial concern over a pressing social issue. Yet, the precise form of collective action through issue-oriented societies emerged *more by default than* by conscious *design*. In their assault on society's ills, churchmen of that era swiftly concluded that ecumenical organizations represented the most viable means of accomplishing the important business of ministry firmly fixed on their agenda. The judgment adroitly reckoned with the social situation wherein the churches carried out their mission. For in the opening decades of the nineteenth century, denominational structures were minimally developed by contemporary standards, and denominational leaders were largely confined to the functions of dealing with sacerdotal matters and the practical administration required for supporting *local* churches and ministers. And because denominations lacked an established bureaucratic structure replete with extensive programming offices and a technical staff of highly trained specialists, they were wholly unprepared to supervise the sundry projects initiated by radical and evangelical religious visionaries.

Other factors, in concert with the underdeveloped state of denominational structures, also contributed to the popular growth of ecumenical societies during this era. Most notable in this regard were the combined forces of separatist polity principles and frontier social experience, which together served to reinforce the voluntaristic character of American church life.[6] Initially, of course, only a minority of churches subscribed in principle to the notion of "local church autonomy," but the frontier created an environment of isolated social relations wherein the majority of parishes enjoyed the heightened freedom of local independence. And once congregations had experienced the latitude of self-determination, they tended to assert the propriety of this pattern and guard their autonomy against the incursion of even the benign arm of their *own* denominational authorities. Gradually, then, as the distinctive orientation of free-church localism subtly infiltrated the patterns of governance for even the more hierarchically organized churches, ecclesiastical officials found themselves operating with markedly attenuated power for exercising strict social control over the behavior of churches still formally under their jurisdiction. These circumstances would have seriously undermined the effectiveness of any opposition which denominational officials might have mounted against ecumenical endeavors. On the whole, however, such constraints on denominational resistance to interchurch participation were not required in this historical instance. The reason was really quite simple. What was a potentially conflictual situation pitting denominations against ecumenical societies was largely ameliorated by the fact that none of the early, issue-oriented societies seriously *threatened* denominational bailiwicks *by competing with* ongoing programs the *denominations* had previously launched. Thus, while the relative sense of independence fostered within local churches smoothed the path toward ecumenical participation, further impetus was added to the movement by the approbation freely extended by denominational leaders who regarded the success of benevolent societies as entirely *complementary to* the success of *denominational* organizations.[7]

With only modest countervailing dissent, therefore, the pristine and decentralized ecumenical enterprises of the nineteenth century moved vigorously toward the achievement of those goals for which ecumenism still strives in the 1980s: they enjoyed lively grass roots support, the blessing and cooperation of denominational spokesmen, a wide-ranging variety of ministerial and reform programming which generated little rivalry with denominational activities, and a liberal recognition by the churches of their need for one another in carrying out the grand mission of the church universal.

THE ECUMENICAL CONTRIBUTION TO THE GROWTH OF DENOMINATIONAL BUREAUCRACIES

In one of his more famous pronouncements, Karl Marx once asserted that the capitalist system was not only destined to destroy itself, but in the same process it would also nuture its archenemy and heir-apparent, namely, socialism. Ironically, a similar situation has obtained, *mutatis mutandis*, for the ecumenical movement. For apart from the specific new forms of ministry spawned by the ecumenical ferment of the nineteenth century, the largest single upshot of the movement—although this function was latent and *un*intended—inhered in the *impetus* it generated *for* the *growth of denominational bureaucracies*. The nature of ecumenical influence on denominational development may be briefly sketched in the following manner. Once the cooperative societies had successfully demonstrated the relevance and practicality of new ministerial forms in such areas as foreign missions, home missions, Sunday schools, tract publication, and so forth, denominations swiftly followed suit by creating their *own* denominationally controlled organizations *modeled after* the *ecumenically initiated* programs.[8] By the dawning of the twentieth century, then, the major accomplishments of the ecumenical movement had experienced permanent institutionalization—not, however, under ecumenical auspices, but through the *assimilation* of these programs *into* the organizational structure of the mainline *denominations*. Through a process of cooptation, therefore, the confessional churches at once appropriated and brought under their administrative management a succession of program breakthroughs pioneered by ecumenical agencies.

This turn of events redounded with the most unfortunate of consequences for the ecumenical movement. The unprecedented burgeoning of denominationalism proceeded *at* the *expense of* its chief *benefactor*, ecumenism, a movement now crippled and in the process of being rapidly superseded. For the dramatic expansion of denominational structures irrevocably transformed the religio-social environment wherein members of ecumenical agencies expressed their faith and practice. Hereafter, ecumenism would have to reckon not only with individuals and local churches, but also with increasingly powerful denominational judicatories. Since denominations—as institutionally discrete organizations—carried with them a separate set of allegiances, aims, programs, and professional staff, as well as an innate and ever deepening set of vested interests,[9] the ecumenical movement could never again return to those innocent days enjoyed during the era of its beginnings.

THE ADVENT OF A FEDERATED
ECUMENICAL ORGANIZATION

Sensitive recognition was implicitly accorded the altered institutional character of the religious environment when a self-conscious ecumenical movement appeared on the horizon early in the twentieth century. Riding the crest of Social Gospel fervor, the Federal Council of Churches emerged in 1908. From the outset, this new organization was predominately constituted of denominational bodies. By reason of its crucial linkage with liberal Protestant theology and its bold attack on sensitive social issues,[10] however, the Federal Council failed to marshal a solid consensus around its overriding goal of demonstrating ". . . the essential oneness of the Christian Churches of America, in Jesus Christ as their Lord and Savior."[11] According to its initial design, the Council sought to fulfill two specific and intimately related functions: "social service as defined by the Social Gospel movement and the coordination of the activities of members in an effort to avoid wasteful competition."[12] The overt Social Gospel orientation of the early Council officials, however, promptly resulted in *more* attention being focused on the *social service* concern *while slighting* the corollary interest in *coordinating* denominational efforts. Consequently, top leadership among the denominations eventually came to regard Council programs and deliberations as largely irrelevant to their on-going concerns. This judgment produced two significant effects: (1) constituent denominations gravitated toward the practice of appointing representatives to the Council who were already well-known for their Social Gospel sympathies, and (2) denominations manifested a definite reluctance to allocate substantial funds to the Council's several programming agencies.

Ultimately, both these actions served to garner for the Council a greater measure of freedom from denominational constraint. Denied an adequate allocation of denominational monies, the Council raised two-thirds to three-fourths of its annual funds from sources *other than* its *member* bodies.[13] And the uniform outlook shared by delegated members facilitated prompt and concerted action by agency decision-makers. Yet, the price exacted from the Council for its freedom from denominational interference in the framing of major policy positions was in the long run substantial. Above all, it meant that the Council persistently represented a minority viewpoint and thus could not speak effectively for all the member communions of the federation.

Meanwhile, under pressure from external forces reshaping the secular environment and a subtle reordering of the movement's internal composition, the Federal Council gradually modified its basic orientation, especially along the dimension of its programming activities. By the 1940s, the Council—noted earlier for its bold, though often unpopular stances—had lost much of its controversial character. The old social issues had either waned in importance or been tentatively resolved by governmental action—represented primarily in the enactment of social legislation introduced under New Deal auspices—and as new designs for interdenominational cooperation had begun to surface for serious consideration by denominational and ecumenical policy-leaders alike.

These changes set the stage for a major reformation of the organizational structure of the national ecumenical movement. Consequently, in the wake of the organization of the World Council of Churches in 1948, the Federal Council was stimulated to take the lead in forming the National Council of the Churches of Christ in the U.S.A. Predicated on essentially neo-orthodox principles, the new Council tended now toward a closer approximation of the theological center of American religious life.[14] The organizational design adopted for the N.C.C.C. in 1950, however, produced a cumbersome, decentralized structure. The Council was fashioned out of a series of *previously independent program agencies*, each of which maintained a measure of ". . . autonomy within the larger N.C.C. structure in terms of staffing, office location, and relations with constituents."[15] A more centralized internal structure emerged from reorganizational changes accepted in 1965, whereby funding and planning were unified and separate agencies were regrouped into larger departments labeled "Divisions."[16] With reference to constituent members, however, the National Council became more explicitly a *council of denominations* (as opposed to the previously implicit pattern of a *council of agencies*). The result was a loose-knit federation of denominations bound together by a rather simple confession of faith and a commitment to "conferencing" and cooperative action.[17] The least controversial activities undertaken by the new structure were the information and research functions, while the most problematic emerged in the effort to devise joint policy positions over against governmental action and/or the solution of public social problems.

Unfortunately, the progressive advances on the organizational front—occasioned by the rationalizing and integrating of the ecumenical structure—never quite brought to fruition the attainment of those lofty ideals relative to cooperative action articulated in connection with the movement's renewal. Somewhere between dialogue and action, ecumenism faltered and then perceptively broke down. Although, to be sure, naive idealism graced the launching of this new phase in ecumenical life, nonetheless, something more structurally debilitating than mere cockeyed optimism confounded the movement's earnest efforts to accomplish its joint mission. The elusive flaw featured in the organizational design adopted by the National Council of churches comes vividly into focus when we assess the *liabilities attending* social *groups federated out of autonomous bodies* which vehemently refuse to relinquish their hegemonic claims to power. The following analytical section clarifies some of the more salient problems and inevitable conflicts thrust upon the Council by virtue of its organizational style and the distinctive character of its linkage with denominational collectivities.

THE ORGANIZATIONAL MODEL OF
THE NATIONAL COUNCIL: FEDERATED-
CONCILIAR AND NORMATIVE

The ecumenical movement in all its diverse manifestations embraces a succession of organizational styles ranging as follows: the *intra-family* models (such as the Baptist World Alliance, the World Methodist Council, or the World Alliance of Reformed Churches);[18] the *consultation* type (which explores the possibility of organic union and/or heightened understanding among judicatories);[19] the *coalition* model (whereby two or more denominations agree to move on a common agenda, such as those projects funded by the Joint Strategy and Action Council, more commonly known as "JASC"); and finally the *conciliar* model (a federated body in which the members maintain organic independence while cooperating on issues of common concern). (See Chapter 1 for further discussion of these types in the history of American Protestantism.)

For our purposes in analyzing the organizational dynamics of the National Council of Churches, the federated-conciliar model clearly represents the most relevant point of reference. Broadly speaking, this model

... includes councils, associations and conferences of churches at the local, metropolitan, state, regional, national, and world levels. Its goal is the broadest participation possible among the churches in mission which will lead hopefully and ultimately to unity. It is inclusive. It sees itself as laying the foundations for a larger ecumenical future. ... In theory a council is an arena where the diverse parts of the church can take common counsel and then implement those decisions. On the American scene this model has been given significant organizational modification. The result is that it has tended at times to develop a highly bureaucratized form—not unlike participant denominations.[20]

One of the more pressing issues thrust into the foreground by the appropriation of federated-conciliar structures, it should be noted, concerns the *means for achieving compliance* from member bodies to the aims and decisions enacted by the composite organization. Etzioni has supplied a typology of compliance structures for complex organizations which skillfully illuminates the peculiar difficulties encountered by the National Council and similarly constituted organizations. This model divides groups into the categories of coercive, utilitarian, and normative mechanisms of compliance. *Coercive* organizations, such as prisons, use *force* to maintain control over participant's behavior. *Utilitarian* organizations, whose best representatives are to be found in economic enterprises, employ *remuneration* as the major source of social control. But *normative* organizations, like churches, rely on *normative power* as

> ... the major source of control over most lower participants, whose orientation to the organization is characterized by high commitment. Compliance in normative organizations rests principally on internalization of directives accepted as legitimate. Leadership, rituals, manipulation of social and prestige symbols, and resocialization are among the more important techniques of control used.[21]

In the competition between ecumenism and denominationalism, therefore, what one discerns is the articulation of opposing claims advanced by two normative collectivities with quite different control resources over their constituents. Moreover, these circumstances place ecumenism in a decidely inferior position. For in the absence of legitimate, coercive authority and without recourse to economic sanctions, leaders of ecumenical agencies are forced to rely on their skills of *moral persuasion* in order to motivate the constituent parties to participate in cooperative endeavors. Not only are the opportunities for conciliar schisms omnipresent in this situation, but there also exists a heightened probability that mere exhortation will not be effectual in constraining denominational action. Indeed, whether in the long run constituent denominations will be persuaded by the periodic appeals from ecumenical leaders probably hinges less on the cogency and sincerity inherent in the appeals themselves than on the relation of these appeals to the perceived self-interest to the denominations in question. As Reinhold Niebuhr so trenchantly understood and sociologists have so repeatedly attested, *complex organizations*—unlike persons—*are incapable of sustained, self-sacrificial activity*. Consequently, those expectations—currently shared by participants in both denominational and ecumenical quarters—which hold that denominations will exhibit disinterest toward their own goals in order to fulfill the aims of an ecumenical consortium have the effect of condemning ecumenism to an existence of endless frustration.

This pessimistic judgment, of course, presupposes that the interests of ecumenism and denominationalism are largely inimical—although the very existence of an ecumenical movement might well seem to impugn the cogency of this assumption. Certainly, none of the denominations takes pride in the disunity of the churches, and the abiding interest in dialogue palpably witnesses to the force still exerted by theological critiques decrying the scandal of a fragmented church. Nevertheless, it may very well be the case that dialogue around the conference table has served in the past as ample propitiation for the church's guilt over separation, while motivation for cooperative action requires a stimulus fashioned out of much sterner stuff.[22]

THE CONFLICT BETWEEN ECUMENISM
AND DENOMINATIONALISM OVER PROGRAMMING
AND FUNDING

If we pursue the question of rivalry further along the lines already introduced, then the countervailing interests of denominations and ecumenism plainly emerge with regard to the practical matters of programming and funding. For it is difficult to gainsay the fact that these two sorts of institutions press opposing claims over essentially the same limited resources of time, money, and personnel. Or, to put the issue more concretely, the funding of ecumenical programs necessarily limits the amount of monies available for underwriting denominational programs.

Moreover, the contending organizations enter the competitive struggle over funding with markedly different potentials for promoting their respective causes, a differential which is ultimately rooted in the fact that ecumenical funds derive in large measure *from* denominational appropriations.[23] Additionally, not only do ecumenical agencies complain of too meager an allotment of the church's total financial resources—even in "normal" times—but also during periods of economic stringency when denominational budgets tighten up, ecumenical contributions are generally one of the first items reduced or eliminated from denominational disbursements. Herein lies an ironic inversion for contemporary ecumenical endeavors in comparison to our earlier experience. That is to say, in the *nineteenth* century, one of the soundest reasons for acting ecumenically resided precisely in its *economic* efficiency. All the churches lived with relative poverty, and therefore, *nothing* could really be accomplished *without* a *pooling* of funds. Later, when accelerating affluence in the wider society translated into increased affluence for the churches, denominations no longer had to worry about the expense of reduplicated programs—particularly if this reduplication achieved another goal, i.e., denominational control over programming. Curiously, then, *modern ecumenism* has fallen *victim* not to poverty, but to *affluence.* And indeed, as long as surging prosperity persisted, the American churches could afford *both* denominationalism and ecumenism—in about the same proportion as the national government could afford both guns and butter. Meanwhile, during periods of short-term retrenchment, ecumenical agencies have typically been the first to experience a drying up of their financial resources. If ecumenical leaders felt their programs had not received an adequate hearing before denominational tribunals, their only recourse lay in resorting to diplomatic jawboning and their only sanction in the tender persuasion of the Council-planned, interdenominational "joint consultation."

Alongside the conflict on monetary questions, there has persistently loomed another *equally troublesome competition over* the time and loyalities of *personnel*, even when—as has usually been the case—these personnel are sympathetic to both the denominational and ecumenical causes.[24] Yet, ecumenical agencies have seldom been able to extend material and prestige rewards equal to those proffered by denominations. The clergy, in particular, are constantly confronted with the intractable fact that voluntary participation in ecumenical activities garners little professional benefit over personal costs. For career advancement, professional status, regular salary increments, indeed, all the standard measures of achievement—to which clergy are subject like all other members of an achievement-oriented society—are distributed almost exclusively through the channel of the denomination. Thus, it may be concluded that, until ecumenism is able to offer rewards within a comparable range to those provided by denominations, it will remain a weak competitor for the time and energy of parish clergy whose participation is essential to a dynamic ecumenical movement.

THE CURRENT IMPASSE BETWEEN DENOMINATIONALISM AND ECUMENISM

The acknowledgement of these hard facts relative to the plight of ecumenism lays the foundation for drawing the ineluctable conclusion that the *contemporary ecumenical movement* is *structured around* a fundamental *contradiction*. On the one hand, it possesses goals which presuppose a homogeneous social structure capable of disciplined, concerted action; yet, not since the early ecumenical societies has such an institutional framework and supportive social environment prevailed. On the other hand, a confederated alliance of autonomous denominations signifies by its very structure that only the most modest of goals will realistically fall within the range of its attainable functions. Given this present configuration of social reality, two avenues appear to lie open before the ecumenical movement in our time: either (1) the goals of ecumenism must be scaled down to realistic proportions in light of the limitations imposed by the rivalry between denominational and ecumenical organizations; or (2) denominations must be fused into an institutional structure commensurate with the aims of cooperative planning and action. And to compound further the difficulties framing the contemporary impasse: the *former* alternative of scaling down ecumenical goals has already been pronounced *theologically unacceptable*; while the *latter* option of denominational fusion has recently been assessed as *sociologically improbable* in view of the experience recorded by the Consultation on Church Union. This means, therefore, that only the latter alternative, a program of church union, has been forcefully raised to the level of critical public discussion in recent days. And in point of fact, the Consultation on Church Union represented, among other things, a tacit recognition of the contemporary predicament in which ecumenism finds itself, and it proposed a reasonable solution for extricating several denominations (the actual number was ten) from the mire of institutional division and immobilization. Many supporters of COCU viewed the early and energetic dialogues as auspicious harbingers of a major breakthrough in church union. Thus, during the mellow days of polite discussion everything went seemingly well. But at the point where real power had to be abdicated, the denominations promptly recoiled from the plan and COCU almost withered on the vine. Despite its recent rebirth, however, COCU does prove something significant—it tested the waters of church union in the full organic sense of the term and demonstrated they are still too chilly and far too inclement to support the fragile life of denominational fusion anytime soon.[25]

TOWARD A VIABLE STRATEGY FOR ECUMENICAL ORGANIZATIONS

The abiding reluctance of denominations to embrace organic union along with the refusal of ecumenism to lower its aims suggest that, unless a third and alternative approach is introduced, the ecumenical movement may simply have to muddle through in the near future, accomplishing what it can in piecemeal fashion. This hapless strategy of muddling through unfortunately finds some encouragement in the rarified manner by which ecumenism has articulated its aims with an eye toward neither offending nor alarming any of its constituent members. The result has been to leave perpetually hanging the status of the ecumenical organization itself. That is to say, how is the ecumenical movement to understand itself over against the denominations? Is it (1) an undeclared *superchurch*?; or, is it (2) a *quasi-denomination*, a first among equals?; or, is it (3) a *specialized service agency* concerned with only a limited range of issues confronting the American churches? The evidence would seem to indicate that, at different times and on different issues, ecumenism has proceeded as though all three characterizations were correct. This sort of basic identity confusion clearly cannot help but jeopardize the movement's effectiveness and becloud its sense of direction.

Although the *interfaith societies* of the nineteenth century never overtly defined their role over against the activities carried on by the denominations, nonetheless the ecumenical organizations swiftly came to function *as* a kind of *"research and development" arm* of the American churches. As soon as a new style of ministry—conceived within the ecumenical context—had stirred the conscience of the church or proved its proficiency in addressing a religious need, denominations promptly appropriated the new approach and incorporated its essential format into their own denominational structure. Hence, the denominations reaped the benefits of ecumenical experiments without ever having to incur the risks associated with developing new styles of ministry.

A similar pattern has obtained under both the Federal Council and the National Council of Churches. For example, the social action contingent of the Federal Council paved the way for the churches to confront the inundating crises occasioned by rapid industrialization and labor conflicts; and in short order, the mainline denominations developed their own departments of social action patterned after the Council's experience. Likewise, the National Council of Churches has functioned as the cutting edge for developing new forms of ministry in such sensitive areas as race relations, war opposition, urban affairs, fair political practices, and so forth. Yet, despite the historical prevalence of this pattern, no functional comity agreements or rational divisions of labor have ever been overtly established between the ecumenical movement and the American denominations.

The overriding question crystallized by the recognition of this historical state of affairs may be phrased as follows: *why* has the *ecumenical* branch of American religious life *stimulated* more *innovative*, issue-oriented programs as compared against the relative dearth of new ministries spawned by the denominations? The answer would appear to be lodged, at least in part, in the fact that ecumenism enjoys the advantage of being able to develop ministry from the perspective of the church-at-large, while denominations must necessarily conceive ministry in terms of their limited institutional perspectives. Just as we would not expect General Motors to devise economic policy consistent with the interests of the wider business community in place of is own particular interests, neither can we expect a single denomination to think as *the* church instead of as *a* church. Operating within a more global frame of reference, then, ecumenism has served as a kind of staging area for the development of new and timely ministerial forms whose effectiveness has generally marked them for later assimilation into the bureaucratic structure of denominational organizations.

A MODEST PROPOSAL FOR REORDERING THE RELATIONSHIP BETWEEN ECUMENICAL AND DENOMINATIONAL ORGANIZATIONS

The foregoing analysis of the institutional character and the social functions of contemporary ecumenism lends itself to the suggestion of a significant policy change for the American churches. The basic substance of this policy recommendation essentially proposes that an *informal* pattern already semiestablished—albeit in a somewhat serendipitous fashion—*be elevated to* the status of a *formal* understanding officially acknowledged by the member communions of the ecumenical consortium. This would mean that by common agreement *the churches* would *allocate research and development*, along with information dispensing functions, *to* the various levels of the *ecumenical* organization. Once developed and evaluated within an ecumenical context, however, programs could be distributed to member denominations—on the basis of interest and new program capacity—for actual operationalizing. Accentuating the research and development function need not mean that ecumenical organizations would cease serving as centers for communication and dialogue, but the duplicate and competitive activities supported by separate programming offices divided between denominations and ecumenism could be eliminated. Moreover, agreement to this division of labor would establish a partnership between these two basic segments of American religious life sufficient to accomplish a number of desirable ends: (1) it would rationalize and legitimate an informal arrangement already to some degree in practice; (2) it would allow the ecumenical movement to define its role over against denominational structures so that clear mandates might devolve to each type of organization; (3) it would facilitate a more cogent utilization of limited resources in the forms of time, money, and personnel; and (4) it would *separate* the *development* of programs *from* the large-scale *administration* of programming—a feature which should allow for a more objective evaluation of the church's various types of ministry. Furthermore, the appropriation of this division of labor would have the effect of establishing an interdependent linkage between ecumenical and denominational organizations, giving each a vested interest in the vitality of the other. Until structural interconnectedness binds the ecumenical movement more specifically to the centers of power located in American denominational organizations, a viable ecumenical movement does not appear a very likely possibility within the foreseeable future.

SUMMARY

There are, to be sure, a host of problems set loose by this cryptic policy recommendation which is a spin-off from our sociological analysis above—problems that cannot be adequately adjudicated with the seriousness they deserve in this brief exposition. The intent of this interpretation, however, has not been to articulate a full-fledged plan for resolving the contemporary ecumenical crisis, but to bring some critical attention to bear on a succession of troublesome problems that mar the effort to achieve cooperative planning and action by American religious organizations. Toward this more limited goal, we sought, first, to demonstrate the inherent conflict and rivalry structured into the very manner by which ecumenical and denominational organizations are currently interrelated. The result has been to frustrate the realization of ecumenical goals and lower the level of cooperation among churches which are endeavoring to fulfill a common mission. Second, our historical analysis has outlined some of the latent functions ecumenical organizations have contributed to American church life by serving as the spontaneous fountainhead for innovative styles of ministry. Ecumenical efforts in this regard have also unintentionally fostered the rapid growth of denominational bureaucracies as demonstration projects of ecumenical origin have been assimilated into the ongoing program departments of the mainline denominations. And finally, we have broached a promising new avenue for extricating ecumenism and the denominations from their contemporary, immobilizing impasse by proposing an alternate mode of interrelationship which encourages a division of labor and partnership between these two sorts of organizations in place of their present competition. This policy recommendation contains—so we have suggested at this stage of its formulation—both a propitious measure of sociological cogency and a generous degree of practical feasibility, given the present parameters of that organizational environment wherein the American churches carry out their ministerial functions.

Moreover, unless some decisive modification of the institutional structure of ecumenism is undertaken—whether along the lines suggested above or some alternative scheme for organizational transformation equally as comprehensive in scope—the prospects for the genesis of an authentic ecumenism do not appear auspicious. For if the movement continues down its present course without a major redefinition of its structures and functions, ecumenism may never become anything more than a noble ideal whose historical fulfillment is seldom realized in the social experience of the churches. The plight of ecumenical organizations may, therefore, be reduced to this final observation—articulated by means of a liberal paraphrase of Walter Rauschenbusch's famous line— namely, we have an ecumenical spirit; what we need now is an organizational structure rational enough to back it and a differentiated set of functions distinctive enough to sustain it.

Notes

1. Cf. Barrie Doyle "COCU on the Shelf," *Christianity Today*, XVII, no. 15 (April 27, 1973): 40; and J. Robert Nelson, "New Life for COCU," *Christian Century* XCI (November 27, 1974): 1117-19.

2. Cf., Jeffrey Hadden, *The Gathering Storm in the Churches* (Garden City, N.Y.: Doubleday, 1969).

3. Eugene Burke, Arleon Kelley, and Nathan H. VanderWerf, "Struggle and Hope: the Search for an Authentic Ecumenism," *Living*

Ecumenism Series, Series I, No. 3/Part 1 (National Council of Churches, 1975), p. 2.

4. See Robert K. Merton's classic discussion of latent functions in *Social Theory and Social Structure* (New York: Free Press, 1968).

5. Several of the more important analyses of these groups include: Winthrop S. Hudson, *Religion in American Life* (New York: Scribner's, 1965), pp. 134-57; Gilbert Hobbs Barnes, *The Anti-Slavery Impulse, 1830-1844* (New York: Harbinger, 1964), pp. 17-24; Sidney E. Ahlstrom, *A Religious History of the American People* (New Haven: Yale University Press, 1972), pp. 422-28; and Alice Felt Tyler, *Freedom's Ferment* (New York: Harper, 1962).

6. On this issue, see Seymour Martin Lipset, *The First New Nation* (New York: Basic Books, 1963), pp. 159-69.

7. Sidney E. Mead, "The Rise of the Evangelical Conception of the Ministry in America: 1607-1850," in H. Richard Niebuhr and Daniel D. Williams (eds.), *The Ministry in Historical Perspective* (New York: Harper, 1956), pp. 228-29.

8. Barnes, op. cit., pp. 162-163.

9. Cf., Peter L. Berger, *The Sacred Canopy* (Garden City, N.Y.: Doubleday, 1967), pp. 140-45.

10. Martin Marty, *Righteous Empire* (New York: Dial Press, 1970), pp. 182-85.

11. Ahlstrom, op. cit., p. 803.

12. Henry J. Pratt, *The Liberalization of American Protestantism* (Detroit: Wayne State University Press, 1972), p. 48.

13. Ibid., pp. 49-51.

14. Cf., Roland Robertson, *The Sociological Interpretation of Religion* (New York: Schocken, 1970), pp. 212-13.

15. Pratt, op. cit., p. 31. See also organizational chart, p. 32.

16. Ibid., p. 43.

17. Cf., Forrest L. Knapp, *Church Cooperation: Dead-End Street or Highway to Unity?* (Garden City, N.Y.: Doubleday, 1966), pp. 1-32.

18. See Burke, Keeley, and VanderWerf, op. cit., pp. 12-16, for a discussion of these four types.

19. Cf., Nils Ehrenström and Günther Gassmann, *Confessions in Dialogue: A Survey of Bilateral Conversations Among World Confessional Families, 1962-1971* (Geneva: World Council of Churches, 1972).

20. Burke, Kelley, and VanderWerf, op. cit., p. 14.

21. Amitai Etzioni, *A Comparative Analysis of Complex Organizations* (New York: Free Press, 1961), p. 40.

22. Cf., Knapp, op. cit., p. 215.

23. Pratt, op.cit., pp. 51-55.

24. Cf., Oliver S. Tomkins, "Regional and Confessional Loyalties in the Universal Church," in *Man's Disorder and God's Design* (World Council of Churches, New York: Harper, 1948), pp. 143-146.

25. For a background analysis of the events which led up to COCU, see Eugene Carson Blake, *The Church in the Next Decade* (New York: Harper, 1966), pp. 117-24.

Conclusion

12

Epilogue

Ross P. Scherer

We are at the end of our survey. It has been somewhat narrowly focused—this book is not a complete "sociology of religion," not even a "sociology of religion in America." Its aims have been more modest—to suggest a new viewpoint and simultaneously to provide a survey of some aspects of the organizational forms of some mainline religious bodies ("denominations") in America. The Editor and authors have sought to interpret these forms in terms and concepts which would make present and future comparison more possible. In the process of doing this, we have intentionally ignored other religious groups important in contemporary America, especially sects, cults, and other independent religious movements. And furthermore, we have focused primarily on *structure* (or organization) perhaps to the neglect of *substance* (or culture, belief, mission). Perhaps it has been an error to treat structure without parallel emphasis upon substance (since, as Sister Kim notes, the Second Vatican Council meant primarily a change in meaning/substance rather than form of Catholicism). Nevertheless, it has been difficult to go about comparing the different ecclesiastical *forms* in view of their particularisms and avowedly sui generis character, let alone dealing with substance as well. Thus, we have erred in the direction of trying to discover how the various traditions might be treated as organizationally *alike* and so have perhaps too much separated form from meaning. Furthermore, we have assumed that functionally there is no "one best way" for ecclesiastical form, that operation of such structure is best judged on pragmatic grounds as "means" to an "end." In point of historical fact, however, while various denominations have indeed adopted various "ways," structural "means" has frequently been transformed into "end," a process which sociologists have termed "goal displacement." Thus, means and ends may not be all that separable. Differences of structural form have frequently become a source of "scandal" and major barrier in the search for a common formula for church unity (cf. the near foundering but recent reformulations of the Consultation on Church Union).

"Openness"—Descriptive or Normative?

Besides providing a descriptive survey of some ecclesiastical forms in America, this book has essayed to present a new look for visualizing denominations as "open systems." "Systems" implies interconnectedness—from parts to whole, whole to parts, and part to each other. Few have a problem with this. "Open," on the other hand, implies the unavoidability and necessity of a role for external environment—a relationship of wholes to other functioning wholes! Does an approach which sees an influential role for external forces upon denominations imply the *normativeness* of environmental demand? Must the rule for denominational playing in the "environmental game" be that the way to "*get* along" is to "*go* along?" Not at all. Need *structural* openness be correlated with *substantive/theological openness*, or may they be independent of each other? We prefer that the answer to this question be left to research.[1] The present volume takes neither environment nor denomination as prior, but does regard environment as a potential source of influence, but which in turn is mediated by a denomination's theological tradition, intellectual and other resources, leadership, member qualities, and so on. Conversely, denominations, in turn, may be partly determinative for the social order (as they were for civil rights legislation in the U.S. in the 1960s).

As noted in the introduction, one of the outstanding characteristics of American denominational organization is the seeming fragility of its basically coalitional, cooptative nature. While mission may be "of God," the eventual execution of such enterprise basically takes place in local congregations of "people of God" who are volunteers, part timers, and spiritual "amateurs," and who are frequently marginal in their commitments. Such local church members can and may withdraw their support at any time since it cannot be compelled. Denominations in America must thus operate with the "consent of the governed." This means an extraordinary proportion of effort must be spent in "persuasion" and firing such member commitment (some may deem this a type of goal displacement). The bargain which is thus "made in America" is exchange of participation and suppport by lay members for a major voice in defining mission—in effect, those who "pray" and "pay" need not merely "obey." European observers note that such localistic domination (when coupled with a situation of non-establishment like that in the U.S.) tends to divert "mission" to "triviality,"[2] and others add "privatization." Is this question of mission vs. triviality, however, so simple? Are there no circumstances in which, in a pluralist situation, high commitment cannot be hooked up to a broad concept of societal mission?

Roman Catholicism—Deviant or Normative?

There is, however, a major exception to the above pattern of operation, and that is the Roman Catholic Church in America. The RCC, in American terms, is a "deviant." While, as Sr. Kim relates, it has made some modifications in its structure, the major changes wrought by Vatican II have been in meaning, rather than structure. The RCC still operates generally without formal consent of the governed and from the top down (vs. the modal Protestant-Jewish pattern of operating from the bottom up). One might be tempted to term the very flat, coalitional, Jewish model of church polity as the wave of the future. On the other hand, we still see the more Americanized, Protestant, COCU denominations striving for some formula to express their joint oneness. We see the various Lutherans still continuing their discussions concerning some formula on which to unite. All have been and are in dialogue with Roman Catholic theologians and episcopal committees to somehow find ways to manifest the unity which they say they have discovered already to exist. Many Protestants too have expressed themselves in favor of a need for some sort of universal "primacy" but what? Thus, is it possible to manifest unity and oneness on a basis which simultaneously avoids the fragility of coalitionism which heretofore has seemed to be the lot of religious organization in America? The theologians would say that the answer to this question must be "a creation of God and not of men." Perhaps the real contribution of Roman Catholicism to American church form is still yet to come.

CONSIDERATIONS FOR FUTURE RESEARCH

We hope this book will serve not only to inform but also to stimulate research upon denominations. Before that can be done, we need an adequate summary and codification of what we already know about denominations. But even before such codifying can be done, we need to make explicit a number of kinds of decisions and distinctions which we often take for granted. Beckford's world survey of the research on religious organization[3] and Takayama's discussion and list of propositions (in Chapter 9 of this volume) are good starting points for this work. In the last decade social scientists have given much attention to sects and more recently to cults, but relatively few have been studying denominations as complex systems of organization.

What kinds of preliminary distinctions do we need to make in order to design a fruitful program of researches on denominations?

1. We need to be more creative in our combination and application of what are now termed "paradigms" (see Introduction). We need to deal with denominations both on the macro-level as economic-ecological competitors for a share of the nation's populations and discretionary income (factist paradigm), but also as smaller sets of people searching for and sharing meaning within congregations, movements within denominations, and special agencies of mission (definitionist paradigm). There is nothing right or wrong about the use of any one paradigm or combination of them, but we ought to be more self-conscious of what we are or are not doing as we carry on research.

2. Another requisite is that we should be studying religious organizations more comparatively and crossculturally. Studies of denominations one at a time may be good, but comparison of *several* at a time would be better. Perhaps simultaneous, intensive study of individual cases of congregations, judicatories, and denominations should go hand in hand with abstracted, mass comparisons. The one sheds light on the other. One of the shortcomings of the present volume is in assuming that we can best understand "American denominational organization" by focusing exclusively upon denominations in the U.S. On the contrary, we cannot really see the effects of the American brand of pluralism upon religious organizational operation here *without* comparing American Protestant, Catholic, and Jewish structures with their equivalent structures in *other* national settings.

3. Another distinction we need to make clear is which organizational level we are focusing upon—the personal/individual, the suborganizational or contextual, or the organization-as-a-whole? Each exists within an environment appropriate to it, and each may in a sense also constitute an environment for its own constituent parts. Many studies, for convenience, have via survey methods studied only individual/persons and have tried to project these data to organizational units. But since organizational entities as social emergents have lives and identities almost of their own, we ought to secure data appropriate to these levels and not rely solely upon personal data.

A contextual-level study which this volume has neglected is study of *internal movements* within denominations and their effects upon the parent body. Zald and Berger[4] offer an imaginative scheme for doing this which could be applied to the study of denominational faction formation and schism. Hargrove[5] notes that such movements may be "nativistic" and exclusivist in operation and oppose change, while others (for example, charismatic movements) may push the denomination to more openness and inclusiveness. Here it might be helpful to borrow ideas from anthropological study and political sociology. Further creative comparisons of "functional equivalents" as, for example, Catholic religious orders and Protestant mission societies (as was done by Winter in Chapter 5 of this volume), would add to our understanding. The migration of seminaries to university-related "clusters" (reported in Chapter 6) and the concomitant changes occasioned by this merits further study. How, for example, do social interaction and learning within such a cluster school differ from these processes within a freestanding school?

The local congregation level has perhaps been studied the most, but such studies frequently study the congregation more in relation to its environing community than in relation to its overhead, parent denomination. Both need to be done. There are far fewer studies of the higher levels, including the ecumenical or "interchurch" level.[6] Garret (Chapter 11) suggests that the whole interorganizational field for religious organizations in the U.S. has changed from the late 19th and early 20th centuries to the present. The effects of such historical shifts need to be explored through more longitudinal studies. Kelley's comparisons of rapid and faltering denominational growth patterns are provocative and suggestive but not the final answer.[7] What assumptions concerning quantity vs. quality does he make, and what norms does he take for such for organizational evaluation? Are they valid?

4. A final question arises concerning the so-called functional imperatives of organizations. As noted in the Introduction, there is not a lot of agreement on which ones are essential. An open systems perspective suggests that the major tasks are coming to terms with the environment and procuring resources, establishing structures and processes for doing something with these raw materials, and then exchanging the outcomes for further resources, and so on. If it is valid that organizations must somehow *simultaneously* meet the various organizational tasks as they pursue mission, how do denominational decision makers determine priorities, and how does the solving of *one* imperative compete with the solving of *others*? During periods of economic and member growth, decision making is relatively easy, but how do leaders make decisions during decline? (See Johnson's treatment in Chapter 10.) How is the decisional behavior of denominations different from that in other voluntary structures?; in purely business structures? Is it possible for denominations to propose and implement imaginative proposals for social action upon the environment (adaptation) and simultaneously to maintain strong, internal esprit de corps? How do denominational size,

selectivity, educational level of members, theological tradition, type of church government, etc. affect the implementation of social action programs?[8]

The above are some considerations to bear in mind as we plan for more concerted, international study of denominational organizations.

Notes

1. See Barbara Hargrove's discussion in *Sociology of Religion, Classical and Contemporary Approaches* (Arlington Heights, Ill.: AHM, 1979), pp. 58-62 and 282-286. This is a profound introduction to the sociology of religion, utilizing a historical perspective, and much more inclusive than the present symposium; highly recommended and well written.

2. Hargrove cites Bryan Wilson as to the indictment of triviality, ibid., p. 57.

3. James Beckford, *Religious Organization* (The Hague: Mouton, 1975).

4. Mayer N. Zald and Michael A. Berger, "Social Movements in Organizations: Coup d'Etat, Insurgency, and Mass Movements," *American Journal of Sociology* 83 (Jan. 1978): 823-861.

5. See Hargrove, op. cit., chapters 14 and 15, in which she discusses the recent literature on movements, especially the writings of Richard Quebedeaux on the types of neo-evangelicals, charismatics, et al.

6. Henry J. Pratt's *The Liberalization of American Protestantism* (Detroit: Wayne State U., 1972) is one of the few treatments of the National Council of Churches, although not fully satisfactory as a study in the sociology of complex organizations.

7. Dean M. Kelley, *Why Conservative Churches are Growing* (New York: Harper and Row, 2nd ed., 1977).

8. James R. Wood of Indiana University is concerned with this problem. See his review of Beckford in the *Review of Religious Research* 20 (Spring 1979): 233-236.

INDEX